WE'LL
NEVER
HAVE
PARIS

WE'LL NEVER HAVE PARIS

Repeater

Published by Repeater Books
An imprint of Watkins Media Ltd

Unit 11Shepperton House
89-93 Shepperton Road
London
N1 3DF
United Kingdom

www.repeaterbooks.com
A Repeater Books paperback original 2019
2

Distributed in the United States by Random House, Inc., New York.

Cover design: Francesca Corsini
Typography and typesetting: Frederik Jehle
Typefaces: Meriden LT Std, Libre Baskerville

ISBN: 9781912248384
Ebook ISBN: 9781912248391

Printed and bound in the United Kingdom by TJ International Ltd

To my father, François Gallix — an inveterate Parisian, forever reading or scribbling away in cafés.

To my son, William Gallix, who was born in Paris. The light of my city.

To my mother, Carole Jessop, née Wanless (1942-2017), a Londoner who once resided in Paris. I miss you so much.

CONTENTS

"When I look at the city of Paris I long to wrap my legs around it."

— Anne Carson, "Short Talk on Hedonism", *Short Talks*, 1992

Introduction

Andrew Gallix

In February 1993, the *Times Literary Supplement* devoted a special issue to France. Articles on all things Gallic, from Louis XVI to Roland Barthes, were announced on the cover, illustrated by a black-and-white shot of a young woman on the banks of the Seine. It was taken surreptitiously by Robert Doisneau, as part of a series for *Paris Match* documenting the heatwave of 1948. The young woman is sitting on the cobblestones of the Île de la Cité, a typewriter balanced on her lap. With her stylish sunglasses, short skirt and bare feet, she seems to epitomise Left Bank bohemian chic. In fact, she turns out to be English author Emma Smith, hard at work on her second novel.

Fast-forward to May 1968, and one of the most iconic images of *les événements*, captured by Jean-Pierre Rey for *Life* magazine. You can just about make out an elderly couple surveying the march of History from the fifth-floor balcony of a typical Haussmannian building. Below, on Place Edmond-Rostand, a tidal wave of students. Another young woman, perched on a friend's shoulders, rises above the fray, brandishing the Vietcong flag. Her attitude is reminiscent of the equestrian sculpture of Joan of Arc that stands on Place des Pyramides, although her steed is almost completely obscured.[1] All that remains of Jean-Jacques

---

1   This gilded statue is now a rallying point for far-right activists on May Day. See Richard Kovitch, p. 190.

Lebel, the avant-garde artist who translated Burroughs and Ginsberg into French, is a raised fist and shock of hair. The young woman is not chanting slogans or singing "L'Internationale" like her fellow demonstrators, as though her ability to be spoken through — to channel France's revolutionary spirit while conforming to the allegorical, muse-like status imposed upon her by the male gaze behind the camera — were predicated on her own silence. Or is it simply that she does not know the words? This is a distinct possibility. After all, who better to embody the figure of Marianne in this improvised re-enactment of Delacroix's *Liberty Leading the People,* than Caroline de Bendern, an English fashion model of solid aristocratic stock?[2]

A few years ago, as I was having a drink with Christiana Spens in Montmartre, a middle-aged American couple alighted at the next table. After a while, the woman, who kept looking over, plucked up enough courage to ask Christiana — not in so many words, but through a series of gestures — if she could take her picture. I was tickled by the idea that they would now go home, to deepest Wyoming or wherever, with their faith in glamorous Parisian women firmly reaffirmed. What they say is all true, they would tell them back home, producing the likeness of a British author as incontrovertible evidence.[3]

---

2   Caroline de Bendern was disinherited by her grandfather because of this photograph that was reproduced the world over, losing an estimated £7.5 million in the process.

3   As reported in *The Times*, there were 23 British showgirls at the Moulin Rouge in January 2019 — out of a total of 60 — against only 6 from France. See Heidi James's short story, p. 74.

It is this incident which put me in mind of Doisneau and Rey's famous pictures, setting off a train of thought about the extent to which our vision of literary Paris has been shaped by anglophone writers. By "literary Paris" I do not mean the city's depiction in works of literature (Hugo, Balzac and Proust will always trump foreign competitors on that front) or even Saint-Germain-des-Prés' café society, but rather the more nebulous notion of Paris as the very space of literature.[4] A place, crucially, that you have to *go to* in order to become, be recognised as, and lead the life of a writer. As Julian Hanna puts it, "We left our provincial towns and descended on Paris like the chosen ones, wearing black polo necks, in the hope we'd be recognised by others like us" (p. 171). In Geoff Dyer's *Paris Trance* (1998), a novel haunted by Scott Fitzgerald, Luke relocates to the French capital, from England, for the express purpose of writing a book, which he abandons as soon as he begins leading the life "intended to serve as its research, its first draft". The inference, here, is that Luke is a bit of a poseur, but also that Paris is a city where literature can actually be lived out — where you can be a writer without writing. This fantasy of Paris as the locus of an art-life merger recurs throughout the present volume. The narrator of John Holten's short story decrees that "making an art of everyday life is the aspirational art of living in Paris, everything else is tourism" (p. 307). The young Brian Dillon used to dream of "a city that bristled with profound, radical, stylish thought" (p. 539). Lee Rourke would conjure up Parisian streets that

---

4   See Stewart Home: "'literary' 'Paris' is a simulation, a series of signs that have no relationship at all with a so-called 'reality'" (p. 273).

were "alive with intellectual conversation, in that uncaring, fuck you kind of way you've always wished existed, those long-winded conversations about Proust with crazed taxi drivers trundling across the *arrondissements* in wild abandon you've always imagined happened" (p. 352). Lauren Elkin's English character ascribes a young man's abstract cast of mind to the city he was brought up in: "It seemed easy for him to think that way, having grown up right here, in Paris, near the Jardin du Luxembourg, with all of that literary and cinematic history steeped in his everyday life" (pp. 386-387). "Can you imagine that in England?" enquires Nicholas Royle's incredulous protagonist, "Streets named after abstract ideas, things that don't exist?" (p. 241). For the likes of Tomoé Hill, travelling to Paris is a pilgrimage, not a city break: "We go to Paris reverent: as if the city was a heart in a reliquary beating with the words of writers instead of blood" (p. 114) — words which are not, of course, necessarily French ones.

My contention — and a contentious one it is too — is that the bohemian Paris people think of most readily outside of France — the ur-cliche, if you will — is anglophone. It is the Paris of Hemingway, Joyce, and Shakespeare and Company before being that of Rimbaud and Verlaine or Sartre and de Beauvoir. If we accept this as true, or at least partly so, it is doubtless due to the hegemony of the English language and imperialism of Hollywood as much as the appeal of Hemingway's blueprint. Scandinavians, say, or Latin Americans, have their own take on this myth, revolving around their own writers' interaction with the French capital, but these versions are mainly consumed locally. Enrique Vila-Matas provides an interesting case study. In the mid-Seventies, he spent a couple of years eating croque-monsieurs at the Café de Flore and writing a novel (what else?) in a *chambre de bonne* belonging to Marguerite Duras (a dingy garret for which he never paid rent). *Never Any End to Paris* (2003), the autobiographical novel that chronicles this period, reads like a roll-call of French intellectual life — the Spanish author cannot nip out to the Drugstore Saint-Germain (now a fashion emporium) without bumping into Roland Barthes — and yet his role model, throughout, remains American. It is the desire to lead a "writer's life" à la Hemingway that brings him to Paris in the first place, and the whole novel (as its title suggests) provides a running commentary on — and failed re-enactment of — *A Moveable Feast*.

How many French authors does Hemingway encounter, or even mention, in *A Moveable Feast*? To be honest, apart from Blaise Cendrars, I cannot name a single one off the top of my head. All those that come to mind are either American (Scott Fitzgerald, Ezra Pound, Gertrude Stein, Alice B. Toklas, John Dos Passos), Irish (James Joyce) or English (Ford Maddox Ford, Wyndham Lewis, Aleister Crowley).[5] Paris, for Jonathan Gibbs when he was growing up, was akin to "the drop-in sets of a cardboard toy theatre: the ideal backdrop to whatever drama you imagined you might one day star in" (p. 67). It was also, above all, a cheap-as-*frites* backdrop for the Lost Generation, which is one of the reasons why the city could be construed as a moveable feast. Will Wiles's astute observation that the

---

5   Hilaire Belloc was Anglo-French, but spent most of his life
     in England.

French capital is a "uniquely memetic city" — that its "distinctiveness has been paradoxically easy for other cities to emulate" — also applies to historic bohemian areas, such as London's Soho or New York's Greenwich Village, which almost invariably have a whiff of Montmartre or Latin Quarter about them (p. 337). Hemingway described Paris in the 1920s as a place "where there was a way of living well and working, no matter how poor you were," adding that this was "like having a great treasure given to you". That treasured lifestyle was swept away by the onset of the Depression in the 1930s. As Will Ashon remarks, artists thrive where there is "affordable, preferably semi-derelict, real estate. Which is to say, you can't be an artist in Paris, anymore, or in London either" (p. 301).

Paris used to have the added advantage of offering a rather laissez-faire attitude in matters of morality that was conducive to artistic creation, especially if you were writing in a foreign language. Jack Kahane, the self-styled "booklegger" from Manchester launched his Obelisk Press in 1929, just as the Lost Generation were packing up, in order to circumvent and cash in on Anglo-American censorship. Subsidising serious, albeit often risqué, literary works by flogging "db's" (dirty books) — some of which he tossed off himself — Kahane published the likes of Cyril Connolly, James Joyce, Lawrence Durrell, Anaïs Nin and, perhaps most famously, Henry Miller's *Tropic of Cancer* (1934) that was banned in the United States. His son, Maurice Girodias, went on to launch the Olympia Press, which released the first editions of Nabokov's *Lolita* (1955) and Burroughs's *Naked Lunch* (1959), as well as the works of that notorious

Scottish émigré, Alexander Trocchi.[6] National characteristics are not set in stone, however, as Stuart Walton reminds us: "If the perduring English cultural temperament is a rumbustious pleasure in living, its French counterpart is seen as glacial contempt, the aridity of an over-bureaucratised polity, notwithstanding the fact that Victorian England invented the chilly reserve in social manners for which the British have been noted ever since, while pleasure in living went by its proper name, *joie de vivre*, across the Channel" (p. 334). Jeremy Allen recounts how, in a surprising reversal of stereotypes, it took "some *rosbifs* from across the Channel" (Ian McEwan and Andrew Birkin) plus a fervently Francophile Scot (Gilbert Adair) "to juice things up and consummate the relationship" between Cocteau's terrible twins (p. 198).

Due to a variety of factors — the launch of the Eurostar in 1994, the growing presence of American and British universities, the rejuvenation of Shakespeare and Company, Brexit — Paris is once again at the heart of the anglophone literary scene. It is increasingly a sort of neutral meeting ground for writers and readers from across the Anglosphere, hence, I think, the timeliness of the present experiment. Out of seventy-nine authors included here, only eight currently live in Paris. Many of the others have resided in the French capital for a period of time (running from several weeks to several years), either recently or,

---

6   Tom McCarthy's *Remainder*, which marked a revival of interest in experimental fiction in the UK, was first published, in 2005, by Metronome Press, a small Paris-based publishing house inspired by Maurice Girodias.

in some cases, decades ago, often seeking out a sense of cultural and linguistic estrangement. The remainder is split between those who have at least visited the city and those who have not. The inclusion of the latter category was essential to the overall project, not only because they are very talented writers, but also because the remit would, of necessity, become an Oulipian-style constraint in their case. (Incidentally, Georges Perec is a recurring figure, notably in Andrew Robert Hodgson's comic quest for the ever elusive "Perec café" on Place Saint-Sulpice, p. 345). In Wendy Erskine's short story, probably set in Northern Ireland, a schoolboy seeks daily refuge in the Parc des Princes stadium on his FIFA video game (p. 83). In Ashton Politanoff's contribution, Paris makes a cameo in the guise of a French movie watched by a character on TV (p. 88). Under Kathryn Scanlan's pen, Paris fades further into the background, only appearing through the brief mention of street scenes on lithographic prints (p. 94). "There are many ways of not going to Paris," writes C.D. Rose (p. 218), and one of them is to claim — like Nathan Dragon's protagonist — to have gone there without actually going ("None of the fuss and trouble"). The City of Light he imagines is like "three famous monuments from different parts of town stuck in a snowglobe all next to each other in yellowing water" (p. 80). In *Midnight in Paris* (2011), Woody Allen uses a similar technique, juxtaposing bits of the Left Bank with bits of the Right Bank, thereby cutting out the boring, unpicturesque bits in the middle, so that the characters might be in Montmartre one minute and the next strolling along the river Seine.

Francophilia is often linked to what Jeremy Allen describes as English speakers' "undisclosed inferiority complex" vis-à-vis French culture — a feeling that may well date back to the Norman Conquest (p. 201). It is symbolised, in Susanna Crossman's story, by the contrast between Hélène's sophisticated lingerie and Charlotte's "mismatched bra and pants" (p. 141). Max Porter evokes the "ever-burning shame of the Eurocentric Englishman abroad" (p. 36). Stuart Walton argues that what "the Anglo-Saxon temperament hopes to find in Paris is the apotheosis of high culture, of a culture it is sportingly willing to admit he lacks, for a weekend at least, in the encounter with its essence" (p 334), or as Stewart Home puts it, somewhat more bluntly, "Francophilia is so often a silly snobbery cultivated by rich idiots and would-be social climbers who want to project an image of being refined" (p. 274). S.J. Fowler's boyhood antics in a city he experienced as "full of itself" and inimical to kids from Cornwall are "vividly placed in cultural terms" by his "aspirational working-class family": "What will the French think of English children?" (p. 56). At Les Deux Magots, Greg Gerke's narrator replays the opposition between robust New World vulgarity and effete Continental sophistication in ironic mode: "The popular cliché about the French, a cliché restated by my countrymen, is that they think Americans don't know how to live. We are savage and deficient in certain refined aspects pertaining to composure, compunction, and, certainly, culture and its expression. As I primped for my wife's picture of me, tipping my miniature cup of coffee with my pinky pointed out and cheeks sucked in, we could come close to the pitiful, ugly American, miming the etiquette he is so destined never to encompass" (pp. 56-66).

As a subgenre, the expat memoir or novel frequently follows a narrative arc that takes us on a journey from euphoria (the possibility of escaping, and reinventing oneself elsewhere) to disillusionment (the failure to escape oneself and go native). Fittingly, Jonathan Gibbs's piece is entitled "Every Story of Paris is also a Story of Disillusion" (p. 67). Tristan Foster parodies the impossibly high expectations of the honeymoon period: his character, we are told, expected nothing less than "sleepy cherubs from the fluffy clouds of Renaissance paintings. Expected to be welcomed by them, almost as if they would be reclining on the linoleum at Charles de Gaulle when she walked through the gates, chubby and rosy-cheeked" (p. 110). Christiana Spens's heroine states that "Paris had always been a good escape [for her], the best escape of them all" — until now (p. 147). This theme is actually so prevalent that Gavin James Bower fears he may have become a walking (or running) cliché: "I run away to Paris — am I sure I'm not a trope?" (p. 151).

In *Dream Machines* (2017), Steven Connor observes that "one travels to the Grand Canyon, Niagara Falls, the Taj Mahal in order to be transported, in order to experience an intensity of being there that is a kind of transport, a departure from oneself". Paris often seems to hold out that promise of radical transformation. When asked why he moved there, Luke, in Geoff Dyer's *Paris Trance*, responds, "To become a different person". Natalie Ferris points out that Christine Brooke-Rose also conceived of Paris as "a place of renewal, rejuvenation, even rebirth, offering her the chance of a 'second career, a second life'" (p. 284). For the narrator of Heidi James's story, the idea of going to live in Paris is an existential choice as opposed to a simple career move: "The other girls were talking about hairdressing, or office work or even going to university, but they were just choosing a career. I felt that I had a choice about what kind of girl I would be, about the persona I could inhabit. That I could choose a me" (p. 74).

"I should never be a Frenchman, never be one of them," laments the protagonist in Daphne du Maurier's tale of Anglo-French doppelgängers, *The Scapegoat* (1957), echoing all those for whom the metamorphosis fails to materialise. In *Love Like Salt: A Memoir* (2016), Helen Stevenson comes to realise that her move to rural France was "hopelessly English," just as D.H. Lawrence was aware that his stridently anti-English sentiments were, in fact, a typically English form of self-loathing.[7] Disappointment, according to Stuart Walton, is actually a "constitutive factor" in English speakers' experience of France, and its capital in particular: "It is at least as important to the British, for example, that Paris should fall short of what they expect of it as it is to the Parisians that *les Anglais* have never really understood it" (p. 332).

In a 1964 letter to Diana Athill, Jean Rhys railed against what she dubbed "America in Paris" or "England in Paris", dismissing Hemingway and Miller's take on the city as

---

7   The move to rural France by many British people does not take place in space so much as in time, the cliché being that their new rural idyll is like a prelapsarian Britain from fifty years ago.

inauthentic: "The real Paris had nothing to do with that lot. As soon as the tourists came the real Montparnos packed up and left".[8] Where to, she fails to say. In *L'Assassinat de Paris*, published in 1977, the historian Louis Chevalier also attacked this process of gentrification which, in his view, was turning the city into "a place only Americans could love". One may wonder, however, if that had not been the plan all along, or at least since the Second Empire (1852-1870)? Perhaps the "real Paris", if there ever was one, disappeared with Baron Haussmann, whose sanitised, homogenised City of Light — partly designed to prevent the erection of barricades[9] — strives a little too hard to be beautiful. For Walter Benjamin, Paris, in the nineteenth century, had been the capital of modernity (understood as reality "dominated by its phantasmagorias") on account of the "dreamworlds" conjured up by its shopping arcades.[10] An early subtitle to his work, that would grow into *The Arcades Project*, was "A Dialectical Fairyland". It was also in this *Ville Lumière*[11] that the Frères Lumière showcased the very first motion pictures. Even May '68 — ostensibly an insurrection against the society of the spectacle — started

---

8   Quoted in Lauren Elkin's *Flâneuse*. Vintage, 2016, p. 52. See Susanna Crossman's story (p. 144) and Anna Aslanyan (p. 280).

9   Barricades reappeared during the Paris Commune and in more theatrical/referential form in May '68 and at regular intervals ever since.

10 Two versions of "Paris, Capital of the Nineteenth Century" (which was the working title for *The Arcades Project*) were written in 1935 and 1939.

11 Paris's sobriquet, *la Ville Lumière* (the City of Light), is often said to have originated in London.

at the Cinémathèque. Dylan Trigg thus argues that the tourists who repair to the Starbucks in Montmartre's Place du Tertre do so "not with a view on effacing the soul of Paris, but precisely in order to preserve the city's *genius loci*. Theirs is a Paris that is best viewed from behind the veneer of artifice, and for this reason, theirs is a Paris that is more Parisian than the city itself" (p.323). Tom McCarthy conjectures, in a similar spirit, that the nostalgia for a "real Paris" may actually be "built into the experience of ~~being~~ (that is, of failing to "be" authentically) in Paris in the first place" (p.342). The Paris we know was always already a beguiling simulacrum, a facsimile of itself, and possibly a dream — "the fever dream of Paris," as Julian Hanna puts it — from which we should try to awake (p. 168).

"Is it possible to become *blind to a place*?" enquires Owen Booth, "Doesn't everyone remember going up the Eiffel Tower, at least once, whether or not they actually ever did?" (p. 44). Paris is either too much of a cliché, or not enough (in which case it is no longer recognisably Paris). G.K. Chesterton established a cogent distinction between travellers, who see what they see, and tourists, who see what they have come to see. A traveller, like Jonathan Gibbs, will see that Paris's famed walkability "is made possible by the shoving of huge swathes of its population, including many generations of immigrants, to the outskirts" (p. 68). In so doing, Will Ashon observes, the French capital has "hollowed itself out and become a theme park, a Disneyland of beauty and culture, a palimpsest of a living city" (p. 301). Although the museumification of Paris is often overstated, perhaps the city, like Eurydice, can only be contemplated nowadays by turning away from it. It is striking how the following pages abound in alternative versions of the French capital, from filmmakers' "parallel worlds" (Richard Kovitch, p. 185) like Godard's "futuristic dystopian landscape" in *Alphaville* (Jeremy Allen, p. 202) to Ian Nairn's 1968 guidebook, with its tantalising insights into another Paris glimpsed at in the interstitial spaces between the tired tourist attractions (p. 294). Susan Tomaselli outlines the decoy Paris "built during the First World War to confuse German bombers, complete with a sham Champs-Elysées, Gare du Nord, wooden replica factory buildings, illuminated by Fernand Jacopozzi (the man who went on to light the Eiffel Tower with the Citroën logo)" (p. 392).[12] C.D. Rose describes Tativille, "a vast Potemkin city, a facsimile Paris, not only with its own concrete buildings, tarmacked streets and functional traffic lights, but also a number of huge trompe l'oeil facades. The scenes at Orly are stage sets with backdrops made entirely of giant blow-ups of the airport. The images reflecting in the endlessly swinging plate glass doors of *Playtime* (the Eiffel Tower, the Arc de Triomphe, the Champs Elysées) are photographs. *Playtime* takes place in a replica, a city of maquettes and projections, one more like the city it needed to be" (p. 224). Jeffrey Zuckerman is more familiar with the "pixel city" on Google Maps than the "real-life one" (p. 509). The Orphic underworld of the Catacombs — that subterranean, "secret version" of Paris, which Sophie Mackintosh describes as "the ghost

12 See Xavier Boissel, *Paris est un leurre : la véritable histoire du faux Paris*. Editions Inculte, 2012.

of the city like a photographic negative" underneath our feet — continues to exert a great deal of fascination (p. 111). It is high time we made our descent.

I give you Paris, *en anglais dans le texte*.

Even As We Plunged Down the Hill

Max Porter

Ce qui est marrant, on leur a dit, c'est de descendre la colline à fond, vers les lumières de la ville. Les Anglais étaient défoncés et surexcités; ils essayaient de nous impressionner et on les a regardés s'élancer dans la pente, s'éloigner de la fête et des lumières de l'école, et ils riaient, ils criaient, ils couraient en file indienne comme des animaux en fuite.

Vous les avez prévenus, pour le grillage ? demanda Magalie. Non, on n'en avait pas parlé. On n'en parlait jamais du grillage. Même à ceux qu'on aimait bien. C'était génial d'entendre le grillage s'étirer à mesure qu'ils rentraient dedans, les uns après les autres. La surprise et puis les rires. Tous les ans ils s'écrasent contre le grillage, dans le noir.

I insist on buying him a beer by the empty canal; he insists on a discussion of the newest electronic music, the wittiest rappers, the way he turned my story inside out, so the girls were laughing at us, as we laughed at Arcadian wallpaper, French kitsch, at the ever-foolish English, and my translator knows I'm joking, this hasn't happened yet, I'm simply on pilgrimage to *L'Oeil cacodylate*, and I know this was years ago anyway, before Océane from Egly, before Abdelhamid Abaaoud, before our honeymoon when my parents paid for us to stay in the smart hotel on the Île de la Cité, and we were so lost and my publisher — this is fifteen years before I wrote a word that might be published — took us for a meal made of coloured mousses, and said sorry, again and again, for the ridiculous traffic, for the Americans, and I thought a high-heel fetish would be the saddest thing here, and I spent an hour in Musique Musique, before the men with scarves around their mouths started throwing bottles at the police, and I said please, really, I loved seeing that, I loved that they let me sleep in George's room, with the cat, I loved that Magalie wrote to me, it only breaks my heart I lost the letters, it pains me to think of how good I was, back then, aged thirteen, at ping-pong, in the Marly-le-Roi gymnasium, when my name was Michel and my legs were browner, and I strolled past myself, years later, clutching my Cixous, smoking a Camel, kidding myself, I couldn't know about Journiac's mass before I was born but I took it as a sign, something unpleasant was coming, such clarity, such glorious wandering loneliness, the English boys were giggling at *L'Origine*, trying to impress us, but the pollen blocks the French kids crumbled into their little pipes were so strong, the nervous son of the American diplomat was sick, pretty cool, she kept saying, pretty cool, this new way of presenting the colonial art of the past, my friends have long gone, lost in Pantin, and she said she didn't think we had a future but we should enjoy Paris and we had such nice sex after that, running our fingers along rows of identical beige spines, stopping for a little beer on the way home, the ever-burning shame of the Eurocentric Englishman abroad, the sense of the swelling drill scene, the clumsiness of GCSE French, of the terrible poem "Bodies in the Seine", of the flimsy memory that perhaps we could hear them laughing even as we plunged down the hill in the darkness, desperate to impress, collecting memories like Victorian diarists, and the taxi driver said They are not Parisians They are Africans ruining this great city, and I fancied saying Let me out I'd rather walk, but I didn't, because I was pathetic, in Paris, and late for the train.

French Exchanges

Chris Power

My whole family went to Paris when my brother was on his French exchange.

My brother's French exchange lived in Meudon. His name was Christophe. My memory of the house is a lot of wood, and a living room on the upper floor, which was something I hadn't ever seen before. Looking back, I think the house, and the leafy street it was on, were built in a style informed by the Bauhaus.

But why did we go to Paris when my brother was on his French exchange?

Christophe's mother, Uti, was the most European woman I'd ever met. I never saw her without a cigarette, even when she was eating. But my memory of her almost certainly bears no relation to who she is now, or maybe even who she was then. She is a fiction I've created by remembering, by forgetting, and by inventing what was forgotten. At one time I thought about her a lot, but now, when I really think about her, I find she barely exists, and the more I concentrate the less of her remains. She is a name and a pair of clogs, a denim skirt, a cigarette and a tanned but indistinct face. I have neglected her and she has disappeared like breath on a mirror. Or like the reason why we went to Paris when my brother was on his French exchange.

A couple of years after we went to Paris, when my father was working overseas for several months, Lutz, Uti's husband, told my mother she should take a lover. Lutz said this over the phone, from another country. It would have been different if he and my mother had been face to face, within reach of each other.

I have never been unfaithful, but I have been with people who were being unfaithful. This is adultery, but is it also infidelity? And does it bring us any closer to working out why we went to Paris when my brother was on his French exchange?

I text my friend Bart and ask him what his French exchange was called. *Laurent Sulpice*, he texts back. *Nice guy, odd clothes. He disapproved of a lot of things. He came back when he was sixteen and I took him to the Tumbledown Dick a few times. After that I never saw him again.*

A streetlight could be seen from the long, large window in the living room of Christophe's house, glowing yellow and shrouded by leaves that were black in the night, lime-flesh green near the light, and black again when they were positioned directly between the light and anyone who looked out of the window after nightfall, whether in admiration or anticipation or sorrow or horror, or lost in thought, not even aware of the streetlight, or the street, or the Bauhaus.

If the reason why we went to Paris when my brother was on his French exchange were a leaf, it would be one that is either too far from the light to be seen, or one positioned directly between the light and myself, standing at the window staring out with an indeterminate expression on my face.

I text my friend Rob and ask him about his French exchange. *Fadil Aimetti,* he replies. *He has not the stature of a rugbyman.* That's what Fadil wrote in his introductory letter, Rob reminds me: *I have not the stature of a rugbyman.* He was pretty, with long brown hair. I remember wishing my face was like his face. *He was a nice fella,* Rob writes of Fadil. *My two weeks in Paris were good. Great house. Lovely sister.*

Sister? I text.

No, Rob replies, *that's not what I meant.*

It was hot in Paris that summer, and our hotel on Rue La Fayette was a shithole. So we didn't go to pamper ourselves.

I email my friend Ben about his French exchange. He says he never had one, but I know he did. I was the only one who didn't have one. I was useless at French, and dropped it before the exchanges ever happened. I know he had one, I just can't remember who he was.

I do remember watching *Dallas* at the house in Meudon. JR spoke in an incredibly deep French voice. Have you ever thought about how the careers of some voiceover artists are tied to the actors they voice? Will Smith or Robert Downey Jr. stop getting hired, and some Frenchman who they never met, or even thought about, has to sell his house and drinks himself to death. Why did we watch *Dallas*? How much time do you need to spend at a stranger's house before watching a soap opera becomes viable? You don't just get through the introductions and then, when the first awkward silence comes along, say, "Well... *Dallas?*" Not even in the Eighties, when everyone watched it and one of my brothers had a "Who Shot JR?" T-shirt.

Of this I'm certain: we didn't go to Paris when my brother was on his French exchange to take an additional trip, via the TV, to Texas.

I don't contact my friend Neil because I'm ashamed of what we did to his exchange. One hot, clouded afternoon we went into the woods near Neil's house, Neil and Rob and Fadil and me and Neil's exchange student, and we threw rocks at this boy, who even before we started throwing things at him had something wrong with his leg, and who limped along behind us, wanting to leave, I'm sure, but having precisely nowhere else to go. I remember his name as François, which I hope is true because otherwise my imagination is a disappointment: François the French boy. Why not slap a beret on his head, tie a string of onions round his neck and be done with it? "My leg, my leg," he called to us, falling further and further behind. We acted like he didn't exist. Like his cries couldn't reach us through the thick, still air. Neil told us that at night François would put some kind of oil on his bad leg, and that one time he had asked Neil to help him. "I told him to fuck off," Neil said, but I hope that was a lie. I hope that in reality he showed that boy a kindness the rest of us lacked.

Céline, a great writer and a vile person, died in the suburb of Meudon. "You can lose your way groping among the shadows of the past," he wrote, but he has nothing to do with why we went to Paris when my brother was on his French exchange.

The Things I Don't Remember

Owen Booth

It's 1999 and I'm going blind in a hotel room in Paris. Paris, for God's sake! The City of Light! The irony isn't lost on me. Even in my condition I can appreciate the absurdity of it.

My travelling companion at the time is less sanguine about things. He wants to go out and see Paris, having never visited the city before. He doesn't understand, because I haven't told him, why I don't want to leave the hotel room, why I don't even want to get off my bed. Eventually he gives up trying to persuade me and goes out by himself, leaving me to wrestle with my awful future. He comes back a few hours later having had a perfectly pleasant time.

That's when I tell him that I may have looked at the eclipse for too long — which was why we came to France, how we ended up in a field on the Normandy coast with six million other people — and without the appropriate eyewear.

It turns out that my friend did the same thing, has been worrying about it too, and we laugh, and probably feel a bit better. In the event, I don't go blind, and neither does he — although nineteen years later I still have this *thing* in the corner of my vision, in my left eye, so...

And also: this incident will somehow end up being my last clear memory of Paris, despite my going back to the city a number of times since. That August evening in 1999:

burned into my memory (although thankfully not onto my retinas). Everything else: blurry, vague.

So, in some ridiculously handy metaphorical sense, isn't it in fact right to say that maybe I *did* go blind that night? Is it possible to become *blind to a place*?

There's a story in my family about the time my brother, who doesn't speak French, went around the Paris Métro, by himself, while on a family holiday — at the age of eight, or six, or four. He gets progressively younger every time the story is told. And, depending on who tells the story, this is either evidence of terrible parenting, or how different things were in those days, or my brother's wild and adventurous streak, or something about Paris itself. I don't really remember anything about the trip in question — I would have been three years older than my brother, however old he actually was at the time — except, possibly, going up the Eiffel Tower. And that may have actually been on another holiday altogether. Or not at all. Doesn't everyone remember going up the Eiffel Tower, at least once, whether or not they actually ever did?

My parents — the same parents who let my brother travel around the Paris Métro by himself at the age of eight, or six, or four — had hitchhiked to Paris in 1968, just after they'd got married in a registry office without telling their parents. Neither of these were particularly common things for young working/lower-middle-class people from Leeds to do at the time, and I love them both for that. In the streets of Paris all the cobbles had been replaced after *les événements*, and the only remaining sign of the unrest was a piece of graffiti reading "La chienlit, c'est lui". After asking a surprised gendarme to recommend a place to stay, my parents were directed to a by-the-hour knocking shop ("pas cher!"). As my mother remembers it — "We were youthful and energetic and walked and walked and thought we had arrived", and I love them both for that, too.

I've only been to Paris with someone I was in love with once, and all I can remember about that trip was going to a museum that, for some reason, had a live crocodile (or alligator) in the basement. Did this really happen? There's a story that an Egyptian crocodile was captured in the Paris sewers in 1987 and may or may not now be on display in the zoo at Vincennes, although I'm fairly sure I've never been to that part of the city. Another version of the tale suggests that it was 1984, and the crocodile was sent to an aquarium in Vannes, Brittany, where it lives in an enclosure modelled on the Paris sewers. I have been to Vannes, but not to any aquariums there, so I can't categorically confirm or deny this. There were also reports of crocodiles on the loose in the canals of Paris following the floods of 2016, but that's more than ten years after my last visit to the city, and the stories are widely considered to have been hoaxes.

Worried that I'm doing my ex-partner a disservice (she's a very nice person), I get in touch to ask her what she can remember of our Paris trip. It turns out that she remembers even less than I do. "Emile Zola and the graves," she tells me. "That's all." She has no memory of the crocodile/alligator.

Neither of us can remember whether or not we went up the Eiffel Tower.

I hitchhiked *through* Paris once. On the way to see another ex-girlfriend who lived in the Loire valley (this was well over twenty years ago, and does not in any way reflect the person I am now — I haven't had an ex-girl-friend in over fifteen years, and don't plan on having any more). I used to hitchhike everywhere *back in those days*, but France turned out to be a challenge. I spent about five hours stuck on the edge of the Paris *périphérique*, trying to get a lift and staring at a giant promotional poster for the Jean-Claude Van Damme film *Double Impact*, in which the Belgian action hero plays estranged twin brothers who team up to fight the Hong Kong triads. I can't remember what the film was called in French, but I remember the strapline, referring to the two brothers, was (roughly translated) "one has a weapon — one *is* a weapon".

Thinking about it now, there's a narrow possibility that this was actually the strapline for one of the films in the *Lethal Weapon* series, but I'm not sure the release dates match with my trip.

And, of course, I ended up inappropriately falling back in love with that particular ex-girlfriend, who lived by a vineyard and whose father used a shovel to swat the hornets that gathered outside their back door in the evenings, because this was France, even if it wasn't Paris, and if you can't end up inappropriately falling back in love with an ex-girlfriend in France — a *French ex-girlfriend* — then where can you? Although in the event the timings were all off, and I was still involved with someone else, and so nothing too untoward happened, and also I was only in my early twenties and *what does anyone that young even know about love anyway?*

Around that same time a university friend and I were briefly obsessed by a TV documentary that the writer and broadcaster Clive James made as part of his *Postcard From...*

series. In "Postcard from Paris", the middle-aged James returns to the city he visited as a struggling and idealistic young writer, interviews beautiful French women including Françoise Sagan, Béatrice Dalle, and Inès de La Fressange, and ponders the life he could have had, and the man he could have been, and the women he could have loved, if things had turned out differently.

My friend and I were both hugely moved by this programme. Clive James, it appeared, *knew all about love*. Love and loss and longing and regret. Here was Clive, balding, overweight, in a loose tie and ill-fitting suit, his life apparently pretty much over, almost laughably mismatched with all these beautiful French women, warning us of what things were *really* going to be like. We, too, would end up looking back on our missed chances, our failed and doomed romances, our youthful relevance. We, too, would ache with regret for our own lost Paris.

And this, we understood, was what it meant to be *old*. Well.

I re-watched "Postcard from Paris" the other day. It's on YouTube. It still holds up. James and his crew knew how to make good television. It's funny to see the boxy Eighties cars and the cheesy title font and the clothes of the BCBG Parisians. And all the smoking. James comes off as a little bit letchy (but only a little bit), and a product of his age, and keeps describing women as "creatures" and so on, but he's a good writer, and *it was a different time*, etc.

And, of course, it was as I was watching it that I realised that I am now almost the same age that James was when he filmed the programme. I spent a lot of my late teens and twenties worrying about how I would feel when I was older, expecting to be spending most of my days full of melancholy sadness, remembering Paris, and cities like it. Constantly looking back.

I'm almost surprised to find that life doesn't turn out like that.

I have children. Consequently, I am not, and could not be filled with regret. Absolute terror of the future, yes. Most of the time. Worries about my failings as a parent, certainly. Tiredness. Boredom. Frustration. Desperate concerns about how to maintain the romance in a long-term relationship. Sometimes despair. All of that. For God's sake.

Maybe it's in the editing, in what we do and don't remember. I certainly miss... the certainty I used to feel about things. The knowledge of where I was going and how it was all going to turn out. But the rest of it, like that time with the crocodile (or alligator), I sometimes suspect it could all have happened to someone else, in a different city — or to no one, and not at all.

My brother, incidentally, grew up into a fine man, and seems largely unscarred by his experiences on the Paris subway system. He has children of his own now. When I ask my mother by email about his youthful solo adventure she digs out some old photographs, and establishes that he was actually ten years old at the time, and only days away from his eleventh birthday. She adds that "he was a very bright kid and the world was a safer place then". She's worried about herself and my father being seen as irresponsible or neglectful parents.

I promise her that I won't use their real names in this piece.

Always Fourteen

Rosalind Jana

Valentine's Day and all the fountains
frozen — each a miniature, bluish rink. City
of fur coats and hats and hiked hotel rates and
every breath made visible.

Valentine's Day and me — fourteen,
in long white boots in a flat. First time
in Paris — still spindly, never kissed,
enthralled by my own glamour.

No reason here for roses. Instead,
a rail of clothes with names that halt
my breathing. Romance enough to run
my hand along a slackened
shoulder; to shiver at the
slink of cold silk.

I am fourteen, playing dress-up, playing
fairy story elegance for a lens, while
my mother, in a corner, watches quietly,
baffled by this fussing over hair and
whether heels convey a mood.

I stare into the camera's black, gobstopper eye. On
the pages of the magazine I'll look poised
but very young.

I'll seem assured — a leisured lady
sprawling on pale couches in long skirts.
I'll stand coolly by a shelf with hands in
pockets; sit by a porthole window, wearing
shorts. I'll be frozen like the fountains,
always fourteen. Always Paris,
with a perfect circle view of rooftops
behind my head.

I have only just started my periods.

Tomorrow we'll be tourists — Mum
leading the way, unraveling
an eager parade of churches, graveyards,
markets, a length of sealskin Seine.
Then I will be teenage, tentative on
unfamiliar streets, hungering already
for the person I'll become — the one who'll flit,
no, stride under fierce, bright skies with
the poise of a woman in long white boots,
who wears her own body with ease.

Free Man in Paris

Jennifer Hodgson

Things had sort of spontaneously coalesced into a kind of dreadful shit tip around here. I had begun to think that maybe all of this would look better in a lot of that dove grey light. But I wasn't even in Paris any more by the time I listened to it, but another city I had gone to afterwards so as not to be in Paris any more. It can't have worked out that well for Joni, either, since she's got that other song, the one about being in Paris and wanting to be in California instead and, in any case, the song is about someone else. Anyway, as I stuffed the buds into my ears I found myself inducted into a very tender world of other resigned people, all rolling their eyes at one another in sympathy. It was a lovely thing to shelter under — everything felt quite redeemed for a minute.

*

People from the place where I'm from are forever putting the things they would like very much, but cannot allow themselves to have, quite nearby but just beyond their grasp. Then they pine after them, but in such a way that they always seem to be taking the piss out of them. Into Paris we've sequestered a job lot of dreams of muckiness, permission to talk about philosophy on the telly and most versions of romance.

It used to seem like you weren't allowed to actually go there. As a child, I would find myself swung around the ring road in an executive coach on the way to somewhere else, with an empty cool box by my feet to vomit into if need be. Or I'd be on a school trip, staying in a youth hostel in the far-out suburbs, on my way to somewhere else again, having my eyebrows tweezed into little spermy commas on a bunkbed fashioned after the Pompidou Centre — which I knew all about because I'd seen it in pictures.

Later, someone told me Paris was *just like a crap West London really* and I thought to myself, right, I'll have that, that can be what I say whenever anyone mentions anything about it. And at the time I knew precious little about either of those places — certainly not enough to make any kind of judgement about their relative crapness. But it seemed like a thing I could say that would prevent me from having to say anything else, and so I would say it. Saying very much of anything was quite difficult then, so I found it useful to have something ready. And being casually disparaging can feel very nice sometimes. Anyway, I know West London much better now. I like to walk around it every now and again, smearing things with my lack of ease and comfort. And Paris isn't like it at all.

*

People have told me very often that I *will* speak French — quite as if it were some ancestral skill that will be be visited upon me at some point without any effort of the will at all. They made it sound like playing the harpsichord or doing competent embroidery. I thought, I'm not having any of that. At school they would try to round out these flat, silty vowels by having me sing this one exceedingly melodramatic French folk song over and over. I just started singing it out loud into this empty room and to my surprise, there it is: deep woods, unhappy love, extreme horror — all of it, just coming out of my mouth like that. They said I talked like a little fishwife, and since then I've taken great care to make it worse on badness.

In the end I think the only way I would be able to speak French passably would be if someone could insert both of their hands inside my mouth and use their thumbs and their knuckles to completely reshape its cavity as though it were Play-Doh. But even back then I suspected that my refusal might well make me even more tediously from the place where I'm from than anything else, and if you can't win, it's often best to say nothing at all. And so, when I'm there, I go more or less mute and the whole city becomes an analyst or a monk and will not take any of my usual bullshit.

This one time I had gone out in the morning to buy a baguette because the day before I'd seen several people carrying those flimsy red or blue striped carrier bags with large baguettes sort of protruding out. This small act, the carrying of the bread, was charged in my mind with a kind of endless and deeply desirable insouciance that I very much wanted a bit of. They weren't those crap baguettes you get here, either, those ones that are all solid crust with the sawdusty, desiccated insides that crumble to nothing when you slice through them. And it was about 37 degrees outside, and the first time I had been anywhere that was 37 degrees outside, and I felt quite vaporous. I think I was striding, yes I was probably striding, down Boulevard de la Chapelle towards a *boulangerie* when a man appeared out of nowhere and took one tit in each hand and squeezed as hard as he could, as if I was an old-fashioned car, and these were my old-fashioned car horns, and he was making me go honk. And I thought at the time, I am having a madcap, humorous and irreverently cruel sexual experience, just like in those films — which I hadn't seen but could well imagine.

This other time I was outside Serge Gainsbourg's house with my cousin, for whom, I think, he wasn't even that mucky Frenchman who was on *Wogan* and did that one mucky song. Words like "provocateur" and "men's dark inner lives" and "untranslatable play on words" were coming out of my mouth and immediately melting down my chin as we sat on the kerb next to that graffitied wall. We shared a Gitane in his honour and then left when I felt like she had had to humour me for long enough. I still go there when I visit Paris, although having walked all the way over I'm never quite sure what I'm meant to do once I'm there. I sort of walk up and down a couple of times and then stand there for a minute, before going away to buy face cream at the pharmacy nearby that they always talk about in magazines. I can't help but keep going to Serge's, although I'm never sure what this little pilgrimage is really about. Years ago in an ASDA car park a song from *Melody Nelson* came on the radio and it made the dimensions of my dad's Ford Ka seem to sag and go all languid. Some days, I'll play it through my headphones as I go up the escalator on particularly dour mornings to try to reproduce the effect. But I can't still be paying homage to that. There's this other song of his I like very much but one minute forty-one seconds in you start to hear a woman weeping on the track underneath. I don't know whether I used to listen to a different version, but these days it's all I can hear and I have to turn it off.

Even now, sometimes I get the train home from St Pancras and I'll find myself walking out of my way to pass through the Eurostar departures area and it's like I'm cruising — I mean, I think in a way I am actually cruising — but I'm never quite sure what's sexier: a person or the departures board.

Laisse Tomber

S.J. Fowler

Looking up from the centre of below. Begins nightmares about space itself, it's fact, how one might travel through it if it folded. In a race car bed, waking up screaming, pulling a stereo down on to my own face. That begins below the tower. Paris is not a city for Cornish children.

My brother is built, back from Afghanistan. He seems fine. The family goes to Paris for a day, which is an enormous pain, travelling in and out from a gîte east of Rennes, but still, proudly, in Brittany. I jacket wrestle with a boy two years older than me who throws me like a doll. I am distracted by his sister. I don't speak a word of Breton, but there's live music. Paris seems unduly hot but an abstract collection of things to do. I can recall my first understanding of the concept of Napoleon, for which there is no English equivalent. I start to stamp my feet and even cry in an art gallery. This forces the entire party to bitterly leave, but in a typical act of stubborn defiance against its children the unit drags me to the Louvre. I become so incensed that I kick my father in the leg. Thinking back to this, what a gentleman he was to not slap my face. My embarrassing behaviour is vividly placed in cultural terms. What will the French think of English children? The same thing they have always thought. My savagery forces the aspirational working-class family to exit both the gallery and then the city, everyone throwing their tools to the floor. As we leave the Louvre I race out of my mother's grip and make for the outdoor seating of the museum's café. I grab the first glass bottle I can and throw it, without hesitation, at a flock of birds. It smashes into many pieces and birds expand into the air. This is the scene in chapter three of *L'Assommoir*, which Huysmans loved, where the working-class family discovers, in the most humorous manner, the impossibility of escaping the environmental fatalities to which they will inevitably succumb. I am instructive to the reader. I am a matrix of symbolic and thematic codes. I am a boy foreshadowing without crisis. Paris is an outlandish landscape, full of itself, needing to have a bottle thrown at it and its birds.

I'm old enough to be introverted. They offer me wine at the dinner table. It's a package holiday. Just three of us. I am unable to understand it but I recognise, drenched in acne, that my family is without cynicism. We're staying by the Sacré Coeur. The Gare du Nord is daunting. The waiter says I should try barberries. On the menu, I ask? No, he says, for your face. Any Middle Eastern grocer will have them. They use them in their rice.

I'm with three friends who are not my friends within one year of my visit. I cannot recall their surnames. I comprehend, in an attractive rented apartment on Rue Ramponeau, that people are not as comfortable around me as they are around each other. They are scared of something I might do. An argument sours the air at the midpoint of the trip. I end up shouting. I mock them for being sincere, overtly earnest to the point of being, in my eyes, categorically, stupid. The world needs balance. Balance in the universe, fuck these earnest shits. Shut up and sit down. The world needs people like them, who are sincere and in touch with themselves, they're perfect for a quick Paris weekend break. I shall not come to the city again unless I am alone or with someone I can have sex with to mitigate the conversation.

She is typing into Google, how to expand a shirt that's shrunk. She doesn't add a question mark. I definitely shouldn't, but I'm going to. To whom should I compare myself? Is there anything more foolish than an old man with a young woman? Her boyfriend, whom she refers to as a partner, without irony, is exactly double her age. I would imagine, instinctively, considering myself one of the unwashed, almost illiterate, that anyone who thinks they can resist an offered body is a bigger fool than those ageing across young women. Who do you like? I ask, with trepidation. She says the name of an American. Oh shut up, I respond. She doesn't, and seems hurt but also convulsed by my volatility. She has a tattoo on her thigh. It's writing. What the fuck is that I ask? Why are you so abusive, she replies, and I break into laughter, though I intended to maintain my reserve as long as possible. Why did I message her on Facebook? Because I cannot be in Paris alone. My Paris is specifically not a place to be alone. So anybody as company will do. How many times will this be why I am with someone? How long will I linger in the bar with her, trying to massage its fixtures into atmosphere? She orders me a very strong drink, which is the only thing she will ever do that surprises me and I don't like it because I'm a sweet drunk. Have you read *Lasomwar*, she asks? I don't even reply. She's pointing to a plaque. We don't even spend the evening together, I can't take it. I walk from the Rue de la Goutte d'Or where we've been all night to the Boulevard Barbès, following it south down Boulevard Magenta. I'm intimidated by the side roads. I have no sense of this city, I realise. But hailing a cab seems worse than being lost. I find myself on the Rue de Turenne and cross the Île Saint-Louis. The Boulevard Saint-Michel is busy and I feel more confident, though I'm growing weary. I have the feeling I have so far to go. It made me proud to choose hotels randomly.

He begins a strange kind of wrestling with me, softly pushing his fingers into my face, as though they might disappear within my mouth, through my cheek. He doesn't want to hurt me. I don't know how to respond because he's an Arab. I've been to Algeria, I say, and this is true. To Oran. This actually works: it stops him and while we don't become friends, there is no more trouble. This comes into my mind every time someone chastises the practise of asking "Where are you from?" as racist. Cyril Abidi is fighting Jérôme Le Banner on a small television in a café. When I sit at the back, expecting to be welcomed, naively, someone mutters something about me and there are stares. My friend Alexander waits for me in the car. There's the book in the car, but I never get beyond page thirty.

We take the Eurostar. I've known her for three weeks. It's felt like longer. We stay two nights. We visit the catacombs. I'm reading *Là-Bas*, which makes more of an impression on me than her. How can some people be so... She takes a

59

private phone call and puts it on speakerphone. She posts everything we do to visual social media. On the last day, I, for only the second time in my life, leave her in a shop and walk away. We never speak again. She listened to music in public without headphones. She ate loudly. She drank too much wine without knowing she was getting drunk, when I wasn't drinking, then denied she was drunk. She liked to dance. She belongs in Paris as a visitor, a perfect guest to Paris. I hope she's moved there.

A disrespectful smile. An unforeseeable wave. An unhurried pose. I'm not a *Parisien* so I can't use the French words for insolent and languid, not having the linguistic context to walk in muddy footprints. It's studied, and fraught. It's anxious, the attempt to be effortless. An invisible dog, that makes me follow its lead. It's all attractive though. I miss what I'm used to, clumsy efforts to not look away, grips like a Bulgarian. Inevitably, this is expunged with a desire for something new. It's very nimble, very fluid. Like a minor electrical discharge from a cattle fence. She says she hates other women. I don't know what to say. I know not to agree. There is a forced smile. Is it even a smile? A grimace at my not agreeing. Everything imperceptible is a test. I'm just going to look away, I think. I turn around, my back to her and look at nothing. I feel a hand on my shoulder. That's unexpected. You've slipped, I say. There's a certain danger. Do you think you can make a woman orgasm without touching anything on her body from coccyx to navel? she asks, emphasising the anatomical vocabulary. Why would I try? I reply. Impressed as I am that she was born here, I cannot help but be put in mind of a literary critic who has no love for writers, whose criticism is not an enhancement of understanding, an invitation to read the book again in the light of her interpretation, but simply an instrument of destruction. The peroxide works, but I can smell it. Hair that smells a little like a chemical toilet. This is affecting, even arousing. This is also deliberate, I think. We make our way down Rue Condorcet, she stops at a patisserie and eats what she buys in three bites. The butter, she murmurs. I get nothing. Feeble applause. I'm quite tired. No one wants to talk to me. Her chin in her palm. She's so senseless, she's doing it deliberately. I have a good memory for clothes: she's cut off one of the shoulder straps. She smells strongly; it's acrid, urine is in there. This is why people shave, I say. To look like a little girl, she replies, or asks? I take a handful of her pubic hair and tug it firmly upwards, towards her belly. I end up drinking her blood and think this is standard, associate it from then on with Paris. That that is Parisian and not French. It doesn't work as well back in England, makes me retch. I imagine I can feel cells between my teeth like fish eggs.

Some ill-advised gallery reading with name-droppers. I am not many things. This feels like the first time I've walked around Paris alone. Things haven't changed here, though. I've never stayed more than four days. I'm not necessarily sad about that. First time on business.

I'm now aware of what being in love is and am kinder because of the fear it will depart. I sit in a hotel on Rue Henri Barbusse and write as she sleeps. There's a picture of me upon Paul Éluard's grave I've kept. Why did I choose the city for a honeymoon? I'm a hypocrite. Not worth recounting much else, love is repetitive.

Martin has arranged a reading at the Cirque Électrique, on the Place du Maquis du Vercors. No one attends.

Paris Doesn't Belong to Us

Greg Gerke

On the third day of our honeymoon, we wandered back across the Left Bank. We walked the narrow blocks near the Sorbonne with their small expensive apparel shops, where a pair of woman's shoes cost more than our two high-speed train tickets from Amsterdam, and their specialty stores, including a number devoted to antiquarian books. Only after I followed my wife into these establishments did everything about my person seem ill-fitting. My $50 coat from Uniqlo, my discount Merrells' from DSW, my $16 haircut from Luigi at Astor Place Hair. The male and female handlers at these stores had the skin of porcelain sculpture and from that skin I extrapolated their existences in nanoseconds. They enjoyed their espressos (one couldn't say "drank" of such a minute cup of liquid) with the distancing brio of the acculturated, they spoke of their trips to the Alps and Spain, and they had sex late at night with the aftertaste and acids of $50 dishes coursing through their blood. Years before, in another arrondissement, I walked into a small museum dressed in my 1999 outerwear, that is to say an ensemble fabricated by my station in life — I made minimum wage — and my place of residence, Eugene, Oregon, a bubble that held nothing against holes, screwy pastels, or crossknits in one's rags. Dressed in some such unseemingly outfit of earth tones, I passed two well-heeled men who worked at the institution. They spoke to each other garrulously, but as I hove into view, the eyes of the more sophisticated locked on my form and I saw his head move up and down as he pored over everything I was to outer appearance. This motion ended with a strong look of dissatisfaction that he pinioned to my soul across our eyebeams and I convulsed like a David Lynch shibboleth, as I was now ruled by his implanted disregard. Outside of my parents and a few lovers, it was the first time I had the mind of another person inside me, feasting on my ego after an easy kill. Years on, it is a moment or rather a confluence that stays stapled to me like a lifetime achievement demerit slip. No matter where I go or what I do, the stain of that delicately cutting encounter lingers, pointing at me like a convict flaunting a knife at the next heart his life will harm. It is deep set, disappearing for a few years and then rearing like it gained strength all the while.

To embrace the Saint-Germain quarter of the city, we sought Les Deux Magots, being emblazoned in the guide book thus, "Its name refers to the two *magots* (grotesque figurines) of Chinese dignitaries at the entrance... Sit on the inimitable terrace... Sip its famous shop-made hot chocolate, served in porcelain jugs." Joyce, Sartre, Stein and Hemingway went there when they were not so well known, escaping a dim limelight only cast after success. To sit in the dining room, given our blue jeans and the shortage of euros or applicable credit in those jeans' pockets, would have required a caliber of effrontery we didn't possess. We took a table inside, under the retaining vinyl plastic shield, facing the Church of Saint-Germain's nave. The stiff-faced waiter in his sixties, short and fey with thin wire-rimmed glasses and a bow tie over his white serving coat (the repertoire of any stereotypical barista at a fine establishment), mercifully listened to our order of a café and a cocoa — the most affordable items, six and nine euros, respectively. The patrons were what one expects when paying astronomical prices for things McDonald's and Dunkin' Donuts sell for a song. There were certainly tourists about, and also Parisians, but everyone was there to look or be looked at. Fine fittings, expensive outfits, the latest phones, the latest primary-colored handbags, eyes glazed by bullish calories, skin as soft as butter left out overnight. The elderly man next to us, who had padded in with multiple bags of papers and periodicals, decorated his table with a hand-sized journal and a shiny pen with an ink fuselage, though he did not indite, but fixed his eyes easterly to the church, and to those hundreds of people passing in an early evening growing cold. An American mother and daughter came in and sat before us at the table by the window, though the mother could have been an older sister in a certain light — her beige leather boots doubtless still smelling of the box that housed them on the Rue Dauphine the day before. Blonde from blonde, they were clearly chuffed at their outing and held a phone high to capture their faces close upon the other in happiness at Les Deux Magots. Could these people be thinking about us? Though a few feet away, did they even see us? If they did, what did they see? A married couple? Two people in love? Two people at odds? Two Americans at odds? Two Americans against all odds?

The popular cliché about the French, a cliché restated by my countrymen, is that they think Americans don't know how to live. We are savage and deficient in certain refined aspects pertaining to composure, compunction, and, certainly, culture and its expression. As I primped for my wife's picture of me, tipping my miniature cup of coffee with my pinky pointed out and cheeks sucked in, we could come close to the pitiful, ugly American, miming the etiquette he is so destined never to encompass. At times, my wife and I act goofy together — there is no other word for the spirit of our connection. The best approximation in French is *joie de vivre*. This goofiness enables the easefulness that is our love. I told the audience of our marriage this was the "most important reason" we were before them. Once I might have dreamt of sitting in the Les Deux Magots, sipping coffee and smelling the cigarettes of a proper philosophically-enamored female, aka Susan Sontag, but I am happy to report this is not my life. Wrongly, I once thought I needed someone to speak of Plato with to be happy. Uniformity is what I had been looking for all along.

Every Story of Paris is also a Story of Disillusion

Jonathan Gibbs

If you were brought up, like me, in a middle-class, reasonably cosmopolitan household in the south-east of England in the late twentieth century, then Paris was just *there*. Mostly you went camping in Normandy or Brittany, but you got to go to Paris, you had been there, before you even knew what it was, and what it might mean. Then gradually you learned what Paris had to offer — to you, personally — and it became established in your mind like the drop-in sets of a cardboard toy theatre: the ideal backdrop to whatever drama you imagined you might one day star in.

Yet when I think back on my experience of Paris, what comes most readily to mind is a series of mildly self-deprecating anecdotes.

The time I went to Paris to promote my first novel, translated into French, for a prize it didn't win, and spent most of my time looking for presents to take back for my family. The time I took my wife, when she wasn't yet my wife, to Paris for the weekend, and I was so intent on showing off my French to the waiter that I didn't notice I was ordering steak tartare, and subsequently spent much of our romantic weekend on or near the toilet. The time I house-sat my

67

uncle and aunt's lovely house in the western suburb of Louveciennes for a couple of weeks — I think this must have been during the year after my A Levels — and spent whole days wandering lonesomely around the city looking for adventure, or just connection. I visited the *Marché aux puces* and bought a beret. I went to see *La Cantatrice chauve* at the Théâtre de la Huchette. I tracked down the Beat Hotel and found it was just a hotel, on the outside at least.

I did eventually find some form of connection in a boy of about my age who was sitting on his own on the edge of the huge Grand bassin octogonal in the Tuileries. Or else I was sitting there, and he found me. And we got chatting, and met again the next day, I think, to walk and talk some more. I have no idea what we talked about. I could never work out in the years afterwards if he was just lonely, like me, or was nervously trying to pick me up, or both.

But here's the thing about Paris: it is forgiving of those who come to it looking for adventure and fail to find it. (Paris is not equally forgiving of everyone, obviously. Its unsurpassable walkability — the sheer reasonableness of the size of its centre — is made possible by the shoving of huge swathes of its population, including many generations of immigrants, to the outskirts.)

No one can live up to their expectations of Paris. The precedents are simply too insanely unachievable. But Paris forgives you for not living up to it. It is the most merciful of cities. That said, I'm glad I had tried and failed to measure up to the possibilities of the city before I ever read Geoff Dyer's 1998 novel *Paris Trance*, which plays on exactly this conundrum, of the gap between the expat fantasy and the reality. What would have been the killer would have been the realisation that, not only could I not live up to the Parisian adventures of the early- and mid-twentieth century, I couldn't even live up to the failed adventures of that second *fin de siècle*.

The Au Pair

Emily S. Cooper

I got off the overnight bus. You met me, jeans tied together
at the waist.
You took me to the Amélie café and told me under her face

that sugar sticks were designed to be snapped in the middle
and the inventor
killed himself when everyone ripped them at the ends.

The family left for summer. You moved from your
apartment to the 16th.
Their kitchen counters tortured you. Liquids seared
the wood.

We slept in the children's beds, toys arranged neatly on
parquet floors.
We never fucked. Even though it was Paris.

Even though, when I was a teenager, you told me in the
John Street taxi queue
that you loved me and that I must, must love you too.

Even though we fought for hours and you told me that
your philosophy degree
qualified you to tell me that I was terrible at arguing, I still
did not fuck you.

We bought cheap wine from Carrefour and went into an
expensive *cave à vin*
to ask them to open it for us. At the fountain, you confessed
your crack habit.

On the Métro I told stories about the other passengers.
You cut me off.
That's weird. Stop it. Nobody does that. We squeezed
through the barriers.

I got to the bus station and found that I had printed the
receipt and not the ticket.
As I hugged you goodbye, each rib under your coat bent
away.

French Lessons

Heidi James

Gemma's son has died, tragically and out of the blue. I don't have the details, though I've seen photos of the memorial service: held out at sea, the mourners floating on surf boards in a bobbing, shifting circle. From the comments it seems he went to bed one night and just didn't wake up. It happens sometimes. He was only eighteen years old, strong as a bull. Even so, it's not as rare as you might imagine.

She found me through Facebook: liked some of my photos, made comments about my weight, the usual. She was always posting about her husband and his successful business, photos of her huge, immaculate house by the beach, her beautiful kids smiling with their tanned arms looped around her neck. I hate how social media does that, returns people you hoped you'd lost forever; reveals *your* hiding places, *their* gilded lives — but how do you avoid it? You have to at least try to take part or what's the point?

I'm still not sure why she messaged me about her son; it's not like I live nearby and could drop round a casserole or anything. Perhaps she just wanted to share her grief, dilute it a little, have it witnessed. It was heartrending. The broken syntax and fragmented phrases too painful to repeat. I even cried, though I'd never met the kid, but then I cry about other people's children I read about online all the time.

She was the first one to like me at school. I was a weird kid. A joke really, desperate to fit in, to be liked, morbid and maybe a fantasist. Maybe. I remember that time mostly through the clothes I had to wear and my total discomfort. My aunt gave me sacks of my cousin's cast-offs: old-fashioned, hot nylon, itchy wool or too tight. I hated the rub of waistbands, cuffs or collars. I just wanted clothes that didn't show how poor we were or how disgusting I was. I just wanted loose things that didn't remind me I had a body; a shameful body that invited hurt and ugliness. I remember a fist around my foot, holding me still, tugging at the lace on my ankle sock. I remember a lot of things lately. Not all of them correctly. Gemma had great clothes. She was tall and slim and had great teeth without having to have braces. She was popular, even though the other girls called her a slut behind her back, and she sat next to me in French class. We were in the top set, and I was top of the class.

She told me that actually, if I tried, I could be pretty. I laughed at her; and focused on translating the sentence Madame Walsh — who was really French but had stupidly married an Englishman — had chalked on the board.

"No," Gemma said, "I mean it. Come stay over and I'll show you."

It turned out that she was right. She smeared stuff on my face, and shook out my hair, and replaced my clothes with some of hers, and just like that people seemed to forget I was weird and ugly underneath. She took me out with her, to watch boys play pool at the youth club and then later to hang around outside the Chinese takeaway, and even though I didn't say much and just waited for her while she got off with a couple of boys, nothing bad happened.

Gemma and I had plans to move to Paris when we were sixteen. She said we were too good for our shithole town. We practised our French and choreographed dance routines in her bedroom to songs by Prince. She'd seen a TV show about the Moulin Rouge and decided we were going to be showgirls, shimmering in sequins and living in a chic flat in Pigalle. We were going to be bad and glamorous. We were going to be sexy. We were going to party and drink and have lovers. I had read a couple of Jean Rhys novels and had started listening to music by Bikini Kill and L7, so it seemed like a good idea. It might seem a strange way to go about it. The other girls were talking about hairdressing, or office work or even going to university, but they were just choosing a career. I felt that I had a choice about what kind of girl I would be, about the persona I could inhabit. That I could choose a me.

It was around this time that I first met my father. He drove a cheap sports car, drank a lot and had a beautiful girlfriend who wore tight black clothes and red lipstick. They talked about sex like it was architecture — an essential infrastructure, but one that was aesthetically pertinent. They would pick me up from school, the top down on his car, and the other girls turned green with envy as they climbed into their mother's Volvo estates. They loved dogs too, and I would go visit them and sit on the floor of their untidy cottage with their three Great Danes and dream that I could move in with them and never see my mother and her pristine flat again.

They took me to a party to meet their friends, it was boring until everyone jumped naked into the swimming pool. A famous boxer laughed at me for keeping my underwear on, then put his arm around my waist before shoving the meat of his fingers inside me. That's not important and not what I want to tell you, so forget I mentioned it.

They wanted to meet my friends, so they could know me better, so I took Gemma along one night. They made us dinner and let us drink vodka and coke. They told Gemma she could be a model. I just sat and listened and watched. I watched the way my father looked at his girlfriend, the way he laughed at her jokes. I watched him stroke her thigh under the table as she parted her legs. Something twisted in my gut and I felt sick. I could watch him undetected because he didn't really notice me.

"So, Gemma, what can you tell me about this one?" he nodded in my direction, "Is she really naughty in school?"

"As if! She's top of the class,"

To which my father replied, "She gets that from me. I've got a very high IQ, haven't I, babe?" His girlfriend nodded. "I never bothered with college though, the school of life has taught me all I need. I bet you're naughty though, aren't you, Gemma?"

All my other choices — frumpy scholar, cloistered penitent, wife and mother — disappeared. I don't know when it became an option to choose being broken, but it seems I did. If I really chose at all.

He let us choose the music for the drive back home. Gemma put on The Cure. He drove fast, overtaking two cars at once on a narrow lane. Gemma laughed hard, her wide mouth exposing all her teeth. He laughed with her, and watched her in the rear-view mirror, before accelerating harder. I let my head fall back against the seat and gave in as the vodka pressed me into a new shape. He asked if we wanted to smoke and chat for a while and when Gemma nodded he turned the car off the main road and parked outside the supermarket. Dark and locked up for the night, the trolleys corralled like cattle — we were the only ones there. Then we were talking, as he rolled a joint and so that we wouldn't be sick, he blew smoke in our mouths, his face kiss close. I could smell his lemony cologne, and a heavier, animal scent. My hands were numb. Then he asked if we'd ever kissed each other, and we laughed and said no. He said we didn't know what we were missing, and that we should try it. He wasn't looking at her, but me; he was watching me and so I kissed Gemma's soft lips and she kissed me back, her tongue broad and metallic in my mouth. After a few seconds I started to pull away, but he pushed me back, his hand cupping the back of my head, saying "Don't stop, you've only just started". So, we carried on. Apparently, we were so beautiful he could hardly breathe, we were the most beautiful thing he had ever seen.

He dropped me off two streets away from my mother's in case anyone saw us, then took Gemma home alone.

We never got to Paris, but I was a stripper in Soho. It's not as bad as you think. It was an old club run by two men who'd been there since the Fifties when the girls had to stand still and could only switch pose when the lights went down for a second. They would joke about the good old days and how professional the girls used to be. John would crank the dusty red curtains open and the lights were bright enough to cocoon you in your own light, naked and dancing, perfectly alone on the little stage.

I made a lot of cash and there was no touching which made it ok, and why shouldn't it have been? I wasn't sure. There were the conflicting feminist arguments about who was exploiting who, but the details interested me and I learnt so much. Like how to cut tampon tails so they don't show when you're on stage, how beautiful the body is — cellulite, stretch marks and all. I learnt how to be liked, by the other women, and the men in the audience. I learnt to be quiet but not stand-offish; to look people in the eye and just tell them what I wanted, what I felt. The women were a mixed bunch: single mums, artists, out-of-work dancers and actresses, a couple of academics — all interesting, intelligent women. The audience was mostly made up of men. You'd get the occasional woman, usually there with her partner for a kick. We'd always flirt with her, pay her the most attention: that brought in a lot of tips. Mostly the men were sweet, respectful; a few dickheads, and the odd one or two so lonely they believed they loved you. At Christmas, all of us girls would go on stage together, wearing cheap red Santa outfits and pelting the punters with polystyrene snowballs.

My friends said I changed, that I seemed hard. I stopped seeing them. I'd already stopped seeing my mother and father. I made a new choice, and then another and another.

A French girl joined the strip club. So thin her veins crossed under her skin like a macramé basket holding her together. She could do the splits, her bush fuzzy between her legs. She took a lot of coke, and she was beautiful even though her hair was always tangled. Sometimes we spoke in French together, when she was too fucked up to speak English. It wasn't Paris, but who gets the life they wanted?

I've learnt to want what I've got.

I've left a lot out, but this is close enough. I got the life I chose, and Gemma ended up unhappily married in Hawaii, mother to a dead son.

Some Standard Paradise

Nathan Dragon

He splashed it on and Paris flashed in his head. Something residual. Sprinklets sitting on the surface of his skin.

At least the word — PARIS — at first.

Pointing towards something sparsely surrounded with whatever came with it.

He did what amounted to some research so he could picture it better. And this so he could tell everyone about his trip there, or trips if he wanted to. Sometimes he'd go through a few pages about it in a magazine, some photography books — this one photographer from there he liked with a name like a street. Then it was there when he was standing in front of the mirror or looking out the living-room window. In the comfort and discomfort of his own home.

He'd realized that the label on the bottle of the Florida Water was probably why. He'd been relieved to see, on the back of the bottle, the recent indication, his incantation of this, specifically: *Eau de Cologne*. To himself: Ahhh, right.

Whatever he seemed to know of it he couldn't help. Or what came first.

A place has its placeness, its repertoire of place-things: things you think about if you hear someone talking about some place. Things stick and have the potential to stay stuck over time.

This was an explanation for it.

And how bits dislodge from a focal point, make a mound and scatter; get stuck under those top notes, lose saturation.

Or — something got stuck in his mind that was a miniature bit dislodged from some other original, or archetypal thing, combined with something else. Like three famous monuments from different parts of town stuck in a snowglobe all next to each other in yellowing water.

He could revisit any way he wanted, the way he wanted to, without ever thinking of actually going. None of the fuss and bustle.

There were a few specific things he could think of if he tried. There was perfume and he knew this for a fact. Some other elses, a lot of substitution.

Only to conjure up the idea.

Capital *I* idea, he thought.

And maybe another one to hold it up against.

Once or twice it had been Key West up there, but it was mostly Paris in his head or out his window, right. He couldn't blame himself for the fact that it was, after all, all in the name.

He had all that he needed there to be.

Some standard paradise to agree with, quietly put.

He tried to picture the types of things the people at work talk about wanting to do when they talk about going away. And who talked about what exactly so that way he had something to impress all of them.

He knew about the lack of love in a dream.

Like a hill in front of the sky.

An old cloudless daydream in the shade, but bright in the hollowy breezy way it was. A sip of Vichy water, right?

That's something he'd read.

He would have to take time off at work to pull it off. So that he could mention that he was taking a trip to Paris and he could chime in sometime that he had gone before. Glad to go back.

Glad for himself, glad to have something to tell them.

At work they joked with him, how he needed a change, at least a break. How he had to do something, like really get out.

There was pity.

So he got the idea and the Florida Water in the section of the store with all the bath stuff so he could smell different. A change, there it was, like a shrug. Refined.

When he thought about the whole thing, the combination reminded him of that one famous marine biologist with the musically-named boat. And citrus.

A conflation of all citrus into only limes, he guessed.

He needed to use a specific word or phrase, of course — needed to. For effect. It was easy after that.

Getting to be at home with a new bottle of Florida Water. Get a little fragranted and think about it. Learn the name of something else there.

He could picture himself walking by the names of things. He remembered all the bones they had there underneath. Like an island on top of a reef — another thing.

Once mouthing himself off in the mirror, he pushed all the way through gliding rays in the Keys, to drying himself off in the bathroom of a big hotel on the Seine. The Seine it's called, right?

He figured it was a good start. A perfectly good start. That he could get himself there at all.

81

No, when he thought back and had a chance to correct himself, not a hotel but a hostel.

A place made romantic with anything enough.

Just name the thing.

He had a gist of it now. It passed through him like a membrane. He was osmosissing. What's a place there he'd heard of without having to look it up? Testing himself. Rain falling on him walking his way up the Champs-Élysées. Like a film scene go-to. To get another bottle of *parfum*. He was impressing himself.

Also the Left Bank and whatever that could mean, he thought. Because it depends on which way you're facing on any river.

Just imagine this, but on a park bench, just like his park bench here, the only place out that he seemed to go. Staring at the roots of a tree. A honey locust? No, correcting himself again, a chestnut tree of course.

He could imagine anything already given to him, but nothing from scratch, being a part of a thing or a copy of it. Everybody, anybody there from the neck down when he pictures being there, otherwise he can't picture it. It's a lot to make up faces.

He even thought about dumping out the screw top bottle into a spray bottle and covering his life in it.

A prayer to his fraudulence, that it might make him happy.

Parc des Princes

Wendy Erskine

Bus is rammed, always full on the wet days with the blazers stinking of old dogs' blankets, and that nutter three seats behind him, the heavy guy who elbowed him in the face so his teeth snagged on the inside of his cheek. Had been sucking a big sweet at the time so the slobbers he spat out were blue and red. Doesn't like the two teachers he had this afternoon, Miss Hinds and Madame McGuigan. Hinds didn't let them do a practical today. Come on Miss like! What's the point if we don't make anything? Did about food safety instead, don't reheat this, don't reheat that, but she was pissed off because somebody messed about with one of the bread sticks that was there from the other class, carrying on like it was his dick. Quit that, she said, quit that, you think somebody's gonna want to eat that after your dirty paws have been all over it? Another class made stuff but some of them chucked it in the bin at the bus stop, white sauce, lumpy white sauce running onto the concrete. Then on came the rain.

A crowd down the back of the bus are flicking bits of rubber at people, not sore, just annoying. Hit again, back of the neck. Yous gonna stop that? comes a voice. Yous gonna stop that? Big Dawn, trying to put stuff on her face with a brush. Yous gonna wise up? They repeat what she's saying, high and whingey. Gonna stop that! Gonna stop that!

Sacrebleu! The guy that came in when Madame McGuigan was off for the month told them the word sacrebleu. The guy with the shitty wee car. That your shaggin wagon? No more of that please, he said. *Sacrebleu*. *Sacre Bleu*. Sack my Bleu. Suck my Bleu. Suck my Bla. A bag's just got emptied on the floor, stuff'll get booted around, wee guy is scrambling to try to get it back, wee guy cares about his pencil case, he's not going to get that stuff back.

Why don't you stop that and pay attention? Hinds said this afternoon. Dunno. This is important. To be fair miss, it's not. What did you say, I beg your pardon? Right, out! Wrote stuff on a bit of paper and sent him to see the year head, the guy who looks like Martin Tyler but with a fatter face. Dandered off to see the year head. Jesus, this bus driver must be a learner cos what speed are they going at? Crawling along. His shoes are too small, they're toe-pokers, bought for that cousin's wedding and the marriage is already on the rocks, his ma says. Kick those shoes off when he gets in, take off the fuckin tie strangling him all day, be home soon now anyway, shit, what's that, felt more like a coin hitting him this time, but soon he'll be home, soon he'll be

pressing the white button though
hearing the little flute of sound
toodle oodle oo
the whirr inside ahh ok
switch on the TV and there will be —

two guys in the front seat, taking it in turn to dig each other's arms, hitting on bruises there from the day before. Guy that covered for Madame McGuigan said they don't go ouch they go aieeee! Nobody believed that cos you don't go aieeee no matter where you're from, wise up like. Everybody started hitting each other, aieee! Aieee! Guy went crazy. The bus breaks and they're flung forward and then back like in the car crash adverts, but only just a bit. Somebody drums their phone against the window, quicker and quicker, somebody bangs the seat but

a big paint splash

FIFA 19

English, press that

the swirl, then —

late for Madame McGuigan this afternoon cos of having to see that year head, headed down the corridor to her room past all the flags. Somebody said to the guy that was in for McGuigan, you not got the gay flag? The rainbow flag? No, he said, because gay is not a country. Got a lot of junk in those rooms down that corridor though, that picture of the big glass pyramid, somebody said it was on the TV in a show where you had to find a crystal, that big photo of all those cyclist guys going past that grey thing, the big bridge in the middle of nowhere. Madame McGuigan asked something when he came in, Dunno miss, dunno at all, and she did that dopey fuckin thing, held her hands up to her ears like the words were disgusting, she did that when you tried to speak normal. Tried to explain why he was late but she just made more of the noise and pointed at the free chair at the front. Oh well whatever, suit yourself, but anyway

UEFA Champions League

select country, country France

Angers, AS Monaco, ASSE, Dijon FCO, EA Guingamp, FC Nantes, Girondins de Bordeaux, Lille LOSC, Montpellier

HSC, Nîmes Olympique, OGC Nice, OL, OM, Paris
Paris Saint-Germain, always gonna be,
Parc des Princes, yeah.

When he sat down Madame McGuigan started playing something, it babbled away, everybody wriggling in their seats, Suck My Bla! somebody whispers, then fill in the worksheet. It's down the bottom of his bag now, drink leaked out this morning so it'll have turned to mush. Madame McGuigan's got a big poster behind her desk, a couple sitting at a table in a street, wee waiter coming over with a tray, but so fuckin what, places like that in the town. There was even a place in the town had a rat, somebody filmed it through the window late at night when it scurried around the café. Stinking old rat.

OK, will go with Barcelona
Shooting basics, crappy wee spot like the school pitch
Shooting basics with its wee park benches
alright, Parc des Princes

push and he hits the cold metal of the seat in front, hard whack on his ear so there's silence and then every sound's like at the swimming pool. Don't turn round to look at the big guy as he's getting off, even though he can nearly taste the sweet bloody slobber again, just look out the window, watch that man getting the black bag ready as that big dog crouches at the bus shelter, that one that's always wrecked, the plastic over the timetable bubbled with a cigarette lighter but

Parc des Princes
grey sky but no shadow, dazzle of the lights,
criss cross crosshatch, bright white,
the red and blue squares, *Paris est magique*

86

wraparound, only the grey up above
wraparound the
six dark green stripes six light green stripes
squares, blue and red, triangles of flag
snug in the Parc des Princes, happy shapes of sounds from
the crowd and it's gonna start soon
Revenons plus grands
everything's gonna go grand or something like that
suck my Bla
Paris est magique.

Very Little Romance and Very Little Dialogue

Ashton Politanoff

The Parisian street is dimly lit, all the storefronts dark. Two men emerge from a parked car. They are wearing windbreakers and one of them has a moustache. They each carry an empty satchel. They don't say a word.

We follow these men through courtyards and staircases and hallways. The faint sound of a dinner party can be heard. One of the men grabs the bare breast of a statue as he passes.

One by one, these two men climb through a skylight hatch until they are on a roof. They are silhouettes just like the chimneys. Soon, they are overlooking an empty plaza with a roundabout.

With affixed rope ladders, they climb down until they are level with a high window. They cut a hole in the glass and an arm reaches through the hole to turn a knob from the inside. They enter the building, a bathroom, in this way.

A security guard is level with the handle of a pistol, his mouth taped shut, arms and legs tied tight. A third man appears outside the building in a trench coat. The third man is carrying a guitar case, but we know he isn't here to play music. These two men are able to buzz the third man in right through the front door.

In a room full of jewels, the three men converge. The third man removes a tripod and pieces of a rifle from the guitar case. The rifle is assembled quickly and silently. The tripod is set up. The third man mounts the rifle onto the tripod and adjusts the legs of the tripod so the target, a keyhole the size of a small bullet, and the gun, are perfectly aligned. But then, the tripod is abandoned. The man removes the rifle and aims. The other two men look alarmed. This isn't part of the plan. The man shoots.

The bullet disappears into the hole. There is a moment of uncertainty, but then all the jewellery display cases unbolt automatically and the other two men open their satchels and start filling their bags.

The third man, the marksman, sniffs from a flask of whisky. This is the smell of victory. He puts the flask away without so much as a taste. The two men steal the entire collection and the third man leaves early for the getaway car. The security guard comes-to and is able to trigger the alarm with his forehead, but the men have completed the job.

My wife comes into our home office where I sit with my laptop watching as the alarm shrieks wildly from the film, the first sound of its kind. The men are already in the getaway car. Even though this film takes place in Paris, there is very little romance and very little dialogue.

We have to go, she says.

We get in my car, the present in the backseat, and I drive. I take what I think is the fastest way there.

What were you watching? she asks me.

A French movie, I tell her. I tell her the name, but she doesn't say anything. She returns to the screen of her phone and I look ahead at the road as we climb the hill. The eucalyptus trees hide the sun, the car passing through shadow and light. Soon, the sun will set.

Their house isn't far from an elementary school. My wife thinks I can pull into their driveway, but I park on the street instead. The air is fragrant and fresh. It smells like a different country up here. My wife rings the doorbell before I reach the landing and the door swings open. The husband, Bill, is there. Bill and I were friends before he met his wife Karen and my wife, but now we are all friends. My wife hands over the present, and we follow Bill inside. This is their new house.

Wow, my wife says to Bill.

Karen, I say. Congratulations.

Yes! my wife says. On the house and the baby.

The present is for the baby, not the house, I say. Bill and Karen laugh but my wife doesn't.

The baby is sleeping in a low rocker near the dining room table and my wife follows Karen to the kitchen. Bill gives me a tour. He points at the windows. Those were all redone, he says. The old windows — the glass wasn't tempered. That could have been dangerous.

The house has two floors. I lose count of all the bedrooms. They have a real backyard that overlooks a valley and in the distance, the coast can be seen.

They call this view the queen's necklace, Bill says. At night it's easy to see why, he says. He shows me the fountains with Spanish tiles, and the little koi pond, all that came with the property.

Under the pergola on the picnic table, there are cheese

90

and crackers on a cutting board and a bowl of olives. Wine is served. Like my wife, I opt for the rosé.

Really? Bill says. My wife laughs.

Bill turns on the grill and disappears inside to prep the salmon and side dishes. My wife disappears and before Karen and I can talk, we hear the baby waken and whimper, so she leaves too. I go to the edge of the backyard and rest a hand on the metal railing. The drop is steep and thorny with cacti all around.

Inside, I find my wife in the kitchen with Bill. They don't see me, and my wife speaks in a soft voice — I can't hear what she has said. I don't see Karen anywhere, and I don't want to walk in on her nursing, so I leave and go back into the yard. I expect my wife to appear at any moment, but she doesn't. Instead Bill comes out with a tray of salmon. The salmon is well-seasoned with wedges of lemon and other herbs. Bill lays tinfoil directly onto the grill and then places the salmon one fillet at a time. The transaction is smooth and efficient. He leaves me there. I pour myself more from the bottle and sit in a dusty cushioned loveseat, my wife and Bill appearing and disappearing, sometimes together, sometimes separately. The Brie is stiff and doesn't spread easy. I crack a lot of crackers in the process. By the time the food is ready, I am already halfway full. The meal consists of salmon and instant rice and microwaved veggies with butter — broccoli, chopped carrots, cauliflower. I sit across from my wife, and Bill sits next to me, diagonal from my wife. I look at my wife look at Bill.

How's work going? Karen asks me, the baby now down and napping again near her feet in a bassinet.

Part-time still, I say. But well.

My wife eats from her plate. Bill works in finance. He does very well. The conversation soon turns to him and I tune out.

When everyone is finished eating, I start grabbing plates and serving bowls and forks and spoons and knives. I find their trash and use a knife to clear the plates one at a time. I find Tupperware and place the leftovers inside. Then, I get the sink going and I find a pair of yellow rubber gloves that are a little big for my hands. I use the gritty side of the sponge first and rinse everything under the hot jet of water. The heat gets to my fingers and Bill and Karen assure me that I don't have to clean, I should just leave it, but I ignore them and I continue on. I am focussed on my work.

Seriously, Karen says calling from the dining room.

No, I say.

She says my name. She comes into the kitchen. She slaps my shoulder playfully. She wears a low-cut shirt. This is becoming a kind of game and I grow more obstinate, like this is my mission in life, to clean the kitchen. I grab dirty glasses and small plates that have no association with our dinner — items that were dirtied at another time, probably from lunch — and start scrubbing. Karen tickles me and I finally stop even though part of me wants to see how far this will go. My seated wife doesn't look at me when I leave the kitchen, her whole body turned away and facing Bill holding the baby. I look right at her. Her legs are crossed.

Should we head out? I say.

Let me finish my glass, she says, but she doesn't even touch her glass for several minutes.

The metal screen door of our apartment slams behind us. I fill two coffee mugs full of warm wine and sit on our couch, thinking my wife might join, but she goes straight to the bathroom and shuts the door. I hear the door lock. Soon the shower is running, and I remember the film.

I go into the office and wear headphones so only I can hear this time.

The three men escape from the robbery untouched, but the detective on the case hunts them down. In the final scene, in a meadow, the three men are shot and killed by the police.

Soon thereafter, my wife and I cease face-to-face communication altogether.

Master Framer

Kathryn Scanlan

He said he'd studied under an old master of the trade. He was with the old master until the master died. From the master, he learned all there was to know.

They felt lucky to hire him. They had a stack of lithographic prints — playful, pandering Parisian street scenes — which they intended to sell for tidy sums at a tony local street fair. The master framer began work at once, with an industry they admired from their office, where they looked up from paperwork to nod in approbation.

Then one day he came in gray, disheveled, wearing what he'd worn the day before. They asked what the matter was. His wife, he said, had changed the locks and put his things on the lawn. He'd put the things in his car and driven to the parking lot of a large discount store, where he spent the night. He'd set his shoes outside the car while he slept, and when he woke, they were gone.

They saw that instead of sneakers, he wore stiff leather wingtips, which gave him a professional air despite his rumpled hair and clothing. They suggested he sleep on the sofa in the workshop until he got sorted.

Weeks passed. When they unlocked the workshop in the morning, the master framer snored open-mouthed on the sofa in his undershorts, often with an erection in plain view. His unbathed body rubbed its oily brine — soured by the odor of discount cologne — into the upholstery irreversibly.

When the master framer stepped out for lunch one afternoon, whistling a tune and wishing them well, they approached his work station with caution. He always appeared busy, so they didn't worry. But today they picked a finished frame from the stack and held it beneath the special lamp they'd purchased for this purpose.

Ah, see — very nice! said one.

What is that? said the other.

Beneath the glass, on the white mattboard, was a smear of peanut butter, stuck with cracker crumbs — oozing dark oil.

Disgusting! said one.

An honest mistake, said the other.

But they found some offensive object encased in each of the frames in the master's stack: a thick clipping of ragged toenail — several kinky pubic hairs — a crushed potato chip — dandruff by the handful — a green crust of nasal mucus — congealed blood.

Then they saw that the corners of the frames were crooked. The screws — sent in sideways and too hard — split the wood. Glue oozed in permanent, sculptural drips. Not one was usable. They cried and exchanged bitter words of blame.

When the master framer returned from lunch, his box of things sat soggily on the sidewalk and his key would not unbolt the lock. No one answered when he knocked. He put his ear to the door. He looked up and down the street. A dirty little white dog with an upturned snout lifted its leg on his box. He gave chase, but the dog outpaced him without effort. Winded, the master framer heaved the box into his car and drove away.

He never saw them again — his employers — but he did see one of their prints hanging in a bathroom of the house of a wealthy woman who hired him for odd jobs some years later. She needed her trees trimmed and her leaves blown and the crap of her dog removed from the lawn, where she liked to walk barefoot.

When he'd performed these services tolerably well for a few weeks, she offered him the modest guest quarters above her garage. She liked the master framer — liked him even better when he told her he'd framed the print in her bathroom, which she prized.

What an amazing coincidence, she said. What fine work. What a man of many talents you are.

To Disturb So Many Charms

Utahna Faith

Theatre.

We alone are happy to recognize vibrations running in the abyss of black paused ground which we followed. The vast theatre rose before us, and we entered, barefoot in silk and velvet. Hands held in the transitioning dark. Eyes pinpointing the distant stage.

Too distinct to be killed, and too luminous for dementia, the spouses will remember two major acts, performed hastily in front of royalty; the aftertaste of disappointment. The sigh unnerved them. There were no inquiries, no smiles, and no ringing of tiny bells as the red velvet drapery fell.

They will forget these and remember the many dazzling performances met with expressions of moonlight, of unveiled desire, of something perhaps nearing adoration.

She collapses in the side wing. Unseen. He carries her with unquestioning love.

The day after the phenomenon, my companion awakens sewn into a shroud nature had never before imagined. Overloaded secular clairvoyance, tarnished pagan mysteries of union, deeper than mundane supposition.

The so-called Great, replied of temperance: obey your gospel. Smile under sovereign dimensions, aided by the fabric, silent virtuoso. Sad humanity can never control the atmosphere; disorder touches all living things, a sharp knife, a glint of rose gold. Beautiful monsters whisper, of women who sleep in strings, float with the rustle of opportunities, wonder. Veiled accounts of a scientific era.

Silence became the law, was carving a space for future proclamations, the sleeper going at full speed.

Memory.

The man who captured the veiled accuracy of one apparent summer afternoon, seemed to be the center of gravity. I handed him my red guitar. A white couch appeared on the rooftop.

Noise. Heavy applause. Knowledge of ways to make a fortune. Troubled, irresistible, undeniable.

Superstition struggled luminously with the problem, mathematically guaranteed to disturb so many charms. Deviations from a standard: miraculous perfection.

A film crew arrives and carries the couch away.

Back and Forth.

The taste of a thousand pardons, you kicked gravely the engineer of the eyelids. Hidden reason, hands strained, puzzle fingerprint.

He strives to shine. Purple wool, moth-eaten, jaunty around his neck. He raised his blue eyes, whose appearance reflected mysterious creatures, the fire in the taste of woman, self, species emanating, heedless.

She asked him of monsters. He spoke of money, an edge no word can define.

Sexes shall breathe unfamiliar things of the heart, until the process succeeds. Dazzled, I will speak of a cure.

She is eye. She is I.

The Red House, and Onward.

Some guests fired up liquid extensions, blended colors, while others lolled about engaging in myriad glinting perversities. Absorbing mental courage, held knotted behind your vision, we proclaimed to all of unnecessary physics and overall suggestion.

Later that night, before sunrise, we jumped out of the frame, all inflamed. Powerfully redeemed, where light imbues the vastness of energy.

No sarcasm. Nothing bitter.

We knew it was time to go.

This secret, realizing the dream of homogenous delight, unimagined flowers crossing the threshold, put us lifted. We landed on the wax-splotched mantle, unfazed. Immutable even. Safer than all roses.

Tumbling onto the floor made entirely of bedding. Each other. Home.

Time passed unnoticed, humid and gardenia scented, until again we knew. It was time to go.

Destination.

But, Oh! Why? Why did we bring him here, his brain and his shoulders and his pale blue eyes and all the rest of it? Why here, distancing, to Paris of all places? Those arms to embrace remained a great delicacy. The parts of him. We swear to betray their secret ideal.

Some days later I can only despise the crackling acid in his brain. The pale eyes submit now, for us alone.

Rewind.

I did not know, at first, the cause of her fascination with me, nor from whence she had come.

She was nowhere and then, all at once, everywhere. The café, the stoop, the walkway along the river, or our favorite abandoned hideouts along the wharves.

(You were reported missing, we read in the *Picayune*. It was the day after she and I disrobed and pressed every silken pore of our skins together.)

We continued, she and I. Nights of bicycles and bars and dark chocolate kisses were infinite, but only in the imploding manner.

We lived in silk kimonos.

"We" then equalled: she and I.

Still radiant, we were once young girls, whose rare fruits lied, pitching such charming lines in the cockpit of the last 747.

Once, "we" had equalled: he and I.

What is there to say?

The three of us: Inevitable.

Of Him. (To Her.)

That first night, as I chose to summon him in your presence, we were shaking. We waited, your insane beauty emanating.

And he, retrieved at long last, entered spewing his fiery venom. Nothing new as a reverie. Then unconsciousness.

Transported, innocent, sand-foam speech. His voice, between moon rays and clouds, impossible. Powerful, fantastic, and true.

Your presence handles the decision.

And he, just sitting, those wild eyes lifted and clinging. I watch him watch you, helplessly, as your essential talent, your notes ringing out, a shadow moving atop the temporary but beautiful winding staircase. You descend one step, slowly, and then another. Violin at your shoulder, bow sliding, impossible notes sounding out. Even the red walls and black painted floor were quivering. Your faded violet dress left behind as though you had never known even a single stitch of clothing. Your nudity, as tremendous as moonlight, led my friend to all your instruments. To you.

On the spot. Spot on. Creation.

The outcome he despairs consists of your cheeks, your breath. A subtle flare of your nostrils, not artificial.

One remembers standing in the kitchen, confronted with old possibilities: I would not suffer this time. Zero humiliation. No prisoner of love, whatsoever his investigator divided, and holding that box in his hand despite. Person. The incomparable creature peering out.

You both will leave me. Wounded. But not mortally.

Interlude.

The perpetual slenderness of vocabulary suffered similarly, in reverie. Restless from the masterpiece, you played all imaginable hunches.

The last accident, fast and tangible, left us nothing but lips, and the illusion of a grave.

Since now found, asleep, beautiful and demolished, we have seen eyes floating in the sky like a torn away and flapping billboard.

The depth of the underground, pure and weak, was far too subtle to hold you.

Two adventurers contemplated shadows. One dressed in flowers, eyes radiant and motionless.

We dance on the newly packed earth as petals fall.

Sublime Conundrum.

The shrieks first, and then the smile.

Know that divas are invisible tonight. Garter belt grips. The angle of a straight-backed velvet chair.

Dramatic talent assured him many accents. Conditioned by illusion, spectacle, sudden magic.

And you, princess of feathers and steel.

The Tragedy.

They had contented themselves. Then, one autumn evening is turned on its head in astonishment. The afore believed impossibility, the numbing and bitter reality which cannot be.

We all search for that one Irish grandparent, search Caribbean islands that welcome, that allow dual citizenship, or more. We contemplate the weather in Canada.

It is necessary to avoid all screens in this so-called presence in which we have, temporarily, landed. The creature on the screens! We turn away, holding one another from falling. Horrific: Head so large, hands so small, heart withered to nonexistence. Inexplicable failure of the system. In entirety. Perhaps explicable in myriad long-ignored ways, but feels inexplicable in situ.

Digression.

Women, intelligence, freedom, seeing what remained of work from the centuries.

The years and decades had sufficed to overcome some or many obstacles, and now. Calling all Goddesses. Eve, even, don't give up. We call your Lilith. The temples and sanctuaries; they are yours, hers, ours. Let myth be myth, understood as such. Essence confused with their monotonous moral nothingness, their futile attempt to tarnish, to extinguish, to deny.

We shall put back in place enchantment, charms, personal approaches worth seeing. Rebuilding our temples, regrowing our forests. And good men, not tarnished by the idea of the sword as violence. Not insensitive. Not unmoved. And completely without the desire to see us desecrated.

With these, our magnets, theirs and ours and nothing less than shared desire.

Feel their presence, on to disastrous, even in those who approach presence adapted. Reinstated. Bringing with them equal electricity, whilst mutually attending to ours. As we attend to theirs now. It shall be worth seeing, worth living; strange rapture, this affirmative [affirmation?] which lacks, whatsoever, a system. Which lacks any manipulated sense of shame.

It was time to go.

Powerfully redeemed, with sarcasm bitter, we jumped all inflamed out of frame, where light imbues the vastness of energy. This secret, realizing the dream of homogeneous delight. Unimagined flowers crossed the threshold, landed on the mantle, unfazed. Immutable.

Safer than all roses.

(We put the horror we have left behind where it belongs. At the center of an imaginary black hole.)

Post-Digression.

Us. Again. We are three. Running through the Louvre even though the act has been done and overdone. One of us, we chant together, shrieking and laughing, echoing and dissipating. Security has changed over the decades, and yet we are out, down the stairs, turning the sharpest corner into the smallest alley. It is day one.

But Oh! Why did we bring him here, his brain and his shoulders and his pale blue eyes and all the rest of it? Why here, distancing, to the actual Paris? Those arms to embrace remained a great delicacy. The parts of him. We swear to betray their secret ideal.

Some weeks later I can only despise the crackling acid in his brain. The pale eyes submit now, for us alone.

Wherein I Speak To Her Again. Before.

I did not know, at first, the cause of your fascination with me, nor from where you had come.

Nowhere, and then, all at once, everywhere.

The café, the stoop, the walkway along the river, or our favorite abandoned places along the wharves.

Your insane beauty emanating. Always. Your espresso eyes touching me, your dark curls hiding your secrets no more. Our conversations.

(*They meet.*)

And him, at last, spewing his fiery venom, nothing new as a reverie unconsciousness and transported. Innocent sand-foam speech, his voice between moon rays and clouds, impossible, powerful, fantastic, and true.

Your presence handled the decision.

And he, just sitting, those wild eyes lifted and clinging. I watch him watch you, helplessly, as your essential talent, your notes ringing out, a shadow moving atop the temporary but beautiful winding staircase. You descend one step, slowly, and then another. Violin on your shoulder, bow sliding, impossible notes sounding. Even the red walls and black-painted floor were quivering. Your faded violet dress left behind as though you had never even known a stitch of clothing. Your nudity, as tremendous as moonlight, led my friend to all your instruments. To you.

On the spot. Spot on. Creation.

The outcome he despairs consists of your cheeks, your breath, a subtle flare of your nostrils, not artificial.

One remembers standing in the kitchen, confronted with old possibilities: I would not suffer this time. Zero humiliation. No prisoner of love, whatsoever his investigator divided, and holding that box in his hand despite. Person.

The incomparable creature peering out.

You both leave me wounded. But not mortally.

Fast Forward; Fast Down.

Back in Paris we lie flat on the round top of a tall tower. An outer arrondissement. Difficulty swallowing human indifference tonight as we kiss. Sublime pleasures hindering. Sacrilege. There is wine, carried in backpacks as we climbed. My knee and his cheek bleed, scratches from razor-wire. She and I admire one another's bruises from the straight up metal ladder. They will change many colors before leaving us.

The metal we have climbed on, that we lie on, is rusting in spots and all faded a pale mermaid blue. As the sun rises, so does he. We share.

He dances a tarantella in the center of the tower, then, laughing, guzzling wine from the bottle, he closes his eyes and dances faster, outward, taunting the edge. We crawl on our bellies, but we cannot catch him.

Addendum.

Magnetized poles have been challenged. We adore the equator, but also love our seasons, after all.

To Sing

Tristan Foster

The wardrobe offered by the club could have been inherited
from a wealthy old aunt. Dresses and coats and robes from
a forgotten era in excellent condition. Kept in plastic in a
darkened room, smelling of fragrant soap. She meant to ask
where they had all come from, who had brought them here
and why, but then she got used to them, made the outfits
her own. Thought it was luxurious to wear a different old
gown every night. Because this is what we do.

She wants to glow. Actually. This is what she thinks
as she waits in the dawn for sleep. Pulls the sheet back
and reaches for her phone to check the time. Watches the
light cutting in from outside but not for too long. Decides
to escape to the seaside soon, and the slow march into
the waves. This city is hostile to the sea, she can feel it in
her blood.

Midday waking. The noise of the city outside, not enough
rest, conscious of edges. She stays in bed till her feet start to
sweat, then throws the sheet off to begin the day. A ticket
to the Picasso Museum and she winds her way through,
eventually getting stuck in the stuffy, wood-panelled room
with a sculpture of a man holding a sheep. Bronze but looks
like it's made of mud. Like it formed here with time. She
feels tears welling in her eyes and wonders if crying is OK.
Hides in a corner, back against the wood, out of the light.

I can feel you
drifting away
drifting drifting
away

In the room the women come and go because what else is there to do.

*

Came to sing. That's why.

To sing all night in clubs and come home in the cold dawn. The walk slow, head clear by the time she unlocks the door. Returning like a cat. Maybe saw it in an old movie. Old actresses wearing old outfits, necklaces sparkling in black and white. Knew well the lies that Hollywood tells but still wanted to believe. Because that's what it is to be human, wanting to believe. Saw it, probably, as a little little girl. But here now. Saw, too, *Pont Neuf in the Snow* at the gallery back home. Stopped in, passing through, regretted it later. More aware of the tension in the air than the art on the wall and thought she should have spent the time lying in the grass outside. Anyway, stopped at the painting. Tempted more by its name than what it depicted: barely in the snow but it was the *in the* that mattered, as if it had a choice, as if it could slip in and out of snow like a jacket or dress.

Had a local teach her manners. A girl who waitressed at the club. Learnt from her the things you do, the things you don't. Laughed and smoked together on days off, leaning out of windows. Tried on expensive dresses together in perfumed boutiques and thought that she had finally arrived in Paris. Visited the Catacombs again, this time not a tourist. Dislodged a skull and threw it to each other like it was a toy then played chasings down the rows and rows of bones. Told in French by the guards to behave. Hell is very boring.

Sang lullabies of monkeys and jungles to baby brothers when young. In their room pool-water blue. Held one to her chest, usually. Taking turns from night to night like good boys, accepting their warmth and their weight as they drifted away to sleep.

Heads in the crowd. Each a galaxy of its own. Each filled with needs, wants, longings. With ideas of themselves. Here to escape them or maybe sink into them more deeply. Whispering and ice tinkling in glasses after she has finished singing and the applause fades. The clink of cutlery on china plates. She's seen more than a few tears running down cheeks. Knows the demons that dance around each head as, after the show, these people lie in the dark staring up at the ceiling.

The things she thinks about now that she never had to think of before. Words for things, street names, everything. Repeating them as she walks home like prayers. The discovery of new niches in the brain, like the cavities in Byzantine churches for the worship of some melancholy saint. The patron saints of new notions.

The ways we find comfort in things, in places, in time, in a particular moment of the day.

In the room the women come and go and maybe steal a kiss because what else is there to do.

*

Came here expecting angels and got devils. The same ones she left behind. Expected sleepy cherubs from the fluffy clouds of Renaissance paintings. Expected to be welcomed by them, almost as if they would be reclining on the linoleum at Charles de Gaulle when she walked through the gates, chubby and rosy-cheeked. *Voice like an angel* she was told all her childhood. How silly.

Hasn't visited the Pont Neuf. That she's aware of. Dated an architect who wailed in his sleep, night terrors. They lived on reverse hours so sometimes she was there for it, able to hear his calls from the other room. She asked him about the bridge, expressed a desire to go, but then his midnight screaming became too funny. She began to imagine what a building would look like in ruins. Thinks of the Tower as the skeleton of Christ the Redeemer, the colossal statue on a Rio hillside she has seen only in photos. Of the two men who made these things on opposite poles. Their profound unhappiness and the monuments they have left behind to mark it.

She wants to glow. Actually. So perfect that when she sings they could turn the lights off and there would be a candlelight flicker. If the lights were cut, the audience would mumble first their frustration, then their concern, all but ignoring the glowing, singing girl.

That's what she wants. But she wants many things.

Not even in a way that is impassive. Because what else is there to do.

Catacombs

Sophie Mackintosh

We queued for three hours in January to get into the Catacombs, chill wind, crisp, no rain. We knew that passersby were laughing at us waiting in the temperature, revealing ourselves as bad tourists, and we could have avoided the queue if we had paid extra but we were too cheap, our money was going on bread and small glasses of jewel-dark wine. The winter sun flickered and moved position. My phone was running out of battery but I wasted some watching videos and images of lakes under the ground, of people feeling their way through the maze of tunnels and writing graffiti on the stone walls. We moved from foot to numb foot. All day we had been walking around the city. The rain would not begin until the next day, when it would hit us in the cemetery, when it would fill our shoes and we would have to search for any shelter before our train. We did not yet have knowledge of the rain. The rain would leak into the earth of the city and the lakes, the oceans, filling the tunnels. Underneath us, the ghost of the city like a photographic negative. I was ashamed to be queuing but I wanted to be in that city below us, the secret version, where the air was hard to breathe, and the skulls were tight as teeth in a mouth. We would walk down into the ground together. Nothing here but the cold at the end of my fingers and my nose. I had decided I would not wear gloves in Paris for it was not chic, but then I had queued for three hours anyway which is the least chic thing you can do. We were in love, and it felt good and unfamiliar. And yet the dark was coming up like a wave. The skulls would shine out towards us like beacons. I was waiting for them. I strained to hear the noise of the subterranean bodies of water and the people feeling their way, people making chipped marks against the stone, people with ropes and breadcrumbs to create their own intricate ways back. I wondered how long you could survive in the tunnels, how long you could stay pressed up against the bones, and in the queue I had read also about the collapsing cemeteries, the overcrowding, the necessity of putting your dead underground. Please don't ask me to marry you in Paris, I had said when we were drunk, Please don't, I need to know that you won't ask me or anything, and that felt good and unfamiliar too, and the weight of being drunk pushed on my chest and on my limbs like a warm and heavy blanket. On my dying phone I read everything I could find about the Catacombs, as if it could stop the sun where it moved, the people openly laughing at me as we queued, to who I could then say: I know about this, I know history! I know! My legs were so heavy and cold by the time we walked down, my lungs were tight and I was afraid, but I thought of the swimming man I had seen on a video, in the subterranean lake, how he had slipped through the blue with his head above like a seal, and a light strapped to his forehead, and it had been beautiful, and how nothing had dragged him down.

Pilgrimage

Tomoé Hill

Les Halles, sing-songed the automated voice on the Métro, a beat too long between words. The fast shuddering halt of a train that knew its purpose — doors opening, doors closing — a mechanical act that, for me, was imbued with eroticism as I watched the surge of bodies entering and leaving. *Les Halles*. I sat in the narrow plastic seat and clenched violently — a last gasp stifled, as were all my gasps then — spasming as if possessed; another hidden orgasm in a city where I should have been luxuriating, unabashed, in layers of literary and actual sex. Instead I was coming alone on the Métro, in a crescendo of solitude. There is a line in *Henry and June*: "Writers make love to whatever they need". Love seemed like a puzzle piece that did not belong to the rest of me: I do not know if I was making love to myself in the hope that I might understand my life — the distant poles of desire and its opposite that I seemed to both inhabit — or because I wished to be a writer, another impossibility. The only thing I could do was conjure up the fantasies and act as if they were real; as real as the ebbing shudder of my swollen heat and the waning image of the man seated next to me, no reader, indifferent to the Paris in my beloved books.

Paris exists within two amorous dreams for those who do not reside there: pristine hotel rooms, the duvet-thick quiet broken by intimate laughter, tourists expecting to be intoxicated by love literally in the air; or its dirtier shadow, illicit delight, a carnal feast within walls and on surfaces permanently marked by the bodily signatures of pleasures past, a guestbook of ecstasy. If I daydreamed in vain of the first, what I craved with a desperate ache was the second, the kind of fucking that overloaded the senses with its greed: the great sexual ego Henry Miller stunned by Nys in *Quiet Days in Clichy*, her Renoir body his animal match; clever enough to take his cock — "Ça c'est quelque chose" — as well as all his money with her cunt and her charm. We go to Paris reverent: as if the city was a heart in a reliquary beating with the words of writers instead of blood, in the hope that to be here will be enough to grant us the kinds of love we, too, desire. If we believe in this form of divinity it is because being unable to define the ache within us would be more unbearable than the ache itself.

I was no Nys or even Nin, married while finding adventures with other men. I read and despaired at how I could almost smell the scent of sex on the pages of these books, the entwining of writing and carnality, how the heart of its orgasms was always Paris: a sexual epicentre whose tremors I imagined I could feel across the Channel, living in a nondescript, new-build house in Kent, on an estate ubiquitous with its duplicates. My sheets were not like the "massive red silk eiderdown, covered in dubious stains" as they were in Duroy's love nest with Madame de Marelle in Maupassant's *Bel-Ami*, only pale blue cotton, streaked with the ghosts of my late-night, secretive orgasms; stolen while someone slept unaware next to me, oblivious to my desire for other men and women. If my sexual life was based on fantasies from literature they were no less powerful than reality: they enveloped me in pleasure I hadn't known in years, the softness of my clit under my fingertips becoming blurred with the turning of pages — fingers sliding off, a book falling, an ending.

I took my furtive pleasures in crowded public spaces as I wandered the city as if alone those few days, a pilgrim-voyeur not looking outward but inward to what could have or should have been: relief in the privacy of sexual gratification, without the guilt of the silence of that room and the other person it held, impossible to touch, as was I. "I could come with anybody just now," said Hugo, Anaïs's husband, as they gazed aroused — another kind of reverence — at two women putting on a private sex show for them, a tangle of flesh and heat. So could I, but there was no one; because of it, I chose to come with everyone, where everyone was, the inverse of what the Paris of romance and sexual desire on the page meant.

I wondered if passengers could smell the animal change in my body as it peaked, the musky sweat that gathered under my arms and between my thighs; if there was a glimmer of recognition at my lips now swollen and reddened beyond decency, the way I tilted my neck upwards slightly as if I were offering it up to be bitten; if my unspoken litany of *just fuck me, please fuck me right now* jolted into the thoughts of fellow passengers like a stray radio signal. I wanted someone to intercept it, look at me, know what it was I needed and longed for — too damaged both physically and mentally to give or receive anything those six long years with someone, untouched. I wanted someone to feel those dirty vibrations in the Métro carriage

— dirty only because they were not within those pristine, duvet-quiet rooms — and give me a sign that they, too, were moved by the force of my hermetic desires; held in a kind of reliquary but wept over by no one but myself.

Those few days I stayed in Paris that first time, Métro Line 4 became almost Pavlovian: I would stare out the window into the darkness, or else at other passengers, the floor, the black accordion-like rubber sections between carriages which flexed when the train went around curves while I slipped into a lustful reverie, listening to nothing but the automated voice that came at intervals: *Saint-Placide. Saint-Sulpice. Odéon. Châtelet.* And on. It was a metronome to my building arousal; where I could not use my fingers to press my swelling clit, inflections of words replaced them. *Sssa*int. O*dé*on. *Le*s H*alle*s. *Shh...*âte*l*et. I pretended the lilting, dancing, clipped letters — drawn out or bitten with relish, at other times hissing with a disciplined sibilance — were an aural stroking of my hidden, yearning flesh. The fragments brought back a long-buried memory of reading e.e. cummings's poem "Doll's boy 's asleep" when young, curious about the haze of sex in the words I read:

you take his mouth
for his eyes are mine

I learned later that he was living in Paris a couple of years prior to the publication of *Tulips and Chimneys*, and I murmured lines out of order in my head between the slow call of stops — their solitary, intimate wisdom becoming suddenly clear to me:

his lips drink water
but his heart drinks wine

Les Halles. Les. Halles. I used those words to cover my quick breath, and then I stood, imperceptibly shaking, too aware of the wet cling of soaked panties to my fur. Catching my reflection in the glass before the doors opened: face impassive but pupils dilated, still dreaming like Doll's boy. *Just fuck me now.*

I walked out into the crowd — legs trembling, cunt still aching, looking in vain for my Paris.

Les Halles — once a grand food market immortalised in Zola's *The Belly of Paris* — is now an ugly covered mall, or it was at that time. You had to go through the Forum des Halles upon exiting the Métro train to get outside, and once in the open it was full of restaurants, keeping the ghost of the market alive. I was disappointed the first time I walked through, wanting only to see overflowing stands of produce as far as the eye could see. There were still some shops that offered consolation, and so I devoured the sight of ripe cheeses, green and red-brown piles of *mâche*, *feuille de chêne*, and *frisée*, the scent of newly-baked baguettes in standing baskets. I fingered leaves and soft fruits unseen, inhaled the hay and animal scents of unpasteurised cheese and the underlying, almost unconscious one of rotting food — because where there is freshness, decay follows. Everywhere I looked reminded me that my desire was growing and blooming but only to wilt and decompose, serving to re-fertilise my imagination, my only source of nourishment.

No fingers pressed into my flesh as if testing a sun-warmed piece of fruit or skimmed through my dark fur, wet with moisture like newly-plucked lettuce; no nose waited by my skin to smell that ripeness that silently sent the message *I'm ready... open me, devour my cunt*; no teeth bit into the soft flesh of my inner thigh as if it were a delicacy to be savoured. I conflated food and sex because there was no sex, or no fucking, but always food in abundance. "When he reached the markets night was falling, and there was a suffocating smell. He bent his head as he once more returned to the nightmare of endless food...": to Florent, in *The Belly of Paris*, the market that first saves him ends up destroying him — a wondrous, monstrous thing that feeds on the people it itself feeds. I was aware that I was looking for a Les Halles that perhaps existed only in my imagination: if I did find it, that meant I was too far gone to be saved, to come back to pleasure with another person. But looking at food was like looking at bodies in their infinite naked variety, and I was ravenous in every sense — looking for myself in all that excess, all the while knowing that where I lay was in a rotting corner pile, undesired.

At the end of Jean Rhys's unfinished autobiography *Smile Please*, there is a section of words she had planned to somehow use — her death meant that they remained fragments. They speak with astonishing rawness of the emotional weight that presses on us all at times plainly on the page, the heart exposed. "I never once thought this is beautiful, this is grand, this is what I hoped for, longed for." She was speaking of London, although she goes on to say she did feel those things (positively) in Paris. When I read that, a horrible ache surged through me again — those words echoing what I felt and was unable to articulate sitting in loneliness, coming alone in that Paris Métro seat.

It seemed like all my desires, all the things I'd read and longed for, died at Les Halles that day — or perhaps, unlike Doll's boy, I simply woke from my dream. For a few years after I remained convinced that I was past tense, fictional; I could write myself *because* I wasn't real, only a character on a page. In its way that was reassuring: I existed more wholly trying to piece together the story of me than I did when I searched for who I really was in the non-existent market, or pleasuring myself long ago on that train.

Why do we read of Parisian love and then go to Paris like travellers on a pilgrimage, going forth in hope and returning in despair, knowing now that love is suffering and that the promises of the page are not for us? Are only some few destined for that true divinity? The rest of us drift like ghosts between states of ecstasy and heartbreak, but always going back to the word: the faith that we can attain the happiness we have read about, to live perpetually high, at the peak of joyous orgasm, at the moment of *I love you*. We are forever pilgrims, forever wandering; cummings's brief lines sum up what it means to look for love in Paris and never find it — a lifetime's journey, itself a kind of life.

for every mile the feet go
the heart goes nine

Marlene or Number 16[1]

Yelena Moskovich

MARLENE, she looks older than the men, the daylight, how it accuses contours.

MARLENE got a new lavender coat, it hangs down to her calves, long over the jean skirt held lopsided at her waist like a hula hoop with a studded belt. She's had a double espresso from the barman who says, Don't you want to take off your coat, Marlene? No, thanks, Marlene replies, I like it on. How do I look?

MARLENE is turning in circles, the clean hem floating up and tickling the skin behind her knees.

MARLENE took a couple of aspirins during her shift yesterday afternoon 'cause there was nothing else, then cut her index finger trying to get a slice out of the tight lime, and the gash wouldn't clot because, as the man-from-the-back told her, aspirin thins out blood. The man-from-the-back closed the industrial dishwasher he was loading, brought over a hand-towel and wrapped it, gracefully, around the gash, cupping his own two hands at the stem and holding her towelled-finger like an orchid-head. She followed the edge of his hands, a beckoning, a teacup, then up at him, and he at her, and

---

1   *"Marlene or Number 16" won the 2017 Galley Beggar Press Short Story Prize.*

then he looked away and said I'll find you some band-aids Marlene, but began to feel mannered against the baggy intimacy between them. His head turned away, eyes lingering on the postcards taped one next to another in a series on the wall above the stairway leading to the basement where the toilets are.

MARLENE's been pointing the finger. She's been blaming her younger brother. Didn't I change your pooped-un-derwear when you were a chubby little Messiah, though? He hung up. Marlene whispered into her iPhone, lipstick smearing on the plastic, *and you are supposed to be my blood...* The men are speaking Albanian over the TV in the corner of the café. This café where Marlene works, and the barman, and the man-from-the-back, who's in the toilet just now. It's early afternoon, the man-from-the-back rarely goes, but when he does, he urinates for a long time. The barman's thrown out a couple of jokes already and now he's just coughing like a dandelion between sips. He reaches for the remote control beneath the counter and turns the sound up on the TV as the garbage truck thuds on the street, right in front of the couple of tables on the terrace of the café, one empty, and one with two young women, just arrived. A black man gets off the garbage truck, hazard-green trousers, neon yellow plastic vest with silver reflective strips, he rolls the green bins from the curb to the gaping metal trunk, hooks them up to the lever, which lifts, dumps, and sets them down. He rolls the bins back to the curb, where he stops to look at a stream of sun falling out from the parting clouds, white hairs curling in the dark crown on his head. There's a white man in a white truck behind him, honking. At the bar, the milk is frothing. The white man's pounding his black-leather steering wheel, screaming, *Allez!*, Come on! A young mulatto with orange hair and freckles across his honeyed complexion pedals past them both on his bike, singing Françoise Hardy to himself in a high-pitched voice, *Tous les garçons et les filles de mon âge...* "All the boys and girls who are my age..." Well, this street's global, but concretely it's in the north of Paris. The fruit and vegetable seller's an Arab. The tobacco shop, where you get your cigarettes and Loto tickets, is run by a Chinese man. And across from him is Bombay Nights, previously Tandoori Nights, previously Rajpoot, previously Kasimir House. And this bar, named after the street, Le Saint Denis, is an Albanian hangout, so no one can say why they serve that cheap green Portuguese wine, but they do, fizzy vino verde €2.50 a glass, Marlene'll bring it over.

MARLENE's not Albanian. She's not a child of the eagles: *Shqipëri* as the Albanians call their own country, meaning Land of the Eagles. That's why there's the two-headed eagle silhouette on the solid red flag taped to the side of the cash register. Marlene did have a child, though. Well he was her partner's boy, and hers, when they were together. He was panic-stricken by pigeons. They couldn't get past the arch of Porte Saint-Denis without him peeing himself in his modest terror. The man-from-the-back comes up from the basement toilet, past the rows of taped postcards. Naples, Marseilles, Barcelona, Athens, Palermo, Rotterdam, Brussels, then a dense red tulip field with a Dutch woman bent over to pick one, pantiless in a miniskirt, her sun-kissed ass-cheeks next to the cursive writing, *Beautiful View From Here.* The man-from-the-back goes around the staircase to the corner, where the extra orange-brown leather stools stand, on top of one, the metal fan, turned off, it's three blades still within the wired caging, looking out as if cherishing a long-passed insult. He turns the fan on, and goes back to the back.

MARLENE's leaning on the bar, her hip curved out, pointing across the street to the grass-green Carrefour supermarket with the homeless man slumped outside against the low-grates and the front window, shirtless, belly out, chin down, hands which have lost their sense of humour upturned at his thighs. He's warming at the surface of consciousness, stinking of daydreams. Nextdoor's a small four walls with wooden booths, a phone each, fifteen-cents-a-minute to call Senegal, for example, *Taxiphone* spelled out in flashing blue and white lights. A thin man in a faded black sweater and wrinkled grey khakis walks past, holding a half-eaten cob of corn, white napkin crumbled over the stem in his hand. Another man, rounder, blue short-sleeve button-down, bow-legged in his stiff jeans, grey hairs on his arms, his hands missioned with carrying nothing but a standard #10 envelope. *Deux*, Marlene says to the barman and he gets out two wine glasses and places them on the counter in front of her. The two young women on the terrace turn their heads towards Marlene. One's got a tall neck with a mess of her brown Norwegian hair knotted into itself, and the other, hygienic-faced, shining blonde hair behind her ears, silver hoops in her plump lobes. They are both studying at the theatre school down the street, blue door. They're waiting for their glasses of the cheap vino verde.

MARLENE, this past weekend, was dawdling through Montmartre for no reason. She stopped in front of the man with a thinning ponytail, a wooden easel between them, he looked up, she said, draw me. The man drew a caricature of Marlene, her eyes puffed and sliding open, her mouth a squeaking pickle about to snap in two, her cheeks like flattened candy wrappers. She handed him the fee in euro coins, counting it out.

MARLENE's sauntering through the bar towards the terrace with two glasses of vino verde, trying to get her lavender coat to catch a breeze and ribbon around her legs. A couple of the men wave their hands and say, Come on, Marlene, you're blocking the TV... The man-from-the-back reties his white apron twice around his waist. His worn purple cotton T-shirt hangs at the sleeves and sticks to his shoulders, the sweat in the form of angel wings. Sorry, Marlene says and moves out of the way, but what do you think? Think of what, the man with brown leather loafers says and picks up his pint of beer. Think of my new coat, Marlene's smiling shyly. Oh, yeah, the man says. That's right. It looks nice, Marlene. Good colour for you.

MARLENE's still blushing when she returns from the terrace and the two women are sipping their wine behind her and she joins the men and watches the TV screen. An enormous stage is lit up with crossed beams. The camera zooms in like an eagle swooping, then abruptly cuts back to a panel of judges. A woman in a corseted canary-yellow dress, petite, reddish-orange lips, says Hello, she waves. The next judge, tight white button-up, glasses like an architect, a cleft chin and a shiny forehead someone forgot to powder, says Hello, *Hello there Albania!* The first act is a young man in loose white soccer shorts and a red-and-yellow team shirt. He spins two soccer balls on his index fingers, then takes one spinning ball to his chest, bounces it to his foot, then his heel, then up to his knee, clocking his hips to the traditional Albanian song playing in the background. The third judge is a short man with a clean buzz to his dark hair. He's disappointed. Then the words burst through the screen: *Albania's Got Talent!* and cuts to the commercial break. The man with loafers puts down his pint glass, smoothes out his thick steel-wool moustache, then goes outside to smoke. The others pick up their conversation.

MARLENE's watching the commercials as if they were a continuation of the talent show. Her mouth's loose and her eyes glaze and her fingers curl in, even the one she cut yesterday, with two band-aids taped around it. Are you okay Marlene? the barman asks. Marlene looks over to him. Am I okay? Marlene repeats it. She thinks about it. I'm just, Marlene takes a couple breaths, I'm just…

MARLENE! The man-from-the-back yells. Your phone's ringing! You left it on top of the cash register. You're lucky no one stole it. Oh I don't think anyone'd steal it… It's an iPhone, Marlene! I mean I trust everyone here. But there are guys that come in and out. I mean I trust people. *You* shouldn't! But I want to. If you wanted to trust people, Marlene, you should've gotten a Nokia. I'm just looking out for you. That's nice of you, thank you. The phone's still ringing in Marlene's hand. Answer it, Marlene.

MARLENE, hello. It's Marlene's ex. Her voice is low. She doesn't want her son to hear. He's nine and he's sad and she doesn't want any more messes. When are you coming over, Marlene's ex asks her, to pick up the last of your stuff? Marlene's ex lives two streets down from the bar, between the Japanese massage place, windows covered with posters of bare backs and orchids, and the corner-store *épicerie*, she's on the third floor, where you can yell from the street, phrases like WHAT'S YOUR DOOR CODE AGAIN? and I JUST NEED TO SEE YOU.

MARLENE, I'm putting it in a box and I'm taking it to the bar and I'm dropping it off. Alright, Marlene agrees, because she wants her ex to see her in her new lavender coat and maybe she'll bring the boy, even though he's not her biological son, after five years, he called her Mama Marlene. Then she hangs up and realizes her ex is on her way, carrying a cardboard box of her stuff, the last one, the final trinkets of ways she couldn't explain herself and that plant, the small cactus she never watered and yet, it lived on, without a grudge. On the TV screen the next contestant is up. A boy in suspenders and a black bow tie. He's missing his two front teeth. He's singing Leonard Cohen's "Hallelujah", voice splintering from him, eyes pinching and cheeks flushed as he's reaching for the high notes. Next is a boy in a Muslim cap with dark skin and blue eyes, blowing the trumpet like Miles Davis while serving baklava.

MARLENE's ex shows up with a cardboard box in her hands, she's got blue jeans and a silky shirt tucked in, her flour-blond hair parted in the middle, strands of grey hidden, her lipstick applied, a tired rose.

MARLENE, her ex says, here take this. She hands her the box. Marlene takes the box and says thank you then puts it down on the curb next to the now-empty green garbage bins. You don't want any of it? Marlene's ex asks her. I don't think so, Marlene replies. She's wondering if her ex has noticed her new lavender coat.

MARLENE waits. She waits. She turns a little left and

bends her knees as if she's about to curtsey. Marlene's ex is staring at her, pulling her eyebrows together. If you didn't want any of it — but Marlene's ex stops herself because she doesn't want to get into it.

MARLENE is now doubting whether her ex will notice the coat at all and suddenly, the boy's back in her thoughts. She really wants to see the boy. She misses that little boy. That little peanut nose, that little wobbly-eyed boy, that vigilant stare and high eyebrows, Marlene misses that little boy more than anything, she could almost take off her new lavender coat and throw it into the green bin. Well, goodbye, Marlene's ex says, they kiss on the cheek, and she is walking away. The two young women left change on the table, and the empty wine glasses side by side.

MARLENE swallows because her mouth is getting dry. She's done with her shift but she decides to stick around at the bar until it's completely dark. The sun sets. The bobby pin's hanging down on a couple of strands from her head, she's stroking her dark hair messily with her band-aided finger, mostly missing the hair and bumping the plaster into her chin. It's the night-time now, there is no shame.

MARLENE steps outside to make a call on her iPhone; it's ringing and ringing, then the call's picked up. Marlene says, It's me again, to her ex. Her ex breathes out, Marlene, please, she says in a quiet voice because the boy's asleep now, You can't do this. Marlene is just listening, wondering if the boy heard the phone ring and woke up and is listening just like her, his small body crouched against his bedroom door. We said we were going to respect each other, Marlene. Marlene's ex is taking her time now because she's getting angry. You're only thirty-eight, but I swear, Marlene, at that bar, you look — about fifty, and I know, that's an awful thing to say, to someone you love, but now, we have to love other people.

MARLENE likes poetry, and it's almost 2am, and they're closing up, so the man with the steel-wool moustache stands up and recites a stanza he remembers from Lasgush Poradeci, "Why I Need to Love You":

Because I chose to love you.
And I chose to woo you.
And I chose to
kiss you.
That's why.

Then the bar owner shushes him and says to Marlene, you should read Ismail Kadare, Marlene, he's our guy. He even stops wiping the counter and clears his throat, and announces, "Poetry" is the title of this poem. He moves the rag to the side and begins to deliver the lines carefully, translating them from Albanian in his head for Marlene:

Poetry,
How did you find your way to me?
My mother does not know Albanian well,
She writes letters like Aragon, without commas and periods,
My father roamed the seas in his youth,
But you have come,
Walking down the pavement of my quiet city of stone,
And knocked timidly at the door of my three-storey house,
At Number 16.

Not bad, the man with the steel-wool moustache says. Marlene smiles but can't look up at the barman. She says Thank you to the floor.

MARLENE's walking down Rue du Faubourg Saint-Denis alone, with her iPhone in her hand, because the barman locked up the café and they all said goodbye. It's cool now, the wind is blowing up her jean skirt, and ruffling her new lavender coat. The homeless man at Carrefour is awake, he says, *Psst*, to Marlene but she's got her eyes semi-closed, walking towards the arch of Porte Saint-Denis, smiling to herself. The homeless man forgets Marlene and starts picking at his belly button. She's already down the street, alone and humming, to herself and to her new coat, the lavender fabric dancing in the gusts of wind, her left hand bobbing to the melody she's humming, and her right cradling the iPhone between her band-aided finger and palm. He's behind her, the shadow, speeding up, his shoulders in, narrow hips, quick steps. He lunges at Marlene.

MARLENE's face down on the cobblestone circle beneath the arch. There's pigeon shit and cigarette ash smeared on her coat, torn hem. The shadow's sprinting far into the darkness, one hand moving the wind, the other clutching her iPhone, which is, suddenly, ringing in his grip.

MARLENE, do you, want to, come over? I'd like to see you. He'd like to see you too. He can't sleep. He wants you to sing him something. After, we could lie down, together. I miss your body. I don't think I can, just stop, loving you. Also, I'm ready to talk about my responsibility in what happened. And your brother called me. He says he doesn't know how to say he's sorry, that's why, but he'd like to give it a try. I was thinking you could go back to school. I could take care of us for a bit. You looked so beautiful this afternoon in your new lavender coat, please. Come home.

MARLENE, near the curb where it smells like stone and urine, is pushing herself over, onto her back. She opens her eyes and begins counting the stars, fourteen, fifteen...

Yulia

Donari Braxton

i.

She said she "liked the idea of an American in Paris."
Romantic, she said. But she ate syllables and the word
comes like: "rustic," her tongue curling a little noose. *Lynch
z'ie foreign dip'zong!* Friction seppuku, an air-raid siren.
Notes like from a dog whistle, pinching scales through the
fashionable gap-tooth of her upper rows. Irresistible.

Especially when she breathes. Especially in Trocadéro
at night, where we've always hated Germans, and in my
family, still do. She was one, half naked under a bright
neon-red Pepsi Cola LED sign attached to the wall, and
she had no idea what she was talking about.

We were catching our breath still: one of us was panting,
one just sighing but rapidly, so. You blend into places. You
don't take things too seriously. You peel off a limb, bits and
pieces. You enter a pool, get out of the pool. The water you
take with you: you don't like that water. You shake it off like
a stray, *there-there*. You wrap yourself in blankets to suffocate
the fire; you trade wet for the itch and a roll in the grass.

ii.

For me, there was no other way to make love. If there was
one, she didn't seem to know about it or care. It was the

silence afterwards, stung. An unusual silence — a somehow personal one. And war every night waiting out that she'd break it:

"C'était bien?"

"I thought you fell asleep."

"Look at this picture."

"If you like dogs so much, get a dog?"

"C'est *toi* mon chien."

About dogs, she was vocal about liking them. If there were a dog in the street and she thought you were watching, she'd approach the dog just to *show you*, or something. She trafficked in luxury vehicles and self-analysis, and had a playlist of conversation readymade for the bakery, *Vavin*, Veronese.

I remember sometime around her seventeenth year, her parents objected to nose jobs, so she sold her BMW, and paid for one herself. She explained that surgery in small-town Germany is no small cross to bear, how she'd dealt with the experience, how she'd prevailed (this was in line at the bakery). Then, she waits for your surrender — just picks at the almond croissant, small bites.

"Brave of you."

"Well, now I regret it."

And on and on, processed and repurposed — no feelings, instead packageable facts. Transactional trauma, a virtues ledger. And about bakeries: once or twice a month, she'd bring home bagels and lox; this was *extremely* pandering of her. You'd have to take really large bites. You'd have to spit nothing out.

iii.

In France, Germans speak French. A lot of people do, *Verfremdungseffekt*. In Hebrew, there's no word for that. We'd walk the Canal Saint-Denis and I'd scan the window menus, look at the prices, calculate. Once we were seated, she'd somehow find a "special," or something in fine print, or she'd combine a dish or two or three — in the end, she'd have to chip in for the bill. That day, she'd have the steak, where I'd eat mostly bread, between our dates, to afford the lies that I'd told.

While that morning's another story entirely: I'd laughed during lovemaking, and this was the final nail in the coffin. You can't redo these things ever.

You stand instead to attention: *zu Befehl!*

You do sex in a serious way; this is a *serious* time. You give your partner your undivided *attention*. You stomach that attention's a word for what it's not. That it's not the thing; it's every other thing your brain's fucking off about — then you get to get the erection; sometimes you get to keep it. The cerebral cortex does that.

It blocks out the hum in the room. The beats of blood pulsing in your neck, your heartbeat. You're dying. The cotton fabric lightly resting against your skin. Black Blazer, Button-Up, Banana Republic, $59.99. Miraculously the world melts away, and now you pull focus, the little lens in your mind's eye stopping down, to the one thing you do, and poorly at that. Women. And that, my boy, is all that you do, *l'man ha'Shem*.

"Regarde moi!"

I have to look around the room sometimes, too. I have to look down:

"Non, mais regarde!"

"Arrête."

iv.

After sex is the part she seemed to like the most. She reveled in silence, but only then. She was analytical at night, while I lived in constant fear of laundry. What remained of her fashion sense — Michael Kors Leopard Calf Hair Mini Skirt, $312.28, Gucci Marmont Belt Black $299.99, either a red or blue one Juicy Couture Long-Sleeve Tee — these careful statements now just bunched at her hips, like a loincloth collage. I wore the rest of her makeup on my neck and my shoulders, and wondered if her eyes were closed, really. She love-talked in French, but the *oui* came like *wee,* so to American ears, you're less stud than spinning teacup. Then in postmortem she'd caress and say: *Mmm?* Over and over, as if she were asking me a question. If I would reply to her: *Mmm?* Or if I would reply: *Mmm.* or *Mmm!?* She'd just reply, by going: *Mmm?* to me again. As if I were the one who had asked her *Mmm?* to begin with — which, I have to say, I hated about her more than anything else.

"Tu veux que je m'en aille?"

"Speak English."

"Did I say it wrong?

"It's just better that way."

"Do you want me to go?"

"Oui."

"Hahaha," she said.

But I had no sense of humor. I hadn't told a joke deliberately in some forty years. I *was* who she thought I was; she just didn't know it. That's why I *always* looked away when she looked at me too closely.

Here, I break off to go fetch the towel. I had to clean myself off. That's your job after sex. You're a man and your ecstasy makes garbage. Play stupid games, win stupid prizes. You're a housewarming guest in the valley; your cocktail's spilt on the new crimson Bombay, $3990. You pat at it kind of. You wait for the help to arrive and take over, for the host to spirit you away, *Hé hé hé héééééééééééé! Donari, non non nonnnnn, t'en fais pas Donariiii, pas de soucis Donariii, allez!*

But here, no one comes. No one saves you from your fluids, your vulgarity, your Jewishness. You sit patting forever and ever and ever — she's kept her eyes open. She wants to see to the task's done. Your disease is one thing, your kin's another entirely. It almost hurts my feelings in retrospect.

"Water if you like."

"Mmm?"

"Mhm."

"Mmm?"

"Mhm?"

Music was playing from a gramophone in the other room. The music was inappropriately modern or unironically not.

"How old is this music?"

"It has a USB port."

"I said *music.*"

"1960's, I said."

"I want to go out."

"I'll walk you home then, come on."

135

v.

We dressed individually, separate rooms. It was fall/winter and we needed long socks, heavy scarves, gloves and coats. I wore mostly black, while she wore blacks, reds, a purple headband.

I locked the door behind us with a heavy gold latchkey, the old-fashioned kind still in use in parts of the Latin Quarter. We set down the corridor together, the stairwell, mostly in silence. I put the gold latchkey in the brown tote that she'd taken, shaped like a hand, so that I wouldn't lose it. It had a fancy silver zipper that I was always scared that I'd break, because the corner fabric was tearing. I offered to carry the bag for her but she declined.

Outside on the street, South Montparnasse, there should have been all the familiar sights, or smells at the least. Paris smells like many things, but our street Rue Le Verrier, especially in the fall, had the papery taste of a library. That night, there was no library, but smoke, instead. Paris had grayed out, and all you smelled was smoke. You didn't smell a fire, and truth be told, I didn't know that smoke *had* a scent. It does: it's metallic. It smells as if an army tank were parked in the desert, hollows out like a prune, and now is slowly evaporating into vapors. That night in Paris, to stand on the street was to breathe in those vapors.

Yulia couldn't tell if it was her imagination, but I could. She saw a tank on the boulevard transforming by virtue of the prism into a mirage on the sand. She told me: *I am hallucinating things.* Nervous, I agreed with her mostly — really I *knew*. For I saw the same tank go, too. I watched an armored caravan melt pavement before the Archangel Saint-Michel with my *eyes* — it rolled north toward Châtelet, as the now toy-sized Citroëns scrambled to make way.

And escorting the machine on its flanks was a column of very matching soldiers. The tank's camouflage itself was not matching; it wasn't the right camouflage for urban, more jungle camouflage, instead. To me, this suggested that the French had had no time to prepare.

Yulia scanned my expression for clues, but I had none. I was busy searching French airspace above for an operation. I could see only stars and commercial flights in the sky. We walked a few blocks toward the high ground of Edgar Quinet, where there was a restaurant, *Tournesol*, that we fancied. We took one of the outside tables that lined the restaurant, intent on ordering tea, being normal. But of course the waiter didn't come. Instead, he was on his phone, flailing about, talking to colleagues, to patrons, to passersby.

"Ah, monsieur! Monsieur, s'il vous plaît!"

He gave me such a *look*. When Yulia wasn't herself looking, I physically checked around my eyes — that they were intact, that they weren't bleeding. I didn't know if bleeding eyes were a sign of insanity, but had they been bleeding, I'd have assumed that they were such a sign. Then when she did finally look at me again, I only looked away.

I wiped my glasses off by using the bottom right corner of my shirt, which first made them blurrier, but when you do it right, eventually it makes them less. Then I looked past her, over her shoulder, toward northern Paris. That was the last time Yulia looked toward me for answers.

It was the Sabbath and there were many Chassids running away. We saw many birds flying in the opposite direction. Yulia wasn't speaking anymore. I asked the waiter:

"When will we find out what's happening here?"

He said:

"Can't you see for yourself?"

I looked out into Paris, but everything, except for the tank column advancing, looked normal.

"I don't see anything."

"Look at the Tower!"

The Eiffel Tower was very far away, at that point. You had to stand on something to see that north into Paris. You could stand on a bench and maybe see it. The waiter was standing on a table. I stood on my chair.

And in the distance, I found it. The Eiffel Tower was on fire, and it wasn't just a little. It was burning like the wicker man in a pagan sacrament. From base to the top of the Tower, flames took to every direction. They were mostly orange, but there were also blues and yellows.

"Was there a terrorist attack?" I asked.

"No," he replied.

"But then, what?"

vi.

Probably there wasn't an answer. I put my hand on Yulia's hand. Neither of us cried or anything. We just watched and waited for the Eiffel Tower to fall, or to slowly wither away into nothing. I didn't know how long it might take. Should we leave the restaurant, head west through the police state, and try to get closer to the scene? How close do you need to be to watch the Tower fall down? What does it matter if you're close or if you're not? Already I couldn't remember what color the Tower had originally been. Like a moth, you don't remember the flame, you go to meet it. But the longer we watched, the longer nothing happened at all. The Tower burned and burned and burned. None of its pieces fell off.

Wear the Lace

Susanna Crossman

This place that Proust slowly, anxiously comes to occupy
anew every time he awakens: from that place, as soon
as my eyes are open, I can no longer escape… My body.
— Michel Foucault, "The Utopian Body"

They were driving to Italy. It was April. Unexpectedly hot.
Charlotte planned to sketch what she called An Impossible Balance. The hoisted four million bricks of Florence's
terracotta Duomo. On the way, the car broke down. It
was a stupid fucking idea, her now ex-boyfriend, Steve,
said, and took the first plane back to London. From Nice,
Charlotte escaped on to a train bound for Paris. Everything
tumbled. Arriving at the Gare de Lyon, she found herself
stuck overnight, rang her new French landlady, Véronique,
blurting out, "Sorry, I've only known you for six months.
But I've no money. Nowhere to stay." On the phone,
Véronique's voice, encased in red lips — a smoker's, tarry,
treacle growl — told desperate Charlotte, "Stay with my
niece Hélène in the Marais. She's a real *Parisienne*".

Now, when Charlotte thought back to that day, it was as
though she had begun to snip through the thousand ties
to her past, one by one.

On that April afternoon, Charlotte observed Hélène slide
open the top drawer of her wooden chest, catching her first

glimpse of French lingerie. A collection of curves and lines, hooks and straps. Velvet and tulle. Vertiginous lace. Hélène was freshly-showered. Dew-wet. Long hair up. Enveloped in a man's blue dressing gown. Charlotte stood by the door. Crumpled Sonic Youth T-shirt. Two day-old sweat. Bleach blond hair in greasy spikes. An overfilled rucksack by her side. Reaching into the drawer, Hélène said, abruptly, "My *Tata* Véronique said you arrive this evening. Sorry, I busy now. I—"

Charlotte hadn't listened. Couldn't think. She knew she should have been admiring, even sketching, the zinc-clad Paris rooftops Véronique described as "A Lofty Grey Field in the Sky." But Charlotte only saw the drawer, Hélène's lingerie, garments exposed in pairs, one cupping the other. Tops and tails. Row upon row, like precious jewels, or buildings awaiting inhabitants. Ivory white, burnt gold and black. Scarlet red. Bottle green. Knots and holes. Criss-cross. Bows. Taut and silky. Charlotte longed to reach out her hand and touch. Hélène caught Charlotte's gaze and giggled, saying, "Ah this is my collection".

Charlotte laughed too, but her laughter was a cover. In that instant, it was as though Hélène had seen Charlotte's old, mismatched bra and pants through her clothes, her awkward, sweaty arms and skinny legs, seen the British women in white cotton underwear that had brought her up. They wore functional garments on their skin, things put on top of other things.

Then, Hélène pushed the drawer shut. Charlotte blinked. The vision was gone.

Hélène waved red lace in Charlotte's face, said, "Sit, I be getting dressed". She disappeared behind a curtain.

Charlotte didn't know where to go. Her rucksack slipped to the floor, pulled a coat off a hook. Behind the curtain, Hélène hummed a tune. Sweat trickled down Charlotte's back. The studio, an old maid's room, was honed like a sharpened pencil. In one corner, pans hung neat as soldiers on parade. A shelf was stacked with columns of coffee bowls. In front of Charlotte was a low table with aligned papers. Post-it Notes with a pen on top. Things waiting to be written, Charlotte thought, and she longed to grab the pen and scrawl in her own diary that she wished she'd never come to France to study Architecture, hadn't invited Steve. She wished, she thought, she wasn't in this perfect fourth-floor Marais apartment.

Charlotte, slumped on a chair, she thought of her Manchester student house. No one ever washed up. Once, maggots had invaded the sink, swarming delicately in a pan of congealed beans. Little white forms, like ballet dancers, writhing amongst the red. In the student house, every open vessel, cup or plate, became an ashtray, blooming flowers of butts.

In the Paris studio, beside Charlotte, was a pile of books. "Hélène", Véronique had said, "studies literature". Yet the first volume Charlotte picked up was on lingerie. A litany of words and illustrations tempted and taunted her: *culotte, cuisse, négligé, parure, liseuse*… She wriggled. The vocabulary was doubly foreign, strange two times over. Since she was ten, Charlotte's mother, a doctor, had read her books on menstruation. "Vagina", her mother would say, "is a six-letter word." Diagrams explained intercourse. Rules to be obeyed. Before she had sex, Charlotte informed men gleefully, as she had once told Steve, "In case of pregnancy,

I must make it clear, I'm pro-abortion". Charlotte was twenty, raging and polite. There was no room for lace.

She snapped the lingerie book shut, lurched forward, knocking over some papers. At the sound, Hélène emerged from behind the curtain, in red underwear and jeans, but nothing else. *"Désolée"*, Charlotte tried to rectify her mistake, but the papers slipped again, and a sea of disorder swamped the tidy space. Hélène kneeled before her, so close Charlotte saw the freckles on her breasts, red lace fringed with a meadow of flowers. Hélène smelt of waves and buttery cake.

Then the doorbell rang.

Hélène rushed to open it and made introductions, saying, "Julien, Charlotte is my aunt's tenant". Standing, Charlotte laughed again. She clutched her rucksack straps, as Julien came and kissed her, placed his cheeks on hers. His lips touched her skin. Stubble. Rough. Smooth. The French *bise*. Once. Twice. Three times. Four. "Can you two collect the clothes from the laundrette?" Hélène had a large, empty cloth bag in her hand. She pushed them both out the door.

Two minutes later, Charlotte found herself with Julien, in silence, watching a dryer go round. Julien was dark, slight and small. He was wearing an ironed shirt and jeans. He held himself straight, contained, as though a distance must be kept from his sealed outside. Véronique had said, Hélène's boyfriend Julien is an anarchist. Charlotte had expected him to look like her British friends: a shaved head or a mohican and Dr. Martens. To break the silence, she babbled, "Great of Hélène to let me stay. Bloody car broke down. Tomorrow, will leave early. Catch a train to—" Julien raised his hand, interrupting her: "I must take the clothes. Now!"

143

The dryer had stopped turning.

Swiftly, he crouched down, placed the empty bag at a right angle to the machine. One by one, Julien removed trousers, T-shirts and men's underwear. His slim, long fingers turned socks into parcels, crumpled T-shirts into Euclidean folds. Julien built towers out of square blocks of pants. His cloth architecture reminded Charlotte of Haussmann's Parisian boulevards. Just recently, a lecturer had told them how, "after the chaos of the French Revolution, Haussmann had steamrolled the narrow winding streets, replacing them with wide avenues. The Archbishop of Paris claimed the new architecture was bathed in light and would improve morality. It was restrained, controlled elegance. Nowhere to deviate or hide."

By the dryer, Julien let out a sudden sigh, examined the folded clothes and zipped the bag shut. For the first time he grinned at Charlotte and she tried to smile back. Later they returned to Hélène's studio, and later still, they took Charlotte to a Polish restaurant. Friends came, borscht was ordered. A woman with eyeliner and immaculate curls conducted an in-depth conversation on strikes, Vorticism and Saumur-Champigny. The men flocked around Hélène, like urban pigeons by a fountain. After several glasses of wine, Charlotte loudly told a story about getting drunk and fainting into Steve's arms at a wine show in Bordeaux, but nobody laughed.

Hélène placed her hand, gently, on Charlotte's leg and said, "You are cute. Your hair." So free. Hélène looked suddenly sad as though the lines of her perfection had formed a cage. But Charlotte didn't understand. The words "cute" and "free" took her this way and that, into a labyrinth. Lost, Charlotte told another, louder story about hitchhiking to Glastonbury Festival with a pervert. She spilled purple soup on her lap. Wanted to dance. Saw Julien frown as she gulped down her wine. As the Parisian evening drew to a close, Charlotte felt everything slipping, pulling away. France kept making her feel like this — raucous, out of control, as though she exposed the wrong parts of herself. She was trapped in the outline of her skin.

At midnight, as she fell asleep on the apartment floor, she caught a final blurred glimpse of Hélène's red underwear.

The following morning, Charlotte woke at five. Got dressed. Found clean black cotton knickers. Slicked her blond hair back. Before leaving, she glanced at sleeping Hélène and then at the chest of drawers. She stared at the top drawer ardently, longing to cloak herself in another façade. That April morning, Charlotte promised herself that one day she would own a similar collection. Wear the lace. She flung her rucksack on her back, and opened the door. It would be her revolution.

The Blues, the Yellow Sheets

Christiana Spens

Couldn't get out of bed, then, as if standing would be falling. I stayed there so long that the details began to taunt me. The skulls on the navy scarf, fading in the light by the window. Teeth chattering and migraine sickness, cigarette nausea and weak tea. Lilac nail polish —the only sympathetic smell, it seemed, then. Respite from swirling pain, confused nostalgia, those fevered visions. Could I find it in a walk around the block, a tiny little bath, a Nespresso pod?

I continued to not get up. I stayed in an old-fashioned bed, in an old-fashioned room, with old-fashioned rose pink wallpaper that I liked very much, certainly more than getting out of bed. I was happy enough here, I thought at first. This would do, this pretty Parisian cell. It would do until I was forced out of bed by hunger, at least.

When at last I was hungry enough to get up, I put on some clothes and went down the street to the supermarket. I had always disliked supermarkets, even French ones, which seemed slightly better than the British equivalents on account of a decent range of coffees and fruits and flowers. And yet now even the Parisian supermarket made me uneasy. I wondered if I had a phobia of supermarkets: the glaring white strip lights and too many items and decisions to make. Things I wanted and things I couldn't really afford or were too unhealthy, or had something that

I may or may not have been allergic to. All the problems, all the futile, everyday little problems that I loathed. They didn't even need to be problems: I had made them into problems. It was entirely my fault that I was wandering around a French supermarket wanting to die.

Eventually I picked up things that I needed: milk, coffee, wine, bread, some vegetables and fruit. I felt sick of these things upon buying them. The idea of having to cook anything filled me with dread. I was hungry, but couldn't really imagine eating. I passed the flowers, suffocated in cellophane, hanging by the side of an aisle, wilting incrementally.

I reached the checkout and spoke minimal French. I used to enjoy the challenge of improving my French, but now it was one more handicap. I piled the foods into a canvas shopping bag and paid the money and smiled and left. I felt desperately inadequate. I was hungry but then I was sick. And if I could be sick and bored here, in Paris, then there was no hope. If all I wanted to do was stare at the wallpaper and lie in the bath, and I was still miserable, then something must be wrong. Paris had always been a good escape, the best escape of them all. But now, here I was, wanting out. Anything would do. I thought of options that would be easy, things in pill form.

There were no painkillers, though, and no people to bring them. It always takes sickness to realise you're alone. Voices in the music, matching my own regret — but why? How could I try any harder? How could I stop my heart racing for no reason? Where did my flatmate keep her Valium? She talked about her breakdowns, and the tablets for emergencies; this seemed to measure up. I'd fit her size.

I'd manage two.

It dragged on — more pear juice and headaches, wound-up thoughts and make-believe. Fantasies, scratched down with good intentions. Quickly, it came to that.

I found the Valium, in a little white bottle. The language of languages, medical terms. Drug names. *Diazepam* in any country. I walked into a dream, where I did not feel guilty for not leaving my bed.

*

The blues, the yellow sheets. Crumpled and lonely, dust in the sky where you should be lying alongside me, best friend and love, always, love in empty spaces — in imagined skies and letters outlined in colour. Better than the other ones, surely?

Letters fading into smoke and work and paint dust. Imaginary, but something I could plan around, at least. Pencilled into the diary, flights booked, looks learned. A whole story, sketched out too quickly.

I sit alone all day waiting for you to come back, strike lightning and chaos and remind me who I am, who you think I could be. Because that matters, now.

Stroking your hair as you try to sleep, you stroke mine when I can't.

*

Can't get the bed sheets straight enough. Sheets, walls, curtains, bag — all colours of vanilla ice cream. Sickly sweet, bile like ice cubes. Something chic now makes my stomach turn. Outside the window — caramels. A coffee sky. A broken chandelier. Pastels for every surface and emotion. Old things, told they were elegant, happy to keep breaking. Cigarettes losing their attraction; writers losing their looks.

I longed for night and the lights out, for imagined colours that must be better than these, I was sure of it.

Away from sickly nausea and dumb respite, wild animals beat at the door and did not listen when I said I liked domestic bliss and straight cream walls that didn't move and blur. Love to stop the ground from swelling, revealing itself as the sea beneath my toes.

It didn't come, but I forgot the symptoms, the shakiness. I blamed myself, or other things. I called them names I'd heard before. I opened my arms to an emptiness I could not contain, but which sounded right, sounded like the answer to the problems. *Love,* from a record, too much love, packed away and dusty. Something to want and want and want and want and leave, some day.

Living Without

Gavin James Bower

I self-diagnose the way a friend of mine self-diagnoses sucrose-intolerance, the way I swear I don't, or won't, Google my symptoms when I feel unwell.

It takes months before I admit to admitting, important, like seeing my dad in the chapel of rest, but not anything like a resolution. There's no closure in looking at a dead body. A circle both can and can't be closed.

Somewhere between abuse and dependence, that's me. I'm not a trope. I don't binge. Sometimes, I drink a few beers and leave it at that. I don't drink every time I'm stressed.

Not at first, anyway.

I give up alcohol when I'm eighteen and don't drink again until after university. I grow up in a town where one wrong look and it's a glassing. I accumulate a few too many bad experiences, the worst one after talking to someone's girlfriend and that someone blind-siding me in a club. I pull on the girl's tie, overstep the mark and blame it on the drink — foreshadowing the morning after, guilt and shame, and what I later become. A friend of hers tells me I'm a creep. This should matter more but it's enough, even then, to make me stop.

I start drinking again in my twenties, progressively more and more with the only problem years, before the most recent, during a bad break-up. This is at the end of 2011, beginning of 2012.

I run away to Paris — am I sure I'm not a trope?

You can walk across Paris in two hours, and for two months I do nothing but walk around and write bad poetry and letters telling her it's over. She tells me the same. We fight to have the last word, like when we were together.

In August that year, she says she wants to try again. By then and only then, I'm over it.

I'm over it because of walking in the snow, the bitter cold of Paris. I'm not a father, not married, not engaged, not in a relationship with anyone or anything but me. Not any more and not yet. My misery. My pain. My solitude.

My self-indulgence, more like.

This is my first experience of grief as I come to understand it years later – my dad dead now but alive and at home then. Here I'm mourning a failed relationship, lost romance, in a city that's nothing if not a mausoleum to Love.

"I've lost that part of you — the part that was mine," she says, just before it's really over.

I miss her when she leaves. To admit it, the sentiment somehow distorts; an abstraction hollow now by confession.

"There is no such thing as autobiography," Winterson says. "There is only art and lies."

Then the confession of a lost love's the greatest deception of all.

Back in 2012, I want to move on. People tell me I have to, like my dad in a letter he writes at the time — one letter from my dad I don't lose — urging me to move on with my life.

But I can't replace her.

In Paris, a sublet from a friend, I lean out of the window, fall against the frame in the cold — unbelievable cold that winter, a single heater on wheels positioned wherever I am in the apartment — and smoke. I think of her, the way we are or, rather, were. She isn't with me. And there it is. There, in that ephemeral place, transient space.

Life goes on, as stupid people say — as if the suffering of loss can be ignored simply because, for everyone else, it doesn't matter.

I fill a notebook I'll later destroy, like another letter from my dad — one letter from my dad I lose deliberately. I fill it with my fears, fears I'll never be able to love again, when in fact I'll never be able to love her again.

A perfect sentence.

I will never be able to love her again.

In that first glimpse of loss, grieving a dead relationship, I discover a self-destructive side of me that never really goes away. That side can only, I think, be suppressed — my not drinking meaning my lack of inhibitions has to take on an altogether different shape.

Sober, I don't go near strangers, take my turn, follow them into cubicles, or wander down alleyways and hidden corners of city streets after dark, my battery dead and my head spinning, no idea how or why I got here.

With practice, I manage to get to the same level as friends who drink. I get progressively looser over the night. I can't fake the chemical, though — the one I've got a problem with, the one that, no matter what I say or do as I negotiate ways I might one day drink again, long after I no longer live in Paris, I can't live with but can just about live without.

The Hanged Man

Joanna Walsh

The Hanged Man shows a man suspended, upside-down, from the living World Tree, rooted in the underworld and supporting the heavens. Given the serene expression on his face, it is believed he is hanging on the tree of his own will.
— www.biddytarot.com

Do you know the streets I like
In Paris?
They are the streets along the top
Of the cemetery wall.
The cemetery walls are white; they don't know what to do with themselves
So all of them turn from each other.
At steep angles
Still I like them
Why?
Because they are always going away from something.

I am going away from something in order to be here. Here I do not go away from something. I am in the first place I have been in not in order to get away from something. Does this mean I am going toward something? If so, I do not put it like that.

153

I have generally gone away from men. But wherever I am, I find another.

1

Here are some things men have said to me during sex:

██████████████████ *body.* ████████ *soles* ██████ *feet.*

████████ *time.*

████ *dirty* ██████ .

██ *not yet.*

████ *it* ██ .

████████ *?*

We're ████████ *out.*

I ██████████████ *in your mouth.*

████████ *good,* ██████ *first time.*

In each case, I have not known what to answer.

I am in this city to pay homage to
The god of skylights. There is one in my bathroom. As it faces the sky that is all I see out of it.
The sky is white.

I am here now *pour de bon*, or so they say, unsure how to cope with such fulfilment.

I look up and see the branches over the cemetery wall: they say nothing to me. Looking

takes the place of hearing.

...

The small woman stopped outside my door and knocked three times. I answered, wrapped in a sheet. She said, *do you have a man?* I said, *yes?* And she said, *I need him.*

It turned out she needed him to lift her father who had fallen from his bed and could not rise. She could not lift him and, watching her look at me, I knew she did not think I could, and that she did not think that we could lift him together. She did not ask me any of this, she could just tell by looking. And she could tell without having ever looked at my man that he could lift her father. I got my man and we went to her father's room and her father smelt quite clean, though he was wearing an adult nappy. He was fat from sitting and inside his thighs were two long white scars from an operation, his belly button was out and round from perished muscle, his belly also a dome and he was solid. It took us time to raise him, all three of us, two of us not even men, during all of which time he smiled, and was entirely mute. She said, thank you, she said, *I called the fire brigade, the first time they came, the second they said, don't you have a man?* She said, *thank you* again, and *I must make you a couscous, how long are you here for?* My man said, *we are going tomorrow.* We did not tell her we were coming back next week, and that her father was still lying on the other side of our wall.

He did not smell bad, her father. That's what I'd been straining for. A spicy smell: cologne, no body behind it. He could have been made of wax.

...

We went into the cemetery and the only grave we could find was Merleau-Ponty. It was white with a crack in it. ████████████████████████████████████
.A few weeks later someone in the building died and we were asked for contributions. My landlord wondered if it was the wax man. My landlord said he had not been the small woman's father but her husband.

We crossed from the cemetery on the crossing with the hanged man on green, the usual light suspended upside down. I only saw it as day crossed to night. It looked like a hanged doll. This morning after you left the river was up over the *quais*: the lip on the edge of each *quai*, exposed, and I saw a man and his son (aged about nine) walk along the lip, as it seemed, between two bodies of water. And though the water on the land side could not have been more than a few inches deep, it kept level with the Seine on the other, which made the whole thing artificially appear an entirely terrifying enterprise. Instead of only half so.

...

I am physically distressed that ██████████████.
(See how bodies displace so quickly into writing!)

Sometimes I look up ███████████████ underneath of your upper teeth. White, no fillings: and don't they look lovely!

Again, ███████████████ though repetition were addition. As perhaps it is.

Of Père Lachaise, On Business

Eley Williams

I'm thirty-nine, many people spell my name incorrectly and in these ways I think I have much in common with Elisabeth Demidoff.

She died aged thirty-nine in 1818. I died in 2018 — *JUST KIDDING*. My parents died in 2018. If you write **1 8 1 8** with a thick black marker on a cheap whiteboard, the lines and sweeps of ink squeak with a sound that goes something like this: *weep woo-weep, weep woo-weep*. If you draw the number **3 9**, the squeak is more like this: *woo-woo woop-weep*.

There were nine different guidemaps to Père Lachaise available online, so one can visit the cemetery with the following discrete approaches in mind:

ENGLISH / FRENCH / SPANISH / ITALIAN / FAMOUS WOMEN / ARTS / GASTRONOMY / LITERATURE / COMMUNARDS

Elisabeth Demidoff is buried in one of the biggest mausoleums in the grounds of the cemetery. It's a romantic, dead, moss-spackled place, and this huge structure looms large on one of its tiered hillsides. The mausoleum has lovely pale masonry and the whole thing is far taller than my house back home in England. I slip a little on black, wet leaves as I make my way around the building to try and find the entrance or a door, catching my balance by placing a hand on the stone of its walls. The stone is neither warm nor cool. There are little ferrets or stoats or polecats chiseled in roundels all along the walls of the mausoleum, their tails bristling in relief. It looks as if they are chasing one another through a series of tossed quoits, or as if they have been modelled spraying one another with terrified or territorial urine.

Weird animal to have on your grave, I think. The printed guidemap in my hand is crumpled and the ink bleeding a little in the light rain. *Ermine* is too close to *vermin*. I consider which animal I would have on my heraldic crest. Something mythical or chimerical but at least pretending that strength or nobility is a theme: a lion crossed with a bull, say, or a leopard crossed with an eagle. A shark with a pair of crossed secateurs. At school, my best friend's surname was Coglione. His official family crest bore "per fess argent and gules, three pairs of testicles counter-changed". We drew our idea of this crest on each other's textbooks. I once went to his house and saw what the actual crest looked like. At the time I didn't know what shape testicles might be, or should be, or could be. They looked like brash bulbs of garlic or a deck of cards' hearts sinking in on themselves, deflated.

I hadn't thought about those testicles for a long time. I hadn't thought about testicles generally for a long time. Funny the way your brain twists and turns when it should be concentrating. When I'm excited I almost can't control the way my mind goes, I'm so sorry. Back to the *business at hand*.

Having found Elisabeth Demidoff's resting place, I push the printed map into my pocket alongside my flask and sandwiches. I look at the ferret-creatures on the masonry again, and check on my phone, fingers skittering a little.

Ferrets bush up their tails to try and make themselves appear more intimidating if frightened or on the defensive.

This is my first encounter with *bush* as a verb like this and I try bushing my jacket and shoulders. The sky is stained with post-storm, the clouds grave-coloured and moving like something curdling, amontillado shaded, humming and emptied just above the cemetery's lampposts. I kept reading on my phone.

A bushy tail can also show excitement or interest, and learning to tell the difference is important. If the ferret is hissing or backing-up then one might assume that they are frightened or annoyed and the handler must proceed with caution.

A group of ferrets is called a *business*, I read. That suits me just fine.

It is not just the print-out that is in my pocket. I feel the familiar edges of the newspaper cutting that sits hidden in there with the tips of my fingers, touching it as if it is the ear of a beloved, companionable dog.

The cutting is from back home. It's old. Not as old as *weep woo-weep, weep woo-weep* 1818, but we're talking the same century. I was clearing out my parents' house — they were dead, I'm no thief — and this wadding of paper was being used to flesh out and enplumpen a teddy bear's collapsing face. I noticed a corner of it and tugged it free. This was the kind of teddy bear no child would ever want to hug with its one livid eye, its fur worn away to scrofulous nothing and body making strange creaking and crackling with old newspaper. I gutted the teddy and laid its innards across my knees. The newspaper was cramped with text and in a typeface I didn't recognise.

Daily Tribune, 25 October 1893, 4

A newspaper older than the concept of teddy bears, I thought. Downstairs, I heard my parents groaning. (I messed up the tenses before — I apologise: *I was clearing out my parents' house — they were dying, I'm no thief*.) There had been a disagreement about their Will and I was upset or something. That was on the Friday. I did some things I regret, horrible but fair things, then found this newspaper on the Sunday as I was upstairs in the attic. It's all a bit of a blur, really, but I had scrubbed myself and the house pretty clean by then. Not scrubbed the room they were in, of course, as that really was beyond a mess. Anyway, imagine! We'd be arguing about a Will, and then in my hand was this tattered scrap of newspaper about a Will. A sign: that's how I interpreted it. I have it committed to memory, testing myself on the precise wording as I sat in my first-class Eurostar seat and played with my complimentary orange juice, watching the Kent countryside streak by. I took a snapshot on my phone too, just in case.

Singular Provision in a Will.

A curious Will contest, according to Paris papers, is about to be tried in the Seine courts. Five years ago a Russian Princess died, leaving a large fortune. There was great surprise among her relatives when the testament was opened. By one of its clauses she left 5,000,000 francs to the person who would remain a year in the chapel to be erected above her grave in the Père-la-Chaise. The body of the Princess, according to the legendary report, lies in a crystal coffin, in a wonderful state of preservation. No one of her relatives has been able to remain longer than two or three days in the chapel. What will become of the 5,000,000 francs is the question.

I haven't felt this calm for years, I realised, as I chanted this final line to myself for the umpteenth time and slid my hands against the mausoleum's masonry. I haven't done the calculations nor worked out the exchange rate, but I reckon that I'm in for a pretty penny. A year in the dark, all time to myself.

Of course I dug a little deeper into the story. I researched on my phone that whole day in the attic until my parents were finally completely quiet downstairs and even the flies fell silent. Online I found out that another American newspaper had something to say about this Will. *The Boston Herald* had scanned its archives and in 1893, I got this hit for "crystal", "coffin", "Paris" as search terms. It claimed that it had documents obtained from the American Ambassador to France:

Five years ago a Russian princess who died in this city, left by will $1,000,000 to the person who would consent to remain for the space of one year in the chapel which is erected over her tomb in the cemetery of Père Lachaise. The princess lies in a crystal coffin. Thus the whole body is distinctly visible and this is what causes so much fright to all who have as yet attempted to gain the prize. But the will forbids all visitors. The candidate must be alone with the dead for a whole year before the $1,000,000 is won. No work is allowed. Books and newspapers, however, are permitted, and a servant brings meals regularly to the watcher. One hour's walk a day is allowed, but this must be undertaken before 5 o'clock in the morning in summer and 8 o'clock during the winter months. Several Frenchmen have assayed to win the prize, but all have given up after a short trial. One lasted out nearly three weeks, by which time he had completely lost his reason, and remains a jabbering idiot. The will makes no mention of foreigners being ineligible. There is every chance, therefore,

for a strong-minded American, who fears neither ghosts, ghouls nor gravestones, to become rich in the short period of 356 days. Application is to be made to the municipality of Paris.

This added some interesting details, I think, especially about the walking. It was only a matter of more idle Googling to work out which grave or mausoleum they might possibly be referring to. I remember that as I formed a plan, excitement crackled up my spine and into my stomach. I realised that I had not eaten the whole weekend. I went downstairs, booking train tickets to Gare du Nord as I went. Thank God for phones. I stepped over my parents on the kitchen floor and made myself a sandwich, drinking old milk from the carton because no one was there to tell me that was vulgar. With a flick of my thumb on the phone's blue screen, I learnt more about Princess/Countess Elisabeth/Elizaveta Demidoff/Demidov, née Stroganoff/Stroganov. She was married off aged sixteen, her husband building his fortune through modernising infrastructure and mining. That sounds good. My parents owned a stationer's and they made a fair bundle, so I reckon a Russian Count was good for a few bob. The reason why I couldn't see a red cent of my selfish parents' money I really couldn't say. Unfair, basically. I'll be candid with you now, as I use my phone's blue screen to illuminate the cobweb-jammy door of the mausoleum: it's entirely unfair the way my parents cut me out. I feel sick now just thinking about it. And still angry, even though I showed them what's what. 300,000 graves in this graveyard, and I still find myself so angry that

I feel the urge to kick down every stone, set fire to every tree and patch of ivy-bedecked masonry.

As I stare at the mausoleum door, considering how best to gain entry, some tourists pass by my spot. I duck behind the ferret-laden wall but couldn't be sure they hadn't seen me. It was a pair, man and woman I think, slumped over each other in matching red cagoules. He was wearing a Jimmy Morrison T-shirt and sobbing theatrically on his partner's shoulder. *Still drawing crowds*, she was saying in French, patting his hair. They were holding cheap plastic flowers in their arms. Honestly: Apollinaire, Éluard, Stein and Toklas — all these graves and you choose *Jimmy Morrison to fawn over*. I suppose for most people it is not so much the graves that draw you there as proximity to the idea of who might lie beneath them, marking the mark they made on you.

I am pretty sure that they did not spot me, but one can't be too careful. I had been lucky so far because of the rain: no one had seen me scale the wall in the CCTV blind spot and enter the site, and all of the paths I had taken were tumbled down and grown-over, completely empty of the selfie-stick hordes. This couple was the only problem I had encountered. That was fine: I had time and it was worth my while to be scrupulous. I set my mouth in a straight line, made sure all my paperwork was safe in my pocket, and watched them as they rounded a corner away from me.

I stalked them for a while, picking my way over the reaching elbowing tree roots and avoiding the more vocal crows that were strutting about. We passed Balzac, we passed Chopin. They bickered and sobbed the whole time — it was quite extraordinary to watch. *What a business*, I said to myself as I smelt the air and hopped from grave to grave charting their progress. They checked their guidemap about an hour into their walk and after a huge row — voices raised, raised hands — they went in different directions. I hope the wife left to go apply lipstick and make her way to Oscar Wilde's grave to give it a big old kiss. That's the tradition, isn't it? Anyway, the now-lonely man's sobbing was very rude and distracting and louder than ever, putting me off, making me angry, so I ran up to him and broke his neck, etc., etc., and dragged him off the path. I propped him up beside a grave where the name had been worn away, off the beaten track. The weather did something Gothic, the crows turned their backs, the trees shook heads or hands above me in the wind.

No challengers, you know, I whispered to the cold man. *No hard feelings*, pas de sentiments forts. *I'm thorough about these things.*

I stayed with him for a while to make sure he would be quiet for ever and ever, and told him about my ideas for spending the money, how I'd spend the year with Elisabeth. I told him about my whiteboard in my parents' attic where I'd set about making my plan — the plan about all those powerpacks in my rucksack to keep my phone going as long as possible, the plan to send an email automatically to the officials who control the Père Lachaise site about where to send the money once the year is up. I told him and his now-greying hands about the gun, and how I'd keep anyone out if they tried to remove me. I emphasised the word *they* with a ferret-like hiss. I told him even about my parents and I think I cried a little on his Jimmy Morrison t-shirt. Then I dried my tears and told him about heraldic testicles and we both cheered up, I think, and all in all it was very pleasant until the flies came, *always so quick*.

I made it my business to leave.

Paris: A Manifesto in Twenty Arrondissements

Julian Hanna

1.

We met at a hostel on Rue Mouffetard where I was staking out the ghosts of my literary idols. "How many *arrondissements* have you visited?" she asked. Never having registered the existence of any *arrondissement* except the fifth and sixth, I answered: "Two". She said: "You should really learn to drift [*dériver*]. Paris is like a vast board game, suitable for endless play. But when you die it's over — for you!"

2.

Will I ever collect the letters you sent *poste restante*? The narcissism of love drawn out by the fever dream of Paris is insatiable, it has no end but death. Nothing has faded in the least: every visit to Paris is as fresh and vivid as the moment I last walked these streets, dreaming awake. The post will wait for you — but for how long? How many dead letters can it hold? I drank too much and forgot to collect them; you wouldn't tell me what they said. I wrote from Paris: *I'm in Paris*. I wrote to another woman, missing you both (such things are possible). All those letters are dead now, and Paris is still Paris.

3.

Never have I found out what I want from Paris, or what Paris wants from me.

4.

Have you read *À rebours*? The yellow book that corrupted Dorian Gray came from Paris. When Wilde was convicted of gross indecency he resisted the temptation to take the night boat with the others, choosing to stay and fight the philistines. When he was freed he returned to Paris, finally having no alternative. London was left to those without sin, while the sinners went to Paris. (That is why this is about Paris and not London.)

5.

Paris is Wilde's tomb in Père Lachaise: fame, sex, death. Robbie Ross (who now lodges in the same tomb in a convenient little cubbyhole) gave the job to the sculptor Jacob Epstein. Epstein was a true cosmopolitan: raised by Polish Jews on the Lower East Side, he moved to Paris to attend the École des Beaux-Arts and was later sucked into the Great London Vortex. Why the modernist Epstein? Epstein, whose next project was *The Rock Drill*, a terrifying transhuman figure fused with an actual drilling machine; Epstein, who served in the Jewish Legion and left after a breakdown without firing a shot. When he finished it, the tomb was declared obscene by French customs police. Unveiled by Aleister Crowley it wore a bronze butterfly to hide the Sphinx's balls — now it sits encased in glass to keep out the necrophilic kisses of adoring fans.

6.

We discovered that Latin Quarter cafés were too expensive and intimidating, so instead we wandered in cemeteries for free. We nosed around Shakespeare and Company, still grubbily bohemian under old George's stewardship, with army surplus sleeping bags laid out in the upstairs rooms. We bought cheap editions of Colette and Duras and Sagan.

7.

Will it ever be like that again? Then it all felt like a different era: the Paris of my dreams, the Paris of Proust and *Pierrot le fou*. But now it seems like the same era: cinemas projecting celluloid, cafés without laptops, letters written and received *poste restante*, photos that remained unseen till you returned; heavy stacks of paperbacks, cigarettes anywhere you liked (except at Le New Morning), ignorance of the world beyond the city walls, so beautifully cut off from anything except Paris. The timeless analogue city spread out in front of you, international but not yet global, the city in the age of mechanical but not yet digital reproduction.

8.

Never was there an authoritative source for anything — only occult tips passed from stranger to stranger like secret passwords, like currency between young lovers. We left our provincial towns and descended on Paris like the chosen ones, wearing black polo necks in the hope we'd be recognised by others like us, smoking idly in cafés while we waited to be sucked up into the mother ship of Western culture.

9.

Have you ever been a local? Emma Bovary, stuck in the sticks, dreamed of Paris:

> In the city, with the noises of the streets, the hum of the theatres, and the bright lights of the balls, they were leading lives where the heart had space to expand, the senses to blossom.

I know the feeling of walking through somebody else's fantasy on your way to work. But when I go to Paris I forget myself and fall headlong into the dream.

10.

Paris is a firecracker exploding in a carriage of the Métro with a deafening bang, then another and another, as smoke fills the enclosed space and the bomber-jacketed boys who lobbed them in at the last second, just as the automatic doors slid shut, stand doubled over in laughter on the platform. You suddenly realise you've arrived on Bastille Day, this isn't just any normal day in Paris — or is it?

11.

We drank cheap wine at an outdoor table, watched the stack of little saucers we'd read about growing higher by the hour, noted the warm feeling of rising intoxication — reading, writing, eavesdropping, looking — all perfectly manageable until you try to stand and pay the bill, and you miss the step and fall down into the moonlit cobblestoned street.

12.

Will I write a letter to the new lover whose room I just left, her scent still on my clothes, and another to the old lover, who is still unaware of being "the old lover"? Caught in my romantic reverie, standing on a bridge in Paris like so many others have done forever into the future and the past, I think: yes. And I will send a third letter to the wife I haven't met yet, warning her never to let me go to Paris.

13.

Never had I breathed air and drank wine like this. I grew up in a city of a few thousand, less than a hundred years old. The people there never thought to do anything but live and work and die. How does a city like Paris exist with this level of romance? Doesn't it interfere with everyday life? How do people go on with *Métro-boulot-dodo*, surrounded by the scent of sex and the sight of the Sacré-Coeur, steeped in the sound of the language spoken by Stendhal and de Sade, Sartre and Simone de Beauvoir?

14.

Have you ever stayed out all night, wandering between the banks of the Seine, smoking unfiltered Gauloises and talking to stray dogs, killing time in never-closing cafés?

If you have serious ideas about life,
If you make artistic discoveries
and if all of a sudden your head begins to crackle with laughter,
if you find all your ideas useless and ridiculous, know that

IT IS PARIS BEGINNING TO SPEAK TO YOU

15.

Paris when you were free to travel and nothing was recorded, no one saw the band except the people who were there in the room. Travelling was a dream, because nothing could be verified and nothing made any sense or had any purpose and no one could even find you for weeks or months at a time.

16.

We never really had Paris, but we didn't want to have it anyway. We only wanted to breathe the air of Le New Morning for a while and drink overpriced coffee at Le Select.

17.

Will we ever have it again? Let's meet somewhere cheap and dirty and far from the tourists. In a basement bar where we can kiss and not be recognised (but still be seen).

18.

Never has there been anything like Paris in the brief gap between the fall of the Soviet Union and the rise of the internet, when the poor could finally travel and everyone saw the City of Light for the first time. Maybe there were other times, but this was one.

19.

Have you read Perec's *An Attempt at Exhausting a Place in Paris*? He is sitting in a square, Place Saint-Suplice in the Latin Quarter (where you'll likely sit). He describes everything that happens, which is to say nothing (just as you'll do in that pristine notebook you've got hidden in your bag). The book could go on forever but it stops after about fifty pages. Three days drinking coffee and brandy and watching buses and pigeons and nuns. Does he exhaust Paris? No — Paris exhausts him!

20.

Paris is inexhaustible — there is never any end to...

Paris Montage: Coincidence is the Mystery of the Metropolis; Montage Crystallises that Chaos

Richard Skinner

i. Gare de Lyon, twelfth arrondissement

These people are fools, but did I have the nerve? I was scared at first but, after a while, there was an ecstasy in it. We lifted wallets, handbags, watches even. The best time of year was during summer when the station was crammed full with tourists, travellers, merchant stands, porters and station agents. Me and my accomplices (whose names I never knew) worked all through the summer. Every day was the same— "Can I do it?" — and every day I managed it. It became an addiction. They say you should never return to the scene of the crime but, when my two accomplices were arrested, I couldn't resist. I pushed my luck too far at the Hippodrome. I got sloppy. I lifted a bundle of cash from a woman's handbag while she watched the horses but, as soon as I left, two men appeared either side of me. It was Jeanne who taught me that prison is a model of the soul. That's where I found love.

ii. Champs-Élysées, eighth arrondissement

"New York Herald Tribune!" There she is. My little elf with her petite figure and short hair. It's crazy, but I love her so much. But she doesn't love me, I know. That's a pity. What a fox she is. She seems happy to see me. She smiles. I buy a paper and ask her to come to Rome with me. I hate France. She doesn't answer. I know she lies. I caress her silly lies, she's got brown eyes. Sometimes, I get furious because I'm sad. That cop. He shouldn't have got in my way. It's too bad but you have to live dangerously till the end. Life's pretty funny, you never know what's around the corner. I guess I'm weak. I pass my idle days with my idle ways. I wonder why she never wears a bra. Later, after I've seen the guy who owes me money, we'll make love, I know we will. I want her too much. I've got jazz playing in my head. It's nice to wake up next to a girl. She keeps me warm, but we never kiss. And later on, maybe I'll tell her my real name.

iii. Boulevard Raspail, sixth arrondissement

It's horrible to have to wait for bad news. I know it's bad news, I can feel the cancer in my stomach. It changes the way you look at everything, like someone has reached inside your brain and wiped everything clean. I have always felt the desire to be desired — my singing career, my fans have meant the world to me, defined me — but now I just wish people would leave me alone. I feel like an accidental tourist in my own life. Everything feels strange, new. My dress feels silly and whimsical. My lover doesn't really love me, my friends don't really care for me. I now realise a great many things that I should have before. But I couldn't see them and, even if I could, I didn't want to admit them to myself. It's time to face up to a lot of truths. I'll live every day as if it's my last, because it could be. Time has stopped. I'm wandering aimlessly in the city. Perhaps I'll go to the Dôme for a cognac. I'll kill time before it kills me.

iv. Saint-Germain-des-Prés, sixth arrondissement

I'm sick of it. Why is my luck so bad? I was born under Leo, the luckiest sign of all, but no luck for me — it's pathetic. Where are your friends when you need them? Gone. *Disparus.* Just like that. When the news came through that my aunt had died and left me all her money, I was going to be a millionaire. I was going to have it all. Instead my lousy cousin got it. I'm penniless and on the streets. The sole of my shoe flaps. It's embarrassing. I have to search through bins for food, or I steal. A street vendor beat me up the other day for stealing a tomato. Just one tomato. The last straw was spilling that sardine oil on my trousers yesterday. That bothered me more than anything. The nights are the worst. Sleeping on the hot streets and blocks of stone and then, when the vicious sun rises yet again, the light bounces off them, blinding me, burning me. There's no escape. The sun is a monster, the city a cage and I am a clown.

v. 1 Square Albin-Cachot, thirteenth arrondissement

Oh, where's the house? Is it this one? Yes, this one, but I don't dare ring the bell. Instead, I walk on by and pretend to look in a shop window. Oh, who's that entering the building? She must be one of the girls. She looks normal, like me. I imagine her climbing the stairs, going into a nice bedroom, undressing and getting into bed ready for a client. I picture a man hitting her, then holding her down roughly. I'm hot with shame. But I'm excited, too. There's a bench over there. I sit down and take a deep breath. What am I doing here? For no reason at all that I can think of, the tears come. My husband is a kind man. He treats me well, but he treats me as if I were a child. I'm not a child. I have to do this or else I know I will leave him. I am damned if I do and damned if I don't. I dry my eyes and put on my dark glasses. I'll try again. I walk to the door and ring the bell. It buzzes open. I think of the priest and his wandering hands. The stairs are many and spiral. I climb them.

vi. Rue Mouffetard, fifth arrondissement

I came to my new home here in the city with just one bag and a cardboard box. I left everything else behind. The country villa, the piano, my life. Everything was gone. When I arrived, the first thing I did was take my daughter's mobile out of the box and fix it to the ceiling. The blue crystals remind me of her. The café on the corner is nice. I spend a lot of time there. Well, I have nothing in the new flat, just a bed. One day, just outside the café, a street musician played one of my husband's pieces on a recorder. I hear the music in my head all the time. It was a sign. I'll finish my husband's piece. Then the young man turned up with my cross, which he found at the scene of the accident. He wanted to meet me to return it. I agreed to meet him for a coffee. His earnestness was absurd. He told me my husband's last words, but they were a punchline to a favourite bad joke of ours, which I repeated. I told him to keep the cross. Some months later, the numbness started to go. Then it was just pain. If this is Liberty, I'd rather be a prisoner of love again.

vii. Eighteenth arrondissement

I'm so sick of it all. The world is ours? No way. No life here, no jobs. Just trouble. I'm so bored. That's why we go into the city and fuck things up a bit. This time, we called in on Saïd's crazy drug-dealer Astérix. Kung fu? Fuck that shit. He was an asshole. Then we got jumped by the police. Just like that. Saïd and Hubert both got nicked but I escaped. I watched a movie. Can't remember what. I smoked a joint. I saw a cow. I fell asleep. I saw them again at the station. We missed the last train. We walked around the streets. We crashed a gallery with its shit art. Saïd and Hubert chatted up some girls. They were stuck up. Everyone was. Hubert lifted a credit card though. Ha! We tried to use it to get a cab back but no go. We tried to steal a car but some drunk guy interrupted us. We went to the mall and saw on the news that Abdel died. Then we beat up a skinhead. Hubert told me to shoot him, but I couldn't. I gave him the gun. I don't want it no more.

viii. Rue des Iris & Rue Brillat-Savarin, thirteenth arrondissement

Who is doing this to me? Why? What I have done to them? I have worked hard to get where I am and I'll be damned if they destroy everything I've earned. They are watching the house round the clock but why can't I find where they're filming from? It doesn't make sense. Then more tapes and stupid drawings arrived. I know very well what they mean but I'm not going to tell anyone until I've found out who is terrorizing us. It has to stop. But why now, after all these years? Why not just let sleeping dogs lie? It's driving me mad and Anne looks at me funny these days. She suspects something's not quite right, but I can't tell her anything. Not yet. What are they complaining about? He had a life, didn't he? If it wasn't for us, he might not be here at all. He should be grateful for everything we did for him. But, instead, he turns against us, biting the hand that fed him. Some people. What have I got to hide? Nothing. Nothing at all.

ix. Gare du Nord, tenth arrondissement

Every night, when I get home from work, my daughter is there. Her latest thing is her rice cooking machine. She loves it and we have rice every night. She's my treasure. She's my light, my heart. I love her more than anything in the world, but she's growing up. I drive trains out of Gare du Nord. I retire in two weeks and the guys are planning a send-off involving lots of rum. I'll miss work, but I'm tired, too. I'm a little tired of everything, to be honest. And she is growing up and will leave home soon. There's a young man courting her but he'll have to try harder — she's a tough cookie, just like her mother. She has a temper on her! I don't want to give her up, but I know I'll have to. It's the way of things. She doesn't want anything to change either. But, I will have to force her to leave, if necessary. She needs to have a life of her own and move on with it. She's my heart. I will miss her.

Paris at 24 Frames a Second

Richard Kovitch

Cinema is the truth at 24 frames-per-second. And every edit is a lie.
— Michael Sabor, *Le Petit soldat* (Dir: Jean-Luc Godard, 1963)

I

The images my mind conjures when I think about Paris are, by any measure, extraordinary. Here are some examples:

A beautiful woman walking along the Champs-Elysées, illuminated only by the light from shop windows.

A hit man lying deathly still in a decaying apartment in the Quartier de l'Amérique.

A BMW hurtling towards oncoming traffic in the Champerret Tunnel.

East European hustlers encircling businessmen outside Gare de Lyon.

A man's head being caved in with a fire extinguisher in a sex club on the Rue de Penthièvre.

You will be reassured to learn none are first-hand experiences, and yet they occupy my mind as if they were. But in reality I have only visited the French capital twice. Once in my early teens, when I found myself camping — yes, camping! — on Haute-Île State Park. Then again in my twenties, when I finally infiltrated the bohemian city to mingle with filmmakers and designers, stumbling through the Catacombs by day; clubbing under Pont Alexandre III at night. Ultimately my lived experiences of this extraordinary city remain as limited as my mastery of the French language. And yet Paris still feels immediate to me — intimate even. How is this possible?

In a sense, it is because I am always visiting Paris. The French film industry remains the third largest in the world, producing over three hundred titles a year. As the national capital, Paris inevitably dominates cinematic representations. To this roster of indigenous talent we must add filmmakers from overseas, moulding the city to their own ends, be it art-house doyens like Michael Haneke (*Code Unknown*, 2002) or Hollywood thrill-seekers like Tom Cruise (*Mission Impossible: Fallout*, 2018). Paris has also hosted some of the most memorable spectacles of the media age, from the euphoric (the student riots of 1968, *les Bleus'* two World Cup victory parades in 1998 and 2018) to the harrowing (the 2015 *Charlie Hebdo* massacre and Bataclan terror attacks). Given the unavoidable amplifications, distortions, omissions and prejudices that ensue whenever a camera rolls or an editor cuts, I would be unwise to take any of these depictions at face value. No doubt the Paris of my imagination does not exist. But that does not necessarily render it fictive.

II

The Paris air did him in.
— *Paris nous appartient* (Dir: Jean Rivette, 1961)

It's 1965. General de Gaulle flies high above Paris in a helicopter. Alongside him is the politician Paul Delouvrier. Beneath them Greater Paris sprawls. 4,661 square miles. 8.5m citizens. The city looks bleak from the air. It is shabby, fragmented, still liberating itself from the shadow of the Second World War. After an hour, de Gaulle turns to Delouvrier and complains; *"Delouvrier, remettez-moi un peu d'ordre dans ce bordel!"* ("Clean up this bloody mess, Delouvrier!"). Cohesion is sought; beauty is desired; chaos rejected.

De Gaulle's lament immediately puts us in mind of Jonathan Raban's *Soft City* (1974) and its key insight that the raw urban landscape ultimately awaits the "imprint of identity". For filmmakers, both local and visiting, this presents great opportunities. Cities may harbour radically different zones in reality, but fictional interpretations can make them cohere. The director Claire Denis has presented the French capital in many different, contradictory ways over her twenty-five-year career — from the transient romance of *Vendredi soir* (2002) to the hellish dread of *Les Salauds* (2013) — and each is as plausible as the next. This variety is even more evident when we consider the wider history of French cinema. From the stately *Cinéma de papa* of the mid-century to the youthful energy of the *Nouvelle Vague* in the late Fifties; from the pop hedonism of the *Cinéma du look* in the Eighties to the violent transgressions of the *New French Extremity* in the Noughties. Far from achieving "cleaning up this bloody mess", filmmakers compound the sense of chaos by building parallel worlds that readily contradict one another.

First impressions count though, and my earliest impressions of Paris came via the Roman Polanski thriller, *Frantic* (1988). A minor work in the director's canon, but a film that remains dear to my heart. Prior to watching *Frantic*, my only sense of the French capital had been its cameo in the James Bond film *A View to a Kill* (1985). But where Bond used Paris as glamorous spectacle — replete with Grace Jones parachuting off the Eiffel Tower — Polanski revealed something darker, framing Harrison Ford's desperate hunt for his wife against the dominant anxieties of mid-Eighties urban life: terrorism, race, narcotics. From its opening scene *Frantic* establishes Paris through an exile's eyes. Two Americans, Richard (Ford) and his wife Sondra (Betty Buckley), are slumped in a taxi that has broken down on the Boulevard Périphérique, a ring road that runs like a noose around inner-city Paris. "Do you know where we are?" asks Sondra, half-asleep. "No, it's changed too much," replies Richard, surveying the heavy traffic. The city feels hostile, alien... mysterious. We are a long way from the city of romance the couple honeymooned in decades earlier.

Polanski later insisted he was reaching for something more mundane: a "lived in" quality. Paris, after all, was his home. But Polanski being Polanski, the darkness inevitably found its way in. And in emphasising the daily grind of Parisian life — the indifference of strangers, officious bureaucracy, the erotic potential of the city after dark (embodied by the leather-jacketed, gum-chewing,

twenty-two-year-old model Emanuelle Seigner) — Polanksi
cemented in my mind ideas about Paris that resonate to
this day. Here was a very adult city. It felt seedy and intimidating. Nothing could be ventured upon lightly. And yet
its pleasures were numerous. It was also seductive. Exotic.
Enticing.

As my interest in cinema grew through the Nineties, my
ideas about Paris deepened. This wasn't the result of a
conscious effort to immerse myself in French film history —
that would come later — but via random VHS rentals that
piqued my curiosity (Tartan and Artificial Eye proved significant allies), or if I stumbled across late-night screenings
on UK television. As a result, the Paris I encountered owed
less to the canonical works of French cinema, far more to
the fresh talent that emerged in the Nineties. Claire Denis
and Olivier Assayas would prove to be lifelong devotions,
but it was random films that caught my attention at the
time, such as Pierre Salvadori's surreal, black comedy from
1995, *Les Apprentis* (starring the late Guillaume Depardieu),
replete with its mysterious apartments; or the raw, explosive
energy of Mathieu Kassovitz's *La Haine* (also 1995).

More than any film from this period, my most vivid
memory is watching actor/director Cyril Collard's *Les Nuit
fauves* (1992) late one night on Channel 4. How could a
film be so erotic and harrowing all at once? Collard's Paris
is fluid with possibilities, evoked in the driving scenes that
depict him hurtling in his red Porsche between disparate
lovers as if they were Stations of the Cross. When I later
discovered Collard had died weeks after the film was
released, aged just thirty-five — from the same HIV-re-

lated infection that doomed his on-screen persona — any semblance that cinema could only ever be "make believe" was completely undone.

Fundamentally, these Paris-set films made it abundantly clear the city's international reputation for escapist romance — emblematic in films such as Vincente Minnelli's *An American in Paris* (1951) or Woody Allen's schmaltzy *Midnight in Paris* (2011) — simply didn't hold. In fact, it was a mystery that it had ever been established in the first place. Not only does this postcard Paris feature surprisingly little in indigenous French films, but other motifs occur with a far greater frequency: the anonymity of crowds, heavy traffic, the cavernous apartment, raw sexuality, a love/hate relationship with American culture, even traces of the Occult. More a city of darkness then, than a city of light.

III

Lives will cross, their destinies disconnected...
— *Bob le flambeur* (Dir: Jean-Pierre Melville, 1955)

These themes found their apotheosis in Bernardo Bertolucci's *Last Tango In Paris* (1972), a film I first saw on VHS in the mid-Nineties. I knew of its reputation through hearsay, but when I finally watched it I was quickly availed of any ideas it was "soft porn". Opening with Marlon Brando cursing God underneath the Pont de Bir-Hakeim, and climaxing with a bullet to his back in a dingy apartment in Passy, it is a film fixated as much upon death as sex. Pauline Kael's review upon the film's release argued it was "the most powerfully erotic movie ever made, and it may turn out to be the most liberating movie ever made". I'm not sure that still holds — *Betty Blue* (1986) and *Blue is the Warmest Colour* (2013) are subsequent contenders regarding eroticism — but it continues to exert an extraordinary power. Paris's wintry exteriors evoke a harsh solitude; hot, Francis Bacon-inspired interiors incubate Brando and Schneider's spiral of abuse and anonymous sex. Significantly, it still feels like a story that could only play out in Paris.

But then, isn't that how I always feel when watching my favourite Paris-set films? They all seem to locate something that's essentially "true" about the city, even as their aesthetics diverge dramatically from one another. How can Claude Chabrol's dark thriller, *Juste avant la nuit* (1971), and its unearthing of the moral turpitude of the French bourgeoisie, feel as equally "Parisian" as Claude Sautet's playful Nineties romance *Nelly & Monsieur Arnaud* (1996)? Why does the sci-fi dystopia of Jean-Paul Godard's *Alphaville* (1965) feel in some way connected with the ominous modernity of the *banlieues* depicted in Céline Sciamma's *Girlhood* (2014)? Or consider Jean-Pierre Melville's extraordinary *noirs* starring Alain Delon (*Le Samouraï*, 1967, *Le Cercle rouge*, 1971, *Un flic*, 1972). These films construct a coolly modern Paris, inscrutable to outsiders, otherworldly even. We sense the city's fluidity as, over the course of the trilogy, Delon effortlessly ghosts between roles as both criminal and police officer, his on-screen persona enriched by off-screen entanglements in *L'Affaire Markovic* (1969) that connected him directly to gangland Paris. "I always lived my roles," he would claim ominously in 2018. "I've never acted." And yet for all the "reality" Delon implies, we must not forget how Melville's films heavily pastiche

US noir, or that they bare zero traces of the late-Sixties counterculture disrupting the boulevards of the city at the time of their production.

IV

> What facts? This is the supernatural. Nothing is clear.
> — Henri de Maublanc, *Le Diable probablement* (Dir: Robert Bresson, 1977)

This then is the chaos that frustrated de Gaulle when he looked down on the city and demanded order. And yet it is this same chaos that fuels Paris's creative life. Films set in Paris might provide scant assistance to anyone attempting to navigate the city on foot, but as guides to our inner lives they are invaluable. The best even alert us to media deceptions, challenging our perceptions, warning us of the implicit bias that exists in us all. Consider Michael Haneke's assault on media and memory in *Code Unknown* (2000) and *Caché* (2005). Or the near-virtual worlds that converge in Leos Carax's *Holy Motors* (2012). Or the consumerism and political stasis that lurk at the heart of Bertrand Bonello's *Nocturama* (2016). In Antonio Campos's *Simon Killer* (2012), Brady Courbet's eponymous loner travels to Paris seeking romantic renewal, only to end up masturbating alone watching internet pornography. Paris is resistant to his fantasies. Reality has failed him. But in its place deeper truths are unearthed.

And so I continue to understand the French capital through disparate, but extraordinary images. I may still know very little about the real Paris. But the freedom to get lost in images of this great city has proven invaluable in shaping a deeper understanding of the modern world:

The crack of gunfire as a young man makes a bid for freedom on Rue Campagne Première.

Chewing gum stuck carefully to an iron railing as a man draws his last breath on a balcony in Passy.

Nico's "Janitor of Lunacy" playing over the dying embers of a teenage party.

A Mercedes-Benz speeding towards a rendezvous with the driver's lover as twilight falls.

The statue of Joan of Arc outside Place des Pyramides engulfed in flames.

The Past is a Foreign City

David Collard

In the 1980s I had a poorly-paid job in London but, living frugally in cheap digs off the Tottenham Court Road and with few overheads, I could afford to nip across to Paris quite often, although "nip" was hardly the word back then.

Before the tunnel opened in 1994 it took a day to get there, catching the ten o'clock train from Victoria to Dover, a slow ferry or wallowing hovercraft to Calais and then another train, arriving at Gare du Nord in the early evening. Next (in my case) the southbound Métro and the warm urban *sillage* of garlic, saucisson sec, Gitanes, brake dust, rubber, urinals and fermenting sweat. Ten stops to Odéon and a no-star hotel. In my duffel-bag a spare shirt, a bottle of duty-free cognac, thermos flask, earplugs, books and cigarettes. We all smoked then, everywhere, all the time. I remember students from Marcel Marceau's School of Mimodrama on Rue René-Boulanger milling around outside at lunchtime, none of them miming but all of them *actually* smoking. Skinny in leggings and leotards, they looked like Giacometti sculptures.

I never visited the Eiffel Tower or Notre-Dame or the Sacré-Cœur and still haven't. What a friend's father, a dashing young man in the late 1920s, called "Gaypers" — a flapper-era contraction of "Gay Paree" — was not for me. No champers on the Champs-Élysées, no B*elle*

Époque hankie-pankie, no *Folies Bergère* or *Moulin Rouge*, no *ooh-la-la*. By the 1980s all that was for chortling Brits who referred to "the Continong". I had other priorities.

What drew me there were the films made by a cohort of directors between the late 1950s and early 1970s — the *nouvelle vague*. I'd sat transfixed through a trailblazing Barbican retrospective in 1984 and, now hooked, I wanted to see everything, by everyone: Robert Bresson, Claude Chabrol, Jacques Demy, Jean-Luc Godard, Alain Resnais, Éric Rohmer, Jacques Rivette, François Truffaut, Agnès Varda, the lot. I was a discriminating glutton or, like Isabelle Huppert's character in Hal Hartley's *Amateur*, a nympho-maniac virgin. Asked how this is possible, she replies: "I'm just choosy". I was choosy, but I wanted it all and in that pre-digital era you had to go to Paris.

In the mornings I would haunt a handful of stores selling back-issues of *Cahiers du Cinéma* and scripts and press books and lurid Belgian posters, spending many hours contentedly riffling through thousands of dog-eared lobby cards and glossy Studio Harcourt portraits. ("*En France, on n'est pas acteur si l'on n'a pas été photographié par les Studios d'Harcourt*" wrote Barthes in *Mythologies*.) I remember the dozens of cardboard boxes tightly packed with tatty manila envelopes on which were scrawled, in thick black felt tip, the name of the star, or director, or film, or genre. I recall the thrill of expectation when teasing open a packet labelled CARETTE (Julien), or MODOT (Gaston) or VIGO (Jean) or BARDOT (first name unnecessary), or my namesake COLLARD (Cyril), director of *Les Nuits fauves*, who died aged thirty-five from an AIDS-related illness three days before his only feature film won a clutch of Césars.

Afternoons and evenings were spent either at the rather formal Cinémathèque Française or sprawled in the dark on lumpy seats in a Left Bank *salle obscure*, raptly yearning. As a sedentary *flâneur* I'd watch four or five films a day, not only New Wave but Popular Front productions from the 1930s and cult American movies admired by the *Cahiers* critics, such as *Shock Corridor* and *Hellzapoppin'*. Back in my hotel room after midnight, I'd guzzle whatever food I'd picked up on my way and scribble some notes. I was measuring out my life in fleapits and flophouses, creating new memories. I needed to stock up.

A particular memory is of a damp November evening in 1987. I was twenty-six and in Paris for three nights. Cars with warm yellow headlights swoosh by as I trudge along Rue Saint-Jacques. In my overcoat pocket is the weekly listings magazine *Pariscope*, the many pages dedicated to film annotated with ticks, crosses and question marks. I'm heading for one of the small cinemas clustered around the Sorbonne — L'Accatone on Rue Cujas, which, as we cinephiles knew, had been managed in the 1960s by Truffaut himself. Recently refurbished, it featured a gallery, a tiny bar and a bookshop stocked with Baudrillard, Barthes, Kristeva and Foucault. I arrived to find the bright lobby packed with damp overcoats, their occupants poring over copies of *Pariscope*, smoking.

We had gathered for a rare screening of Jean Eustache's *La Maman et la putain* (*The Mother and the Whore*), shot during the summer of 1972 and regarded by many as the New Wave's last gasp, perhaps its apotheosis. It's a *ménage à trois* involving a self-absorbed intellectual called Alexandre (Jean-Pierre Léaud, perfectly cast), his older girlfriend Marie (Bernadette Lafont) and a young Polish nurse, Veronika (Françoise Lebrun), a plotless three-and-a-half hour epic exploring their private dilemma through a series of meandering scenes accompanied by long stretches of dialogue — the kind of cinema Hitchcock derided as "photographs of people talking". It's like life, in other words and, documentaries aside, there are few better depictions of how things were for many of us in the 1970s. For one thing (and this may seem absurd today) nobody seems to own any furniture — when not in bars or cafés or wandering around the boulevards, everybody hunkers down on the floor, or on mattresses or beanbags or cushions, until one minor character, played by the director himself, somehow acquires a wheelchair.

Lafont, then in her early thirties, captures perfectly the pain and rage of a woman losing her lover to a younger rival. She came from Nîmes and had a raspy Arlesian accent, made raspier in her later years by drink and tobacco. Her screen debut at eighteen was in the sun-drenched seventeen-minute short *Les Mistons*, directed by Truffaut in 1958, and in the same year she appeared in Chabrol's *Le Beau Serge*, a gloomy low-budget melodrama widely regarded as initiating the *nouvelle vague* movement. She remained a wonderfully durable talent on stage and screen for more than half a century, usually playing tough, raucous, ballsy, independent women with sharp wits and a sharper tongue. There was something of the *soixante-huitard* veteran about her as she grew older. She had a watchful, sometimes predatory expression, pursed lips giving way to a wide smile, an explosive laugh. She was an absolutely terrible off-key singer and while she made her share of bad films she was always the best thing in them. My *Pariscope* said that she would be present at the screening, which explained the crowded lobby. French audiences adored her and so did I.

She didn't turn up. I can still hear the collective groan in the packed auditorium (which seated about a hundred) when the bad news was announced, but when the lights dimmed we all settled down and were soon enthralled. (On its release *Le Figaro* had denounced the film as "an insult to the nation" and *Télé 7 Jours* called it a "monument of boredom and a Himalaya of pretension". If that doesn't snag your interest you won't have read this far.) I think I may have glimpsed Lafont a few weeks later, surrounded by friends in a queue outside another Latin Quarter cinema — the Saint-André-des-Arts — platinum-haired, wearing a bright Inca poncho and beret. But it might have been somebody else.

The past, for me at least, is a foreign city, and a city that changes with every passing year. The mime school near Porte Saint-Martin closed down in 2005 and the building is now a flashy mid-range diner called Bristol Renaissance. Marcel Marceau died two years later. The Accatone closed in 2012 to be replaced by, of all things, *"un espace d'information financière"*. These days the *nouvelle vague* seems a rather blokeish enterprise, and is far less of the vital cultural force it once was. Auteur theory, which used to inform much serious thinking and writing about film, no longer has much traction. The movement's directors grew older and in some cases sold out; critics and academics moved on. Smokers are now fewer in number and more furtive in behaviour. Bernadette Lafont died, aged seventy-four, in 2013.

I recently watched *La Maman et la putain* at home on DVD. It's the same film I saw at L'Accatone that wet November evening, but it's not really the same film at all. How could it be? The past is a foreign city that changes year by year — we do things differently now. I glumly realise that I've been writing about my adult self as it was more than thirty years ago and I am therefore now, by any objective measure, old, or oldish, and certainly old enough to be the father of the film's three characters, and its director, and with the perspective that time and age and disappointment bring. The French have a way of seeing the Biblical allocation of threescore years and ten as a week, each decade corresponding to a day, so if you're in your mid-thirties, dear reader, you're already on Thursday lunchtime. I'm on late Saturday afternoon and braced, more or less, for *Le Dimanche de la vie* (the title, as it happens, of a Raymond Queneau novel filmed in 1967, directed by Jean Herman and starring Danielle Darrieux). I shan't be around much next week, but would like to see a movie on Monday. A matinee.

Waiting for Godard

Jeremy Allen

The 1988 novel *The Holy Innocents* starts and ends at the Cinémathèque Française, during the tumultuous year of 1968. Along the way the story by the late Scottish novelist and film critic Gilbert Adair takes in the Langlois Affair, the May uprising, plenty of cinematic references (particularly *nouvelle vague* references), a Charles Trenet chanson played on repeat and three young people having an abundance of wayward sex together. Aside from the author's nationality, the novel could hardly be more Parisian were it based on a Jean Cocteau novel made into a film by Jean-Pierre Melville, which of course it is.

Les Enfants Terribles — the original novel by Cocteau (1929) and Melville's faithful screen adaptation of the same name (1950) — is the cornerstone of *The Holy Innocents*. It's a story that keeps being told, and with each telling mutates and becomes more sexually transgressive. Cocteau and Melville are both regarded as the fathers of the New Wave, and the former gave the latter his blessing by narrating the picture. The film was made with a meagre budget and starred Nicole Stéphane and Édouard Dermith as the star-crossed brother and sister — two beautiful, androgynous Jedwardians with exquisite cheekbones and curly blond quiffs. Their presence on the screen was a youthful antidote to what François Truffaut called the *Cinéma de papa* prevalent at the time, which the *nouvelle vague* would later attempt to wash away.

The forbidden sexuality is always implicit in this 1950 adaptation, and unusually it takes the watchful gaze of some *rosbifs* from across the Channel to juice things up and consummate the relationship between the titular siblings: first in Ian McEwan's novel *The Cement Garden* (1978), then Andrew Birkin's 1994 film of the book starring his niece Charlotte Gainsbourg. Adair puts his own spin on the story by bringing in an American interloper and turning a taboo tryst into a reckless love triangle. It doesn't quite end there either. Adair, troubled by the flaws he saw in *The Holy Innocents,* refused to allow it to be adapted into a film, at least until renowned Italian director Bernardo Bertolucci's people got in touch with his agent. Adair readapted his own novel as *The Dreamers* (2003), which appeared the same year as the Bertolucci film of the same name, starring Eva Green, Louis Garrel and Michael Pitt. From the implicit idea of incestuous union in Cocteau's original work, it becomes a three-way fuckfest in the hands of the Italian, as you might expect.

The Cinémathèque Française obviously doesn't feature in the original Cocteau work, given that it wasn't set up until 1937 by the French archivist and cinéaste Henri Langlois, and Georges Franju, who later directed *Les Yeux sans visage* (1959). Cinephilia would have been a fledgling and very niche condition in 1929. Turning the leading characters into *enfants de la Cinémathèque* was Adair's idea, and his attention to detail regarding the *nouvelle vague* tips over into Francophilia too. In the opening credits of the third Antoine Doinel film, *Baisers volés* (1968), Truffaut briefly shoots the scribbled note taped to the Cinémathèque window notifying patrons that the building is closed. The sign, though only in shot for seconds, inspires the conclusion of Adair's *The Dreamers*, while the Charles Trenet song featured in *Baisers volés*, "Que reste-t-il de nos amours?", is also the song that soundtracks the trio's sequestered world away from the student insurrection on the streets (Bertolucci chose to use the better known "La Mer" in his version).

The trio's games involve re-enacting scenes from movies, and when they do venture outside of the house, they set out on a mission to create mischief, running through the halls of the Louvre like the trio in Jean-Luc Godard's *Bande à part* (1964). One assumes Bertolucci's interest was initially piqued not only by the sex, but by the plot revolving around the sacking of Langlois. The Italian filmmaker became a disciple of Langlois' when he lived in Paris during the late Sixties, as were Godard, Truffaut, Jacques Rivette, Claude Chabrol and Alain Resnais. And so too the three central figures in *The Dreamers*. Without films to lose themselves in each day, the latter trio disappear into a *demi-monde* of sexual adventure to pass the time.

The Cinémathèque Française now lives in a geometrically melty Frank Gehry building down by Bercy, but the residence was at the Palais de Chaillot in the sixteenth arrondissement back when Langlois was fired. Before moving into its permanent home, it swapped Parisian addresses a number of times, including downstairs at what is now the Palais de Tokyo, taking up residence there in the late Eighties and early Nineties when Jack Lang was culture secretary. In fact, if you keep your eyes peeled while wandering around the art gallery, you can still see some of the old calligraphy on the wall: letters appear to have been chiselled away while some remain, giving the remnant display the look of a job started then abandoned after someone thought better of it.

The Palais de Tokyo is a ten-minute stroll from the Avenue des Champs-Élysées, where the French New Wave's most universally recognisable scene took place. The black-and-white image of Jean Seberg wandering down the avenue with Jean-Paul Belmondo, selling American newspapers as she goes, has become representative of the whole *nouvelle vague* — at least in the Anglosphere — possibly because *À bout de souffle* (1960) is the only New Wave film many Brits and Americans have seen. The fact that the scene also features an American enunciating words that are recognisable without subtitles might also be a factor. "Do you know what my first words were?" asks Eva Green's Isabelle in *The Dreamers*. "*New York Herald Tribune*!" she shouts, with the intonation rising as she imitates Seberg.

Other scenes that have taken on a certain postcard virality include Jeanne Moreau in baggy jumper and chequered newsboy cap running across a bridge with *Jules et Jim* (1962), or Anna Karina and her co-stars dancing in *Bande à part*, famously inspiring the dance scene in *Pulp Fiction* (1994). The final shot of Antoine Doinel in Truffaut's *Les Quatre cents coups* (1959) has also become well known thanks in the main to the many copycats it inspired. But no other shot is as synonymous with the French New Wave as Seberg and Belmondo sauntering nonchalantly along the Champs.

And then there are those other things associated with *Breathless*: the jump cuts, the cross-referencing of other

New Wave films, the obsession with American culture — particularly a fetishisation of Humphrey Bogart in Howard Hawks' *The Big Sleep* (1946) — the circular dialogue, the handheld camera, the Parisian *mise-en-scène*, the Breton top, the cigarette protruding from Belmondo's lower lip, the driving around the city in a Peugeot 403... these are all present and correct and have become the hallmarks of the French New Wave, which can lead to disappointment when only a few of them show up in other movies.

If Brits have an undisclosed inferiority complex regarding the French and France itself — a vague notion of suave uniformity — then the *nouvelle vague* compartmentalises the country into two categories: Paris and non-Paris. The city itself is the cynosure of everything important: chic, arty and worldly, and also a very dangerous place to be. Everything outside of Paris works differently. Ennui reigns, citizens are unreconstructed and family life dominates in the provinces, like in Roger Vadim's *Et Dieu... créa la femme* (1956), where Brigitte Bardot — a sexually liberated and progressive youth, ergo: *jeunesse dorée* cruelly displaced in a parochial backwater — is demonised and punished for her wickedness. Paris is often juxtaposed with non-Paris to highlight how enlightened it is, and how backwards everywhere else is. In Claude Chabrol's *Les Cousins* (1959), Charles (Jean-Claude Brialy) is a naive country boy whose urbane cousin Paul introduces him to a world of libertines, beatniks, lesbians, card players, carousers and seducers. That things end in tears should come as little surprise to anyone but Charles himself.

201

In Godard films, Paris is a place of alienation, possibly due to the amount of time the director spent growing up in Switzerland. Characters are often on the run from the capital, to escape the authorities (*Le petit soldat*, 1960) or the bourgeois lifestyle (*Pierrot le Fou*, 1965). Anna Karina plays a stripper in *Une femme est une femme* (1961) and a prostitute in *Vivre sa vie* (1962), though both are more symptomatic of Godard's lack of trust in his wife than a desire to paint the city as a modern-day Babylon. In *Alphaville* (1965), he escapes Paris by transforming it into a futuristic dystopian landscape (that looks a bit like Paris in 1965). In *Une femme est une femme* (1961), Paris becomes the set of a musical, but the characters are too cosmopolitan to engage in such high jinks (there are a few songs performed a cappella), unlike the Norman working class in Jacques Demy's mind-melting *Les parapluies de Cherbourg* (1964), who are always singing in the streets as if life were a giant opera soundtracked by *nouvelle vague compositeur du jour*, Michel Legrand.

Truffaut's *Les quatre cents coups*, his first autobiographical Antoine Doinel film — which dramatises moments from his difficult childhood — portrays the ninth and eighteenth *arrondissements* as dingier and more undesirable than the postcard Paris projected in *À bout de souffle*. Varda was never afraid to shy away from gritty topics, in *Cléo de 5 à 7* (1962) tackling an impending cancer diagnosis in real time, and her *chef d'oeuvre, Le Bonheur* (1968), exploring infidelity and suicide with the Île-de-France never looking so beautiful, but Paris always treacherous underneath. Éric Rohmer's love affair with the city is at the other end of the scale: an idealised dreamscape of charming affairs and sporadic dialogue where strangers' eyes meet in cafés or on buses and lead to meaningful, if fleeting, congress.

The further away from Paris one goes — especially if it's abroad — the more surreal everything becomes. Outside of France, the rules of the game are less easy to define. Alain Resnais' *Hiroshima mon amour* (1959) is wrought with psychogeographic symbolism, with Paris the sophisticated hub that binds the horrors of Hiroshima with Emmanuelle Riva's naive childhood neverland of Nevers; while his landmark *L'année dernière à Marienbad* (1961) is a nonlinear Bohemian hinterland, suffused with enigmatic dialogue and gratuitous luxuriance (Blur's "To The End" video from 1994 brilliantly recreates its peculiar ambience).

If anything binds these films, it's youth. The *nouvelle vague* unleashed a deluge of youthfulness; a celebration of the transience of juvenescence; less a wave, more a tsunami. By 1968, the New Wave was all but over, but there was enough residual energy to get Henri Langlois reinstated at the Cinémathèque Française. What's more, the Langlois Affair is often looked upon as the catalyst for the events of May '68, a fitting dénouement for a French cinematic movement that ultimately changed the world.

Paris Belongs to Us

Elsa Court

1.

I grew up in Picardie, about an hour's drive from Paris when traffic is good. From my childhood I remember our family's yearly day trips to the capital, traditionally on 15 August, with a mixture of fondness and embarrassment. My father chose the date specifically because, with half the locals on holiday and most shops and museums closed in observance of the Assumption of the Virgin Mary, it promised to be the ghostliest day in the year. As if animated by a desire to excavate historical Paris from the omnipresent assault of present day distractions and globally imported goods, Dad would drive from the Concorde to the Arc de Triomphe, past the myriad inactive boutiques of the Champs-Elysées, and play a CD recording of Charles de Gaulle's Paris liberation speech, a speech in which, I couldn't help notice, France is imagined as female, but Paris is masculine.

Paris may well have been "abused" and "broken" ("outragé", "martyrisé" in de Gaulle's words) in the not so distant past of the Second World War, but it was, and still is, hard to understand how my father, who had turned eighteen only a few weeks after May '68, could have been so immune to the spirit of his own generation that he had remained a fervent and unapologetic admirer of de Gaulle since his childhood years.

Ironically, it was through the counterculture of his generation — more specifically the post-war filmmakers of the New Wave — that I developed my first alternative impressions of the city of Paris, long before I had a chance to explore the city on my own terms. My father shared, without knowing it, Godard's contempt for the *société de consommation* and its omnipresent language, but he couldn't have cared less about the self-fashioned radical cinema that a group of Hollywood-enamoured film critics started shooting in the streets of the capital in the late 1950s. He had a "certain idea of France".

Our annual Paris trip would usually culminate on the Île Saint-Louis, a quaint island in the middle of the Seine — and another postcard favourite — where, after we'd parked the car, we wandered almost alone, as if in the past. "Paris nous appartient," my dad would say, triumphant, knowing he was borrowing the phrase from somewhere, but not thinking particularly of Jacques Rivette. For a long time, it felt like my Paris and my dad's would never intersect. But eventually they did.

2.

In Agnès Varda's New Wave classic *Cléo de 5 à 7* (1962), Florence "Cléo" Victoire, a pre-*yéyé* pop singer played by Corrine Marchant, anxiously waits for the results of a biopsy which may reveal a diagnosis of cancer. Dread sends her on a journey of emancipation and self-discovery across the streets of Paris, from Rue de Rivoli to the Café du

Dôme in Montparnasse, then from Vavin to the Salpêtrière hospital via the Parc Montsouris in the fourteenth *arrondissement*. It is 21 June, the longest day of the year.

Cléo is the portrait of a woman inscribed within a documentary about Paris, as Varda puts it. She is, to use Lauren Elkin's term, a *flâneuse,* as well as an adopted Parisian. Her fear is not only of death, but the provincial fear of the big city, which was Varda's when she first moved to the capital. Standing on the Boulevard de l'Hôpital as she leaves the park, Cléo observes that the thirteenth and fourteenth *arrondissements* contain the largest number of hospitals in Paris. Because she has carried the fear of illness with her along her itinerary (which the viewer has witnessed through flashback images, conspicuously meaningful street signs, and the omnipresent gaze of strangers), this realisation forms another uncanny dimension to Cléo's world, which seems to be closing in. It is, she quips sarcastically, almost as if "one were better cared for" in these arrondissements than anywhere else in the capital.

Today, as if to confirm this supposition, a private clinic on the Boulevard Jourdan, the Institut Mutualiste Montsouris, takes its name from the park where Cléo meets Antoine, a young soldier about to return to the war in Algeria. It is where my father was admitted on 12 May 2015 on the eve of his scheduled esophagectomy, a surgery procedure to remove a cancerous part of his upper stomach and lower oesophagus. Papa had already undergone chemotherapy for a few months and we were informed that he may not survive the operation.

When I speak to him on the phone on the night before the procedure, I try to sound calm so as to be the support

I tell myself that he needs. By this point, I am in London, where I have lived for years. The name "Montsouris", pronounced by the receptionist, makes me think of Cléo, who puns on the name in the film. I try hard to think of France and everything that once felt like home, but to no avail. The home country means little in this moment, because the everyday feels out of bounds.

3.

If you type "Paris" and "everyday" in the Google search bar you'll be directed to blogs promising to instruct the reader on how to "do Paris like a local", and American Express-sponsored travel sites explaining in a short paragraph that the French *art de vivre* is ubiquitous. You too, New Yorker, it seems to say, could learn from this subtly alternative (passé? out of time?) way of life. Witness for yourself the locals taking the time to go for a stroll on the banks of the Seine, wearing perfectly chic yet casual clothing, or simply walking to the local *boulangerie* to buy a baguette, or else meet a friend in a café in the middle of the afternoon as if work deadlines were not piling up. I too, used to look at Parisians thinking I could learn something about either style or belonging or both.

In my student years, I experienced the Latin Quarter as a hub filled with people who were just passing through, where my efforts to feel attached required constant negotiation. Populated by a few key Métro stations, the iconic Saint-Michel fountain, two Sorbonnes, and the bridges that lead to Notre Dame, the heart of Paris looked and felt like an open-air museum celebrating the cultural energy of days gone by. Its smell was the smell of its antique book stands, showcasing reprints of Janis Joplin gig posters among yellowing Louis-Ferdinand Céline paperbacks, wrapped in plastic. Not being a Parisian, I had a desire for some sort of connection which for a moment I hoped to find among Paris's international population. In those days, I studied English at the Sorbonne and, like many of my peers, I only cared for American writers, but this was no port of entry into the Anglosphere: when I applied for a job at Shakespeare and Company, I was told politely that the shop preferred to give work to international — Anglophone — students. Being neither a Parisian nor an *émigré*, I felt completely out of step with the *Quartier Latin*.

In my spare time I took to exploring regions of the capital where I had nothing particular to do, in search of a neighbourhood where the elusive everyday, I firmly believed, would be restored to Paris: what George Perec defined as "what happens when nothing happens, except for the weather, people, cars, and clouds". There, via Monge, then Gobelins and beyond Place d'Italie, I experienced, as many others have before me, a city living the life of a provincial town, filled with non-iconic street names and quieter everyday lives: children leaving school, acquaintances starting conversations outside local pharmacies while trying to make each other believe that they're in a rush; tower blocks here and there, looking on to the suburbs, with their sparse communal gardens, the young and multicultural families.

By the time of my father's operation, I had traded the hope of becoming a Parisian for the certitude of being a foreigner in London. Travelling across the Channel to visit him sent me back to the fourteenth arrondissement with a new-found sense of purpose. No longer a *flâneuse*, it seemed fit for me to use public transport. Dispatched by the Eurostar in raucous and familiar Gare du Nord, I took the RER B and got off at Cité Universitaire — the southernmost station in Paris *intra-muros*.

The clinic, a five-minute walk from the gates of the Parc Montsouris, was a bright transparent building which, on that day in May, let quantities of warm daylight shine through. In the gastroenterology department I was instructed to wait outside a set of steel doors before entering the sterilised post-op recovery room, where, once I was let through, I found Papa very much alive but recording signs of physical and emotional shock due to the anaesthetics. My mother and brother were beside him, but neither of them seemed to register my presence. Only my father did. "Oh no," he said to me as soon as he saw me walking in. "Now you too are going to see me like this."

4.

In the months following my father's diagnosis at the beginning of the previous winter, the idea that his life was threatened had affected my world with an odd and insidious violence, making me wonder by what mad set of circumstances I had found myself living outside the home country independently of my parents' bodies.

In recent years, a surge of new writing on motherhood (Sheila Heti, Jacqueline Rose, Lara Feigel, Chris Parker, and a few years before them Maggie Nelson, among others), has given way to a renewed discussion of what it means politically to inhabit the female body. It seems obvious, but equally inescapable, that mothers are the sites of an original belonging, and that to address motherhood is to address the space, the powers and limits of the female body. It is also to address the physical labour of parenthood, and the structural inequalities to which these bodies are subjected in their labours. Fathers, in society, seem to occupy a symbolic — aristocratic? — space in comparison. A father historically is a name and a status. The elusive assurance of protection. Closely intertwined with the duty of financial support, the father's commitment to a child's life is historically, socially, what gives it value.

Annie Ernaux's father in *La Place* is a stature, a Sunday suit, a figure of repressed tenderness and reliable material generosity, the photographer's shadow on a holiday snapshot. And what further form of closeness is, from a father to a daughter, desirable or appropriate? Among the few moments of closeness that my father and I shared independently of the rest of the family were the evening walks we took after dinner when I was a teenager. I remember this ritual fondly, because it enabled me to enjoy the strange climate of our streets after sundown. The low buzz of electric cables. The odd fellow wanderer, always male, always alone, who would give my father a nod as we crossed paths, but always ignore me. My father was not obviously built to be a protector, but there was no doubt that the fact that I was walking beside him meant symbolically that I was safe. Through him, I imagined and wondered at what it must be like to feel free of one's movements, to not live in fear, to think of oneself as an agent, sufficient, mobile.

Cléo de 5 à 7 deals with a subject that was certainly unpopular among French audiences and producers in the 1960s: cancer. But the dimension of the film which has endured in cinema's collective imagination is that of a woman walking alone through the streets of Paris, owning her right to look out on to the world — no longer guided by the consciousness of her own body as a visual object. "Pour moi," says Varda, "le premier acte féministe c'est de lever les yeux de son nombril ou de sa cuisine et de se mettre à regarder autour de soi." The first feminist act is to look up from one's navel or kitchen and start looking around. It makes a lot of sense to me that, among the more or less generous reviews that the film received upon its original release, *Arts* magazine immediately compared *Cléo* to Virginia Woolf's *Mrs Dalloway*. The perspective of the female subject asserting or inventing her perspective through her walks in the city did not have an obvious precedent in French literature.

In Varda's only other full-length film set in Paris, *Daguerréotypes* (1975), Marcelle, the wife of the perfume-maker on Rue Daguerre, watches the hours bleed into the evening from the boutique's window and manifests the physical impulse to go out as soon as it gets dark. Off camera, her husband calls out to her, asking her to come back in. "She always seems to want out after dark", he explains to the invisible filming crew, while the camera shows Marcelle walk out, close the door behind her, anxiously look up the street, and immediately come back in. She does not actually want to leave.

Paris is the first city where I ever felt free to take evening walks unaccompanied by my father.

5.

Long were the months when I was inhabited by an odd and helpless desire to wrap my arms around my father's shoulders, to hold him like a child and protect him against an ill that was in fact internal and against which I could do absolutely nothing. That feeling never completely receded after Dad survived the operation and entered what we would be encouraged to call "remission", after another round of routine chemotherapy would permanently take away his taste for coffee and red wine. For the first time, everyday life struck me as a fiction we briefly believe in when loss has not yet occurred.

I stayed in Paris for a whole week following the surgery and visited my father daily, sitting beside his bed on the large windowsill, basking in the light that heated the room and accentuated the smells of uncollected urine, watching the medical fluids coming in and out of the drain and tubes that traversed his lower abdomen.

My mother and brother were there too. We were at peace; we hardly spoke. Now and then I would lift my eyes from the pages of a magazine to stare out the window and survey Cléo's park in front of me, the lush greenery Varda had chosen as the setting for her heroine, to protect her against the odds.

I imagined Varda shooting the film there, not on the first day of spring, as she originally intended, but on the day of the summer solstice. She did not regret, in hindsight, this delay, mainly because of the dappled light it produced under the trees of Montsouris.

Men, writes Simone de Beauvoir in *The Second Sex*, are favourably conditioned to regard their bodies as objective points of contact with the physical world. This neutral body which is not weighed down by the burden of being specific or other, she writes, believes its connection to the cosmos to be legitimate and natural. For that perspective to be granted to a woman in narrative cinema is rare and valuable. This, I would like to be able to share with the men of my family.

After Agnès

Niven Govinden

I had this idea to photograph the same street where Agnès
Varda filmed *Daguerréotypes* in 1976. The documentary
had left a deep impression on me since I'd seen it several
months earlier, reflecting an interest in communities and
their loss. The spark was something both romantic and
sociological, most keenly felt in the quotidian for artisans
and small businesses. During my regular trips to Paris I was
in the habit of photographing everything, from the food
on my plate to the graffiti I'd hunted out as a teenager,
using various tags to map my way across the river. Early
on I recognised that my interest was in the inanimate;
how my Polaroids were strictly mineral and vegetable over
animal (bar cute dogs). I loved the street scenes of Brassaï
or Doisneau but was unable to replicate that, my eye more
easily caught by rusting ironwork or crumbling stone.
Similar to my writing, my best photographs came once
the blood had been drained. Still, I was obsessed with the
Varda film and its characters. The shopkeepers were long
dead, but the totems of decaying storefronts would be how
I paid homage. For the same reasons, Detroit was always
on my mind; desperate to see in person and through a lens
how the great civic buildings of the last century had been
abandoned and reduced to shells in the wake of the collapse
of the auto industry and the fleeing middle class. I wouldn't

find this on Rue Daguerre, but if I looked hard there would be similar ghosts. However, as much as I wanted to, my feet wouldn't take me to that side of the 14th. I was scared of what I would find: perhaps a Carrefour Express in place of the perfumers. Worse, I was scared of being disappointed, that the ongoing renewal of a street would decimate any onscreen recognition I had. The regeneration of Soho posed a similar problem but there I clung on to what I knew: low winter light rising over Berwick Street; the maze you cross from Poland to Dean Street; that Ronnie Scotts and Bar Italia would be going nowhere. I was too late to create a similar landscape for Rue Daguerre because it had never been part of my Paris life since I'd been coming over as a teenager. My certainties lay in the doorway of my stationers in the 4th, there since the mid-Seventies, in the marble and tilework of the Boulangerie Murciano on Rue des Rosiers, and on the cobbles of Rue Viollet-le-Duc where I once saw a boy who made my heart stop beating inside my chest. Wood, ceramic, stone, my equilibrium gleaned from these and what I record: my daguerreotypes.

In Search of the Grinning Cats

Adam Scovell

A pair of cats are relaxing on the concrete in Rue Courat. One is an orange tabby whilst the other is a radioactive yellow with very white teeth. Both are on stilts and grinning with rebellious mischief. I had come what had seemed a long way to see them, all the way from Montmartre in fact, in the stifling heat, a few days before 14 July. The cats are an artwork created by the graffiti artist Monsieur Chat, in memory of the filmmaker Chris Marker.

Marker, one of the pivotal artists of the twentieth century, had lived in the chaos of the house that sits behind the wall; filled with owls, cats and paraphernalia surrounding Alfred Hitchcock's *Vertigo*. It made for a perfect pilgrimage. But I had felt the idea to be subliminally implanted from the previous day's wandering. M. Chat himself had put the idea into my head, having seen his yellow cat grinning down from another wall further into Montmartre, one of the cats actually seen in Marker's *Chats perchés*. "We must go," I said to my partner, "to see Chris Marker's cats." She has my sympathies in hindsight for I had already used our time in the city to go to the house where Michael Haneke had filmed *Caché*, the road that ends Jean-Luc Godard's *À bout de souffle* and Éric Rohmer's grave. Dinner was on me for the foreseeable.

It felt odd to finally arrive at the mural. Marker had

always been such an ephemeral figure himself: the photographer rarely photographed, the filmmaker rarely on screen, the Cheshire Cat that smiled before quickly fading into the ether. Disappearance was part of his endeavour. When his death was announced in 2012, I remember thinking two things. The first was that I couldn't decide if I had previously already thought him dead. His elusiveness gave the impression of a ghostly loss. The second was that I didn't quite believe now that he was dead. He was more like Schrödinger's Cat than other felines: the possibility of both options was always strangely there, the illusion of which was only broken when a new project or film found its way into the world. Seeing the mural on the wall opened the box to show that sadly the cat had left this time for good; not for Tokyo or Vietnam, or the West Bank for wine with Varda and Resnais, but somewhere beyond us all.

I wanted to take a singular photo of the mural, but ended up snapping away most of my reel of film. The trip as a whole felt like compensation for something, not least an escape from England at the time, but also a quiet acknowledgement that I wanted to be here among the grinning cats too. Paris is a city of cinema in a way that no other city really can be. Only Paris could descend into groundbreaking riots starting with the political wrangling of the Cinémathèque. Only Paris would name an underground station after Delphine Seyrig, and squares after Jacques Demy or Jean Renoir. And only Paris would spray its walls in the memory of the most avant-garde of filmmakers. The cats still grin, of course, that ginger tabby and his yellow friend with the white teeth. It's because they know they're home.

Hulot sur la jetée

C.D. Rose

I have never seen Paris rawly waking, crude sunlight on her lemon streets. I have not sensed the moist pith of farls of bread, nor frog-green wormwood, nor matin incense courting the air. The first time I visited Paris, I smelled piss outside the Gare du Nord.

I was twenty-one, twenty-two maybe. Some friends had got a cheap ticket for the night ferry and a train and asked me along. We arrived and walked out of the station, and the first thing I saw was a guy casually unzip and let flow, oblivious to the great city passing around him, briefly catching my eye as I caught his. Such was my great welcome to the *Ville lumière*.

We stayed in the cheapest place we could find, a hot, breathless, flock-wallpapered room in a nearby pension. Now, when I look to see if the Hotel Jarry still exists, I find 40% of TripAdvisor reviewers classify it as "average", 16% "terrible".

I remember little of the rest of the trip, save for standing in queues and getting ripped off. I have no photographs of that time, so perhaps it never happened at all. It matters little; I have not been to Paris many times since then.

There are many ways of not going to Paris. I have done it by reading books, looking at photographs, listening to songs, and watching films. Once I did it by falling in love.

I had had an invitation from a girl I hardly knew. (I had met her at an art gallery in Italy. She had unruly hair and bee-stung lips, and swung an early Seventies Nikon F2 around her neck. What else could I do?) I got the cheapest flight I could find (the intervening years had not been financially generous); she told me she would meet me at the airport.

One of the films I have watched is Chris Marker's 1962 *La Jetée*. The film begins with the screeching of aircraft engines and then pans over a photo of Orly airport's long, peninsular viewing platform. The mechanical roar fades, replaced by the choir of the Russian Orthodox Cathedral of St Alexander Nevsky chanting a piece for Holy Saturday, the one day when Christ is dead, not yet resurrected. "This is the story of a man," a voice (Jean Négroni, tar and sawdust) tells us, "marked by an image from his childhood". As a child, taken by his parents one Sunday to see the planes arriving and leaving, our protagonist sees a "crumpling body" and hears "the cries of the crowd": a man dying, or rather, being killed. He remembers this day, this scene, intensely, and most significantly "the frozen sun, the setting at the end of the jetty, and a woman's face".

More stuff happens after that (Paris, along with most of humanity, is completely destroyed in a massive nuclear war, for example), but it is that woman's face at the end of the jetty he remembers, and so do I.

When I arrived in Paris that second time I did not quite go, I had been expecting something similar. Not a crumpling body, nor anguished cries, and maybe not at the end of a jetty, more probably in a bland arrivals lounge, but a woman with her camera and her fringe, standing there amidst the crowd of taxi-hustlers, conference hosts and other expectant lovers. To be thus met on arrival at a harbour, station or airport is one of life's deep momentary joys.

I scanned the ranked faces, each briefly eyeing me in return. I saw a tall woman with brown, sun-faded hair, but when she removed her dark glasses, she was not the one I sought. Another stood with her back to me and I was sure I recognised her shoulders, so I tapped her, and she turned with disdain. A third had the same jacket and my hopes rose, but then she opened her arms to swoop in embrace on a small and startled child. After nearly an hour, I knew something was wrong.

And then, a series of texts awoke my phone. *Have you arrived yet? Where are you? I'm here, but I can't see you.*

I wondered if we had become invisible to one another, if we were ghosts, slipped out of each other's time streams. But it was not that.

It seems stupid now, of course, but back then I did not realise there was more than one airport in Paris.

Another film I have watched is Jacques Tati's *Playtime* (1967). This film begins with a long sequence set in the arrivals terminal of Orly airport. Two nuns pass by, whether arriving, welcoming or departing, I do not know. We also see a nurse with a baby, a woman with a black hat, a woman with a luggage trolley, a man with an overcoat, a man with a violin case, a man with a raincoat and a man wearing a turban and flip-flops. Then come two older women, a man holding flowers, a priest, and a porter. We see a group of American tourists (well-hatted Midwestern matriarchs), the "President" (of the Republic? I am never sure), a military officer, a group of schoolgirls, a man with a camera, an impressively well-dressed couple, a gaggle of flight attendants, another military man clutching a gift (possibly for the President), a woman in fur with "nothing to declare".

"I want to write about Chris Marker and Jacques Tati, *La Jetée* and *Playtime*," I told M, a film scholar. M looked at me sceptically.

"They're tonally very different, those films," she warned.

Playtime is a high-profile, high-budget comedy, two hours long, a rich satire of modernity replete with a vast cast, an intricate *mise en scène*, thousands of sight gags and deft use of colour, though almost no dialogue and nothing much in the way of a plot. *La Jetée* lasts a scarce twenty-eight minutes and consists almost entirely of a sequence of black-and-white photographs over which a single voice reads a complex story. *Playtime* is in constant motion, endlessly dizzying in its kinetic choreography; *La Jetée*, when it moves at all, moves so slowly its movement is scarcely perceptible. *Playtime* is circadian (the action, such as it is, takes place over one day, more or less); *La Jetée* extends until the end of knowable human time, and reaches back beyond its beginnings. *Playtime* posits modernity, futurity and technology as glitch-ridden, subject to human error, and worthy of endless satire, yet striving for seamless efficiency and at work for the benevolence of humanity. In *La Jetée*, present and future technology is relentlessly barbarous, a force for nothing more than utter and complete human subjugation. *Playtime* is by world-renowned French director Tati, and features the iconic Monsieur Hulot, a synecdoche of a certain strain of Gallicism. *La Jetée* is by the pseudonymous, rarely-pictured, unknowable Marker.

There are two main airports in Paris, and I was at the wrong one. I called the girl who had been waiting for me, but was told about prohibitive roaming charges, and was instead texted some garbled instructions as to how to get into the city, to a place where we could meet.

The rank outside was cluttered, hectic. I did not understand the difference between the various train and bus lines, the signs indicating directions and place names I did not know, but eventually I found a bus which promised to deliver me safely to our hastily-arranged meeting point. The bus took its time, meandering through dull suburbs. It was Sunday. There were works, a road closure, a protest probably. At somewhere called Joinville-le-Pont, just outside the Bois de Vincennes, the bus stopped. The driver got off. I sat there, contemplating the failing battery on my phone.

M was not wrong about the films, and yet: both circle around Orly airport, the place where I had erroneously landed. *La Jetée* opens and closes there, in some sense stays there forever, our protagonist stuck in an eternal memory loop. In the opening sequence of *Playtime*, Hulot arrives along with all the others, but only after a couple of false starts: we see a tall man, raincoat, umbrella, hat, but it is not him, a case of mistaken identity. He appears later, from an overcrowded bus, accidentally, almost surreptitiously, as if by mistake. He is wrong in this world, all gangling angles and mishaps, too human amidst the plate glass and shining steel. Like the man in *La Jetée*, Hulot seems to have come from the past into a present version of the future. Half of him is here, the other half is in the past. ("I remember you from the war!" shouts one of his chance encounters, but whether this is true, or yet another false memory and mistaken identity, we do not know.)

It is at the airport where Hulot, too, spots a woman, one of the American tourists, but an anomalous one, one who stands out from the crowd. He spends the rest of the film trying to meet her again, only to fail. He tries to photograph her, to imprint her memory, but cannot, ending up instead sending her a gift which she will receive, but whose donor she will never know.

Both of these films are about trying to capture the unreachable. Both of these films deal with a man, faintly lost, ever in transit, and an evanescent woman. These films hinge each other, like images reflected in glass swing doors. They are almost contemporaries: *Playtime* began filming in 1964, a mere two years after *La Jetée* came out. And, despite their settings, neither film goes to Paris. The Paris of *La Jetée* is either a memory or has been obliterated, and *Playtime* was not filmed at Orly.

Troubled by intrusive flares and gleams from the steel and plate glass, and disappointed by the impossibility of halting all air traffic to and from the airport during filming (the very traffic Marker uses the sound of), Tati built his own Paris. "Tativille" was a vast Potemkin city, a facsimile Paris, not only with its own concrete buildings, tarmacked streets and functional traffic lights, but also a number of huge trompe l'oeil facades. The scenes at Orly are stage sets with backdrops made entirely of giant blow-ups of the airport. The images reflecting in the endlessly swinging plate glass doors of *Playtime* (the Eiffel Tower, the Arc de Triomphe, the Champs Elysées) are photographs. *Playtime* takes place in a replica, a city of maquettes and projections, one more like the city it needed to be. *La Jetée* is a film which is in Paris, but a Paris which does not exist: the city is destroyed then recreated through memory. Both are constructed from photographs. Despite the fortune spent on its construction, Tativille (like *La Jetée*'s Paris) has been all but obliterated. What little is left now sits beneath the A4 *autoroute*, just to the south-east of the capital, near Joinville-le-Pont and the Bois de Vincennes.

Another driver eventually appeared, or maybe it was the same one back, I could not be sure. The bus started up again and grumbled its way into the city, eventually stopping to disgorge all passengers and their bags at Les Invalides. I let her know where I was and received the words *quartier de merde* texted back to me, as well as the number of a Métro line and station. I headed underground.

Filming on *Playtime* was held up by technical problems and, more frequently, money running out. It took so long that many extras dropped out, frustrated by the slow hours and eventual lack of pay. (Barbara Dennek, the woman who plays Hulot's object of desire had planned a career in film, but after her experience on set with *Playtime*, never made a film again. Hélène Châtelain, the analogous actor from *La*

224

Jetée, went on to have a long and varied career, but never made another film either.) Tati used the same solution for an absent city and absent actors: life-sized photographs. In the crowd scenes in *Playtime*, many of the bystanders are photographs, strategically placed among the living.

The endless white-tiled tunnels of the Métro reminded me of nothing so much as the urinals in British Victorian pubs. I admired their cleanliness, the way they reflected light and sound. I wandered. I took my time. I got lost.

1961, a bright Sunday in late September. Families take their children to the new airport. It is an afternoon out. Crowds gather and scuttle as jet engines roar. The singer Gilbert Bécaud sits in the café and has an idea for a song. "Dimanche à Orly", he will sing two years later: the tale of a man who lives with his parents in a comfortable nearby flat but sees the planes leaving and dreams of a different life. (And twenty-five years after that, Jacques Brel will reference Bécaud in his own attempt to sing down his imminent mortality, a vision of lovers endlessly meeting or separating, "Orly".)

A man with a battered leather jacket and closely-cropped hair, the look of a traveller or a former soldier, the look of a man who has seen things, takes a Nikon F, the best camera he's been able to get hold of through one of his journalist contacts, and organises a small group of his friends, including a man who looks vaguely like himself and a girl with hair which tousles in the wind here, and takes pictures of them, but not portraits. No one smiles in these pictures. As they pass through the arrivals hall and the departure lounge then head out onto the viewing platform, he notices another man studiously taking pictures. This man, taller and more confident, well-dressed in a light grey cotton suit, crisp white shirt and narrow green tie, slips a Focaflex (the latest model, slimline, discreet, beautifully designed) out of and into the pocket of his jacket. The first man sees that the other is taking long shots of the new buildings and the crowds, but not the planes. The tall man snaps people arriving, but also the rubbish bins, the door handles, the stair rails. The two men notice each other, think they may recognise each other (from the war, perhaps?) but make no acknowledgement other than a scarce nod of the head, the taller man apparently not wanting to be recognised, then move on.

If you watch La Jetée, *the scene on the jetty, at about three minutes in, and look carefully, you can see Jacques Tati in the crowd on the jetty. If you watch* Playtime, *look carefully at the crowds in the opening scenes, and freeze the frame, you can see a life-sized blow-up photograph of Chris Marker.*

I cannot remember when I came up out of the Métro. I would like to think it was on one of those faded olive staircases, with Belle Epoque signs guiding me to meet a girl drinking unfeasibly strong coffee in a pavement café, but I seem to think it was a ripe cement stairwell in a rather bland suburb. It matters little, because I have also been there, in that not-Paris of getting lost and endlessly circulating, looking for something that probably does not exist, in the same way that both films are stuck in their loops of time and place and memory. *Playtime* was supposed to end with Hulot escaping, walking out from the screen, as literally as possible, projected in *ombre chinoise* around the auditorium. The idea was dropped due to its technical impossibility and the film instead ends with gridlocked traffic endlessly circling a roundabout. *La Jetée* ends with its beginning.

I still hope to return one day, in the middle of a warm Sunday afternoon, and find the sky and the glass and the clouds, and someone waiting at the end of the pier, but it has not yet happened. The last time I did not go to Paris it seemed I, too, had been marked by an image from my past. I was returning from a conference in Angers and had to change trains. I had had a couple of beers, was tired and running late. Unsure how long the queue for the Eurostar would be and no longer caring, I unzipped and took a piss, just behind the entrance to the Gare du Nord.

Props

Laura Waddell

The spaghetti Alexandre is eating gets right up from the plate and slaps him hard in the face. Individual gelatinous strands ricochet in a backwards bend, flinging pinprick droplets of orange sauce up the wall behind. Like a colony of ladybugs they creep slowly down to the carpet where they will seep into the wool. The soil of a plant shoots from its plastic pot; a confetti cannon of clumps and grains, some hitting leaves on their way up and ending elevation then and there; most reaching the ceiling before bouncing back and raining down over the tiled hearth. A pink balloon pops. The neighbour's parrot squawks.

Again?

The dust brush Nina uses to collect the soil and re-pot it for the next scene is already matted with glitter and hair. The next balloon from the packet is blue, but the colour doesn't matter for a one-take shot as long as it's not green. This balloon bursts too when it is only half blown. The next one is pink again, and she bobs it by the string into place.

The salt and pepper shakers are placed on the table again. All set. Break for lunch. "Spaghetti?" someone offers Alexandre. Everyone laughs. Alexandre laughs loudest of all with very white, straight teeth.

Nina sits in her prop van with the door open and spoons rice from a paper plate into her mouth. The plate is biodegradable. It can go anywhere, which is just as well. There are no recycling facilities on set, only constantly replaced black garbage bags filled with plastic forks, tissues, and bits of electrical tape. At the end of today there will also be a lot of used spaghetti.

A runner walks by, two hands out in front filled with a clutch of bright plastic straws. "No, Matthew, we're not doing the straws anymore. They're out. You were in that meeting." He about turns in response to the disembodied order. Straws hit the inside of a bag in a dull, muffled downpour.

Nina closes the door of the trailer without turning on the light. At one end of the cabin there are rails of clothes. Modern casual to match the customer profile of newly launching, *supermarché* own-brand Strike Sauces, bagged and tagged for each ad segment which will run in the gaps between next season's cable network hit. For Alexandre there are multiple identical pairs of jeans and slim grey shirts. In Agnes' unverifiable illness, Nina has agreed for a small fee to assume the responsibility of dispatching items from the wardrobe as well as her prop store. Typically she works on her own but she knows from watching what Agnes' team does, and that most has been done in advance. Nina steams shirts already picked out so they are hot and fresh before each take. Half of them are now covered in sauce and soil and crumpled in Alexandre's trailer. Someone else takes them away. Nina does not know whether they are laundered or thrown away.

Behind the rails are 1920s relics from a previous shoot. Of dubious heritage but alright in a crowd scene. Silk slips, thick coats and paste jewellery from the Marché aux Puces de Saint-Ouen: where props meets wardrobe. Nina slips past Alexandre's endless jeans, rustling the bagging, and crouches down amongst fur. She sits like that for a little while, breathing in the must and damp. When her calves grow strained she sits down completely, burrowing back, legs sticking out in front. She manipulates an ancient sleeve as if a trunk. Parties. Dinners. Treasures bartered and sold for meat in lean times. Buffeted on either side of her cheeks with old fibres, it's dark and warm.

The door opens. A dart of light hits the ceiling. It closes again. Nina gets up and brushes herself down, smoothing hair from her face where the static grabbed at it. She pulls the light cord, picks up her plate and fork, opens the trailer door, and slips the rubbish and leftover grains of saffron yellow rice into the trash.

"A for change. Ten minutes to shoot," strains through the walkie-talkie on the desk inside. She grabs the nearest bag of jeans-and-shirt and the mobile steamer, and heads for his trailer.

Alexandre is watching make-up being applied to his face in a mirror bordered with lightbulbs. A flourish of powder from a soft brush ricochets off one high cheekbone. All texture is being erased. "Let's do this!" he booms into the mirror when he sees Nina bearing clean clothes. She steps over the last change, collapsed formlessly on the floor, and hangs the new set on an empty rail to smooth out any wrinkles with puffs of warm steam. The plug is tricky. She bends down to tap it with her fist until it clicks into place and the green light of the steamer clicks on. Few wrinkles have appeared since she last steamed this particular shirt at

6am, the first task of the day on site. But there are a *few*. It seems unlikely a man eating dinner would have a pristine shirt. But this is advertising, and the mood board doesn't contain creases. Market research urges convenience and clean lines for the affluent urban Parisians browsing today's *supermarché*. Ralph chews gum into putty while wearing a white tank top. A glass sits drained of protein shake to one side, dull with residue. He has not yet been witnessed eating lunch on set. His tank top is thinly ringed wet under the arms. It clings to him. A hairdryer clicks on.

Outside the sun is high. Nina trips, trying with one hand to catch the rickety rail and failing. A sprawl of black clad arms and legs on the yard's hot, blanched dust surface. Sore spots seep into focus; a knee, her temple. She rolls into a ball and onto her side as someone on a walkie-talkie takes her elbow. Twisting her neck she sees it is Markus and shakes him off, embarrassed. But once she is on her feet she says thank you.

In the distance the neighbour's parrot squawks. The sound is adjusted. It squawks again at optimal volume.

"Are you hurt?"

Markus is a camera assistant reaching the end of a three-month contract who leaves crosses of coloured electrical tape all over the floors and ferries cables back and forward. Often Nina is removing props from a set while he is unscrewing lenses and cameras, but they have never spoken. All equipment is ticked off and put away after a shoot. This ad is due to last until the end of the week. A large blue crate of Strike's Sauce depletes each day, but after-effects will apply more of it, matching the orange-red viscosity and increasing the glisten. Without the hand tossing it, the spaghetti will come alive, digitally manipulated to show the life-giving properties of blended tomatoes and spices for the busy Parisian worker for whom the miracles of modern convenience are invisible.

"No. Yes, a bit. It was unexpected."

"You're covered in dust."

Chalky grey all up one side. Nina brushes herself down. "I've had better shoots." The static on Markus' walkie-talkie grows more frantic in pitch. "I better go, it's dinner time."

"Again and again and again, huh."

"Between you and me, I hope that meatball actor chokes on his sauce."

*

Nina is lying in bed one Sunday morning, laptop paused at a freeze-frame of the balloon bursting. You can almost imagine, if you pause it too, the very tips of her fingers approach from one side of the frame to catch the string. The basil she has been growing on the windowsill drifts in with the sound of a market down the street.

*

One evening, Markus is browsing yoghurt when Nina rounds the corner with a basket on her hip. Set talk gives way to searching for the newly launched sauce. They find it in aisle 6. Markus bobs a jar up and down to mimic the explosion of the advert. Hilarity bubbles up from inside. Nina holds his eye while holding a jar at arm's length. It bursts when she drops it. A grand and jagged starburst appears immediately on the black-and-white tiled floor. A screaming orange scar with shards of glass like cat's eyes. Tomato protest. A real mess. "Strike!" she stage-whispers the slogan while they rush, wheezing with laughter, under the exit sign.

Music For French Films

Nicholas Royle

1.

Some years ago, in a second-hand record shop, I found a CD called *Music for French Films*. I recognised the name of the artist. Christian Miller had been the resident pianist in a pizza restaurant in London where I waited on tables after finishing at university.

I listened to the album over and over. I liked it partly because it reminded me of those innocent times when I was in my early twenties and had, as they say, my whole life ahead of me. But, some time later, when I came to copy it into iTunes, just as in my twenties I would have recorded an LP on to a blank cassette so that I could play it on my Walkman, I unchecked the tick boxes for those tracks, dotted throughout the album, on which Miller sang. He sang well, but I prefer instrumentals and, after all, he never sang in the old days. He just played the piano, solo and as an accompanist to artists performing in the restaurant, which was a popular venue for live jazz.

Was the music on Miller's album even jazz? It featured jazz musicians playing the instruments of jazz — piano, bass, drums, saxophone — but also a string quartet, which interpreted themes I vaguely recognised from films released between 1930 and 1968. Why that particular cut-off, you might wonder. It's a light album, even whimsical. You won't come across anything from Jacques Tourneur or Georges Franju or Jean-Pierre Melville. So why, whenever I think of the album now, do I feel as if the sun has gone in behind a cloud?

2.

I met Marie when we were both waiting at the counter for orders. Jose was reaching into the oven with his peel, pulling out pizza after pizza, which he slid on to plates.

"How do you know which one has extra cheese?" I asked her, staring at two Margheritas that seemed to be topped with exactly the same amount of mozzarella.

"The olive," she said, balancing two plates on her arm. Or, more accurately, *Zee olive*. The first words she spoke to me.

"What if someone's ordered extra olives, or it has olives on it anyway?" I said, wanting to extend the conversation.

Marie put her head on one side, her lips forming an embouchure for an invisible saxophone. With her arms already in the correct position for the classic Gallic shrug, she blew a tiny raspberry then walked off carrying five pizzas, a swagger in the sway of her black skirt.

"Hey, kid!" Jose shouted.

I turned to face him and he gestured at the waiting orders.

Upstairs, there was a back room where waiters could eat and smoke. A French window led out to a tiny terrace. When it was my break, I carried my pizza up there and saw that Marie was sitting outside smoking. I sat inside and watched her through the window. Her cheek was drawn to a point, like sand sinking into an hourglass, as she sucked on her cigarette. Then she reached over the parapet and tapped the ash into the gap between the buildings. When she had finished, she ground out the butt and chucked that over as well.

3.

I was clearing a table near the entrance when Christian Miller came in. He returned my greeting with a smile and headed for the stairs down to the jazz room. Marie was laying a table close to the top of the stairs. He paused and I watched as they exchanged a few remarks. I couldn't make out what they were saying, but I heard Marie's voice. She didn't speak much English beyond what she needed to take orders from customers, so I wondered if Christian spoke French and if he spoke it better than I did. She gesticulated, opening out her body towards him. When she had finished, he laughed. She smiled and I heard him say "See you later" as he started down the stairs.

As break time approached, I could hear Christian getting into it downstairs. Sometimes he would play to an empty room. I imagined that if he had a piano at home, it wouldn't be a grand. I took my pizza down there and sat at the back of the room. It wasn't long before Marie came down also. It was always dark in the jazz room, with black walls and spotlights, so there was no reason why she should see me on entering the room. She sat at a table closer to the piano and lit a cigarette, her pizza going cold on a plate beside her. She turned her head the other way and blew a perfect smoke ring. I watched it dissipate slowly as it drifted through the air. Only after she had finished the cigarette did she turn her attention to her pizza, and it wasn't until I'd finished my own and pushed my plate away that she heard the noise it made and turned around and saw me sitting there.

4.

Marie hadn't made many friends among the staff. She was the only French national and I the only other French speaker — a slight exaggeration, but I had spent four years studying the language, including a year in Paris, living in the 10th; Rue des Vinaigriers, if you want to know. If some of us went to the pub, she would sit with me and we would talk in French. "I wish I was better at it," I said. She asked if I missed Paris. "Paris, maybe," I said. "Not Parisians." She said she was a Parisian and would be going back at the end of the summer. "Oops," I said, in English. "You should come," she said, in French. Or: "You should come back". Or even, "You should go back". Did those remarks carry different shades of meaning? I thought of the girls I'd known in Paris and how I'd never known where I stood with them. Whether I was expected to make a move when I slept on Isabelle's floor. Whether Réjane would have been disappointed I didn't call. Whether a drink with Laurence was meant to lead to anything. They all seemed so passive, indifferent. Perhaps they thought the same about me.

In September, Marie wrote on her order pad, tore the page off and gave it to me. I read it and asked, "Is this real?" "It's in the 20th," she said. It was her last shift. People went to the pub. We sat pressed close together. An Italian waiter said he'd see her in Paris. She smiled. Maybe she'd given her address to everyone. I walked her to the tube and kissed her. She tasted of cigarettes. I couldn't say whether she kissed me back. She turned and was gone.

5.

I buy two CDs by American jazz piano player and composer Bud Powell. Neither of them is one of the three albums Powell recorded while living in Paris, from 1959 to 1963: *A Tribute to Cannonball*, *A Portrait of Thelonious*, *Bud Powell in Paris*.

Looking like compilations, which I normally avoid, they are *The Amazing Bud Powell Vol 1* and *Vol 2*, comprising standards and original compositions, such as "Parisian Thoroughfare". They feature several alternate takes; there are two tunes on each album that each have two alternate takes, in addition to other titles that have one. In recent years, there has been a resurgence of enthusiasm for vinyl. Purists disparage CDs, but it's the perfect format. It has more of that variable of which it takes up less — space. You can copy music from it on to a computer. The only downside, for me, is, precisely because of the amount of space, and perhaps to justify the higher cost (when introduced), CDs are often loaded with alternate — or, in British English, alternative — takes, which I don't want.

When I copy these albums into iTunes, I think about leaving out the alternate takes, on the assumption that they were added when the albums were made available on CD. But, when I look them up, I find this is not the case. Volumes 1 and 2 were originally released on 10" vinyl in 1952 and rereleased on 12" in 1956 with alternate takes on Volume 1.

Sometimes I want to go back to the past because, in my mind, it was simpler than the present. But am I kidding myself? Was the past just as complex as the present?

6.

I hitched to Dover, got a one-way ticket on the boat, then hitched again. Dropped off in the *banlieue*, I was soon in the city, walking east along Rue des Vinaigriers. It was late afternoon; the shadows were long. I thought of Laurence, Réjane and Isabelle. Things would be different this time.

I climbed the steps to the Canal Saint-Martin, which I crossed by one of the footbridges, then hugged the perimeter of the Hôpital Saint-Louis, birthplace of Roland Topor. I remembered seeing Polanski's adaptation of Topor's novel, *The Tenant*, in London and in Paris. At the National Film Theatre there had been laughter during one scene — Polanski as Trelkovsky, dressed as a woman with make-up and wig, looking out of the window of his apartment on Rue des Pyrénées, the regular thump-thump of an unseen object, the slowly bouncing ball, exchanged for Trelkovsky's bewigged and made-up severed head — but when I had seen the film at the Studio Galande there had been silence. Apart from the faint crescendo on Philippe Sarde's soundtrack. London found it funny; Paris was horrified; I thought it was beautiful.

I walked down Boulevard de Belleville through scattered vegetable debris from the day's market. I checked my map, turned left and stopped to take the folded slip torn from Marie's order pad out of my wallet. It had acquired furred edges. I looked at the loops of her handwriting, measured the depth of the impression of her ballpoint on the cheap paper. I ran my fingers over the words, as if they were Braille.

7.

Passage des Soupirs was reached via a set of steps up from Rue des Pyrénées. There was no access for motor vehicles. Some of the buildings had front yards, which residents had filled with pots and shrubs. I found the address that Marie had written down. There was a light on in a window on the top floor.

At first she failed to recognise me.

"You said I should come," I said, in French.

"I didn't know you were coming," she said finally, as if she hadn't heard me or I hadn't made sense. Her blank expression had creased up into a frown.

"Well, here I am."

"Yes. Well. You'd better come in."

She led the way up to a two-room apartment.

"Nice place," I said, looking around at the kitchen.

"We share it. My flatmate is away. Where are you staying?"

"I don't know," I said. "Nowhere."

She took a cigarette from the pack on the table and lit it, pulling the smoke deep into her lungs.

"You shouldn't smoke," I said. "It's bad for you."

"You can stay one night," she said, ignoring my advice. "In Cécile's room. I have to get ready to go to work."

"Where do you work?"

Another pause. Then: "In a restaurant, Place des Fêtes.

Most nights. Do you want a coffee?" She had yet to smile since my arrival, but the offer of a coffee was something. She filled a stove-top espresso maker and went off to get ready.

8.

I asked if I could walk with her when she went to work and then walk back. She gave a shrug, which I interpreted as a yes. She was wearing the same black skirt, with a white blouse. She put on a tailored black jacket and then, knotted at the side, a red silk scarf.

The other end of Passage des Soupirs gave on to Rue de la Chine, where we turned left, eventually finding ourselves on Rue Pixérécourt. These residential streets were quiet; it must have been just before or just after the hour at which men return home and then immediately go out again, for bread, and never come back. It was just me and Marie, walking fast with matching strides. Would I become one of those men? Would we marry or live together? Would I return home one day and then go out for bread? We crossed the end of a street that was angled away from our direction of travel. All I saw of it was the blue sign on the wall bearing its name — Rue de l'Avenir — and I said that that was what I loved about France. The poetry of street names: Passage of Sighs, Street of the Future.

"Can you imagine that in England?" I said. "Streets named after abstract ideas, things that don't exist?"

"You think the future doesn't exist?"

"Yes. Well, not yet anyway."

"So, it will exist — what, in the future?"

"Yes, but then it will be the present."

"What about the past? Does that exist?"

"It used to." I turned towards her but she didn't look back.

9.

Parting from Marie in Place des Fêtes, but not before I had asked to borrow her keys, I wandered up to the Parc des Buttes Chaumont. Exiting on the north side I made my way to Avenue Secrétan, a busy street I remembered had everything, from supermarkets to *boulangeries*, hotels, bars, even locksmiths. I picked up a few things then headed back towards the 20th.

I put Marie's keys down and unpacked my shopping. I opened the Beaujolais, tore the end off a baguette. In Marie's room I sat on the edge of her bed. Pulling back the covers, I got in. Her pillow smelled of washing powder and an aroma I had never known was hers but now recognised. I relaxed and may have drifted off. After some time I got up and opened the closet, which had a louvred door. I held the material of a dress to my face and inhaled traces of perfume, sweat, cigarettes and that same personal scent. I dropped the dress on the bed and opened a drawer, running my hands through knickers and tights.

I took a shower, then walked around the apartment naked. At the kitchen sink I watched people go past along Passage des Soupirs. Back in Marie's room I removed books from a shelf — Gide, Camus, de Beauvoir — and put them back in a different order. I picked up my watch. Half an hour remained before she was due back. I went into Cécile's room, but her things didn't interest me. In Marie's room again I hung up the dress, then pushed back the clothes on the rail. I stepped inside, turned around and pulled the door to, peering through the slats.

From the kitchen came the buzz of the doorbell.

10.

Marie was tired and wanted to go straight to bed. In the morning she made coffee and we sat in the kitchen. She lit a cigarette and blew out the smoke in a ragged stream. I decided she brought out the smoke rings only when she felt relaxed.

"I have to go out soon and I'm working later. Will you head back or…?" She spoke quickly as if she had been rehearsing.

"I might find somewhere to stay, if we can see each other…"

"I'm busy." She flicked her cigarette over the ashtray and glanced at me then turned away. "I have these meetings, for this thing, and then I'm working. It's not the right time."

"What thing's that?"

"Just a thing I'm doing with some people."

"Right. OK, look, I'll get going."

She flicked ash again. "Good. Another time maybe."

"Right," I said.

I got my bag, we kissed on both cheeks and I left.

It was dusk before I returned.

The kitchen window was dark. I let myself in using the keys I'd had cut on Avenue Secrétan. I put a light on and made a sandwich. I'd spent the day on foot and was tired.

I undressed and got into Marie's bed. When I woke, it was completely dark outside. I checked my watch. It was after ten. I got up and showered. I patted myself dry with tissues, then wiped down the shower. I sat on the end of the bed to put my shoes on and while I was tying my laces looked at the door to the closet.

I tidied up, switched the lights off and left.

11.

There's a lot of talk about *defining the relationship*, less about *the defining relationship*. Some people are lucky enough to experience their defining relationship early in life *and* it works out for them. Others experience theirs later. Some never do, or they experience it early and it doesn't work out.

After Marie, after Paris, I don't get close to people, or I get close to them in the wrong way. Things don't work out.

Older now, alone, I live in a continuous, perpetual present. I collect dying media. (I'm not interested in streaming. My life already feels streamed.) With CDs and DVDs, I *have* something. I'm rewatching French films I saw in the 1980s and 1990s when I was too immature or my judgement was skewed. I don't know, though. I watch *Trois couleurs: Bleu*. How hard is it to find a blue lampshade in Paris, or a swimming pool? As for the soundtrack, the Zbigniew Preisner is good, but the way Kieślowski uses it — with these odd pauses — is bizarre. It may not be all bad, but I don't think it's all that.

I rewatch *The Tenant*. The French supporting cast are dubbed into English, with American accents. In that regard, it's a mess, but the scene with the severed head is still beautiful.

I watch *Monsieur Hire* for the fifth time and Michel Blanc's title character listens to the fourth movement from Brahms' *Piano Quartet No.1 in G minor* for the hundredth time as he stands at his window watching Sandrine Bonnaire's Alice in the apartment opposite. It is, I now think, possibly the saddest film I've ever seen.

12.

I figured I had until Friday. Although maybe she worked weekends and had nights off in the week.

I'd grab four or five hours' sleep each evening and get a shower, but, more importantly, I had a space that was my own for part of the day. The effect of haunting the Gare du Nord during the small hours was isolating. Choosing to be alone in Marie's apartment was different. I could sit and think, read her books, smell her clothes. I could be close to her. One night, ten minutes after leaving, I pictured the coffee left out on the table rather than put away in the fridge. My body flooded uncomfortably with warmth. I debated whether to go back and decided the risk that she would return while I was there was greater than the risk that she would correctly interpret the meaning of the coffee on the table.

The following evening I found the coffee in the fridge and, on the table, a postcard from Cécile saying she would be away for the rest of the month. I undressed, put my watch down on the nightstand and got into Marie's bed. I pulled the covers over my head and imagined she was there with me. I was tired but sleep was a long time coming. When I woke, I sensed that something was different. I tensed, listened. The rattle of a letter box. There were two other apartments in the building, but neither had shown any signs of life. I got out of bed, straightened it, grabbed my clothes and shoes and, as I heard footsteps on the stairs, slipped into the closet. I pulled on my jeans as I heard a key being inserted in the lock.

13.

I heard somebody enter the kitchen, deposit a bag, rummage, light a cigarette. The uncorking of a bottle of wine, the pouring of a glass. I stared through the slats, but focused on a mental image of the kitchen. Had I left anything out? Then, what lay in front of me swam into focus. The nightstand — my watch. I heard movement. A shadow entered the room and Marie walked around the end of the bed, passing within inches of me. She put her glass down on the bookshelf and moved to the bed. With the angle of the slats, I couldn't see her top half, but if she were to look at the nightstand she couldn't fail to see my watch. Her movements suggested she was undoing buttons. The white blouse landed on the bed. She moved to the bookshelf, picked up her glass and left the room. After a moment I heard the shower. I opened the door, took three strides, recovered my watch. The door to the shower room was open. Marie was in the shower with her back to the doorway. I entered Cécile's room to get my bag. In the kitchen I saw Marie's glass on the table, the bottle next to it. I poured half a glass and drank it. As I closed the door, the sound of water ceased. I crept downstairs, put on my shoes and left the building. I looked up at the kitchen window, as a silhouette passed across it. Marie would have poured herself another glass, her lips, which I had kissed only once, meeting the imprint of mine on the rim. I waited in the shadows until the kitchen light went out, leaving the faintest hint of another light within. A few minutes later this was extinguished also. I checked my watch and left.

14.

The next time I went back to Passage des Soupirs was late at night. After midnight. The window was dark. I removed my shoes before climbing the stairs. At Marie's door, I paused, listened. Nothing. No crack of light. I turned the key, listened. Nothing. I pushed open the door, stepped inside, closed the door behind me. Listening. Nothing to hear over the thump-thump in my chest. Without my bag (left-luggage locker), I advanced unencumbered. On the table: handbag, cigarettes, lighter, ashtray. Draining board: wine glass, residue.

There was a creak.

I froze.

Deciding Marie had turned over in bed, I moved towards the doorway. There was a hump in the bed, facing away, towards the nightstand. I listened. Deep breathing. I entered, took two steps to the end of the bed. Waited there for a moment, listening to the breathing, which remained the same. I moved to the side of the bed and bent down. Her mouth was slightly open. A lock of hair had fallen across her forehead. I lifted it away. As I removed my hand, a sigh escaped her lips and she shifted her head. I froze again. As she turned on to her other side, her eyes opened — then closed. In seconds her breathing found its rhythm again. I walked back around the bed, took a last look from the doorway and passed into the kitchen. I put my hand into her bag and found something soft. The red silk scarf. I lifted it to my nose and breathed in, closing my eyes. I tied the scarf around my neck and moved to the door.

15.

"Belleville," says the recorded voice on the Métro, with an upwards inflection on the second syllable, as we approach, and then, "Belleville", with a dying fall on "ville", as the platform appears. "Couronnes," asks the voice, answering, "Couronnes," with that same downward cadence. "Ménilmontant." Up on the last syllable. "Ménilmontant." Down.

I ascend to street level and walk up Rue de Ménilmontant, past vape stores, mobile phone shops and Cash Converters, past graffiti on the ends of buildings painted by people born since I was last here. I turn right into Rue du Retrait and left at the end into Rue des Pyrénées. In the plate-glass window of the hairdressers on the corner, I catch a glimpse. Even at night, the red scarf stands out. I take the steps up.

As I walk down Passage des Soupirs, I insert earphones and listen to Christian Miller. There's a light on in the window of what was and could possibly still be Marie's apartment, so I wait for the track to finish and then walk on to Rue de la Chine and then Rue Pixérécourt until I get to Rue de l'Avenir and I see what I didn't see before: Rue de l'Avenir, angled away from anyone walking north up Rue Pixérécourt, is a dead end.

On my way back to Passage des Soupirs, I listen to the Brahms. I listen to it once, then remove the earphones and put them in the left-hand pocket of my jacket. From the right-hand pocket I take out the keys. The window on the top floor is now in darkness. Just as *I* haven't changed much in thirty years, it's possible the locks haven't either.

Paris, You and Me

Gerard Evans

You may say I'm a dreamer / but I'm not the only one.

As a child, hearing John Lennon sing this line, and indeed this song, freed something within me — gave me permission to go beyond what my parents had presented as the harsh parameters of reality, beyond the presumed ridicule of my friends. In my mind, I leapt over fences and obstacles to where I wanted to be. To where I wanted the world to be.

To read later about the events of Paris 1968, made me feel others had also dared to step over a line in their heads. Little did I know that Paris would be the place where my dreams came true.

I mentioned to my mum that I'd been asked to write about Paris and her immediate response was "Ah, city of romance!". Because it is, isn't it? OK, there's the Situationists, the French Revolution, the Left Bank, the artists and Sartre and all that, but my mum cuts through pretension and knows what matters. That's the measure for me.

Some background: I got an email one day, that's how it started, though it wasn't apparent at the time that the two lines within would turn my life upside down forever.

It was from a woman called Joanna, who enjoyed my

250

writing. We started conversing. To cut a long story short, I lost my heart.

It happened over the course of six months, as penpals, before I even knew what she looked like, which was around five months. Emails got more regular and more anticipated. Meeting was the obvious next step. She agreed and my keyboard knees went weak.

I was very angry indeed back then — freed up by punk, years of Thatcherism and bitter political arguing had stuck me on a nihilist cortisol carousel of anger that I couldn't get off, often robbing me of nuance and pleasantness. This was reflected unapologetically in my writing, so the idea that someone could read that, warts and all, and still want to meet me was the chance of a lifetime. I knew the stakes.

But where to meet?

I suggested Berlin. It felt like a geographically generous gesture, being much nearer for her in Poland than me in London. As time ticked on, however, I lost faith in the idea of Berlin: I'd only been once, a week after the wall came tumbling down and I didn't enjoy it at all. It felt aggressive and lacking in the charm that I'm told it now possesses. Berlin was also, more crucially in this context, a psychologically safe place. A place that treads a neutral friends/lovers line. At forty-two, I'd been single for ten years and achingly lonely for most of those — a quiet desperation, a grief without a pang. Life hadn't begun at forty. Berlin felt like a cop-out from what I really wanted. Like playing a 7 instead of a King.

Places in this context demand big questions. Was I about to meet a friend or were we already in love? Can you be in love without meeting someone? Yes, of course you can. You can be in love with an idea of love and you can be in love with the idea of a person. Their physical presence merely adds a third layer to the idea in some ways.

So I suggested a change of venue to Paris, the city of love, and nervously awaited the email response to the suggestive nature of the choice. Cards on the table.

Is Paris actually like that, a city of romance? It doesn't matter. If reality is simply a consensual agreement — as it surely is — then ideas of cities are clearly that. We both saw Paris as the city of love and that was more than enough to make it a subjective reality. There's no such thing as objectivity in love. Or cities. Remember, some people love Stoke.

I emailed Joanna and suggested we change the venue. Her response email simply bore the title "Paris, you and me". I cried. Because I knew. The code was fading into clear text.

We met. I was just a dreamer and she was just a dream.

I wasn't in awe of the bohemian side of Paris, but Joanna's dad evidently was. He was a successful Polish artist, now bedridden with a particularly nasty cancer. A photograph of her basking, with a Cheshire Cat grin, on the Left Bank was a beautiful gift to send him in the final weeks of his life. I will always regret that we never got to meet.

Anarchists in love? Perhaps, but really the only part of that sentence that we were thinking about was love. Neither activism nor Bohemia were of particular interest here. Paris was the city of romance and romance is an open ticket.

We spent three days living in a 1950s Hollywood movie. Paris was the perfect setting. We bought into that idea of reality and made it ours for those glorious days that remain the best of my life so far. We talked existentialism with sincere pretence; we walked lost in our bubble for endless anonymous miles, oblivious to the surroundings — though they generously let us do that. We kissed endlessly in parks and drank wine on pavements and fell in love as completely as any couple could. It was an innocent time devoid of cynicism and cerebralism. It was an innocent beauty all lovers know. I knew. Joanna knew. Then came the new.

Paris was the city where I started to stop being angry, subtly shifted my focus, and started living. Not magic-wanded overnight perhaps, but I can trace back the chrysalis of the person I now am exactly: to midday, 31 July 2005, by a fountain on Place de la Concorde.

Reader, I married her. That was thirteen years ago to the day, as I write, and we are still as in love as we were on that first day. More so. We live in Sussex, in the UK, but we'd love to live and love once more in Paris one day. We dreamed the love and then lived the dream. She's sitting behind me in the room as I write this and I'm reflecting on being the luckiest man ever. Before that, I never believed love could be like the films, but the evidence was overwhelming. Paris was a part of that evidence — the backdrop but also the collaborator. Berlin may have been the same had we ended up there instead, but for reasons unknown to me, Paris made it all downhill.

The Che Guevara quote comes to mind of course: all revolutions are born of love and all true love causes revolutions. Thirteen years on, my feelings toward Paris remain benign, romantic and grateful. Whether or not all this talk of Paris and romance is a construct or not isn't of the slightest concern. Because Paris was the city of my revolution — they can't take that away from me.

As a final aside, I revisited Paris last year with Joanna but also with my band, to play on an eclectic bill in a basement nightclub near the Seine. The line-up was good, but the audience were better: better than any audience we'd ever played to in Britain because they danced, dressed and interacted like the genuine creative freaks we'd always wanted to play to in London. Finally I get to stand on a Paris stage and sing about taking your desires for reality. The next morning, me and Joanna slope away from the band for a breakfast of pizza, espresso and wine. The restaurant has sparrows flying freely to catch all the drops off the table.

If Paris is what you make it, then I must admit I'm kind of pleased with myself. I was reasonable, I demanded the impossible. And got it.

Flogging a Dead Clothes Horse

Thom Cuell

When we came back the next morning with the same news, Malcolm was still in bed. Finally, Malcolm grew tired of it. He picked up the phone and started screaming to Sid about what a useless junkie he was and so on. Meanwhile, Sid had given the phone over to Nancy and while that was going on, suddenly the eighteenth-century door of Malcolm's hotel room flew off its hinges. Sid crashed into the room wearing his swastika underpants and motorbike boots. He dragged Malcolm out of bed and started hitting him. Then Sid chased a naked Malcolm down the corridor intent on beating the shit out of him. The ancient floorboards went up and down like a ship as the chambermaids started screaming "Monsieur, monsieur. Stop! Stop! Stop!"
— John Lydon, *No Irish, No Blacks, No Dogs* (1994)

Paris appears in the English imagination as a city of romance and rebellion. The Parisian spirit of insurrection has rarely been seen on the other side of the Channel. In particular, the general strike which took place in Paris in May 1968, with its heady mix of sloganeering and civil disobedience, has served as a touchstone for a certain vintage of English dissenter. One such dissenter was Malcolm McLaren, boutique owner and manager of the Sex Pistols.

If we believe McLaren's account, the Pistols, and punk in general, were his attempt to recreate a Parisian moment (the 1968 Situationist uprising) in a London context. As the experiment crumbled he sent Sid Vicious to Paris to try to force a synthesis of the two movements. The danger of this approach became apparent one evening, as his hotel room door flew off its hinges to reveal Sid, clad only in underpants and leather jacket.

The *enragés* of 1968 became the template for stylish urban guerrilla because theirs was the first revolution to be globally televised. The insurrection had begun with the occupation of college girls' dormitories — a signifier of the adolescent energy which is common to both rock and roll and revolutionary politics. McLaren and some early cronies, including designer Jamie Reid, attempted a similar sit-in at Hornsey Art School in June that year, but their efforts fizzled out. In December, McLaren was apparently involved in a famous action carried out by King Mob, whose members infiltrated Selfridges dressed as Father Christmas, handing out stock from the shelves to passing customers (later obliquely referred to by John Lydon in the lyrics of "Anarchy in the UK"). Three years later, in May 1971, British anarchist group the Angry Brigade channelled the spirit of 1968 by bombing a boutique. McLaren, by contrast, decided to set one up.

McLaren's next attempt to recreate May '68 occurred when he forced the bedraggled remnants of the New York Dolls to tour the southern states of America, dressed in red patent leather outfits and performing in front of a Soviet banner. Unsurprisingly, the experiment ended with the band's implosion. The right setting was yet to be found.

*

After he returned from New York in 1974, McLaren completely redesigned his store. The interior was crafted to resemble a bomb-damaged London street, but the true inspiration was revealed by the pictures of Left Bank life displayed in one window. Outside, the London of 1975 was beginning to resemble the Paris of 1968: Roger Perry's photographs of the graffiti of run-down West London showed the writing on the wall.

> With his nose for trouble, McLaren liked this volatile atmosphere: he thought it might set up sparks. Yet this instability also caused real damage, not least to the person who thought he was in control. McLaren liked to play with fire but, in entering the world of John Lydon and his friends, he would be dealing with psychic material far more combustible than the stuff he was used to.
> — Jon Savage, *England's Dreaming* (1991)

One of McLaren's famous early T-shirts featured a list of loves and hates, under the slogan "One day you're going to wake up and know which side of the bed you've been lying on". The shirt didn't mention any of the Parisian Situationists by name, but did include the first usage of the name "Sex Pistols". A subsequent design, the "Only Anarchists are Pretty" shirt, explicitly referenced Paris '68 with slogans such as "*Prenez vos désirs pour la réalité*". With his scattergun approach to iconoclasm, McLaren supplemented this with negative images of Marx and inverted

Nazi insignia, creating what Jon Savage called "a chaos of meaning". Later, "*Prenez vos désirs...*" would be used in a Crédit Agricole advert for loans.

McLaren and his associate (and later manager of The Clash) Bernie Rhodes made an abortive trip to Paris in December 1975, attempting to sell their retooled revolution back to the French. They were more successful in September the following year, when the Pistols arrived to perform their only French concert, at the Chalet du Lac. This time, the band unveiled McLaren and Westwood's Anarchy shirts, and the new bondage suit. John Lydon was surrounded by fashion photographers, while McLaren and Westwood were dubbed "*couturiers situationnistes*" by *Rock News* magazine. The response to the Anarchy shirt must have been gratifying to McLaren, who told Paul Gorman in a 2007 interview that the French anarchist movement had "really framed my critique... this particular shirt celebrated that".

Meanwhile, the band was slowly gaining exposure in Britain. Their first press review contains a manifesto delivered by guitarist Steve Jones, but clearly guided by McLaren: "We're not into music. We're into chaos". Early accounts of Pistols gigs, recorded in Clinton Heylin's *Year Zero*, focus on the visuals, which were easier to assimilate and parse than the chaos of the music, showing that McLaren and the band had tapped into an identifiable visual culture with their echoing of Paris '68.

*

The whole point of Sex is that we want to inspire other people with the confidence to live out their fantasies and to change. We really are making a political statement with this shop by attempting to attack the system. I'm also interested in getting people to wear some of our sex gear to the office. 'Out of the bedroom and into the streets!' Now that would really be revolutionary.

— Vivienne Westwood, "Buy Sexual", *Forum*, 1976

Dialectics is not a sterile process: it causes explosions. Mixing Paris '68 and New York '74 in the London of '76 was an experiment with volatile substances and unpredictable outcomes. In its early days, punk was a sandpit for kids to play in, using slogans and gestures to carnivalise economic turmoil, just like the Situationists had done.

There was a tension between McLaren's libertarian views, and his desire to control the nascent movement. Reading *Leaving the 20th Century*, an anthology of Situationist writing edited by Chris Gray, McLaren observed, "the good thing about it was all these slogans you could take up without being party to a movement. Being in a movement often stifles creative thinking". However, with his "cash from chaos" mantra, McLaren attempted to control both the spectacle of punk and its commodification — adding a layer of vertical integration to Debord's theories.

In the early days, McLaren had dominated the discourse around punk, and imbued the early followers with his sensibility. After the Bill Grundy interview, where the Pistols caused outrage by swearing on live television, punk became a mass media sensation, too big for McLaren to control; the press diluted the message and turned the movement into a cartoon. The group was also less pliant than McLaren had hoped: when the Svengali presented them with a list of bondage inspired phrases to insert into songs, Lydon and Glen Matlock, in a rare moment of collaboration, recast submission as a submarine mission.

McLaren attempted to regain control of the message with a Situationist broadsheet called *Anarchy in the UK*. The editorial notes for the second issue state, "no-one is interested in the truth. The fact that what is happening is fluid, spontaneous, changes day by day, living by your nerve ends, chaos". It was never published.

*

As the group collapsed, in a storm of cancelled shows, record company firings, antagonism and addiction, McLaren began work on a film which would retell the Pistols' story with McLaren as protagonist, a Situationist puppet master manipulating the musicians and the media. McLaren couldn't decide whether he wanted to be the star, or the hidden mastermind: the film opens with him appearing in a mask, only to declare, "My name is Malcolm McLaren".

Paris remained a key touchstone in his mythology, and so McLaren sent Sid Vicious to France to film the dénouement. In a scene bizarrely reminiscent of the opening of Welles' *F for Fake*, Vicious strides through Paris in swastika T-shirt and leather jacket, the camera cutting to horrified reaction shots from elderly passers-by. McLaren glories in bringing inter-generational conflict back to the streets of Paris, in a confected, staged setting. Many of Sid's scenes were shot as he walked from Rue de Rivoli to the corner of Avenue Victor Hugo. Reaction shots from passers-by were filmed elsewhere, near Chatelet. The one representative of youth shown in this sequence follows Sid out of a boulangerie, brandishing a felt tip and begging for an autograph, which he crudely graffitis across her chest; a nihilistic negation of the Situationists' utopian slogans. Playing in the background, a French singer performs the band's signature song, accompanied by an accordion: "*Moi je suis l'Antéchrist, moi je suis l'anarchiste*" — a far better rhyme in French.

Sid refused to sing "Non, Je Ne Regrette Rien", but agreed to do "My Way". Three attempts were made to record the song, with Sid, Steve Jones and a series of French session musos. The Pistols were reportedly too drunk to play, and the French so desperate to leave that the guitarist finished the song with only five strings. Jones added overdubs later, and Sid's vocals were stitched together from three different takes. Malcolm was absent, as the project descended into ersatz farce.

The iconic filmed version of "My Way" features Sid in white tuxedo jacket, black jeans and garter belt, performing the song in the Théâtre de l'Empire before an upper-class audience — a cliché of Parisian self-satisfaction, waiting to be flung into the trash of history. As Sid sneers his way through the song, the audience applauds and throws roses, neutering Sid's posturing and sloganeering. Only gunshots provoke real panic, as the punk goes one step beyond what the Situationists offered, in McLaren's fantasy telling at least. The act even unconsciously reaches further back into Parisian history, echoing the actions of proto-Surrealist Jacques Vaché, who interrupted the premiere of Apollinaire's *Les Mamelles de Tirésia*s — dressed as an English pilot and brandishing a gun — threatening to shoot at random. Finally, Sid walks away, abdicating his position as leader of a new youth movement.

As the celluloid avatar of Vicious is unloading on the Parisian bourgeoisie, the real Sid is chasing McLaren through a hotel room corridor, aiming motorcycle boots at his manager's bare arse. Reviewing the film, Greil Marcus says, "McLaren's attempt to show up the Sex Pistols as a con is blown up by the inclusion of several real Sex Pistols recordings" — just as his fantasies of a Situationist prank were blown up by the Pistols themselves.

By the time of the film's release, Rotten had left the band, and Sid was deep into the downward spiral which would leave him dead at twenty-one. With the emergence of copycat groups, punk collapsed into parody, and was supplanted by New Wave and then the Thatcherite excess of Eighties pop, whose protagonists fantasised about Monaco, not the Left Bank. McLaren, however, retained his fascination with the city. After the Pistols split, he remained in Paris, licking his wounds and preparing his comeback with the group Bow Wow Wow. In 1994, he released the album *Paris*, a poorly received love letter to the city. His interests here are clearly more traditional: song titles include "Walking With Satie" and "Père Lachaise". A few weeks before his death in 2010, he completed a film entitled *Paris: Capital of the XXIst Century*, echoing his early, uncompleted film project tracing the history of Oxford Street.

McLaren never really succeeded in creating anarchy on the streets of London. Like the Situationists, his movement left behind fertile images and slogans for subsequent generations to appropriate, but the establishment carried on regardless. His attempts to recreate the events of Paris '68 had descended into farce, self-parody and the early death of a key player.

The Paris that McLaren dreamed of is disappearing fast: although it is still possible to trace the path that Vicious walked, many buildings have been demolished (including the Théâtre de l'Empire following a fire) and areas gentrified. Bullet scars from street fighting in 1944 have been illegally repaired. After the horrors of the Bataclan, the idea of shots being fired at a rock concert has lost the camp charm of Sid's performance. Post-Brexit, the idea of combining French revolutionary dreams with British youth culture seems further away than ever.

London still awaits its Paris moment.

Paris Does Not Exist

Stewart Home

> Tourism, human circulation considered as consumption
> is fundamentally nothing more than the leisure of going
> to see what has become banal.
> — Guy Debord, *The Society of the Spectacle*

When I hear the word Paris, the 1981 song "Party in Paris" by the UK Subs starts running through my head. If I close my eyes, I can picture the promo video too: the oldest punk vocalist in town dressed in a black-and-white striped "Gallic" T-shirt with fake cancan girls in frilly petticoats unimpressively kicking their legs to something approaching knee height around the band. Although I saw the Subs at least twenty times in the late Seventies, I'd stopped going to their gigs by the end of that decade, and it isn't the classic line-up I once almost loved on that song. The tune is crass but catchy, and I guess it is intended to be ironic.

When I was into punk, in the Seventies, there didn't seem to be much of a party in Paris, the global action for fans of super-dumb sleazebag thud was very much centred on London. The first time I visited Paris was in 1978. While there, I wanted to know if there was any of what us cognoscenti called EFM (extra fast music) I should check out from France. Stinky Toys didn't count but the Dogs did — I was familiar with their tune "19" from the 1977 EP

Charlie Was a Good Boy and that rocked. I also liked some of the tracks Little Bob Story had put out, even if they were more of a Sixties throwback. I found some punks in a Parisian record store and they told me Starshooter (from Lyon) were where it was at. When I heard the band's 1977 debut single "Pin-Up Blonde" it grooved me, although this tune was totally eclipsed by their trashing of the Beatles' "Get Back" — "Get Baque" — the following year. Later in 1978 I discovered Métal Urbain who were way ahead of the curve when it came to French rock and roll, and who still sound to me like the best band ever to come out of Paris.

My next trip to Paris three years later was no more memorable than the first. I was with a group of friends into art. We stayed in a cheap hotel in Pigalle and went to galleries — the funkiest groove I heard on that trip was some *musique concrète* at the Pompidou Centre. That's what you get for hanging out with posh kids who don't dig three-chord stomp! What I most remember from that visit is that every morning after I finished my paid-for breakfast, a waitress in her mid-thirties acted like I hadn't had anything and gave me what I'd just consumed again. I appreciated this both coz croissants didn't fill me up and no one else got double helpings. Although I was nineteen and the people I was with were the same age, I looked very young and the waitress may well have thought I was my friends' eleven-year-old kid brother — she didn't speak English. On my final night in Paris the waitress who'd buttered me up with two breakfasts every morning, ran out into the street as I was approaching the hotel, grabbed my hand and... you can imagine the rest.

The third time I went to Paris was in 1989. I travelled

there with Ralph Rumney, a founding member of the Situationist International who for a time was married to Michèle Bernstein, Guy Debord's ex-wife and the real powerhouse behind the SI. I was to interview Rumney for *Art Monthly* about the Situationist exhibition then on at the Pompidou Centre.[1] When we met up, Rumney told me he almost hadn't shown up since he felt rotten. At the ferry terminal, he said I should go through passport control on my own: he was a marked man and I'd have trouble going to France for the rest of my life if I went through with him. It did take him a remarkably long time to get past the immigration officers. Once we were in Paris, Rumney needed to stop at a bar every few hundred yards. If I'd drunk a tenth of what he downed I'd have been too blitzed to interview him, instead I was buzzing on a lot of black coffee.

Rumney took me to a load of galleries, and everywhere I was given catalogues. Before Bernstein, Ralph had been married to Pegeen Guggenheim, and their son Sandro Rumney is a well-known art dealer. We went to Sandro's apartment and other people's homes and I couldn't believe the wealth I was seeing. I'd thought one of the girls I'd gone to Paris with in 1981 was super-posh coz she had a swimming pool in her back garden and a yacht in her driveway, alongside her dad's flash cars. But Rumney's connections took things to another level entirely. Previously when I'd seen pictures by members of the Surrealist and COBRA movements on people's walls they'd been prints: on this trip to Paris, I got to see large original paintings used as decorations. Rumney asked me if there was anyone in

---

1   My Rumney interview is online here: https://www. stewarthomesociety.org/interviews/rumney.htm

Paris I really wanted to meet, and I said Gil J. Wolman. We called on Wolman, but unfortunately the artist was out; Rumney took me to see Jim Haynes instead.

Rumney was staying on in France to be with friends and family, so I went home alone. When I got to customs, two officials grinned at me. They asked what I did and I told them I was an art critic, which really made them laugh. Then they wanted to know if I understood that I wasn't allowed to bring hardcore pornography into the UK and I assured them that I did: back then, it was still illegal. Next, they enquired about what I had in my bag and I said mostly art catalogues. I was asked to open my holdall and show them the "catalogues". They obviously thought they'd caught me bang to rights smuggling hardcore porn because, somehow, they knew I was carrying lots of glossy publications. The look of disbelief on their faces when I pulled out one art publication after another was truly hilarious.

In 1996 I got invited to the French capital for the opening of the big "Brit Art" exhibition I was included in, *Life/Live*, at the Musée d'Art Moderne de la Ville de Paris. Since I was broke, and expenses weren't being paid, I didn't go. Apparently, all the other artists in the show were careerist enough to attend — I can no longer even remember what I had in the exhibition. The arrival of the Eurostar train service around that time made travel between London and Paris much less hassle, but nonetheless there was a decade and a half hiatus between my third and fourth trips to the city. When I finally got round to visiting Paris by train in 2005, the ease of the journey made the place seem more like Manchester in the north of England than the City of Love it got hyped as being. I must have made a dozen trips to Paris by Eurostar between 2005 and 2014, and two of those excursions were particularly memorable. I even blogged about one of them on 11 November 2009:

Searching for someone called François Raymond on the outskirts of Paris is probably a little like looking for a specific John Smith in London. Who is François Raymond? The one I'm looking for exhibited a series of six photographs of my mother Julia Callan-Thompson as part of an exhibition entitled *Exposition Tamrauc* at the Maison des Jeunes et de la Culture (Paris) in October 1967. I have two prints of just one of these photographs, and rubber stamped on the back of one of them is an address: *François Raymond, 37 Rue Gambetta, Puteaux (Seine)*. I'd like to acquire copies of all the photographs Raymond took of my mother, which is why I've been attempting to track him down...

Virtually every town in France seems to have a street named after the nineteenth-century French politician Léon Gambetta — so the fact that someone with a name as common as Raymond's should have an address on one such street seemed psychogeographically apt to me. There is another Rue Gambetta in the neighbouring commune of Suresnes, which is a ten minute walk from the street of that name in Puteaux.

On my first visit to Puteaux I approached Rue Gambetta via La Défense, the Paris business district. Two thirds of this high-rise office development is situated within the Putueaux municipality, although parts also encroach upon Nanterre and Courbevoie. As a consequence, Puteaux is one of the richest municipalities, not just in France but the whole of Europe. Initially I was a little confused by the layout of La Défense, but I managed to walk out of it and along to Rue Gambetta without wasting too much time. Raymond's street was a mix of old and new dwellings, with a monstrous vista of La Défense. The view towards Paris must have been very different in 1967 when Raymond took the pictures he exhibited of my mother.

37 Rue Gambetta turned out to be an apartment block. The outside had been refaced and the balconies replaced relatively recently, but close examination of the structure, the garages behind it, and in particular the doors, led me to the conclusion it had probably been built in the 1950s. It seems safe to conclude that Raymond had lived and/or worked in this building about forty years before my visit. I examined the buzzers to the flats, but none of these were labelled with the name Raymond. Next, I tried stopping people on the street outside the building, but no one knew of a François Raymond who had lived there.

I returned to Puteaux a couple of days later, approaching it on foot via the bridge over the Seine. This time I went first via Boulevard Richard Wallace (presumably the street is named after the illegitimate son of the Marquess of Hertford, a nineteenth-century "philanthropist" and art collector), to Rue Gambetta in Suresnes, since I wished to compare it with the Puteaux street of the same name.[2] This second Rue Gambetta

2   In the 1870s, Richard Wallace designed and funded the Wallace Fountains, which became an integral part of Parisian urban furniture (ed.).

looked a little less well-heeled than the one in Puteaux, and was considerably less ambient. Both lie in municipalities that are densely populated by European standards. This second trip to Puteaux seemed to take me no further in my quest for François Raymond, and his lost pictures of my mother, than my previous one. However, rather than walking back to La Défense, I decided to take the suburban train there from Puteaux.

Approaching the train station I clocked a couple of pissheads who were weaving so erratically on the pavement that I decided to let them get a little ahead of me as we all approached the escalators up to the platform. The drunks looked like a working-class couple in their late sixties, and they were pretty hefty too. As they reached the escalator, the woman — who'd gone ahead — placed a foot not on the first or second steps which were closest to her and still flat, but the third step that was rising; having done this, she quickly brought her other foot up onto the escalator and placed it beside the right one. The man attempted to do the same thing and lost his balance, grabbing hold of the woman as he did so.

I ran forward, catching both the man and the woman. If I hadn't the man would have certainly bashed his head on the metal stairs and this might have resulted in a nasty injury or even worse. The pair of them were heavy and behaved like a deadweight. I thought the woman would pull herself upright, and that the man would then do the same. When this didn't happen another passerby took the woman's hand to help her, but it seemed she was too drunk to stand up. I held this fat and heavy couple up until we reached the top of the escalator, where the woman rolled awkwardly off the stairs and the man managed to get himself upright. The first thing the man did was check that none of the multiple bottles of wine in the plastic bag he'd been carrying had been smashed, and amazingly they were all in one piece. I rescued one of the woman's shoes which had come off, another passerby returned the other. I hoped that once the woman had her shoes on she would get up, but she was too dazed. By this time a small crowd were trying to help the couple, particularly the woman. Since neither of them were able to understand my English and odd words of French, I decided to leave them in the hands of the native speakers who'd come to their assistance after me.

As I made my way towards a train the man shouted *"merci"* at me. My impression was that neither he nor the woman was fully aware of what had happened, but he at least knew I'd caught them both as they were falling. Once I was on the train and speeding toward the centre of Paris, I realised I should have asked the man if he was, or knew, François Raymond. Obviously it is unlikely that he was Raymond, although I guess he was about the same age as the man I was looking for, and if he'd lived in Puteaux most of his life he may have known him... This chance encounter on an escalator seems as close as I'm going to get to the elusive Monsieur Raymond for the time being...

This blog was read by one of François Raymond's friends and he put me in touch with the photographer's family because, like my mother, the shutterbug had died young. Raymond's brother found some pictures he thought might be of my mother, but I could instantly see it was someone else. So while posting the blog solved the mystery of what had happened to François Raymond, it didn't lead me to the photos I'm still hoping may turn up one day.

After this adventure I was back in Paris a few months later for the opening of the *Le Week-end de sept jours* (2010) exhibition at the École nationale supérieure des Beaux-Arts. I wasn't actually in the show, but I had come up with its title. The curator had asked me if I could think of a good name for her exhibition and I'd said re-using the title of the old Gary U.S. Bonds tune "Seven Day Weekend" might work since it wasn't a million miles away from the Situationist slogan "Never Work". Partly on the back of my suggestion being taken up, I had free accommodation for the opening and a few more days in Paris.

Le Week-end de sept jours was a show of postgraduate art students from Paris, London and Singapore, so I expected the private view to be a tranquil affair — but it certainly wasn't. Siu Lan Ko created banners that were affixed to the exterior of the building based on then President Sarkozy's slogan "Work more to earn more". Rather than using the word "more" twice, the term "less" was substituted in one instance. There were two banners with one of four words on each side. How they read changed according to how the wind blew. Two hours after the banners went up, they were taken down since the art school hosting the exhibition deemed them too explosive and controversial to remain in place. This act of censorship caused a media storm in France and was also covered by the *Guardian* in the UK and the international art press. Embarrassed by the furore, the government's education department ordered the college to put the banners back up in time for the opening.

Unusually for a student show, the private view was heavily policed and absolutely stuffed with people claiming to be journalists. These "reporters" wanted to talk to anyone and everyone who was there, including me. It was obvious from their line of questioning that at least some of those who claimed to be working for the press were actually undercover cops. It wasn't a pleasant night, but it had the strangeness I associated with the "City of Love" from my teenage reading of Surrealist novels like *Nadja, Paris Peasant* and *Last Nights of Paris*. After my initial visits to the French capital these Surrealist works seemed to me to describe a landscape that existed in the mind much more than on the streets of any specific city. As someone born in London I felt better able to attain such states of consciousness in my hometown rather than in Paris. The two incidents I've just recounted are the closest I've ever got to the literary representations of Paris I'd been exposed to as a teenager via Surrealist and psychogeographical writings. I want to stress that I see my "experiences" and the texts that helped generate them as hyperreal; "literary" "Paris" is a simulation, a series of signs that have no relationship at all with a so-called "reality".

Moving on, there are those who primarily associate the 1968 uprisings with France, although for me events in Mexico were more tragic, while in Spain the protests may have been small-scale but they really *did* signal the beginning of the end for the dictatorship there. Words and phrases often set tunes loose in my mind and The

Ethiopians' song "Everything Crash" is the earworm 1968 summons up: "Firemen strike! Watermen strike! Telephone company too! Down to the policemen too!" The series of strikes in Jamaica in 1968, alongside the Rodney Riots, really were extraordinary and thanks to the Ethiopians they're the first thing that come into my head whenever anyone mentions that year, not Paris.

As far as Anglo-Saxon literary obsessions with Paris go, I simply don't dig the phantasmagorias that dominate its myriad scenes and which are most typically conjured up around the spectres and spectacle of Gertrude Stein, Henry Miller, James Joyce, etc. I read all of Joyce's *Ulysses* as a teenager but I preferred the 1967 film to the book, even if as cinema it looks pathetic when compared to true anti-classics of the same era like Jean Rollin's *Le Viol du vampire* (1968). I found Miller's *Quiet Days in Clichy* tedious, although Jens Jorgan Thorsen's 1970 film of the novel is hilarious. For me the cut-up experiments of William Burroughs and Brion Gysin at the Beat Hotel on Rue Gît-le-Cœur are a more enthralling way to hallucinate Paris than the words of the old bores championed by those who mistake the ever proliferating margins they inhabit for a "literary" "mainstream".

The issue here is in many ways a matter of class, English Francophilia is so often a silly snobbery cultivated by rich idiots and would-be social climbers who want to project an image of being refined. The working-class population of the British Isles tends to prefer what they understand to be "Spain" to "France" as a tourist and/or retirement destination. Magaluf anyone? Benidorm? Personally I love Valencia and all the crazy stories about that city's post-dictatorship club scene of the Eighties and Nineties, which was dubbed *Ruta Destroy* by the media. Likewise, those who went through the Seventies London punk scene were well aware that France was for a time home to mock rock corporate tax exiles like the Rolling Stones. The dead-on-arrival "music" such greed produced was something the Blank Generation rebelled against. Such guilt by association is unfair, but France as a favoured destination for tax-avoiding rock dinosaurs could make Paris appear uncool to London punks. And in terms of criminal anti-heroes, it was the bungling Ronnie Biggs who attracted the attention of English (and indeed German) punk kids much more than the likes of Jacques Mesrine.

I sometimes wish that when people mention Paris to me the 1966 tune "Paris Blues" by Tony Middleton would come to mind — since he's a considerably more sophisticated singer than Charlie Harper of the UK Subs. That said, there's both more and less to life than sophistication, and it's a huge challenge to consciously control which *rengaine* runs around my head. When "Party in Paris" gets stuck in my brain I am at least able to amuse myself by transforming the lyrics to "ooh-la-la-la-ooh-la-lay there's a piss-up in Plaistow today..." And given the ongoing gentrification and corporatisation of daily life, there is now good reason to wonder whether there's any difference between a part of East London and Paris — regardless of whether we're talking about Paris, Texas, or Paris, France. So let's end with a question: to what extent have Jean Baudrillard's theories of simulation caught on among English-speaking literary Francophiles? That was a false ending btw, since the matter might more reasonably be summed up this way: "Paris does not exist". And nor indeed does literature!

City Not Paris

Anna Aslanyan

"The distinction between journalism and fiction is the difference between without and within," Mavis Gallant says in a preface to one of her books. "Journalism recounts as exactly and economically as possible the weather in the street; fiction takes no notice of that particular weather but brings to life a distillation of all weathers, a climate of the mind." After starting as a reporter in her native Montréal, Gallant moved to Europe in 1950, settled in Paris and continued to write: mainly in English, and mainly short stories. The diary she kept throughout May '68 appeared in the *New Yorker* the same year, and later came out as a book (inexplicably out of print now). Grounded in fact rather than fiction, *Paris Notebooks* is proof that it takes a master of both genres to tread the blurred line between without and within.

"One of the reasons I came to Europe was to understand what happened here during and after the Second World War," Gallant told me when I interviewed her in 2010. Her Paris — all the Parises distilled in her writing — reflects an entire spectrum of perceptions. The expat heroine of the story "The Other Paris" (1953) feels short-changed: "Where was the Paris she had read about?" The 1959 novel *Green Water, Green Sky* has an American youth indulging in his romantic notion of the city: "That was the way he wanted something to happen; that was the thing he was ready for now." Another story, "Across the Bridge" (1993), also set in the Fifties, is narrated by a young *Parisienne*, and for all its vividness, the narrator's experience comes across as a notion acquired rather than spontaneous. To write Paris convincingly, Gallant had to know it better than all her characters put together, and so she constantly moved between circles, talking to shopkeepers and poets, teachers and cleaners, immigrants and born-and-breds, youngsters and their parents. Despite her intimate knowledge of French life, she had no illusions about her own place in it; nor did she believe that being an outsider gave her some special observation powers. Nevertheless, curious and open-minded, she had to see everything with her own eyes while constantly adjusting her focus.

Was May '68 a turning point in her relationship with Paris? During *les événements*, some of her views changed, sometimes more than once in the course of that month. "Everyone has discovered something," she says in *Notebooks*. Most of her own discoveries are clearly described and substantiated (once a reporter, always a reporter). Years later, she told me: "I can't say I was totally objective, because at the time I was very much in favour of changes in France". In any case, she was a sharp observer. In *Notebooks* she wages a war on fake news, annoyed by exaggerations, suspicious of biases, enraged at rumours. Where is the evidence of the organisers' links to the CIA? When did the shortages start, making people stockpile food? "Why always rape in these stories, and why always four times?" "Until I know the names, I shan't believe it." However, this is a diary, so the occasional deviation is permitted: "Dream:

City besieged, strikebound... Faces all strange to me, but distinct. Everyone very polite. City not Paris".

Remembering *les événements* in 2010, Gallant said: "My sympathies were with the young". Childless herself, she often used childhood and youth — including her own — as a vantage point in her fiction; as a reporter, she relied on her ability to see across the generation gap. At one end of it are parents, worried about their children on the barricades. Wouldn't they worry less if they joined the kids? "Perhaps it's none of their business, as a great deal of it is none of mine? But I'm not French and these aren't my children." Walking around the city that May, Gallant learns things that have so far escaped her attention. It turns out that juvenile delinquents, "what used to be called *les blousons noirs*", haven't disappeared; also, that there is an entire "population of rootless, drifting teen-agers, who seem to have no homes, or else homes they don't care about". And then, of course, there are students.

At first glance, these flag-waving, tract-distributing, slogan-shouting revolutionaries look rather pathetic. Here they are in the occupied Sorbonne, with their portraits of Stalin and Mao, "everything tatty, a folklore now — China, Cuba, Godard's films". Here they march with "that presumptuous banner about the handing over of the torch of resistance", preaching solidarity "to a working class in battle for thirty years". Here they are setting things on fire ("A lovely tree. They tried to burn it — the leaves are singed... We waited all winter for the leaves") and then standing there in narcissistic silence, listening to the radio talk about them. But the moment Gallant hears them chanting *"Nous sommes tous des juifs allemands"* — in protest against threats to banish Daniel Cohn-Bendit from France — all is forgiven: "This is France, they are French, I am not dreaming". To her, that's the most important event of *les événements* "because it means a mutation in the French character: a generosity".

Their naivety, ineptness and self-obsession aside, the young are fighting for a worthy cause. At a meeting at the School of Photography and Cinematography, Gallant wishes students at American colleges could see the place. There is not a single photograph here, but the teachers don't care: "their only terror seems to be that these kids will grow up and become photographers". When they claim to stand with the students, she is embarrassed for them: "If they thought these reforms were essential, why the hell didn't they do something about it before the kids were driven to use paving stones?" Another of her stories, "A Painful Affair" (1981), has a flashback to May '68, when the learned protagonist, "pale trench coat over dark turtleneck", watches with "stoic gloom" as students burn copies of his "long-awaited autobiographical novel, *Sleeping on the Beach*". Mistaking him for Herbert Marcuse, they try to carry him to the office of *Le Figaro* so he can set it on fire. When I asked Gallant about the role the nation's great thinkers played in '68, she burst out laughing, sounding incredibly young: "To be honest, I've never had much patience with French intellectuals". She hadn't come to Paris to hang out with the Left Bank crowd.

As the protests pick up pace, Gallant keeps kicking herself: "I used to think that the young in France were all little aged men. Oh!" For her, supporting the young is a natural extension of always being on the side of the underdog. At the height of the clashes, deploring the brutal treatment of the demonstrators, she stops to point out that the "police have been beating people up for years, without the romanticism of the barricades, and… if the Night of the Barricades had taken place in a working-class suburb like Saint-Denis we would have known no more about it". She then turns her attention to the police:

> They stood from noon until two o'clock in the morning without one scrap of food… and they watched the barricades going up, knowing they were going to have to demolish them and the kids behind them. At around two in the morning they were given the order to charge. They had been given clubs to hit with and tear bombs to throw. What were they supposed to do?

Total objectivity is impossible, even if you stick to bare facts, but that doesn't mean you shouldn't strive for it.

Who else needed standing up for? Immigrants had a rough time in Paris during (or indeed before and after) the unrest. If "*juifs allemands*" were in the news, other groups remained invisible — at least until people began looking for a scapegoat. "I have a queer feeling this is going to be blamed on foreigners — I mean the new proles, the Spanish and Portuguese," Gallant writes. "And, of course, the North Africans are good for everything." Soon she is told it's all the fault of some "*commandos d'étrangers et d'apatrides*", and a friend confirms her suspicion about growing xenophobia, adding that even the young, "except for supporting Cohn-Bendit… are worse than ever". Another demonstration gathers, this time chanting "*La France aux*

Français". So much for the "turning upside down and inside out of the French character".

Did her own status make Gallant more sensitive to the plight of outsiders? In one of the diary entries, she remembers an academic woman she met at a *manif*, who kept "speaking to me as if I were a plucky child recovering from brain fever in a Russian novel. Turned out she thought I was an Algerian, and that was her way of showing she wasn't racist". Gallant doesn't take the woman's condescension personally; even if she did, she wouldn't be putting herself on the same misery scale as the real underdog — the one without. She is angry on their behalf: "Brief flash of what it must be like on the receiving end of liberal kindness. The awful sugar. Lesson and warning." Still, that wouldn't stop her from speaking up for migrants, just as knowing how impossible it was to be objective wouldn't stop her from trying.

"No one seems to understand what I want. Furious. Hate all French." Such snaps are rare in *Notebooks*; if Gallant does want anything to come out of May '68, she doesn't dwell on it. When she asks people about their expectations, most say, "*Quelque chose de propre"*. "*Une merveilleuse abstraction?"* she ventures, but gets no reply. "I thought something was definitely going to happen," she told me in 2010. "I wanted to witness it, to be on the streets when it came. I wanted to see changes, whatever they might be; I had high hopes." Were they about Paris per se or about her idea of Paris? Was it ever possible for the two to merge?

By 1968, Gallant had been living in Paris for nearly two decades. She stayed there for another four and a half — the rest of her life — exploring *varieties of exile*, to borrow the title of her 1976 short story. Once an outsider, always an outsider; yet for all her attempts to keep a distance from the place, the better to understand it, she was perhaps too close to it to be fully on the outside. She didn't just want to witness changes: she wanted to be part of them. Some things (if not quite what she'd envisaged) did change in '68. The workers, criticised for drawing the line at economic demands, won a forty-three-hour week and a 7% salary rise. The immigrants kept their role as the troublesome Other. The intellectuals, too, remained where they'd always been. The students eventually grew into boring *soixante-huitards*. Gallant continued to write.

Could she have ever made Paris her own? What would it have taken: writing fiction in French; having a French family; finding more time for French intellectuals? She never did any of these things. But in May '68 she was at the centre of the action, enquiring, listening, watching, waiting, occasionally interfering. A woman she once met around town pointed to a group of students nearby, saying she was frightened of them. "Where my mind would have registered something like 'Students, intellectuals, readers of *Combat* and *Le Monde*'," Gallant writes, "*her* mind said to her, 'Dangerous, brutal, will hurt you'. I took her by the arm and we walked into the group, which, of course, took no notice of us." Perhaps that was the moment she knew she couldn't have her Paris and write it. The moment she had to choose between without and within.

Manna in Mid-Wilderness

Natalie Ferris

As dusk falls, the strip lighting intensifies. No notice, scuff-mark or glob of spittle is exempt from its scrutiny. This light, so sharply white, strikes the darkening windows, sending darting lines across the chequered panes. Every door I pass is closed, the length of my route blurring into the same faded green. Sound seems to shrink, voices drawing further and further from me and bouncing off the walls in dull thuds. Walking down these hallways, deserted at the close of the day, I'm no longer quite sure what I hoped to find. Searching online for images of this institution some days before my arrival, I was met with a stream of black and white photographs immortalising the chaos of its early years; the floors of classrooms awash with discarded pamphlets, the projection screens of lecture theatres slashed, the gardens strewn with glass, the class-rooms densely packed with chanting students. What could navigating these endless corridors possibly reveal, so many decades later? How could my aimless pacing bring me any closer to the writer who had taken hold of my waking hours? In the high exposure of this municipal light, any faint trace of the novelist who made Paris VIII her home for twenty years was bleached from view.

From 1968 to 1988, at the beginning of each academic year, her name, Christine Brooke-Rose, was typed into the

283

tabulated "Liste Alphabétique du Personnel Enseignant, Administratif de Service et Technique" of Université de Paris VIII, Vincennes. A register recording some of the most eminent thinkers in post-war philosophy and politics, her name shares squares with Hélène Cixous, Jean-François Lyotard, Michel Foucault and Jacques Derrida. She taught Anglophone literature at this newly created "experimental" institution on the outskirts of Paris, founded by Cixous and a number of her colleagues at the Institut d'anglais, most notably Bernard Cassen and Pierre Dommergues. The Paris riots in May 1968 had prompted, among other measures, the reappraisal and overhaul of higher education by Charles de Gaulle's new government. The creation of this *Centre universitaire expééimental* in Vincennes heralded a more interdisciplinary, informal and interactive approach to study, as observed across the Atlantic, in an effort to dispel further student insurrections. Strangely, and unlike her colleagues, Brooke-Rose's date of birth is often omitted from these tables, a solitary blank space issuing from her name as if she had sprung from thin air. She thought of Paris as a place of renewal, rejuvenation, even rebirth, offering her the chance of a "second career, a second life". It was deliverance — "manna from Heaven" extended as an invitation to her by Cixous — from a life in London that no longer made sense. Arriving by second-hand car bought with a publisher's advance, she briefly resided in Rue de Picpus before moving to a flat on Rue Saint Victor, in the Latin Quarter. This flat would be her home for most of her twenty-year tenure.

It is difficult to imagine Brooke-Rose at home. I am not alone in this — other correspondents longed to see her in her "milieu".[1] The rooms and routines of the domestic rarely feature in her novels of the 1960s onwards, concentrating instead on transitory spaces of migration, evolution, or theoretical discourse. It is a window at 9 Rue Saint Victor, with its brittle frames and shifting veiled curtains, from which she stares at the beginning of a BBC *Bookmark* programme. The film does not lay her home bare, but stages her in a classroom she rarely occupied and on a walk she rarely took along the Seine. As she later lamented, the British press often presented her as a caricature of the *nouvelle romancière*, all YSL scarves, slender cigarettes and scholarly severity. There is a sense, however, that she cultivated a personal sense of spectacle in Paris: in her correspondence, she mentions the "scarlet" walls of her "marvellously arranged" flat, as well as the tall luminous column by sculptor Susan Glyn that took up residence in her front room in 1974. I am particularly fascinated by this sculpture, a large "seagreen" and blue column of circles, chains and spirals made to Brooke-Rose's exacting specifications. The opportunity to ask Cixous about Brooke-Rose's private space, during a brief visit to her home close to the Paris Catacombs, was derailed by the insistent vomiting of her cat. In the previous months, Cixous had recalled Brooke-Rose's detachment, particularly from the establishment of the Centre d'Études Féminines founded by Cixous in 1974. As the latter made clear, "Christine did not come for women... I was trying in every way possible to open ways for women, and she didn't want to take part in that". They "drifted apart" as a result of these

1   Mary de Rachewiltz, letter to Christine Brooke-Rose, dated
      26 March 1973, Box 19, folder 1, Christine Brooke-Rose
      papers, HRC

"different investments"; Brooke-Rose's in the "semantic and rhetorical aspect of things" whereas Cixous's allegiance was also driven by the "human aspect of things". For her, an engagement with what was "experimental... Robbe-Grillet for example," was not enough.[2]

Brooke-Rose is now widely acknowledged as one of the foremost emissaries of the "experimental" movement in France, writing some of the earliest and most accessible critical essays in English on the *nouveau roman* and penning amusing dispatches for her "Letters from Paris" series in *The Spectator*. Although the majority of these pieces were sympathetic to the kinds of work undertaken by writers in Paris and made pleas for a diligent British readership, some of them betrayed a creeping exasperation with the impermanence of 1970s Parisian culture. In 1973, she described life in France as a kind of tidal existence that could only reap a few glimmering bagatelles:

> [It is] [...] rather like walking around a national exhibition, entering one fantastic and beautiful structure after another, the Levi-Strauss Palace, the Derrida Daedalus, the Lacan Labyrinth, the Kristeva Construct, the Barthes Pavilion, the Planetarium showing the Sollers System. They are very impressive, but there is a temporary feeling about them, not so much in the sense that they may disappear altogether but because the pavilions are apt to look quite different when visited at different times: another wing has been

---

2 Hélène Cixous, Interview with the Author, 15 March 2013, Paris.

added, a fancy bridge or a strange *trompe l'oeil*. And the walk can be very tiring. There is the perpetual *recyclage*, as re-training is called, the getting-acquainted with yet another theory, yet another structure, until one wants to cry out "All systems go", and find oneself on the moon, which is of course very scientific, but lunatic; very beautiful, with unearthly colours, but what does one bring back? A bag of stones and moondust for the analysers.[3]

When Brooke-Rose recollects her first semesters at Vincennes, she speaks of "bewilderment", of "endless meetings [...] astonishing rudeness [...] blind fanaticism" and of a culture of convolution: "everyone having to speak, in several points *premièrement deuxièmement troisièmement* and subpoints a, b, c, d and long subordinate clauses and sudden *d'autre part* and *par ailleurs* whenever the end seems in sight, so nothing is ever concluded".[4] This uncertain climate — in which strings of interrelated code, theories, beliefs, analogues of meaning, "items" that crossed and meshed to build her own "vast powerhouse of knowledge" — produced her most ambitious novel, *Thru* (1975).[5]

Exiting into the chill December air, into one of the many concrete forecourts, I find some small suggestion that Université de Paris VIII is still attuned to one of its own. Language covers almost every inch of these smooth exterior

---

3 Christine Brooke-Rose, "Viewpoint", *Times Literary Supplement*, 3717 (1 June 1973), p. 614.

4 Christine Brooke-Rose, *Remake* (Manchester: Carcanet, 1996), p. 166.

5 Brooke-Rose, *Remake*, p.106.

walls, inflated to human scale or scrawled in empty corners. Names, entreaties, expletives and tags mix and merge to form a constellation of letters and symbols, "Sonibel", "J'amaaaa", "5000", "Texas", "Demandez", "1968". The riot of graffiti across every façade is evidence of the lasting spirit of those radical years, in which language itself began to disintegrate. For Brooke-Rose, the power of recall resides in the acts of "intercepting and decrypting", in perceiving the "thousands of messages missed, or captured but not decrypted, and even the captured and decrypted now burnt or not released". After Brooke-Rose left Paris, she seldom returned, sequestered in her stone village in the south of France. Paris persisted only in the "variable geometry" of her memory.

Central Committee

Owen Hatherley

On my first visit to Paris, in my early thirties, I didn't have high hopes. I had avoided the city for some time, and walking through places like the Marais, I was reminded why. The things I had been warned about — architectural and social homogeneity, self-satisfaction, wearying historical preservation — practically radiated off the limestone. Having grumpily found what I had expected, I was just about ready to return to the vital pile-up of South London, when I went for a walk in Paris's north-east.

The hills in Belleville and Ménilmontant were as full of street life, weird buildings, social housing and odd vistas as anywhere in inner London, although somewhat more architecturally coherent. Further north were genuinely bizarre things like the housing complexes of the Orgues de Flandre or the beige streets suddenly pockmarked with organic concrete outgrowths. Further on, at Place Colonel Fabien, was the headquarters of the Communist Party of France (PCF), designed in the 1970s by Oscar Niemeyer — a sinuous, gleaming building of concrete and glass.

Coming from a country where the Communists were at best a mildly eccentric fringe party with a presence only in a few pit villages in South Wales and Central Scotland and for a time in enclaves of London's East End, such a building is always going to be a surprise. So too, is how it contrasts with the French capital's achingly bourgeois self-image. What is it doing here?

The Communist Party's administrations in suburban Paris built most of the *banlieues*, the (now notoriously racially segregated) modernist *grands ensembles* that, here in the east end, begin already before you reach the *Périphérique*. Nowadays, they're better known for having been one of the most cravenly Stalinist of European Communist Parties, with dissident Marxists like the Situationists or the *enragés* of 1968 far better known and respected, and with their old base often as not voting for the Front National (or Rassemblement National, as it is now called). Once, however, they were a force in French politics, given enormous moral authority by their dominance of the Resistance, and they came first in the polls on more than one occasion. This building would see them finally building that authority into something permanent — finally, a built monument to the political tradition behind the Commune, the Popular Front, the Maquis, and so forth. Commissioning the Brazilian exile and CP member Niemeyer, the creator of the new capital of Brasilia, as architect, was a sign that this was intended to be a monument to the future, not to a glorious past.

If you visit it now, you'll find a surprisingly welcoming place — if you get past the security infrastructure, visitors are encouraged, and merch is sold. Pass a high fence and walk across a concrete bridge over an artificial landscape of mounds, and you get to an opening under a curved curtain wall of glass, housing the Party's offices. Inside, you're in a futuristic cave, a coven for fomenting world revolution. On most days, they'll let you in to see the grand hall that contains the Central Committee, a breathtaking dome that suggests interplanetary Communism has already been reached. You're thousands and thousands of miles in orbit, and well above the Sacré-Coeur.

Quite soon after the building was finished, in 1979, the PCF, scuppered by a shift leftwards by the Socialist Party and the general decline of working-class politics, began its slow, still ongoing diminution. It is as if in order to build this extraordinary monument to French Communism, it had to die in the process.

No Baudelaires in Babylon

Tom Bradley

Remarks Presented to 3:AM Magazine*'s*
International Conference on Electronic Literature,
Held in the Paris Sorbonne at Millennium's Turn,
When "the New Medium" Still Seemed to Hold Promise

E-literati, might we dignify
our *kaffeeklatsch* within a bottle's toss
of yonder bosky *flâneur*'s boulevard,
named for a dragon-stabbing stalwart? There,
some eight-times-four *annìs domìni* gone,
our betters, moral and political,
engaged *gendarmerie* with bones and blood
while chanting hatred of technocracy,
as foisted by the university
now hosting our chit-chat of net and web.

No one among us bleeds; interesting times
aren't everyone's life-lot; Hell's only raised
to that slim *bolgia* history allows.
But time-holes countersunken in the mind
can draw the consciousness further afield
than single thirds of latter centuries.
If yours admits spelunking, let's return

to classically antique days, when this town,
"Lutetia" on milestones, in extent
was but a mini-Patmos on the stream
whose eponym's a Gallic water goddess.

You play the pagan; I'll feign Jewishness.
We'll wander through a chilled *Aprilis* night
with elbows linked, on torchlit cobblestones,
where one big-buttressed fane's destined to loom
one thousand and a hundred twelvemonths hence....

Waiting For Nothing to Happen[1]

Andrew Gallix

It is a testament to the loving preservation of the French capital that a guidebook, published in 1968, should still be fit for purpose. The quaint period detail (snacks "for five or six bob") must not distract us from the enduring brilliance of *Nairn's Paris*, republished by Notting Hill Editions with an introduction by Andrew Hussey. The author's descriptions — crystalline, lapidary — are still in a league of their own. Rue du Faubourg Saint-Martin? "Simple really; just a straight street with something solid at either end and a firework in the middle". La Trinité's façade, he observes, breaks out "into cupolas and groups of statuary on the least provocation". From the side, Porte Saint-Martin really does resemble "a slice of highly vermiculated slab-cake". The buttoned-up naughtiness of Pigalle is, perhaps more than ever, "like a matron of forty-five unhooking her corsets with a simper or two". Conversely, Goujon's nymphs, with their "[f]ull breasts and infolded thighs" do indeed "suggest devotion beyond the line of public sculpture".

Ian Nairn was a celebrity during his short lifetime. He found instant fame, at the age of twenty-five, by launching a high-profile campaign against the blandness of what

---

1   This is a revised version of "A Zen Guide to Paris" which appeared in the *New European*, 27 July-2 August 2017, pp. 38-40.

he called "Subtopia". He soon became one the country's foremost architectural critics, writing a string of essays and books, including his masterpiece, *Nairn's London* (1966). He also produced several travel series for the BBC. Driven by his demons, he drove a Morris Minor convertible around the country, resulting in a very British take on the road trip format. He eventually drank himself to death in 1983, aged just fifty-two.

One of the reasons why Nairn's works were out of print for so long is — as Owen Hatherley pithily puts it — that he was "too modernist for the preservationists, too much a preservationist for the modernists". His travel writing is impressionistic, guided by his "uncommitted eyes"; energised by what moved him, what he "enjoyed". Scourge of "gratuitous notice-boards", he railed "at the way people try to put words all over the landscape". *Nairn's Paris* could thus be seen, in part, as an act of erasure. The city's romance is arrived at adventitiously, like the serendipitous poetry of Métro station names: "What administrator could invent a poetic conjunction as rich as Sèvres-Babylone?" His guidebook is "an invitation not to argument but to discovery". Yet, for all his vision of an uncharted Paris, cut adrift from cliché and dogma, some passages remain resolutely and endearingly English. Apropos of a department store, he writes: "An incautious step will put the male visitor in a landscape which looks as though it is panties as far as the eye can see. The same situation could occur, doubtless, in Selfridge's or Barker's, but it wouldn't feel the same".

Nairn's relationship with the French capital began rather inauspiciously. On his first visit he suffered from a mild case of Paris syndrome — the (then undiagnosed) malady said to afflict some tourists when the City of Light fails to live up to their expectations. Of all the "world-famous attractions", only the Palais Garnier, Louvre Colonnade and Eiffel Tower passed muster. He cleaves to this heretical view in the guidebook, describing Notre-Dame as "one of the most pessimistic buildings in the world". Several entries — including such crowd-pleasers as the Sacré-Coeur — are cordoned off within sanitary square brackets, making it perfectly plain that these landmarks did not appeal to the author, although it would have been remiss of him not to cover them. Nairn's Paris — for that, after all, is the title of the book — is a "collective masterpiece", not "a place for individual wonders". It may be glimpsed at in the interstitial spaces when "travelling from one piece of architecture to another". Paris is what happens, unseen, *in between* the sights, unless you (like him) have the "ability to turn off the main road" in pursuit of a "topographical hunch".

Nairn cuts a rum figure of a Virgil, providing tourists with a supremely serviceable Baedeker while encouraging them to lose themselves in the city, like part-time Baudelairean *flâneurs*. Going off-piste, however, is easier said than done. In a passage reminiscent of Walter Benjamin, he describes an archway, on Rue des Ecoles, "embroidered with posters, inches thick". The name of French Communist Party leader Maurice Thorez — who had died four years earlier — "still peers through", along with far older "Art Nouveau fragments". Nairn muses, dreamily, that "something by Toulouse-Lautrec" may even have been preserved under all the layers. Paris, in other words, is a palimpsest; its cityscape always already written. No wonder, then, that the travel writer should long for a blank slate, or, failing that, one that resists easy decipherment. Something akin to the restaurant menu boards he was so fond of, "written up daily in near-illegible purple ink", or the "inscrutable lettering" adorning bus stops (designed, presumably, to delight and wrong-foot the unseasoned passenger in equal measure). His is not the Paris we will always have, but the one we never will; a city for ever in the process of becoming, like the "magnificent compositions" greengrocers conjure up out of fruit and veg: "a daily, renewable work of art, as valid," Nairn argues, "as any of the creations that come out of art schools".

Defamiliarising Paris — rendering it "near-illegible" — is no mean feat, given the "unthinking respects" successive generations have paid to the city's "acknowledged sights". The author recognises, with heavy heart, that Place Vendôme's reputation is "impregnable", however much scorn he may pour on the "swishest part" of this "swish city". Instead, he limns the liminal; points visitors towards less canonical climes, wondering, for instance, why Ménilmontant's "genuine poetry" remains largely unsung, compared with "over-praised and grossly over-painted" Saint Germain-des-Prés.

More radically, Nairn goes in search of Paris's *genius loci*, which, owing to the city's "homogenous" and "monolithic" nature, is not rooted in any specific locale. "Specific buildings and specific views" are the "least part" of l'Île-Saint-Louis, he declares, "as they are of Paris as a whole". Promoting the joys of the river Seine, he reaffirms this notion of a moveable feast: "The actual place is unimportant: there will always be a view of something.

What counts is water, the gleaming stone kerbs, the angle of a tree, the look of someone else's upturned feet, their view of your own, the perspective of buildings on the other side". Likewise, the author's elegant black-and-white photographs tend to focus on the aura of a site in lieu of the site itself. The Jardin des Tuileries, for instance, is adumbrated by a couple of empty chairs facing each other, like a Ionesco play on a budget.

Nairn has a penchant for undistinguished locations, where "there is almost nothing to look at in the usual sense'; where space spaces out and place can *take place*. In an entry not included in the present edition, he praises Quevauvillers' features, "all lying around waiting for nothing to happen". Nothing happened with a vengeance, when he and his wife, high on hiatus, spent a "very wet day" near a suburban station "*not* going to the Air Museum": "In London it would have been a misery; in Paris it became The Day the Rain Came, luminous and isolated". Numinous too. There is a Zen-like quality to these mini epiphanies — these lulls in the topographer's relentless perambulations — which signals a fleeting sense of arrival: "the moment you give up and relax, the city will accept you. All you have to do is put your arse on a café seat, park bench, or low wall, and look".

Transmuting the infra-ordinary into the extraordinary is Paris's party trick, hence the "magic-city" sobriquet. It is "a memorable experience," Nairn enthuses, "to have banality transform itself into ideal as you sit and look, hear, smell, and taste — the whole city is urging you to greater depth of feeling, the opposite effect of a Birmingham". The humdrum is magicked, by dint of "atmosphere", into the everyday sublime; a transformative experience that leaves visitors feeling "more alive": "You and the city, together, have built an event which is neither personal nor impersonal". Once tuned into, Paris achieves a flow state, where everything is "plugged in" while remaining a "vehicle for the expression of millions of disparate desires". This version of the French capital is resolutely "on the side of life" unlike many of the fusty, musty national monuments — "desexed"and "stone-cold dead" — which Nairn inveighs against. It provides "pure urban freedom"; a framework within which "life can take what shape it likes", allowing "full space for your private world". It is perhaps best exemplified by the Tuileries, where I am writing this, sipping a cheeky rosé: "These are enchanted groves for world-citizens, where each gesture has its own weight and space: absolute, unimpeded by any outside influence: assessed by its own nature and no other — whether it is a kiss or a system of philosophy. [...] Not bad for a thick copse and some gravel; but that's Paris". I think we can all drink to that.

Donut

Will Ashon

1. I don't know much about Paris. I felt like I did, but I was kidding myself.

2. In truth, I don't know much about anything. When I'm feeling bullish about this I wonder why our children are made to sit in school sports halls to be examined on knowledge briefly learnt and soon forgotten when they can look it all up on the Internet. When I'm feeling less bullish I have to admit that, personally, I'm nowhere near young enough to be a digital native, that my phone is not an outboard brain, and that my ignorance is much deeper, much more complete and perfect, than any other part of my personality.

3. But even allowing for my general ignorance, I don't know much about Paris.

4. I've been to Paris. I've been to Paris a number of times. School trips, summer holidays with parents, visiting friends from university, staying with friends of friends, work trips, visits for important parental birthdays, trips with children. I have driven and been driven — in cars and on coaches — travelled by ferry and train, hitchhiked,

flown, and taken the Eurostar, a carriage of which my son decorated with vomit. In the future I will go on weekend breaks to fill the gaping hole created by my children leaving home, weekend breaks to escape from the crush of my children returning to live at home, trips for anniversaries and birthdays too monumental to imagine just yet, trips to visit old friends I've not sat down with and talked to in twenty or thirty or, eventually, forty years, trips with grandchildren, and finally a pilgrimage to visit one last time, unsteady and with shaking hands, my favourite sites from all the other trips.

5.   One of the only things I "know" (by which I mean "have read") about Paris is that by placing all its poor people in the suburbs (*banlieues*) beyond the city's limits, it has hollowed itself out and become a theme park, a Disneyland of beauty and culture, a palimpsest of a living city. What I'm saying is, Paris is a donut. Or rather, Paris is the donut's hole. Living in London, this used to make me feel superior, until I realised that, by different means, the same thing was happening here.

6.   I also know (by which I mean I've read) that Paris used to be the centre of the art world, but that New York took over. And that there was some connection — mainly involving the cost of living — between points 6 and 5. Artists, it is commonly held, like affordable, preferably semi-derelict, real estate.

7.   Which is to say, you can't be an artist in Paris, anymore, or in London either. And if you think you can, you're not

really an artist at all — have never written a manifesto in blood, or run naked in the snow with a belly full of absinthe, or shot someone or yourself or, in general, caused revulsion and outrage amongst the bourgeoisie.

8. Neither can you be an artist inside my head, which, now I come to think of it, has more than I would like to admit in common with Paris. It is the hole in the middle of a donut and all the interesting stuff involving poverty and world cuisine and semi-derelict real estate is going on around it. All the knowledge is certainly going on around it. It is peripheral to me. I am maybe also peripheral to it, but that's less important right now.

9. Not only does that make my head a theme park, a Disneyland of beauty and culture, but it makes me a tourist in it, too, visiting only on important anniversaries, going always to the same café for the same disappointing coffee, drunk always with half an eye on posterity, on the people who sat here before. By which I mean mainly my younger, prettier, more idealistic — and in retrospect, idealised — self.

10. Although, of course, the architecture of my mind is less impressive, and the stories to be told about my mind less colourful, and no one else — no one, not one — travels here on pilgrimage. My streets are empty and hence both ersatz and perfectly preserved.

What Was His Name?

John Holten

I miss my pre-internet brain, but that doesn't help anything. We can only go forward.
— Douglas Coupland

1.

What was his name? Something beginning with S, Samed? Said? He had North African heritage, his father may have been Algerian or Tunisian. So much is lost in the passing of time, and back then — when I was just out of university and once more in Paris to be a language assistant — time seemed slow and I was listless, although looking back, over a decade later, it was anything but empty. Time was full, but that doesn't sound right: things just happened even though boredom crowded in and threatened everything. That's why I became friends with this guy, S, who was training to be a pilot. We met in a bar down the hill from the Panthéon, whose internet I was using as I looked desperately for a flat. It must have been late September and — for whatever reason lost to those winds of time so destructive to the preservation of the impulses which create human will — he started a conversation with me, probably because he wanted to improve his English (of course we never spoke French) or maybe because he was heartbroken and recently single and loneliness and boredom threatened him in a way that made him want to have fun or in any case not sit at home but travel into Paris from wherever it was in the suburbs he lived, driving his parents' car to reach the quiet, boring streets of the Latin Quarter, and we exchanged numbers, and I can't remember what we talked about in that initial meeting, or indeed much about any of our conversations, that is the point, I can't remember anything about what happened the rest of that night, not where I slept even, homeless as I was at the time. So much is lost to memories that only fade because they were never important in the first place.

I realise I can go through my Facebook friends and find this guy, I'm pretty certain that when I joined Facebook, around six months after this meeting, I reckon, we became *Facebook friends*. Indeed, he could have been one of my first friends on the network. But I won't, not for now.

Darkness shadows everything, the edges are bathed in it, because as I recall the next time I heard from him I had found a place, and this would make it October. He probably texted me and suggested we should meet up, and I agreed, bored as I was sitting at home in this, my new home. I was probably happy that someone reached out to me at all, that I had a friend in the city.

We met somewhere along Rue des Écoles, I cannot remember exactly what the meeting point was, but I remember he picked me up in a car and I found this odd, as I had few friends in my life then, like now, who drove cars, especially in the city. And we went for beers. That's mostly what I remember we did. That's all we ever did in fact: sometimes in bars, those tacky bars around the Latin Quarter that were dull and anachronistic in a weird 1980s way, or increasingly we would drink bottles or cans of Kronenbourg bought in an *alimentation générale* on Rue Saint-Jacques and sit on the steps (were they steps or just the kerb?) at the Panthéon, and this felt good as this had been my neighbourhood when I first lived in Paris a couple of years earlier, a student down the hill, an occupant of the embarrassingly named Rue des Irlandais at the former Irish College for Catholic Priests (it's not every day you get to have sex in a building in which you know the Pope had also once dreamed... the same Pope that would die not long after these events).

I cannot recall how many nights we met up, I guess it must have been a good handful: we'd meet, get some beers, drinking either on the street or in his car, then maybe head to a bar ostensibly to look for women to talk to and fulfil the separate dreams we both harboured but surely never fully articulated. The exact details we talked about I have no clue: he slowly revealed that he had lost a girlfriend and still loved her or at least missed her or at least pined for her in that stubborn male way of not having what he thought he still wanted yet was perfectly powerless to regain. Once, we drove to the Right Bank and made a foray north of the city and he showed me her house, or maybe it was the house they had shared, up near Montmartre, on the edge of the city's famous hill, what feels like its only hill, and I remember a switchback street lined with a thick laurel hedgerow (which seems improbable in the city but Paris is like that, it's full of rebus material at every turn — as are memories of Paris, they are the greatest dreams of all) and this hedgerow was lit yellow from the lights of his car (and the make of his car? No idea, though I do believe it was silver, a saloon car, and we smoked in it) and this night-time pilgrimage ultimately made for a depressing and sad trip.

I'm pretty certain that on the way back we drove down another very oneiric road (which makes it a very Parisian road) but whose name I cannot immediately recall and, resisting the urge to look it up on the internet, comes shrouded with the outlines of activity in that city, in the dark of night: buying Kronenbourg beer and mustard-flavoured crisps in a Monoprix en route to some party or other; reading about it in some work of literary criticism as an example of *getting the details wrong* (because we all know that fiction is built upon the ability to deploy *correct* though innocuous details to monstrous ends) and how a writer had the protagonist of his thriller escape the clutches of the gendarmes by driving down its one-way street the *wrong way* which — the observation could be a translator's or Paul Auster's or Douglas Kennedy's, the latter being one of those writers bizarrely so loved by the French if nobody else — proved the point that one must know the city, must observe the details, must transmute the world of knowable facts otherwise we're lost in the world of dreams and bullshit, much like these half-reminiscences of S, a faceless Frenchman I once befriended and haven't thought about properly for many, many years, who indeed I didn't much think about even when I was in his company. I bought a box of condoms from a vending machine — now this is civilisation — some months later, in the middle of the night, along the same street whose name I'll shortly look up on the internet. In my mind this street is always bathed in the green-tinged, art-nouveau-framed dark shadows of night; it is depopulated and the scene to the above useless memories: it is a Parisian street, a boulevard. And who cares, who gives a toss what it is called? What this particular street in Paris means to me and this piece of writing is the half-thought-through maxim: making an art of everyday life is the aspirational art of living in Paris, everything else is tourism and good literature is not comprised solely of tourism.

I know that I'd get lost looking at a map of Paris, I would spend minutes if not hours scrolling over it, peering into its streets that are half-formed in my mind, half-formed because the memory of them was never really there, they were never known even when I traipsed along the very same streets in the middle of the night for hours at a time. When I first decided I needed to go and live there, to overreach the tourism of the literature I loved, when I was a teenager, I would spend time reading novels, all those tourist novels from a hundred years previous, and then mark out the routes of characters on some old family atlas: Rue du Faubourg-du-Temple, Place de la Contrescarpe, Rue de la Montagne-Sainte-Geneviève, Clichy. I read Aragon's *Le Paysan de Paris* before I had ever stepped foot in the place (and before I could properly read): the streets were never going to exist as the mundane streets that real city streets must condition themselves to be, they have function and are functionless at once, everything else, to put a weight on one or the other is to be a soldier or a tourist, two extreme ends along a destructive continuum. The only thing that destroys an old city is the erasure of memory, ergo history will be the destroyer of Paris.

Trying to think about what else I got up to with this guy, this perfectly nice Frenchman who wore clean, light blue jeans and whitewashed runners, who had a tight head of black hair, a trim set of locks... I cannot think of anything at all. That was it, a random set of nights of two people with little in common hanging out because both are young and both are at a loose end, though loose in very different ways, one recently single or heartbroken, the other excited by the city and all that the city had recently promised them. They are young, and open to the world. He was going to be a pilot, and I know from years after, via Facebook, that he did become a pilot.

Later, things happened, time passed: October moved into November and then December came around, invariably I met other people and eventually life took me away from Paris because I found Paris boring.

2.

Now I turn to the internet: I'm going to beat the algorithm and go through all my thousands of connections manually in order to find this distant memory. After an hour of scrolling through these friends, I cannot find him. There is a good chance that I have missed him — a kind of blindness kicks in when you start to go through ten years of Facebook friends. Scrolling through the collection of people I have gathered on this part of the internet, it occurs to me how random, and also how predictable, it is — the defining antinomy of our online lives perhaps. Perhaps he has left Facebook. Or one of us unfriended the other.

The passing of time makes remembering harder, that is an obvious and banal thing to say and yet it also makes it that much more of an imperative. Nobody warns you about that when you're young, just like they don't warn you about many things like how time itself and its passing speeds up or that loneliness never gets any easier. Paris is not the place to be when you're young and poor.

I just looked up the name of the street and the thought comes to me: people die crossing the Boulevard de Sébastopol in the middle of the day. How many exactly, throughout the course of history, is a fact, but it is also anyone's guess.

The Irish Genius

Gerry Feehily

Myers flicked his Marlboro away and walked to the entrance of the Hôtel de Crillon, Place de la Concorde. Two porters stood on both sides of the revolving doors to this august five star residence. *Bonsoir Monsieur!* they cried, snapping to attention, their tone somewhat jocular. Both wore green swallowtail coats, green top hats and white kid gloves as in some terrible alcoholic dream of being chased down alleys by little goblin men.

Bonsoir, said Myers, himself in a vintage tweed overcoat, of uncommon yellow and red weave.

J'ai un rendez vous, he said, his throat tight.

Just ask at the reception, they said as one, in English, their eyes wet with glee.

Myers shoved his way through the revolving doors into the lobby. White and black tile floor, columns, a vast marble reception desk. A group of Brazilians, in baggy jogging pants and t-shirts, ogled the frescoes on the ceiling thirty feet up. On a white sofa, a Chinese couple with two gangling teenage boys sat slumped, surrounded by bags from the swishest fashion designers that Paris had to offer the world. All gazed into their mobile phones, the white light of the future glowing on faces gone bloodless from a day at the boutiques of Avenue Montaigne. All was lofty, all was hushed, long velvet curtains, delicate gold leaf patterns running down pillars, receptionists in tight black suits and Human League quiffs. And somewhere, did Myers not hear the putter of water, and a hand gliding along a harp?

A bellboy came to enquire.

Je cherche le bar, said Myers, kneading the bunched up tissues and Métro tickets in his coat pockets.

Mais bien sûr, Monsieur! said the bellboy, chuckling, and directed him to the lift, pressed the silver button for him. As he did this he sniffed the air a second, looked Myers up and down, and then mutely doffed his hat as the lift door hissed open. Myers sniffed the air too, catching a smell of something. It wasn't a hotel smell. It wasn't his deodorant, but something else.

His sister Aisling sat engulfed in a giant velvet armchair in the bar looking for all the world like the actress she'd dreamed of becoming as a child. A PR consultant to one of the world's largest humanitarian organisations, she had that air of being someone, a name on the tip of one's tongue, the sort of woman you see in airport lounges, going round the Earth, a universal *gringa* at the heart of conflict zones. Hair pulled back into a ponytail, wearing a white dress of ancient Greek inspiration, she was on her way to Venice, but had decided on a stopover in Paris.

Something very special had happened in her life, she'd explained over the phone. She wanted him to meet her fiancé, Hamilton.

I want him to meet my older brother, who lives in Paris, she'd said.

She stood up, they kissed.

Yuck, cigarettes, she said.

Myers' future brother-in-law, Hamilton, was sitting on the sofa opposite her.

Oh hallo Gus, he said.

So here was the multi-millionaire his parents had been raving about — Hamilton, and that was his first name. An Englander for sure, goggly blue eyes, shoulder length limp blond hair, long teeth. Rolling in money, and yet wearing a white hoodie, yellow jeans and scuffed tennis shoes. He had one of those particularly thin English mouths, Myers noted, reminiscent of cruel captains of the eighteenth century whipping the peasants with an ash stick. He got up off the sofa, deploying himself to his full six foot six and they shook hands.

Come and have some champagne, he said.

Well! said Myers.

As he took off his coat, spread it on the back of a giant armchair, he caught that smell again. It was certainly not deodorant. It had something of an attic to it, and also something of a cellar, underground and skyborne, earth and dust. He couldn't put his finger on it.

Incredible hotel, he said.

Hamilton handed him a glass.

I've been hearing so much about you, he said. Travelling the world, and now living in Paris, writing a novel!

I'd like to hear so much more about you, Hamilton, said Myers.

Really? I don't like talking about myself! he said.

He gave Aisling a look and they both laughed.

Well, how did you guys meet? said Myers.

Ah, said Hamilton, putting his champagne flute down on the glass table and giving the bottle of Dom Perignon in an ice bucket a twist. I met your sister at this forum in Los Angeles for Iranian dissidents, and I thought she was Iranian she was so bloody exotic looking and so I started chatting her up, didn't I?

And both he and Aisling started to laugh.

And how's the humanitarian work going, Aisling? asked Myers.

Oh, a bit of this, a bit of that, she said.

Particularly that! said Hamilton, pointing at her champagne flute. On which note, let's refill, he added.

They all clinked glasses, looking out at the view, at the bone grey façades of the inner courtyard, the exquisite iron balconies, with the tip of the Eiffel Tower blinking over it all.

Bloody great view, said Hamilton.

Yes, said Myers.

We were up at Sacré-Coeur this afternoon, said Hamilton. All kinds of knobbly winding streets and peaky roofed houses. You'd half expect to meet a wild haired genius on every corner, spouting poetry into a mirror, wouldn't you!

Yes, you would, said Myers.

But we didn't, did we? That's why we came to Paris, isn't it. But now you're here, thank God, an actual writer.

And here you are too, Hamilton, an actual tech entrepreneur.

There are more important things in life! said Hamilton.

What's that smell in here? said Aisling, looking around.

Oh yes, said Hamilton. Thought I got a whiff of something.

Myers drained his glass and set it down.

That smell, I'm afraid, is my coat, he said.

They went to the rooftop to the hotel restaurant. As guests at the Crillon, Hamilton and Aisling did not need to divest. Myers gave his coat to the waiter, muttering about some accident with a cat. Please, Monsieur, there is no need to explain! said the waiter, holding it out with both hands as though the cat itself had died. They thumbed the menus at a table that gave on to the city below, the Eiffel Tower twinkling, blue searchlights on the tip of it spreading beams 360° over all the world. There were diners from all the continents here, speaking heatedly, the Brazilians, the Chinese family, an Arabian with three veiled wives sipping Cokes. One thing was sure. They were all having a great time.

Hamilton closed the menu. This place got a great write-up in the *Guardian*, he said.

Brilliant, said Myers.

And this is my treat, you can have anything you want.

Hey, that's very kind of you, said Myers.

We just saw Mum and Dad the other week, said Aisling.

I love your parents! They're such great people. Ireland!

While eating the starter, Aisling explained they were going to take the Orient Express to Venice and stay three nights at the Palazzo Gritti before flying out to New York for a script meeting.

Ah, said Myers.

Hamilton's been asked to help finance a film about child soldiers in Sierra Leone, said Aisling.

The script is utterly devastating, said Hamilton.

They plan to actually film it using real former child soldiers, his sister added.

That's really amazing, Hamilton, said Myers. So you're in film production now?

Not just, said Hamilton, looking to his future wife.

He's founded a water charity too, said Aisling. He's going to run a marathon in the Sahara to raise money for it. Digging wells in Africa.

Wow, said Myers.

And what about you, Gus? asked Hamilton.

Me? he said.

Have you heard anything from Irmgardt? said Aisling.

The waiter came over with their dishes, one in each hand, the third way halfway up his arm. The sommelier whisked behind them with the wine. The waiter said, This is the Barbary duck, with a purée of celery, a coulis of fruit of the forest. *Bon appétit!*

This looks very good, says Hamilton.

The sommelier sniffed the cork. This is a dark, rich Bordeaux, he said, with earth and cheese undertones. He poured the wine, which made a tock tock sound in the silence, sloshing about in the crystal glass, making the silence somewhat deeper.

We don't talk anymore, said Myers, taking his glass.

She was Gus' girlfriend, a German, said Aisling.

Oh, where from? said Hamilton.

East Berlin, said Myers.

Gus has always had clever tormented girlfriends.

Yes, just like me! laughed Hamilton. And your book, Gus, what's it about?

Ah, loads of things, said Myers.

About tormented East German girlfriends?

Myers drained his glass, put it down.

Right now, it's about the entrance to my apartment building, he said. There's this prostitute, who must be about seventy years old, who's got the code to the door, and pleasures her clients in there. In my entrance.

Oh dear.

And the thing is, she's a transvestite.

Incredible, said Hamilton. Still working at seventy. There must be a niche market for that!

Oscar Wilde talked about genius, continued Myers. He said genius was half male and half female. She wears this black dress, her face is painted white, but the make-up's cracked. There's something uncanny about her.

Is she a genius then? said Hamilton.

Do you know what I say, said Myers, when I come in the door, and there's a client taking her from behind, his pants down, usually an old geezer? I say *Bonsoir*, and she says *Bonsoir* back, or she says *Bonsoir* first because in this town you've still got to say Good day and Good evening whatever the situation and it's not ridiculous.

He hadn't noticed that the sommelier had shuffled up behind him.

Would you care for more wine, Monsieur? he said.

Thank you, said Myers.

Cool, and is there much of a plot to this novel? asked Hamilton.

No, I suppose there isn't a plot.

That must be interesting.

In the meantime I'm doing the usual stuff, said Myers, turning to his sister. Teaching and some translations.

Great, said Aisling.

Did you know that Les Dawson lived in Paris? said Hamilton.

Les Dawson? No I didn't, said Myers.

He came here as a young man and wrote a novel, a big experimental novel, in the style of James Joyce. But he couldn't find a publisher. So he went back to England and that's how he became a stand-up comedian.

What's the difference between roast beef and pea soup? said Aisling.

That's an amazing story, Hamilton, said Myers.

You can roast beef, said Aisling.

What? said Myers.

That was the punchline. The difference between roast beef and pea soup.

Ah, said Myers.

It was the first joke I ever understood as a child.

I remember that joke too.

Does anyone still read James Joyce? said Hamilton.

No, said Myers, and he explained how Joyce was overrated, how in fact that duo of Paris-based Irish writers, Joyce and Beckett, was just overrated. He had a word for it, Literachore. Literature that is a chore to read, he said.

I wonder whether Les Dawson's novel was a chore, said Hamilton.

With that five hundred million you earned selling your company you could probably buy it, said Myers, sniggering.

I'll buy your novel about transvestite geniuses too! said Hamilton.

They all laughed, in a certain way.

Hamilton paid the bill with a black credit card after his sister had spent about five minutes checking it out item by item.

Myers poured himself the rest of the red wine.

Hamilton said, Well, we're going to take a helicopter to see Paris by night.

Isn't that amazing? said Aisling.

Pity you can't come, said Hamilton. We only reserved for two. I should have thought about that.

Why? said Aisling. Weren't we supposed to have a romantic helicopter ride?

It'll be all spread out at our feet. The Eiffel Tower all twinkly. Gus might have liked that.

No, not at all! I live here, after all. And Paris is such a great place, said Myers, pounding Hamilton on the back.

Yes, it's great, said Hamilton.

They all stood up to go. Myers embraced his sister.

Sort out your coat, she whispered, as she slipped an envelope into his pocket.

He patted it. He was longing for a cigarette. Throughout the meal he'd broken out into a sweat of nicotine withdrawal.

In the lobby he waved to them as the doors to their lift closed.

They were gone.

Myers hadn't been out in the west of Paris for such a long time, perhaps five years. The west just wasn't his sort of place. Or that's what he tried to tell himself. It was actually lovely, though, but he didn't want to think about that. Not now.

The footman saluted him jovially as he walked out onto the Place de la Concorde, where Louis XVI had his head chopped off, like Robespierre, like Danton, in the name of a freer and more egalitarian society. But there were so many cars turning round the Place and heading towards the Champs Elysées that you couldn't get a sense of the historical import of the place, only its regal style.

Danton had said that the French Revolution wouldn't be complete until the last king was strangled with the guts of the last priest, but now neither priests nor kings had any influence on how society worked. It was people like Hamilton now. People like Myers were the children of this Revolution that had opened the world up forever, like the footmen too, but so was Hamilton. However, in stark contrast to his future brother-in-law, Myers had two revolving credits running and about fifty euros in the bank.

He found his bicycle where he'd left it, locked to a pole on the corner of Rivoli in front of WHSmith's. The books in the window had cheerful pastel drawings of young ponytailed women in jogging pants. There were also book covers with birthday cakes, and confetti, and takeout caffe latte cups. The author of a bestselling book about how French women kept their men in check with their devastating sexual technique was doing a signing there the next day.

Myers unlocked his bicycle. As he rode, he detected a clunking sound coming from the mudguard as if a car had clipped it going round the corner, or as if someone had kicked it.

Down Rue Saint-Honoré he rode past high-end clothes stores. Then he cut up Rue du Louvre and turned right onto Rue du 4 Septembre. By the time he'd got to Réaumur-Sébastopol, he passed as through a portal into another Paris, of North African tat stores and Chinese mobile phones shops, West African hairdressers, Turkish kebab joints. He rode up grimy Boulevard Sébastopol and switched into a lower gear to make it up Boulevard de

Magenta and onto Boulevard Barbès. Underneath the overhead Métro, North African lads were selling cartons of contraband Marlboros, bootlegged Rolexes. He locked his crocked bike in front of his building, and then crossed the street.

At the foot of the Sacré Coeur, he sat down. The city beneath, the Eiffel Tower lit up still. He wasn't on his own. There were hundreds of people there, from Asia, from North and South America, Africa, all watching the city with him and taking photographs. Humanity craves heights and vistas. Here was a great one, and it had to be said, the Eiffel Tower never let you down. It just looked so good, its feet, its curves, the way it went up in one mighty Yes into the Parisian night. Myers smoked one Marlboro after another.

A luminous white ball hovered up above the Tower, stopped then hovered around the structure, before fleeing east along the river. It looked like a fairy light. Within that fairy light, his sister sat with her future husband, Hamilton, the first multimillionaire he'd ever met, with his cruel English mouth. They'd be looking at the grand boulevards of the city, the gently curving Seine. They'd be seeing the dome of the Panthéon, the spires and towers of Notre-Dame from above, everywhere sparkling. The flight would inspire in them a meditative state, one of acceptance and quiet joy. They would look down on everything, full of a sense of benediction and think:

I understand.

Myers walked down the steps, then down the hill of Rue Custine to Boulevard Barbès. He punched the code into his building and in the entrance there she stood, her face painted white, scarlet lips, in her black dress.

She had her client, a young man, pressed against the door, his hands against the wall, head down, trousers puddled around his sneakers.

Bonsoir Monsieur! she said, thrusting, panting, her eyes gleaming.

Myers took his hands off the entrance light.

Bonsoir, he said.

Et bonne nuit aussi! said the client, through clenched teeth.

Trying to ignore their groans of joy, he climbed the stairs, up to the fifth, under the roof, unlocked the door. A pair of cockroaches on their nocturnal promenade about-turned and scuttled to the corners of the room. Myers sat down on his bed. He was definitely going to do something about the coat. It was difficult to work out what it stank of though, but rather than name its notes and tones like some sort of expensive wine, it smelled of a quality — neglect.

Thanks to his sister though, he now had a bit of money, a magic dust that when sprinkled improved the mood. He'd take the coat to the dry cleaners tomorrow, and things would come right in the end. Sure, there were debts unpaid, phone calls from the landlord unreturned, disappointed girlfriends, novels — like the one he'd talked about — begun in a fervour that later broke apart like Boeings going down, first engine one, then engine three, but surely one day, and that day would be soon, it would all come right.

Paris Syndrome

Dylan Trigg

Why move… when one can travel so magnificently in
a chair?
— J.K. Huysmans, *À Rebours*

The American and Japanese tourists who descend upon
Montmartre's Place du Tertre do so with astute foresight.
They know that amongst the dense cluster of cultural and
artistic heritage, surrounded on one side by the dizzying
view of Paris from the crest of the Sacré-Cœur, and on the
other by a series of cascading vineyards — that amongst
all this, there exists a beacon of familiarity in an otherwise
intoxicating world: Starbucks.

Looking at it now, it is hard to imagine that when it
originally opened in 2013 in one of Paris's most iconic
neighbourhoods, that the prospect of a Starbucks in
Montmartre would be met with dismay. Back then, critics
anticipated that the introduction of Starbucks would
undermine the ineffable soul of Parisian life so carefully
constructed from the time of Hemingway and Picasso up
until Woody Allen's incisive portrayal of everyday life as
told through the eyes of Hollywood's elite. History has
not been kind to the critics. Tastefully blending into the
surrounding region, the Starbucks at Montmartre's Place
du Tertre has become a home for tourists who, having

exhausted themselves with the grey homogeneity of the Parisian landscape, now seek sanctuary amid interchangeable furnishings and anodyne coffee.

And they are shrewd to have made this move. For them, this is not one Starbucks among many, but instead a site where memories will be forged and dreams fulfilled. In the nostalgia that lies ahead, their recollections will draw back to those carefree afternoons, which in their languid rhythm mirror the days of Rimbaud and Verlaine, but are now augmented — perhaps even improved — with the introduction of an Iced Caramel Macchiato. The tourists who have taken up residence in Starbucks at Montmartre's Place du Tertre have done so, not with a view of effacing the soul of Paris, but precisely in order to preserve the city's *genius loci*. Theirs is a Paris that is best viewed from behind the veneer of artifice, and for this reason, theirs is a Paris that is more Parisian than the city itself.

The American and Japanese tourists who descend upon Montmartre's Place du Tertre know the dangers that lie just beyond Starbucks. Looking out from the peak of the Sacré-Cœur, they will be greeted with a cityscape, as vast as it is iconic. But in the romantic alleys and imposing boulevards there grows a quiet anxiety. Many of the tourists who have arrived in the city have found themselves strangely depressed. The excitement that often accompanies their walk from the anonymous hotel to the Place du Tertre is offset by a lugubrious atmosphere, which is beginning to infect Starbucks itself. At the coffee counters overlooking the venerated square, a young Japanese couple sit with their heads in their palms, their expression of grief visible through the cracks in their fingers while their skinny lattes sit untouched.

Some of the Japanese tourists had apparently taken a wrong turn one morning and discovered a dimension of Paris that they weren't expecting. Emerging from the picturesque squares populating Saint-Georges, it seems as though they strayed too far to the east before ending up on Boulevard Barbès. Overwhelmed by the maddening panoply of sights and smells, a small section of the Japanese tourists entered what can only be called a fugue-like state. For about ten minutes, they lost sight not only of their surroundings but also of their own identities. When they emerged from their slumbers, they were in Clignancourt at the back of Montmartre. Were it not for the sight of the Sacré-Cœur high on the hill, there would have been no small danger that the group would have strayed towards the *Périphérique*, at which point contact would have been lost with the group indefinitely. Of those that did return, several had to be escorted to the Japanese Embassy for counsel.

Might it be that the American and Japanese tourists who seek home at the Starbucks on Montmartre's Place du Tertre have discovered a truth about Paris that the locals themselves are oblivious to — namely, that the city is best viewed through the prism of artifice? The Japanese tourists prone to Paris Syndrome — a term given to tourists who are ill-prepared for an experience of Paris that dissents from their dreams — merely exemplify the need to frame the romance of Paris through the lens of a simulation. The severity of their symptoms and the long-term damage caused by their breakdowns attest to the urgent need to map out carefully delineated pathways that ensure this simulation of Paris is never disrupted, much less erased.

Siren Orgasms: Leftovers From an Unfinished Novel

Fernando Sdrigotti

Siren Orgasms. One more novel set in Paris. But from the title onwards this one is different.

The name refers to a cocktail once served in a nightclub in Ibiza. The connection between sirens and Paris might seem wanton but in the opening paragraph, Alex — the main character — is woken up by the sound of a police car rushing past. *Siren Orgasms* starts with this very Parisian music: the coincidence of sign (siren) and sound (siren) is too obvious to miss. Alex wakes up longing for a beach, recalling in his lethargy the sound of orgasms coming from the ocean. This clash of spaces is unexpected. There are many allegorical possibilities here. This is the kind of thing good books are made of. It's also the kind of thing that makes an unfinished manuscript.

*

Room 29. A hotel at the top of the steps between Rue Lamarck and Rue Caulaincourt, where else if not in Montmartre.

Alex arrived some days ago. Although he seems to be on some journey — in between places — he hasn't left the hotel and will spend a lot of time in his room. There'll be a lot of watching TV shows he can't understand. There'll be page after page of being in a room he doesn't want to leave [CONFLICT UNSPECIFIED]. There'll be moments when the telephone rings and Alex doesn't answer; there'll be moments when he calls an international number and hangs up. There'll be references to a book he's reading — Dostoevsky's *The Gambler* and Alexei Ivanovich in Paris who has no idea what he'll do with his life. Perhaps that's what keeps Alex indoors: maybe he needs to figure out what's going on and what will go on. So he doesn't leave for pages on end and thinks a lot without thinking anything but then he does leave, and heads to a café on the corner.

He orders a *café au lait* and sits down and looks at the photos in *Le Monde*. From the images it seems someone has attempted to kill Chirac in Paris during the Bastille Day parade (which locates the novel in 2002). And from behind the bar, two twins — barmaids, not mermaids — stare at him. There's also a guy operating the espresso machine and he stares at Alex too — the guy moves his arms a lot, he has to be Italian. The Italian guy makes some comment in French to the twins and the twins laugh — the situation is awkward. But just when Alex is about to leave, a middle-aged woman with a poodle walks in and sits at the table opposite him. She looks like Delphine Seyrig in *Baisers volés* and she's elegant and her toenails are nicely done and her feet wave at Alex from behind a pair of high-heel sandals. Then the dog starts fucking the table leg and then it pisses on the floor and the woman leaves, cursing the dog in French. Delphine Seyrig won't return to the bar or the novel, which feels like a missed opportunity.

So Alex goes back to the hotel, masturbates and ejaculates in a sock. Whereupon he recalls the dream, and tries to imagine how sirens might orgasm. Has anyone ever survived hearing a siren climax?

*

Soon Alex starts to acknowledge the existence of other people, beyond their role as props. He meets two Canadian women in the hotel, filmmakers. They're working on the script for a film called *Diary of a Dead Dog*, probably unfinished, like this novel. With the Canadians [DESCRIBE — DON'T FORGET THE BIRKENSTOCKS] Alex spends some hours drinking warm white wine on the esplanade of the Sacré-Coeur. The Canadians are having a great time. But the wine gets Alex in one of his moods. Or maybe he had expected something else, ending up instead hanging out with film students surrounded by tourists — and everybody knows how much students and tourists suck in novels. So he offers a vague excuse and walks away on his own in search of the real Paris [HIS MOTIVATION NEEDS TO BE CLEARER]. On his way back to the hotel, he stops in a tiny café (Café de la Butte) on Rue Caulaincourt. There are old photos on the walls and two or three old punters who look his way. A waitress, old too, comes to serve him and he orders a bottle of wine pointing at the menu with his index finger. The waitress asks something in French and he thinks she must be asking if he wants the whole bottle. Yes he wants the whole bottle — *oui, oui*.

On the telly, a talk show. Alex can't understand a word but it keeps him entertained. He drinks and watches, oblivious to what everyone else in the café finds so funny — *héhéhé, hihihi, hohoho*. It goes on for a while. A lot of effort has clearly been expended on the presenter's hair. And then the telephone rings and the waitress mutes the television and has a heated argument over this or that with whoever called — *je te dis que c'est un trou du cul*. This juxtaposition of French and English is a nice touch, even if it doesn't add much to the story per se. In any event, Alex soon finishes his bottle of wine, stumbles out of the café and into room 29, just around the corner.

Back in the hotel room he'll dream about the sirens once more [DON'T OVERDO THIS].

*

The next day, hungover and forlorn, perhaps anticipating the rather precarious state of the rest of this manuscript, Alex takes the Métro to Père Lachaise, visits some of the dead buried there, in a passage made up mostly of notes [TO BE WRITTEN LATER — PENDING RESEARCH] and then he ends up walking all the way to République [FIND RATIONALE FOR THIS]. Perhaps he needs to be out and about in Paris, looking for those random encounters so many have already written so much about. Yes, it must be that, and at some stage in his peregrinations he stops in another café and orders a beer pointing at the word *bière* on the menu — *une bière s'il vous plaît*, he even says, feeling that he is beginning to master the basics of the French language. The waitress happens to be from Spain — she's called Neva — and they end up chatting in Spanish. When Neva spots his accent, we realise that Alex is Argentinean:

a perfect opportunity to recycle some stereotypes about Argentine men and Spanish women. Then Neva gets him drunk and refuses to charge him. And Alex stays in the bar for several hours, thinking that he should buy a Rhodia and start writing [HE WOULDN'T KNOW WHAT A RHODIA IS, WOULD HE?]. When the bar starts to get busy — this being Friday night — they arrange to meet the following day. Neva jots down her address on a napkin because that's what people do in 2002. And they'll meet tomorrow around 1pm for lunch in her flat, Rue Saint-Maur, near Belleville.

That night he dreams of Neva — Neva is a siren.

*

Alex wakes up early. He has a quick shower and gets the Métro to Assemblée Nationale [WHY?] and then walks by the Seine, on the Left Bank [WHY?]. On some indeterminate *quai* he sits by the river, watching the water for a while [WHY?]. A *clocharde* approaches him, starts chatting him up in French. Alex excuses himself saying, *je ne comprends pas*. The *clocharde* keeps on monologuing anyway, going over something Alex misses but that the reader may be able to get, depending on their level of French, or their inclination to do some translation work [THIS WILL BE THE KEY TO THE NOVEL]. Alex then walks away, and bumps into a police boat by the Pont Neuf. Divers are trying to fish something out of the water. Alex thinks it may be a suicide [INSERT PASSING REFERENCE TO *L'INCONNUE DE LA SEINE*] and he walks away from the scene as quickly as possible. Maybe that was what the *clocharde* was trying to tell him [THIS PART SOUNDS NICKED FROM *HOPSCOTCH*].

At this point the novel starts floundering. Too many mental monologues and narrative lines that go nowhere. Alex is supposed to be meeting Neva for lunch and there's all this disjointed bollocks. And there's even a badly executed involuntary memory scene about his dead grandmother, the aim of which must have been to insert a reference to how the city affects people; how it might trigger different memories and moods [RESEARCH PSYCHOGEOGRAPHY]. This may also explain Alex's dark thoughts at the time [DOESN'T WORK]. It could also simply be some half-baked attempt to fill a few pages with nice, evocative images of Paris.

Eventually he gets to Neva's and they smoke weed and drink wine and click and have a great conversation [TO BE WRITTEN LATER — RESEARCH WOMEN]. And then Alex finds himself infatuated, walking with her around town [TO BE WRITTEN LATER — RESEARCH PARIS] in scenes that several years later will be deemed too corny to even consider thanks to that awful film starring Ethan Hawke and Julie Delpy.

Soon, out of nowhere, the unexpected climax of the novel: Alex tells Neva that he'll leave the following day. He'll be moving to London: Paris was always meant to be a place in between places; a stepping stone in whatever Alex's journey is about. This occurs down in the Lamarck-Caulaincourt Métro station, just as Neva is about to board her train and after they've arranged to call each other the next day. [WHY DOES HE WAIT UNTIL THEN TO TELL HER? MAKES NO SENSE]. What we do know, however, is that Neva's response is *quelle merde*. And with these words she kisses him. The train arrives. She gets on the train. She leaves without looking back. And Alex is left there [INSERT MOTIVATION FOR EXISTENTIAL CRISIS] and the next thing we know Alex removes his shoes, throws them in a bin in [NAME OF THAT SQUARE ON RUE LAMARCK], and walks all the way back to the hotel barefoot [EXISTENTIAL CRISIS SHOULD EXPLAIN THIS].

Siren Orgasms ends with Alex in his room, getting his bags ready. There's another police car rushing past: the sirens — circularity. And then it starts raining. Alex approaches the window and he can't see anything but some trees and a fragment of sky. The next morning he'll move to London and I'll shelve the novel with other literary failures.

And the rest is all fiction.

The Arraignment of Paris

Stuart Walton

The nervous energy of disappointment is a constitutive factor in the Anglophone experience of Paris. It is at least as important to the British, for example, that Paris should fall short of what they expect of it as it is to the Parisians that *les Anglais* have never really understood it. If Paris was the capital of the nineteenth century for Walter Benjamin, and then the frenetic vanguard of the cultural world in the 1920s — when Britain was reverting to insipid realism in the visual arts and turning to American musicals and Noël Coward on the London stage — the Paris that has since emerged is of the white baguette and the insolent waiter variety: the atrocious pop, the substanceless cinema and a culture that swallows its own pretensions, from couture to an insularly defined gastronomy, whole. The British are never disappointed in their disappointment with the City of Light. The disappointment is *tout compris*. In itself, however, it speaks of a cultural ideal to which the concept of the foreign ought to live up, even though Paris has always offered itself as home to every romantic and untethered soul, as well as those broken by alienated experience. Jean Rhys's heroine, Sasha Jansen, in *Good Morning, Midnight* (1939) has returned to a Paris that once nurtured her freedom and that now dramatises her rootlessness, an environment attuned to both liberty and desperation as occasion commands. Its shabby hotel rooms, the gloom of an empty cinema in the afternoon, cognac-and-sodas in dispiriting cafés where the bathroom mirrors are for sobbing in as much as fixing one's make-up: the whole city forms a stage-set on which the reality of crashed hopes can become as intermittently unreal as the speech and behaviour of its actors.

Every pilgrim to Paris from the citadels of Nordic asceticism has longed to find in it the libertinage with which, in the late eighteenth century, France scandalised Europe, by investing it simultaneously in sexual affairs and politics. The same destructive energies unleashed in the orgies of de Sade motivate the continual lopping of heads on the Place de la Révolution. Even the July Days of 1830, which did little more than see off the last of the Bourbon kings, are imaged by Delacroix in the figure of Liberty, her breasts exposed, trampling forward over the corpses of the fallen. If beauty, as André Breton insisted, should be convulsive or not be at all, the desire it provokes should be hotly rapacious to be worthy of the name. Thus does Monsieur Swann whip himself into a squall of jealous misery at Odette's absence in the capital, for "as he told himself, now and then, to allow so pretty a woman to go out by herself in Paris was just as rash as to leave a case filled with jewels in the middle of the street". And yet gap-year students alighting from the Eurostar are doomed to find only an arid *politesse* where they yearn for initiatory carnal adventures, not least because Paris obstinately does not these days give herself to those who are not already acquainted with her.

The curious air of lifeless desertion that descends over the city in the August *canicule* is interpreted by foreign tourists to themselves in accordance with the myth that the provincial French all dislike Paris too. Its harsh *froideur* is an affront to the hospitable Gallic instinct, they assure each other, even if what provokes it is more likely the brash assumptions that the tourist makes. Sprawling in crowds around the pavement café tables, chattering at an abrasive volume, displaying their enjoyment of their own drunkenness, demanding changes to the menu items when they do decide to eat, and assuming that nobody in Paris can understand the English imprecations they utter when the menu items cannot be changed, are all guaranteed to elicit the superior mien of neighbouring patrons and staff alike. Cultured shuddering at the uncultured is as uncultured as lack of culture itself in all cultures, but it is this demeanour that is seen as having been raised to an exquisite proficiency by the Parisian, who looks with mingled pity and scorn on the braying hordes. If the perduring English cultural temperament is a rumbustious pleasure in living, its French counterpart is seen as glacial contempt, the aridity of an over-bureaucratised polity, notwithstanding the fact that Victorian England invented the chilly reserve in social manners for which the British have been noted ever since, while pleasure in living went by its proper name, *joie de vivre*, across the Channel.

Above all, what the Anglo-Saxon temperament hopes to find in Paris is the apotheosis of high culture, of a culture it is sportingly willing to admit he lacks, for a weekend at least, in the encounter with its essence. It was the genius of Paris that it provided a home for both the deification of culture and its overthrow in the century just gone, when the iconoclasms of the avant-gardes after 1918 provoked concert audiences and gallery habitués to foaming dyspepsia, in the self-same locale where the classical ballet and the tragedies of Racine still set the benchmark. In the present day, what iconoclasm there is has nothing to say to society at large, but is enacted purely internally, against itself. The manifest absurdities of the fashion industry, one of capitalism's shameless oxymorons, and the over-conceptualized somersaults of contemporary cuisine, which have resorted to the language of the inorganic and the inedible in order, as they say in the glossies, to "push the boundaries", even while tourists on the Boulevard Saint-Michel are served the same raggy bavettes and clotted sauces with which they have always been sated, speak an unintelligible language. Only in the Salle des États, where Napoleon III once presided over the legislative sessions of the Second Empire, and where *La Gioconda* now skulks behind her protective wooden barriers and screens of bulletproof glass, does culture still feel like culture, an inert object of the transfixed gazing of the masses, to whom she remains as immune as when Marcel Duchamp drew a waxed moustache on her.

If they are lucky, a moment of transcendence on a drizzly day out in the city from the ruthlessly administered magic at Disneyland Paris may break upon the visitors. The cheap glass of Bordeaux *rouge* that turns out to be unexpectedly delicious; a *coupe* of praline ice-cream at Berthillon; the frankly returned glance from somebody beautiful on the cobbles of Montmartre; sunlight washing through the stained windows of the Sainte-Chapelle; the dazzle of the evening scene from the open deck of a *bateau-mouche* gliding sedately along the Seine: such moments arrive like tokens of dreams half-remembered on waking, already fading under the impress of rationality, but bearing witness to what one hoped the surprising world would be before it surrendered to the principle of order. If Paris is otherwise disappointing, it is because it already bears the image of what the entire first world is turning into — a mausoleum of disordered hopes.

Stalingrad

Will Wiles

It was dawn. We had just stepped off a sleeper train at Nord, and were walking the tree-lined nineteenth-century avenues, searching for our hotel. I had never visited before, but it all seemed so familiar, so like my mental picture of Paris: the radial streets, the cobbles underfoot, the plane trees, the tall stone-faced mansion blocks with their mansard attics. Yes, this was the place. This was Bucharest.

Paris is a uniquely memetic city. The City of Light might be unmistakably distinctive, but its distinctiveness has been paradoxically easy for other cities to emulate. It is an idea that can be reproduced, and indeed has been across France, and across the world. Paris — specifically the Paris of Georges-Eugène Haussmann, prefect of the Seine Department under Napoleon III — accidentally created for itself a kind of off-the-shelf urban-design operating system. It is the Microsoft Windows of cities, and any up-and-coming nineteenth-century city that wanted to appear grand, established and modern could install and run it. And they did, from Bucharest to Buenos Aires.

The Paris system had two main features: the 1859 building code, which standardised the appearance of the city's physical fabric and streetscape, and the carving of new, straight boulevards through the irregular mesh of the medieval city. (It's significant that Haussmanization does not only reject the organic layout — it also comprehensively rejects the grid, which in urban planning terms is at least as ancient.) Neither of these principles was at all new; they are familiar precepts of baroque city planning, with antecedents that are even more ancient. In fact, the wide, tree-lined boulevards aren't even originally urban: they began as the shady *allées* and avenues of formal parkland, and were a routine feature of European suburban improvement long before Haussmann started grinding them through the city centre, and he was hardly the first to lay out a new street or two. The accidental genius of Haussmannization in Paris was that it did not reside in a single scheme. Other cities had laid out their Regent Streets and Unter den Lindens. What Paris created was a system, a method, which reproduced itself across the existing fabric of the city.

Today, when cities in the Far East lay out neighbourhoods designed in conscious emulation of Paris or English towns, English broadsheets like to portray them as helplessly gauche and tacky. But cities are fundamentally imitative enterprises, forever copy–pasting parts of each other into their own composition. Urban distinctiveness is a kaleidoscopic, mirrored image, and its every fragment reflects somewhere else.

The Sunday-supplement snark is cranked out in a city that has its own generous slices of Parisian pastiche. Kingsway in Holborn was laid out at the turn of the century as a deliberate ape of the Champs Elysées, with a dash of Beaux-Arts New York thrown in — one of its proposed names was Connecticut Avenue. Just off Kingsway is the even more bizarre Sicilian Avenue, RJ Worley's stab at Naples on a postcard scale, with an oneiric inattention to the source. Is it the two-thirds-scale Eiffel Towers in Shanghai and Shenzhen that makes their Parisian districts just a little too on-the-nose? We almost had one of those as well, at Wembley, but the developers ran out of money with only the first stage complete. (London even has a pissoir, on Horseferry Road.)

There is another kind of direct reference that cities make to each other, and Paris is home to perhaps the most vivid example of it: Stalingrad. I can't remember the first time I saw Stalingrad. The important thing to note is that I didn't see-see it at all; I wasn't there. I saw the name, on a map, either one of the little ticket-sized folding maps RATP gives out, or mounted on a wall. And I think I might have laughed, because it caused what could only be called a surge of non-association. If psychogeography is the exploration of a place through the literature and memories it brings to mind, this was something like the opposite, and all the purer for it: a rush of meaningless half-learned fragments, ignorance nested in ignorance. Sebald inverted. What to do, as a callow teen, but laugh?

To recap: I was in an unfamiliar city looking at a place on a map with a jarringly un-Parisian name. Stalingrad the Paris Métro station was a place I had never been, and I knew for certain I would not be going to; it was named after a place that I had never been, and would not be going to. Furthermore, it was named after a place I would never be able to visit, because it no longer existed: the Russian city of Stalingrad became Volgograd in 1961. Strictly speaking, it is not named after the place but the 1942–43 siege and battle, during which the Soviets withstood, and then encircled and destroyed, a vast concentration of Nazi armies. Even more strictly speaking, the Métro station was not named after the place or the battle but after the place named after the battle, Place de Stalingrad. Just to clarify the distinction between city and battle, the square was renamed Place de la Bataille-de-Stalingrad a couple of decades ago. However the Métro remains plain old Stalingrad.

This was all very satisfying. There was a pleasingly blunt Gallic courtesy in recognising one of the principal scenes of the Allies' victory in the Second World War, even if France had not directly participated in the battle. Despite our recent mania for new war memorials, this recognition is comprehensively lacking in the UK, where remembrance remains a selective, provincial and amnesiac business. But what I remember about encountering the name is how unevocative I found it. I didn't know what Stalingrad (the Soviet City) looked like. I'm afraid my assumptions were crass, based in (not uncommon) prejudices about Soviet cities and, indeed, French suburbs. Grim, right? Tower blocks and that.

My ignorance wasn't total: I had seen, at school, *The World at War*, but of course that mostly shows the city in ruins and, like skeletons, ruined cities are rarely distinctive. In their own era, anyway: the ruined cities of the Second World War are generally unlike the ruined cities of today because of the preponderance of the concrete frame over brick. Pre-1960, urban ruinscapes had a rained-on, melted look, like the stubs of candles, and subsequently they have a more layered appearance, like pastry.

In any case, it was not the urban landscape that the name brought to mind. It was something else, something almost visceral: the distinct human reflex of peripeteia, the appreciation of a reversal of fortune. Stalingrad wasn't the first time the Nazis had been stopped — they had already failed in their efforts to capture Leningrad and Moscow — but at Stalingrad they were not just stopped, they were crushed. Operation Uranus, a devastating pincer movement by the Red Army, turned the Wehrmacht column besieging Stalingrad into a besieged pocket, and doomed it. That was what was so satisfying about the word: the image of it, the gesture, the pincer closing, hacking off the outstretched tentacle.

Beneath the strategic abstractions the human horror involved was vast, so it is best not to succumb to outright pleasure, but we can allow ourselves a restrained degree of gratification from reflecting on Stalingrad as the place where Nazism began to get what it deserved. A name worth remembering for that, even if the city name honoured a monster and even though the memory comes cut with a shudder at the cost.

When I first saw the name, in the early 1990s, Stalingrad was necessarily mysterious — we were just passing through Nord. It was a blob on the map, the intersection of three lines. Today, that kind of mystery is permanently diminished by the digital panopticon. Google Street View — so helpful to research, so ruinous to the dream cities of the imagination — reveals a pleasant pedestrian square and boulevard with an elevated railway running down its middle, a bit of Robida-esque Third Republic heavy technology. It's all distinctly normal, although it could only really be Paris, or somewhere like it.

Paris Perdu

Tom McCarthy

They all do it: highbrow, lowbrow, avant-garde, retrograde, all of them. What do they do? Create a Paris, a "Paris", a glorious Paris, city for the ages, that's been utterly and irrevocably lost. For Marker in *La Jetée* it's been nuked; for Humph and Ingrid in *Casablanca* it's been mothballed inside memory; for Debord in *In Girum Imus Nocte* it's been buried beneath capitalism; for Burroughs ("Paris Please Stay the Same": the essay's title is rhetorical, functioning negatively, i.e. to signal that is hasn't stayed the same) it disappeared with open pick-up urinals and over-the-counter codeine. The "real" Paris, the authentic one, the one before all this alienation, all this fakeness, all this shit.

But what if this were structural? What if the nostalgia were constitutive, built into the experience of ~~being~~ (that is, of failing to "be" authentically) in Paris in the first place? One of the city's greatest twentieth-century exports, Claude Lévi-Strauss, pacing the streets of Lahore in the Fifties, all festooned with electric cables, senses that he's come fifty years too late to see the real Lahore; then, with a sense of *déja-vu*, recognises the same feeling when he's staying among the Amazonian Nambikwara — although, having read the account of the anthropologist who *was* here fifty years ago, before the rubber-traders and the telegraph, and knowing that this man expressed the exact same feeling, and knowing that the anthropologist who'll come in fifty years from now will wish he'd come when *he*, Lévi-Strauss, was here, that is, now, then, whenever... leads him to a revelation: that the "purity" we crave is nothing more than a condition in which the frames requisite for analysis and interpretation are missing; once these are in place — and putting them in place is, after all, the anthropologist's (and writer's) task, their *raison d'être* — then *pouf!* The mystique that drew him to his subject in the first place vaporises.

He gets it. Lahore, the Amazon, the Arctic — it's Paris. Paris is whatever is lost, and whatever is lost is Paris. That makes Georges Perec's 1974 account of the Paris experience the only accurate one. It's accurate precisely because it understands its own irremediable inauthenticity; understands that inauthenticity can be the only proper mode of being/not being in Paris. In *Tentative d'épuisement d'un lieu parisien* Perec sits for three days in a café, looking at the city passing by his window, noting down what he sees. And what he sees, this being Paris, is largely made up of other people looking. There are even hordes of Japanese tourists snapping photos out of special Kodak coaches that themselves are built like cameras, giant lenses. On Day Two, Perec is overwhelmed by a sense of nostalgia — not for "Paris", but for his time in the same café yesterday: *Curiosité inassouvie (ce que je suis venu chercher, le souvenir qui flotte dans ce café)...* He gets it too: there's no ur-madeleine; it's memory of madeleine all the way down.

The square he sits in is Place Saint-Sulpice. Beneath it there is (was then and still is now) an underground car park. *Sous les pavés, le parking.* I, too, recall (*Je me souviens...*)

a *parking* in Paris. I think it was underneath the Boulevard Saint-Germain or Saint-Michel, near a café where famous writers, Sartre and de Beauvoir or some people like that, once used to meet. It had a luminescent poured-tar floor; its yellow bay-lines glistened wetly, even though they were quite dry. Arriving there, stepping out of the car at level -2 or -3, I'm not sure how long I spent standing there admiring it. In real time it can't have been more than a few minutes, while my friend went and got a display-ticket, locked the car, whatever. Real time was up above, though. Down here, artificial birdsong, playing out on a loop, created its own temporality, a duration that, freed from all clocks, oozed and accreted like the tar. The whole ambience was perfectly synthetic, synthesised; in fact, it brought about a synthesis in the Hegelian sense — an absolute suspension of the city, its simultaneous abstraction *and* solidification in the gorgeous geometry of lots, arrows and tar, of singing without origin or end. It was without question the most beautiful place I have ever known in Paris, or perhaps anywhere. I'm not sure if I could find it again, though. I'm not sure it even still exists. They've probably turned it into a fucking library or something.

a mnemopolis, a necropole !

Andrew Robert Hodgson

On the *terrasse* of the Café de la Mairie there Sulpice adjacent I sat and watched the 87, the 96, the 63 pass, and stop, and pass and wondered if he'd taken a taxi. The waiter came, and stopped, and went and I wondered if I'd ordered anything. Watched the chuff of buses offloading. Through four ply of glass panes and intervening space a small boy chasing an older woman chasing a grey dog chasing greyer pigeons, I suppose blue, almost. In contrast, the pigeons. Who ensemble rounded the fountain in the middle there once or twice. Dispersing, somewhat, knocked the photographer's cue over on the church steps where two ranks of friends and family had stood suited, booted, white dressed (faux pas, y'know), and themselves now missed the "Fromage!" moment, and dispersed to do a lap or two of the fountain along the photographer, the dog, the older lady, the small boy and the pigeons there themselves. Before, "You are late, Monsieur !" and Jean Mimi (*dit* Jean-Martin Philippe, and presented with the further elongated short-ening of Jean Mimi Fifi had resolved himself to the briefer hypocoristicon. Saw that as something of a win, I think. He did) and Jean Mimi closed whatever he was failing to read, folded into his lap reveals it to be a bound book or other, and squinted up at myself as I crossed the road towards him there on the *terrasse* of the Café de la Mairie,

345

the quarrel of mammals and birds and photographers all off over my shoulder, through a bus or two, and I realised I was misremembering.

Or projecting as I sort of fell up the stairs of Saint-Sulpice sortie, the Métro, as opposed to the church there. And, operating on "And so, I'll meet you at the Perec café" had, that morning woken a little late, a little, and flicked through *Tentative* (1975), and found three such cafés from which Georges had *voyeured* the buses, and the church, and the old ladies, and so opted for the first, the Saint-Sulpice (tabac). Which I deduced to be in my near corner, furthest from the group there throwing plastic rose petals at a couple on the steps, and found non-existent. And so, well, I thought Mimi will have cigarettes, and I suppose he won't be much interested in a pair of leather chaps what with the heat of early summer (the season in which we here are), thus further deducing that he was not in this *maroquinerie* bygone tabac. I left to wait to cross the road there where the 87, the 96, the 63 stopped and passed, the latter of which parked across the zebra crossing. And so I had to round the back, and dodge through the taxis jostling to line up underneath a large white P painted onto a blue square. Breeching at a pole topped by a weathered plastic diamond that once was orange, still reading "TAXI". Sort of, clambered between the shifting bumpers and onto the place itself where a ring of benches round a fountain that's off when I've been here before, but on today, and I wonder if they chemical the water. As it's a sort of aquamarine, like, a pool, or the sea in Greece "As seen on Instagram". When someone's high key trying to sell me a holiday, or dietary supplements, or yoga classes or whatever. And I wonder this, not all that keyed, but low, to myself, as a small boy keepy-upping by the bike racks misses a knee, a foot, the last-ditch elbow, and the ball comes bouncing over to the blue pool and well. Well, this water is pristine. Or, perhaps, so chemicalled the ball itself would just fizz and melt away. I prefer not to take any chances, and for the greater good, kind of half lunge out a foot, though not removing my hands from my coat pockets (where, NB, they have been all this time), so as not to show too much effort endured if I miss the thing, y'know? And, in all my glory, manage a half shin into a pile of brooding pigeons on the other side of the place and sort of. Well, how are you supposed to come back from that. Shout, "fetch!" Like a joke, that's a terrible joke. Are the pigeons the dog in this scenario? The boy? Various shrieks and jeering erupt from far behind my shoulder as I quickly turn to find the second café, La Fontaine Saint-Sulpice (café), and resolve to never ever think about it ever again.

I approach the corner there, with Saint-Sulpice (church) to my left, and a wedding party lining up in two ranks on the steps, and stop to read the tail end of a Rimbaud poem painted by the Mairie (municipal body) across a wall leading out from the place towards the Rue de Vaugirard and vaguely remember somebody telling me Arthur himself had wanked from the sixth-floor window of a hotel there roundabouts. But these are not the Mnemes we are here theming, and so turn away to the trees and benches of this south eastern corner of Saint-Sulpice (Place).

There I find a boutique hotel with no sign, and quickly run under the yellow and white striped canopy that hangs out from its front to avoid falling ephemera. Inside is brightly lit, mirrored walls, with deep curtains cutting off the light and growing noise outside on the Place. "Is this, was this the Fontaine Saint-Sulpice?" I ask. The girl on the desk flicks a wrist towards the curtains, "fountain over there, over. there!" And, "yes, yes, that's a fountain, is this a fountain too? A fountain (hôtel ([former] café))?" She didn't seem to hear the bracketed caveats, and "no, no, Monsieur, this is the essjayashell". I wasn't all too sure what that was, but it didn't sound all too much like a hotel, or café, or even a fountain, and so I slowly backed away in silence hoping my slow movements would render me invisible to the functions of her eye, and successfully escaped from the corridor of gleaming mirrors through the blackout curtains and out into the day. Where a tramp laid across the floor by the trees, rather than on any one of the benches, and I asked whether there was a café here in this corner, and perhaps whether it might open today, I asked: "Do you know if there's a café here in this corner, and perhaps whether it might open today?" or ever. And he sort of shuffled about and grunted, like I was one in a long line of strange people stumbling into his living room asking if he was a café, if he knew someone called George. "You know, George Perrick?"

And this is mostly worn thin now, so I assert to find the very last of the three, the Café de la Mairie (café) where Jean Mimi and his cigarettes must surely be. I cross the Place by the intervening ground between the church steps and the fountain, where a kind of black-tie pile on appears to be taking place amongst the latter stages of a wedding party. All that Latin, y'know, in the church services here. Heady stuff, I reckon. An old lady clouts a small boy round the lug. A greyish dog chews a deflated football. A photographer fishes in the acid water for his camera.

At the road there is no crossing, and the 87, the 96, the 63 shunt through taxis lining up below the big P, behind the off-orange taxi pastille, and electric cars push Deliveroo riders onto the pavement to access the entry to the underground car park below the Place indicated by both the big P itself, and a smaller sign that reads "Saint-Sulpice (Pay Ah Err Ka Ee En Jay)". Snaking the traffic I make the far kerb more or less intact, where Jean Mimi lets the book he's not reading fall to his lap and greets me with "Monsieur, you are late!" And behind him I see a plaque in the green border blue background fashion of a street sign that reads "G ORG S P R C". Noticing I'm foreign, the waiter comes bustling with, "Welcome to the George Perrick café, sir! What will you have? A very milky coffee?" And I nod and sit, and Jean Mimi tilts the cover of his book out of the sun's glare so I can read that he's not reading Rimbaud, and I say, "I just saw a bit of the poem on the wall there, across the way". And he says, "Yes, it was around here or thereabouts he wanked out of the sixth-floor window of a hotel". And I say, "I swear down I've heard that somewhere before".

Ten Fragments of an Idea of Paris Already Imagined by You

Lee Rourke

1.

You were walking along Rue Saint-Antoine, near Saint-Paul with Maxine, your companion for the trip that year, looking at the people sitting outside the cafés, as they chatted, sipped, and ate. You pointed over to an old man, green scarf around his neck, sitting alone, glass of red wine, breaking small chunks of a baguette which he would dip into his wine before eating them. Look at him, you said, so Parisian, just sitting there, watching the world go by, dipping his bread into his wine. Do you mean him, she said, I've never seen anybody dip their bread like that before and I've lived here twenty-six years, what an odd thing to do. I just thought it looked French, you said.

2.

You remember standing at the bar in Bastille, but strangely you aren't sure of its name, although you remember everything else, especially the way everyone dressed in there: all swathed in black, nonchalantly talking, huddled over tables, the background music quiet, a mere whisper of something electronic and German, way before you started listening to things electronic and German. You asked for a pastis in your best broken French and the barman kept replying to you in French that was too fast, too slick for you, that made you feel awkward, repeating that he didn't understand what you were trying to say, so you spoke to him in English, and he answered in American — the accent of moneyed New York, you remember thinking.

3.

It's funny, sitting in a café in Paris reading a book: there's always the thought that one is playing a part; merely an actor on a very large stage. There's something not quite right about it, like it's been rehearsed, like you know your lines, as does the waiter, and those passing you by, chatting politely on the boulevard. You were reading Maurice Blanchot, translated into English, and seemed acutely aware of this, like it was some type of failure on your part, hypersensitive to each discerning glance you thought was directed your way.

4.

An unfamiliar city is a fine thing. That's the time and place when you can suppose that all people you meet are nice. It's dream time.
— Louis-Ferdinand Céline, *Journey to the End of the Night*

You think of outside your room, of the streets of the town, the lonely little squares over by the station, of those winter Saturdays all alike.
— Marguerite Duras, *The Malady of Death*

Who will wake up at the end of my dream?
— Jacques Roubaud, *The Form of a City Changes Faster, Alas, Than the Human Heart*

5.

You always preferred French novels. Thin and flimsy but full of ideas, the ones which postulate, proselytise, and show off. Two fingers up, you always thought, to those stuffy English readers, those you spoke to, witnessed reading on the bus, the fusty reviews in the newspapers, all of them afraid of that word that doesn't seem to make the French budge: intellectual. How they revel in it, you thought. You would sit in your own room imagining the streets of Paris alive with intellectual conversation, in that uncaring, fuck you kind of way you've always wished existed, those long-winded conversations about Proust with crazed taxi drivers trundling across the *arrondissements* in wild abandon you've always imagined happened.

6.

There's a chapter you like, or interpolation as Jacques Roubaud calls them, in his novel *The Great Fire of London* ("a story with interpolations and bifurcations") in which he discusses, in interpolation, the perfect croissant:

The ideal croissant (and this has to do, naturally, with the Parisian croissant, since in whatever town I've tried them provincial croissants have been a disaster), the croissant that might be labelled the *archetypal butter croissant*, presents the following features: a very elongated rhombus, rounded at the tips but with an almost straight body (only the *plain croissant*, and it alone, has a lunar, ottomanlike look) — golden — plump — not too well-done — nor too white or starchy — staining your fingers through the India paper that wraps or rather holds it together — still warm (from the oven it's only recently left: not yet cooled). [...] It has three principal components, and three interlocking meaty compartments protected by a tender shell that lends it certain similarities to a young lobster. The centre section is, in this croissant-lobster homomorphism, the body of the crustacean; the end parts are the pincerless claws. It's an extremely stylized lobster, a *formal lobster*, in short. For the croissant to be perfect, a simple tug on each "claw" should easily pull them apart from the "body", each trailing along an oblique, tapering excrescence of inner meat, subtracted from the centre, extracted, as it were, effortlessly from the still very warm innards of the croissant, without making crumbs, or any sound, or tearing. [...] Furthermore, among croissant eaters (croissants in general, plain as well as butter) there are two contending schools: the dry school and the wet school. As far as I'm concerned, I belong to the drier part of the wet school. This means: after having prepared a bowl of *café au lait* (I still hadn't given up milk), hot but not scalding, I dipped the croissant wing (the leg rather) (let's preserve a metaphoric consistency) that I'd pulled off [...] in such fashion that it becomes moist, saturated, softens, but without dissolving, *without coming undone*.

You, in homage to Jacques Roubaud, have always dipped your croissants into your coffee the same way (unlike your bread into wine), and you took great delight in doing so for the first time when visiting Les Deux Magots.

7.

The graffiti always struck you, especially in the outer arrondissements, there's just so much of it, like New York in the Eighties you thought, and because you've always had a soft spot for this form of writing you immediately felt at home, even though it was the first time you'd ever walked those particular streets. You thought of *M. Chat*, that cheery, slightly manic cat that appeared on buildings and rooftops all around the city, trying to find one but never succeeding, and then Chris Marker's docu-essay *The Case of the Grinning Cat*, a film (and filmmaker) you've always loved. You suddenly became acutely aware of this new form of protest, Paris and its revolutionary spirit, and just by walking and thinking this way, making these connections, you at once felt part of something, the socio-historico-political events that shaped this particular city. You may laugh, smirk and titter at this thought now, you find it hard to admit such things these days, but back then, walking through those streets, it was completely real.

8.

When Michel Houellebecq, in *Atomised* (a novel you both love and hate) said,

> people often say that the English are very cold fish, very reserved, that they have a way of looking at things — even tragedy — with a sense of irony. There's some truth in it; it's pretty stupid of them, though. Humour won't save you; it doesn't really do anything at all. You can look at life ironically for years, maybe decades; there are people who seem to go through most of their lives seeing the funny side, but in the end, life always breaks your heart. Doesn't matter how brave you are, how reserved, or how much you've developed a sense of humour, you still end up with your heart broken. That's when you stop laughing. In the end there's just the cold, the silence and the loneliness. In the end, there's only death.

You understood immediately that Paris would break your heart in the same way, and you laughed at yourself for being such a stupid Englishman, in love with something that doesn't exist, in love with the idea of something invented by people who've had their hearts broken in exactly the same way, and this wasn't an ironic laugh, nor metaphorical, it was guttural, you felt it deep within, and at once you realised the importance of your own inauthenticity.

9.

There was a time when the idea of a French partner excited you, Parisian being the ideal, the idea being that you could glean something of their very *Parisianness* and wear it as your own, but it never happened. You never met the right people, you thought, the right Parisians, and no matter how many you were introduced to, the language barrier always ended things for you, abruptly, they seemed to suddenly become bored with you, and you became nervous and anxious, and never once were able to say the things you'd imagined you would, everything became a mess.

10.

You've still never been able to speak French fluently — and you've always envied those who do. Everything you think and say is broken in this way.

The Total City

Will Self interviewed by Jo Mortimer

Will Self: If there hadn't been the Roman Citadel in London — the Roman square mile — then London might be more like Paris. What defines Paris is the Medieval walls. That's why you've got this very high density of Métro stations. You've still got a city operating within that idea of intra- and extra-mural. Whereas, once London has expanded beyond the square mile, which happens in the seventh century, it's over, because there's never another wall built. After 1066, there isn't another invader, so there's nothing to stop London from expanding.

Paris has, for a long time, aspired to the condition of what you might call the total city. In essence, it's trying to annul the reality of its physical geography. Yes, the river goes through it. Yes, you have the Île de la Cité. Yes, you have the hills to the north and the hills to the south. Yes, of course, they're all there, but the reality is that the total-ising — the means by which you move around the city and the furniture of the city — is incredibly consistent and well-designed. You see it in French châteaux and wealthy houses. The whole idea of French gardening is also very different to English gardening. The French don't come up with the landscape garden, so the relationship between the urban and the rural in France is profoundly different. The English approach is to domesticate the wild by creating the landscape garden, and then move out into the simulacrum of nature and then into nature itself. The French idea is to close something in walls and make it look like a room. The gardens at Versailles are like the floor plan of a house. So there's a radically different approach to that relationship between the rural and the urban. Britain, or England, because it was the most heavily urbanised society in the world, earliest, has no real wild at all. Did you know that? There is no wild country at all.

Jo Mortimer: That must be fairly recent...

WS: Take Rannoch Moor. You think, come on, there's nothing, it's a wilderness, but it's the result of neolithic slash-and-burn. Otherwise, it would be woodland — it should be woodland. The reason it's covered in peat is because they chopped the trees down. It's an anthropic landscape; all of the highlands of Scotland is an anthropic landscape. It looks that way because of stuff people have done to it; it doesn't look that way naturally. And I think that's embedded very deeply in the British psyche: the British know their country is completely anthropic. It means that the urban has psychic primacy. It doesn't need to cover the physical land area. Everywhere you are in Britain, there is something immediately in your view to tell you about human activity, and by extension, the city. The city is omnipresent. And here's another thing that ties the urban and the rural together in such a way as to eradicate the difference in Britain: the fox is artificially maintained to be hunted. It would have been eradicated years ago if it was that much of a problem.

JM: Why do you think there is such a tendency to use medical and anatomical words and phrases to describe the city?

WS: It may go back as far as Saint Augustine and the City of God, because Augustine divides all of the cosmos into the City of God, which is the realm of the spiritual, and the City of Man, which is the area of the corporeal. In a way, the City of Man becomes synonymous with the human body. But I think that what we're actually doing when we use a lot of bodily and anatomical metaphors in relation to the city, is we're acknowledging the fact that you cannot understand the city while you cling to the notion that it's full of autonomous individuals. It doesn't make sense. If people really, really are deciding to do whatever the hell they want to at any moment of the day, why does the city run with such regularity? And the answer is that people aren't autonomous. It's back to flow dynamics. We're always trying to keep at bay the fact that we know that the city, by definition, deprives us of our autonomy. So once you're deprived of your autonomy, you relocate your feeling body in the city itself. Since you've been annulled, you're just part of this flow — what are you flowing through? So the way to humanise the fact that you're dehumanised is to infuse the city with corporeality. I don't think anybody does it at a conscious level. If you stopped somebody in the Métro, in the rush hour, and said, "Do you realise you haven't chosen to go down here? You haven't chosen to go to work, and you're not even choosing to go home now, you're not acting out of free will. You have no more free will than a drop of water," they'd look at you like you were completely mad, right? Nobody wants to be conscious of that fact. I'm saying that it operates at a subconscious level, that people start talking about the city like that.

JM: Do you think that came about as soon as cities appeared?

WS: No, I think it happens in the nineteenth century. That's very important, and it's to do with what I call the industrialisation of space-time. It's not until you have completely regularised time, and completely mapped space, that there is this total loss of autonomy. Before that, there are still plenty of places left in the city where time runs slower. You can be yourself. It's like the city freeze-dries into being at a certain point — it's total — and then you have to practise psychogeography in order to escape from it. You can't do it just by hoping to do it — you have to take practical measures.

JM: Do you think you could extend the metaphor of the human body and anatomy to death?

WS: In what sense?

JM: In terms of terminality.

WS: Cities certainly can die, though what's more interesting is how resilient they are. I mean, Tokyo. A quarter of a million people killed in a single night by the United States Air Force, burnt to the ground. All the German cities after the Second World War, Henry Morgenthau and the Morgenthau Plan: his idea was that the cities were all to be razed to the ground completely, and it was to be solely an agricultural society forever. Well, that didn't happen — that's why Berlin is such a fascinating city. Berlin was killed and then remained in suspended animation until 1989. It was put on life-support and it's only beginning to come back to life again — properly — now. So you can see all of that happening in Berlin. I think cities — the life and death of cities — call attention to our autonomy, because it's not about what we do. As Marx said, history is made by the great mass of individuals. There's nothing you can do to affect the destiny of the city unless you're part of a mass of individuals who are thinking the same and behaving in the same way.

That's another paradox of the city. If you lose autonomy and accept the rather savage, draconian psychology of the city, and you abandon your autonomy, then you can't die. You don't really exist — you exist as the Man of the Crowd. You don't exist as Jo anymore, in a way. The conception of the *flâneur* and the idea of viewing the city as something to engage with in a ludic manner — in a kind of disruptive manner — is a privilege, really. I mean, it's not open to most people for obvious economic reasons. They just can't indulge in it. What I'm always trying to encourage people to do is to nonetheless make the steps necessary to see what the city is like when you don't regard it in that utilitarian, anonymous, Man in the Crowd way. You step aside from it. The original *flâneurs* who come out of the original bohemian conception in Paris were young people; they were just hippies, basically. They were just young people getting stoned and hanging out. We can't all do that, clearly. Or not as much as we'd like to.

Feeling in Neon

Cal Revely-Calder

London's St Pancras station is a Victorian cathedral of redbrick and iron. For a spell in the mid-twentieth century, it decayed and was nearly demolished — in 1949, the poet John Betjeman feared that it was "too beautiful and too romantic to survive" — but eventually, its fortunes turned. After an £800 million investment, it was reborn as the British terminal of the Eurostar. Paris is 306 miles down the line. Here in this colossal vaulted space, two countries are meeting and parting ways.

The station itself forms the context to Tracey Emin's latest installation, while her text is a single sentence: "I want my time with you". These eighteen letters are written in twenty feet of pink neon, one of Emin's staple materials; the handwriting is her own too, her characteristic swift strokes[1]. *I want my time with you* hangs from the wires above the Grand Terrace, and it's visible from most of the station's first floor, but since it's square-on to the Eurostar platforms, it directly addresses the travellers either leaving for Europe or returning home. Hanging in the concourse where people reunite after

1 (In the event, due to intractable problems with size and weight, the work had to be secretly made with LEDs. These were designed to be indistinguishable from neon and to replicate its effects. But the secret shouldn't matter; it isn't what you see.)

months apart, Emin's words make their intimate feelings a public thing.

In this little romance, who's the "I", who's the "you"? They might be individual lovers, anonymised in grammar; or, poised where they are, they could be abstractions, political entities. "I", facing down the line to France, might be the 48% of British voters who didn't want to sunder themselves from Europe, and "you" might be the continent they're being forced to quit. Which reading do you want to be true? For most of us, it could equally be either — the personal or the political — because *I want my time with you* is a piece of speech, and the meanings of speech start to messily proliferate when feelings are involved. These words are the figure, as Roland Barthes put it, of "the lover at work". The neon gives tangible form to their emotion, and amplifies it with light.

Emin has been making neon works since the early Nineties, and most of them end in one of two personal pronouns, either "me" or "you". Usually her words are unadorned by anything except an emphatic stroke; she puts *People like you need to fuck people like me* (2007) in a doe-eyed loop, and gives *I can't believe how much you loved me* (2010) a double underscore. Each light-tube shows what Roger Fry saw in every calligraphic mark: "the record of a gesture". And Emin adores neon's sensual edge, calling it "sexy", "spangly", "pulsating", "out there", "vibrant". In her strokes, you see the trace of her body itself.

I want my time with you is nakedly honest. That's all the more obvious when you compare it to the permanent piece on the Grand Terrace beneath: Paul Day's *The Meeting Place*, a large bronze statue of two lovers united again.

Train stations may be sanctuaries of romance, but every romance feels, to those who share it, like a unique and private dream; Day's sculpture is everyone's and no one's, a piece of postcard kitsch. Emin's sentence, by contrast, is an exposure of something uncertain and raw. She says she imagines a question mark at the end of her sentence: "I want my time with you?"

The week I went up to St Pancras, London had been under thick cloud all week, and we hadn't seen the sun for days. I arrived in the late afternoon; there was little light coming through the glass roof, and *I want my time with you* was already beginning to glow. By 8 o'clock night had fallen, and Emin's sentence was burning in the air. Its brightness suddenly gave it thrust, as if the words were pushing away from the brickwork behind. In *Flickering Light: A History of Neon*, Christoph Ribbat tells a story from 2010, about Emin going back to Margate to open the Turner Contemporary gallery:

She appeared in front of the Margate Pier and Harbour Company Building, now adorned with a pink-coloured neon installation featuring Emin's characteristic handwriting and the words "I've never stopped loving you". [...] Taking hold of the microphone to give a speech on that spring day, with the audience eager before her and her glowing pink declaration of love to crisis-ridden Margate overhead, Tracey Emin burst into tears.

You can picture *I want my time with you* the same way: the handwritten trace of a woman, leaning forward, imploring a crowd, or a country, or a single person who looks set to leave. She could write a "declaration of love" in ink or paint; anyone could. But romance is a thing with aura, and it needs a certain glow.

Terminus Nord

Adam Roberts

It's 6.45 in the morning and I have positioned myself in a window seat in the Terminus Nord brasserie opposite the Gare du Nord. Soon the August sun will rise towards its apex and crush Paris again, but at this hour the air is cooler, fresher and easier to breathe, and the light strikes familiar buildings from unfamiliar angles. The Gare du Nord glows golden, like a temple to travelling, but today I have no destination adrenaline to jolt me from my fuzzy early morning mindset.

Instead I'm hoping that the "express" breakfast will do the job. An orange juice in a wine glass, a cold croissant sitting on a micro serviette and an insipid coffee, a triptych served up in hundreds of other cafés around Paris. Boxes of oysters arrive for the seafood display — surely not by train — and a clock on the wall is frozen in the wrong time. Outside, the station is waking up. Taxis and hire cars are dropping off heavy eyed passengers, and a street cleaning vehicle, in bright institutional green, sweeps noisily past.

Terminus Nord has seen better days, but I'm not sure when these were. The Art Deco script on the façade insists it began life in 1925, but a painting on the wall inside shows the same place with the same name in 1889. A game of mirrors gamely tries to amplify its importance, but it is much smaller inside than I'd always assumed it to be. There is a hotel above here too, currently being transformed into what is bizarrely described on the promotional website as an *"urban refuge... as colourful as an African bazaar"*.

If, like Georges Perec at the Place Saint-Sulpice, I stay in this seat all day, I might see all of Paris, possibly the whole world even. It is part of the reason I'm here. Paris should be explored in all its corners, but the ordinary should also be experienced at extraordinary times, and above all with no clear reason in mind. In his "Theory of the Dérive", the Situationist Guy Debord suggested an extreme case of a city exploring psychogeographical drift could be "a static-dérive of an entire day within the Saint-Lazare train station". By not moving and simply observing I might capture an essence of Paris across endless coffee cups, beer glasses and ham sandwiches.

Despite innumerable trips through the Gare du Nord, between England, where I was born and grew up, and Paris, my home today, I have never really observed the station's façade before. A statue of Paris stands proudly in the centre, a Napoleonic eagle at her feet. To her left, lower down, is London, an impatient hand on hip, and on her right is Brussels. A little further away are the more distant cities — Warsaw and Vienna — impossible to reach in a single train journey today. Lower down are the more mundane destinations — Cambrai, Beauvais, Valenciennes — but all still reminders that any place served by a train station contains the poetry of possibilities.

This is the second Gare du Nord. The first opened in 1846, but by 1855 was already embarrassingly too small to welcome Queen Victoria's train during her state visit, and the British queen, possibly not amused, was instead diverted to the neighbouring Gare de l'Est. The humiliated Compagnie du Nord immediately started planning for a new station, and dismantled the original building brick by brick, sending it up the line to Lille where it still acts as one of the city's train stations.

Today's Gare du Nord opened in 1864 and was designed by the architect Jacques-Ignace Hittorff, who had earlier been responsible for the remodeling of the Place de la Concorde and the nascent urbanisation of the Champs-Elysées. Hittorff was born in Cologne in 1792, two years before the city was invaded and occupied by French forces. Despite moving to Paris in 1810 and finally gaining French nationality in 1842, Hittorff was still widely and disparagingly known as "the Prussian" when the train station was built. Is it for this reason that his masterpiece is one of the great hidden buildings of Paris? The Gare du Nord was erected during the massive restructuring of the city under Napoleon III and the Baron Haussmann, but it is one of the rare landmark constructions of this period not to be afforded an approaching boulevard with a classic Haussmannian vista. A persistent Paris rumour has it that Haussmann denied Hittorff this privilege after suspecting him of being too friendly with his wife, but financial disputes with the Rothschild family are a more likely explanation.

Six years after it opened, the new station had its first history marking moment. Hittorff had died in 1867, and Napoleon III and Haussmann had been removed from their positions of power. France was now at war — ironically with Prussia — and Paris was menaced with invasion. On 5 September 1870, the people of the city massed at the Gare du Nord, eagerly awaiting the arrival of an unlikely saviour on the evening train from Brussels; the writer Victor Hugo, returning from a near twenty-year exile. According to a reporter from the *Le Rappel* newspaper who witnessed the event, Hugo initially wanted to jump straight into a carriage, but the crowd would not let him leave without a few words of morale-boosting Hugolean bombast. He stood at the window of a corner café opposite the station — possibly in exactly my position this morning — and proceeded to make one of his most famous declarations. "Saving Paris means more than saving France, it means saving the world," he declared, imploring the Parisians to defend this "centre of humanity... the sacred city". Hugo didn't save Paris from invasion.

Already tired of my static position I decide to leave the Terminus Nord and immediately note the number of establishments within a few metres that have names connected to places reached from the Gare du Nord: Aux Villes du Nord, the Hotel des Belges, La Ville d'Aulnay, La Ville d'Arras. Glimpses of linked destinations such as these are less to provide a quick pre-trip taster and more a trace of a previous time when economic exiles from the regions rarely moved far from the place they first arrived and the place that could rapidly get them back home again. The station therefore became a buffer zone, a tiny annex of a beloved distant territory providing protection against the unwelcoming city that began a street or so further away. Today, exiles can still stand in the station, and — as the poet John Betjeman wrote:

...visualize, far down the shining lines,
Your parents' homestead set in murmuring pines.

Train stations are integral functional parts of a city but also an alien elsewhere. The Gare du Nord is Europe's busiest railway station, but a lot of this action is taking place underground. From here I could head down to the three rapid suburban lines that link the city to big centres of population to the north and east. This other world sits underneath the mainline tracks, and is peopled by the inhabitants of these suburbs. The lines spill out into a windowless shopping centre, designed as a place to pass through, but today a neutral territory where groups gather to hang out. It is not their hometown but not quite Paris either, a city they rarely even see. There have been occasional battles when groups from rival gangs clash, but there is nothing to hold on to or possess in this intangible and characterless environment.

"If you live next to a train station it completely changes your life," wrote the author Patrick Modiano. "You have the impression of passing through. Nothing is ever permanent." I see little evidence of people living opposite the Gare du Nord today, but they must do I suppose. It is the ubiquitous train station fabric that is most obvious, the pure transience of places that simply underline the station's role as a location of anonymity and constant movement. There are temporary employment and car rental agencies, fast food outlets and sex shops, their €1 burgers and *"cabines automatiques"* both offering quick, cheap satisfaction.

I decide to make a quick tour of the station perimeter, to see how far this strange atmosphere permeates. Heading northwards on the Rue du Faubourg Saint-Denis, I remember that another urban oddity is situated here. Look closely at number 172 and you will be observing not the banal Parisian building it appears to be, but rather a giant hollow air vent. It is a construction that was made necessary by the extension of the suburban RER E line into the city, and there is another similar building one hundred or so metres further away on the Rue Lafayette that Umberto Eco compared to a "mouth of hell" in *Foucault's Pendulum*. A train station has a visible impact on a city, but much is also going on unseen, in flues, cables, pipes and hidden service tunnels.

How far do you need to walk away from a train station until it is forgotten or unimagined? On the Rue du Faubourg Saint-Denis the Gare du Nord is no longer in sight, although those living on the odd side of the street have sweeping views across the tracks from their rear windows. This is not railway territory but instead one of the city's most vibrant immigrant communities, a neighbourhood of Tamils who settled here after fleeing the civil wars in Sri Lanka in the 1980s and 1990s. The fragrant shops and restaurants have given the area the name of *Little Jaffna*, but the community has not chosen the vicinity of the Gare du Nord to maintain links with homeland and family. Instead travel agents advertise flights to Colombo and Madras on printed A4 sheets in the window, but would any community deliberately choose to live next to an airport?

The top of the street is dissected by the Boulevard de la Chapelle and the iron baulk of the overhead Métro line. The city's Métro system is situated almost entirely underground, except where it crosses railway lines. Although the constructors tunnelled under the Seine, the channels of railway track were considered to be an even tougher challenge, or perhaps scenery that would not be spoiled by conspicuous bridges. These outside stretches though are most people's favourite parts of the journey, and not just because their smartphones flick back to full 4G reception.

I cross the long bridge over the two dozen or so tracks of the Gare du Nord by foot. Emile Zola described a similar view at the Gare Saint-Lazare as a *"vaste champ"*, and the huge expanse — so rare in Paris — is almost pastoral in its scale and perspective. It is a visual treat, but this place is really about the sounds and odours. The tracks sing, the trains clack rhythmically in and out of the station, a bell rings somewhere far in the distance and a robotic voice lists destinations like a freeform poem. Around this on different waves are permanent notes of oil and sparked steel. A line from Apollinaire's poem "La Victoire" pops into my mind: "Be afraid that someday a train will no longer thrill you."

The other side of this bridge is Zola territory, the Goutte d'Or neighbourhood of *L'Assammoir*. Set at the time of the first Gare du Nord, the station was not then significant enough to merit a mention in the book, but Zola himself had a fleeting, unwanted brush with the Gare du Nord later in life. On 18 July 1898, at the height of the Dreyfus affair and facing a year in jail, Zola escaped Paris in the London train, chugging past the Goutte d'Or completely alone and "with only a nightshirt wrapped in a newspaper" as luggage.

In *L'Assammoir*, Coupeau, the husband of the principal character Gervaise, is employed as a roofer at the Lariboisière hospital that was then being built. Walking down the Rue de Maubeuge that dissects Lariboisière and the Gare du Nord, the hospital can only be guessed at behind a high, grimy wall. A recurring Paris question pops into my mind: why are so many hospitals in the city situated next to train stations? This should perhaps not be a surprise. Both have arrivals and departures, waiting rooms, long anonymous corridors and staff in uniforms, and both offer you the freedom to wander aimlessly (and the Lariboisière hospital is an attractive place for a stroll). Nobody questions why you are in a hospital or a train station. After all, everyone must surely have a reason to be there.

The poet and author Max Jacob, who was treated in this hospital after a road accident, also noted such links. "The hospital is a station" he wrote, with "travellers to the country of shadows! Travellers towards different health!" Above all, in what he labelled the "mausoleum of the living", "be wary of the departures from which we never come back."

The close proximity between the Lariboisière and the Gare du Nord has always attracted some of the city's most destitute individuals. The journalist Maxime du Camp already noted in the 1870s that the hospital "welcomed the puniest and most anemic part of the population of Paris," but today the down and out come for the "salle de shoot", Paris's only safe injection site for drug users, which is housed at the hospital. Some of these users gather at an entrance to the Gare du Nord at the bottom of the Rue de Maubeuge. "Do you know who I really am?" shouts one woman continuously as I walk past, but she's not looking at me. Are train stations chosen by people lost inside their own heads because they offer at least the possibility of a destination, the opportunity to get "back on the right track"?

Finally I am inside the station. The glass canopy gives everything an immense scale, but the Gare du Nord lacks that most poetic of locations: the *salle des pas perdus*. The Gare Saint-Lazare and neighbouring Gare de l'Est have these antechambers, once empty spaces where travellers paced aimlessly, their purposeless footsteps literally being transformed into lost energy. Today these halls are micro shopping centres, designed to optimise the time people spend in the station, but the Gare du Nord does not even have a waiting room. Instead, with platforms extremely close to the entrances, travellers arriving early or waiting for delayed trains are forced into tight spaces as train replenishing vehicles ping relentlessly past.

When they began mushrooming in cities in the nineteenth century, train stations were quickly compared to cathedrals. Claude Monet painted both, and Théophile Gautier, writing about the Gare du Nord, noted that "in comparison with recently built churches, we easily see that the railway is the religion of the century." But if the St Pancras station, at the other end of the Eurostar tracks, has the grace of a great temple, the Gare du Nord is more of a crumbling gargantuan shrine.

It may give a scruffy initial impression of Paris, but I like idea of the Gare du Nord as a kind of secular church, a pantheon to function and a shared sense of adventure. Which is the most important in today's city, the train station or the cathedral? Outlining a project for "Rational Improvements to the City of Paris," Guy Debord — him once again — along with other members of *l'Internationale lettriste* movement, had different destinies in mind for both. Whilst religious buildings were slated to be completely or partially demolished, all members agreed that train stations should be kept as they are. "Their rather moving ugliness adds much to the feeling of transience that makes these buildings mildly attractive," they noted. The only improvements they recommended were to remove or scramble all visual and aural information regarding departures in order to promote the *dérive*.

In 2012, the artist Sal Randolph also chose to play with the sensation of both rigour and mystery that is peculiar to train stations. Randolph created the Bureau of Unknown Destinations, a three-month residency at the Proteus Gowanus gallery in New York that encouraged temporary displacements by train. What if you turned up at a station one day and really didn't know when and where you were going? In addition to a downloadable Psychogeographic Destination Kit that anyone could — and can still — use, Randolph also distributed free round-trip tickets. The adventure began with the opening of an envelope that revealed the destination. Liberated from the decision making process, the traveller was free to truly experience small unknowns.

This morning I could go to Amsterdam or Düsseldorf, Cherbourg or Amiens, to another country or to the extreme limits of France. Or why not just take a stopping service and get out at a previously unimagined suburban town? Until the middle of the 1990s I could even have taken a daily train, complete with vintage Soviet carriages, from here all the way to Moscow.

There is the attraction of the unknown, the excitement of discovering a previously unvisited location and experiencing new scenery on the way, but there is also the melancholy of tracks followed many times before. Has the Gare du Nord become my terminus? Looking out to where the tracks narrow and join, it seems that my country of birth is now further away than ever. The steel alloy cords are stretching longer, the tunnel is getting a little darker. The electric pull is now little more than a gentle pulse, but I still stand listening to the tracks and imagine that some of the messages are for me. For who can bear to feel himself forgotten?

Poisson Soluble

Lauren Elkin

We met at the Salon du Livre, and we met again on a street
corner near the Gare du Nord, as I had been wandering
without any particular destination in mind, and he had just
had his hair cut at a barber's he liked in the neighbourhood.
He stopped me with a hand on my elbow. I let him leave it
there, less out of a desire to be touched than out of a lack
of desire to shake it off. *Nadja! Mon âme errante*, he said.

Yes it's me, yes it was very nice to meet you the other
night, I said politely, because he had been very enthusi-
astic about his offer to help me with my writing career,
even though we were standing in the stall belonging to
my French publisher, and even though I thought I knew
what he had in mind, which didn't have much to do with
writing. But I recognized in his enthusiasm a self-regard
that I didn't want to insult: beneath his lasciviousness it
seemed important to him to be someone who could help
me.

The March weather was indecisive; it was mildly cold; it
showered a bit; but underneath my peacoat I was sweating.
Yes yes it's very funny to run into each other like this,
in the road like this, I said in my passable French which
occasionally wandered into fluency but mostly generated
non-essential words and phrases and apologies that left
my listeners confused. Very English, my French, highly

reflexive. We crossed the street together as he told me about his friend whose car had broken down after the Salon and how he had had to drive to Porte de Champerret with jump leads to help him out even though he had been all the way in the south of the city at the convention centre where they held the Salon. He told me about how while he was up at the Porte de Champerret he stopped in a café for a drink and sat in the window where the neon sign advertising the industrial lager served there lit up his table green and yellow and turned his hands green and yellow and he took out his notebook and began to write about green, and yellow, and industrial lager, and jump leads and meeting me. I had made quite an impression, he said, the way my eyeliner had been a little bit smudged under my eye, but English girls always have slightly smudged eyeliner, don't they? he said with a knowing smile. I haven't really noticed, I admitted. That's the sort of thing you should try to pay attention to, as a writer, he told me. Shall we have a drink in this café?

I allowed him to steer me into a place on the corner of a large boulevard. Inside it was very full of people escaping the rain; there was only a table in a cramped corner by a window with two short stubby stools for seats, placed not on either side of the table, but adjacent to each other. We squatted down, and I tried not to let my knee touch his, but there wasn't much space to avoid it. He wore deep purple trousers, and a crisp blue shirt, and a violet and blue scarf was wound around and around his neck, below wavy silver hair that was slightly too long for London, but seemed right here. His sweater, of course, was slung around his shoulders. He asked me what I wanted to drink, and called out our order to the waiter. He all but called him *garçon*. It was impressive to see someone take charge of the café situation that way. I usually waited until someone came over to me, which could take a long time.

He asked me what I was working on, and no sooner had I begun to tell him than he began to tell me about what he was working on: it seemed he saw some continuity between our projects, though I had simply said "by chance," *par hasard*, and he said "chance, *le hasard*, this is the very theme of my next book." It was interesting to see how he pivoted from asking to telling, from genuine curiosity to that state you often see writers enter into when describing their work, as if they had been waiting all day, or all week, to be given the time and space to talk about it at length, and they gratefully settle into whatever time and space you would give them to do it, as if you've offered them a comfortable chair after a long day of standing.

Chance, as he saw it, was less to do with the vicissitudes of daily life or the controlled chaos of the universe and was entirely a question of paying attention. He could just as easily have been engrossed in his own thoughts, he said, crossing the street, having just had his hair cut; he could have been in pursuit of the next thing in his life, but instead he was walking in Paris, attuned to his environment, looking at the shopfronts, and the people, and the things they left strewn on the ground, and he was dodging cyclists in the bike lanes, which, he said, were idiotically inserted into the sidewalks, endangering pedestrians who didn't pay enough attention to where they were walking, and who were often run over in spite of the printing on the asphalt which read *priorité piétons*, priority for pedestrians.

I hadn't noticed the bike lanes, though it did explain why several cyclists had shouted at me or pinged their bells at me. And so in paying strict attention to his surroundings he was able to pick me out of the crowd of people crossing the street at that intersection, and so receive chance into his life, whereas had he not been paying attention chance might not have come his way.

Or it might have, I said. That's the thing about chance, isn't it? Maybe in running into me you're not running into someone else you know.

My ex-wife does live around the corner, he admitted. Better to run into a beautiful and mysterious Londoner than her sour face. He had been married three times, he said. The current marriage was better than the other two, although she could be a bit clingy, and she didn't like to go out as much as he did, preferring to read at home with the dog in her lap and the cat somewhere nearby. He didn't wear a wedding ring, and I wouldn't have expected him to.

He asked if I had come over specifically for the Salon du Livre. I said no, I often took the Eurostar to Paris for no other reason than I liked to be here, it was a good counterpoint to London, and this trip I had come with an open-ended ticket. I started to tell him how claustrophobic London felt these days, as if the city itself were narrowing, along with our futures. I had been toying with the idea of moving to Paris, and thought I still might, though I would need to decide quickly, before I needed a visa or something to do it. It's all very unclear, I said, what is going to happen now.

He looked thoughtful. Some people can't take the feeling of too much space in the world, he said. They want to feel snug. Like babies. You have to swaddle them or they freak out.

I sipped my coffee and imagined the Brexiteers swaddled like babies, slotted into an army of prams pushed by a million Boris Johnsons in bloomers and bonnets.

They are the enemy of chance, he went on. We have them here too.

I didn't really know anyone else in Paris, so I saw him often. Chance became his watchword; he was truly a man obsessed. Always he would choose a street corner at random from his *plan de Paris* (no Google Maps: that was cheating), text me the address, and when we arrived we would walk into the first café we saw. He told me I should let chance guide my work, to be open to what it would conjure on the page. I acted like that's what I always did. He fixated on my name, which he found all the more fascinating because I had given it to myself. And you've never read André Breton, he said. You're sure. No, I said honestly, I just liked the name better than what my parents named me, which was Ashley. Nothing against the name Ashley, it just didn't suit me. And Nadja does, he said. Yes, I said, reddening, at least I like to think so. It's the beginning of the word hope in Russian, he said, and only the beginning. That's why Breton's Nadja picks it. I didn't know that, I said. I thought it sounded exotic, like a woman who would wear brocade and fur. Ashley sounds like she should be wearing her boyfriend's football jersey. It does, he agreed, topping up his pastis with some water from the carafe. And do you wear brocade and fur? Not very often, I said.

How is your French getting on? he would ask, and I would say badly, badly. Oh well never mind, he replied, André Breton lived in New York for years and protected himself carefully from English the whole time, so as to preserve the purity of his French. I lent him a copy of my book in French, and in exchange he brought me a copy of the Surrealist Manifestos. He made me read the *Poisson soluble* section aloud to him in my shaky French, correcting my pronunciation as I went. I looked up a translation at home. *POISSON SOLUBLE, am I not the soluble fish, I was born under the sign of Pisces, and man is soluble in his thought! The flora and fauna of Surrealism are inadmissible.* I was indeed born under the sign of Pisces, but I decided not to tell him as it would only over-excite him.

It was just as well he didn't give me his own work to read; his novels sold very well but had titles like *La Femme sur le balcon* and *Retrouvez-moi ici un jour*. For all that he seemed like such a publishing world operator the night we met, at every meeting subsequently he was like some kind of self-declared priest of literature, never speaking of it as a business, only as a cult he served.

One afternoon we ran into a friend of his, an American writer, a man, of about his age, who was writing longhand in a black notebook in the corner of one of our cafés. This is Nadja, he said, and I held out my hand. Pleased to meet you, I said. You're English, he said, shaking it. What are you doing in Paris? This and that, I said. Well, he said, with what I can't be sure wasn't a sneer behind his friendly façade. Enjoy it while you can. Soon it'll be just as difficult for all of you to go anywhere, just like it is for us. We can go anywhere, but we can't stay. See you around, he said, and turned back to his notebook.

He was always wanting to talk about my dreams, and I was always disappointing him, because I'm a terrible insomniac, and when I do manage to sleep it's with a kind of dreamless relief. He thought dreams were the supreme conduit to creativity. How do you think I come up with the plots for my novels? he said, waving a hand, as if they hung from the walls like intricate tapestries. Wanting to prove my connections with the occult and therefore my unassailable access to creativity, I promised that the next time we met, I would read his tarot. He was in ecstasy at the idea. It's you I've been waiting for, my Nadja, it's sheer marvellous accident that has brought you into my life, you are the one to read my tea leaves and tell me what you see there, tell me and I'll believe you!

I brought my cards to the next café, all the way down by Alésia, and I probably did play up a bit the part of the mystical young woman, which he seemed to enjoy. When he drew seven cards in the form of a horseshoe it was the Knight of Cups who landed at the top, looking so stately in his armour, bearing the grail seriously in front of him, the wings on his helmet making him look a bit like a minor Greek god.

A Knight! he exclaimed, very pleased with this result. Tell me about this knight.

I recited what I remembered from the book that came with the cards. The purity of his horse, the evenness of his progress, all attest to his belief in fated patterns, and his own role in them. The Knight is well-acquainted with his inspiration and his creativity, I told him. He is not the young Page just starting out, amazed by the fish jumping out of his cup. But he may be too engrossed in his own self-perception to notice if a fish did jump out of his cup. The cups are the suit of feelings, especially love, and consciousness of those feelings. They are about nursing your creativity, and your relationships, not taking them for granted, or fantasizing them out of recognition. Yet the Knight can't get down off of his horse without spilling whatever is in his cup. We're all a little bit asleep, I concluded. It's what we see when we're asleep that can guide us when we're awake, he said. I nodded, and moved on to the next card: the Hierophant.

That night at home I drew my own cards. I was going to have to make a decision about where I was going to live. They were inconclusive. Nothing dramatic, all minor arcana. Be brave, they said. At night I didn't sleep, and tried to find my way through the beginning of a new novel, trying to let chance shape the text as it would.

My walks were making me feel ever more emboldened in the city; I could cover so much ground in a day, from the vaulted medieval streets in the 5th, where I'd once rented a very small maid's room, to the packed streets of Château Rouge, where everywhere you turned there were people selling grilled corn on the cob and fish wrapped in leaves and some kind of milky liquid in plastic water bottles. I picked up playing cards I found in the street, intending, later, to think about what they might signify. I passed a lot of attractive women. I thought a bit about the girl I'd left behind in London, who was probably at her judicial assistant job at that precise moment, certainly not thinking of me. I thought about Baudelaire. I thought about how I used to read him in high school by torchlight under the covers like an idiot because I thought it was more romantic, or more rebellious, than just leaving my light on. I thought about the *Poisson soluble* section the writer had made me read, where Breton says that childhood is the closest we come to living our real lives, and that everything that comes afterward gives us a sense of having gone astray. I thought that no one who had grown up in Bromley in the 1980s, who had worn a scratchy brown uniform to school, who had slept in a damp chilly house and eaten boiled vegetables for dinner most nights while begging to be taken to Pizza Hut on the high street, who had rationed pastel-coloured bits of candy on a necklace until they turned your skin pink and blue, who had sat dully by as your friends collected scented stickers, who had waited desperately to grow up and get away, but was vaguely concerned about IRA bombs and Poll Tax riots and not at all sure how one could avoid getting caught up in such things, could ever think that *that* was real life and everything else a wrong turn. I thought about when they opened the Channel Tunnel, and you could suddenly drive or take the train to France instead of taking the ferry, as we had done a couple of wet summers in my childhood, before heading down to some unspeakable and unmemorable camping grounds in Brittany, where none of the other families spoke to anyone outside their caravan group and ate only sausage rolls they'd brought from home, and the only music we could get on the radio was French pop, all the more strange and foreign for the resemblance it bore to our own pop music, all synths and power chords, but sung in an impenetrable language. With the Eurostar it was as easy to get to Paris as it was to get to Bromley from north London — easier, probably. For now. I thought of my writer friend, and the way he seemed to think about adulthood the way Breton did. It seemed easy for him to think that way, having grown up right here, in Paris, near the Jardin du Luxembourg, with all of that literary and cinematic history steeped in his everyday life. He could afford to think about his life however he wanted. He could believe in chance: he had a mould just waiting to cast himself into. There was safety in that. With his scarf, and his quotations, and his raptures, and his trousers, he could not have existed elsewhere — he could not but be a Parisian writer. While the rest of us make what we can of ourselves.

One afternoon down by the Bastille I passed a shop selling precious stones and I ducked in to see if there were any in there that resonated. I looked at all the *pierres précieuses*, yellow and blue and white and pink, and found a banded amethyst, which is meant to protect you against toxic environments. I thought: is this a stone that's telling me to stay in France, or a stone that offers to protect me when I go back home?

I took myself to a café, and ordered a glass of *aligoté* with confidence, and looked out at the world. The café is so permeable to the street; it is so open, life floats in and out with the cigarette smoke. The pub is about enclosure and the café is about flow, flux. There are times we need one and times we need the other, and we should be able to choose.

I met up with the writer again one evening towards the end of my stay. He had a little bit too much to drink and tried to tell me that he loved me. His eyes were sad and I forgave him.

Ghosting

Susan Tomaselli

Art is memory: memory is re-enacted desire.
— Cyril Connolly, *The Unquiet Grave*

Dullthudding Barrels, Umbilicus, Mollydount, all stops on the Calypso, Hades, and Nestor lines of the Hibernian Metropolis, a train ride you won't ever have taken: the railway doesn't exist. A "subversion of Dublin [which certainly exists] via the peregrination of characters in James Joyce's novel *Ulysses*" [same], the Metropolis lives only in map form, and is a merging of Joyce's text and Harry Beck's 1931 design of the London Underground map.

Joyce's novel lends itself well to a mapping treatment — in fact Nabokov sketched one — and Dublin holds a special attraction for Joyceans as both the source and subject matter of Joyce's genius [witness Bloomsday]. It was the author himself who boasted that if the city "one day suddenly disappeared from the Earth it could be reconstructed out of my book".

But I am not in Dublin, I am in Paris after a break-up. It is 2017, and I am walking through parts of Paris, a city I do not know particularly well, using the novel *Nadja* as a map. I am not attempting a Situationist *dérive*, instead stop-offs with photo opportunities I will tweet at some street scenes referenced in the book, a recreational simulacrum if you like. Not necessarily key scenes, but locations I will find using only André Breton's 1928 autobiographical novel of a love affair that I've read in advance of the visit.

Frustrated with the diminished sense of reality the world had produced, Surrealism intended to initiate a new humanism, a hybrid reality: "the poet of the future will surmount the depressing notion of the irreparable divorce of action and dream". Founded by Breton, Surrealism was an idealisation of madness, non-conformism, Freudian free association and "stream of consciousness", free love, and eroticism. "André? André? ... You will write a novel about me. I'm sure you will. Don't say you won't. Be careful: everything fades, everything vanishes. Something must remain of us."

Walking a street in 1926, Breton noticed a young woman coming towards him: "I had never seen such eyes. Without a moment's hesitation, I spoke to this unknown woman". She told him she called herself Nadja, "because in Russian it's the beginning of the word hope, and because it's only the beginning". For several days they met repeatedly, until Breton tired of Nadja's erratic behaviour (she was declared "mad") and began to withdraw.

Can you reconstruct the city through *this* novel? Though the "shape of the city", Breton acknowledges in his afterword, has already changed and disappeared — "it slides, it burns, it sinks into the shudder of weeds along its barricades, into the dream of curtains in bedrooms, where a man and a woman indifferently continue making love" — and what city doesn't, I am confident from the *Surrealist Manifesto* ("if the declarative style, pure and simple... is almost the rule in novels, it is because, as one must recognise, the authors' ambition is quite limited. [...] And the descriptions! Nothing can be compared to their vacuity; it is nothing but the superimposition of images from a catalogue, the author employs them more and more readily, he seizes the opportunity to slip me postcards, he tries to make me fall in step with him in public places") I will find *somewhere*.

Breton saw photography as striking a mortal blow to old modes of expression, allowing artists to "break with the imitation of appearances", and used photographs (not taken by himself) to authenticate his account of Nadja — images of buildings, monuments, shop fronts, portraits, photographic reproductions of letters and drawings — and also reinforce a sense of the pastness of these events, they reflect a particular moment of Breton's history and a history of the city itself, but could prove useful for my walk. I am using only the text to guide me, and am aware this could go horribly wrong, chasing ghosts, but I've made notes.

My point of departure is the Moulin Rouge, Boulevard de Clichy, where I turn hard and head for Rue Fontaine, and to Breton's house at No. 42 squeezed between a burlesque theatre and the Carrousel de Paris offering a "cabaret and diner spectacle" (both closed). The apartment is marked with a plaque that reads: "JE CHERCHE L'OR DU TEMPS". I take a photograph with my phone. I remember reading a newspaper article on the auction of the contents, that it was crammed almost to the point of bursting with a fine collection of Surrealist artworks and had become a museum to a movement that loathed museums. I am looking for Nadja, but so far am finding only Breton. I move on, down the street and through Place André Breton, passing No. 20, where Georges Sand and Chopin lived, and come to No. 6, a location mentioned in the book. Regarding my own reflection in the glass, I read from a passage in the book:

> But for me to descend into what is truly the mind's lower depths, where it is no longer a question of the night's falling and rising again (and is that the day?), means to follow the Rue Fontaine back to the Théâtre des Deux Masques, which has now been replaced by a cabaret.

The theatre hasn't existed since 1924, it has again been replaced and is now a restaurant called, appropriately enough, Les dessous d'Orphée.

Across Rue Saint-Lazare:

> For a change I decide to take the right sidewalk of the Rue de la Chausée-d'Antin. One of the first people I happen to meet there is Nadja, looking as she did the first day I saw her. She advances as if she didn't want to see me. She seems quite unable to explain her presence here in this street where, to forestall further questions, she tells me she is looking for Dutch chocolate. Without even thinking about it, we have already turned around and go into the first café we come to [there is a café called L'Eden on the street]. Nadja keeps a certain distance between us, she seems rather suspicious. For instance, she looks into my hat, probably to read the initials on the band, though she pretends to be doing it quite unconsciously, it being her habit to determine certain men's nationality without their knowing it. She

admits she had intended to miss the rendezvous we had agreed upon.

I move on, take a wrong turn and end up going too far along Boulevard Haussmann, passing under the canopies of the *grands magasins*. I am lost. I pause in a square, tweet a picture, and someone responds, tells me that part of Bertolucci's *The Conformist* was shot there. I'm starting to wonder how authentic Breton's *roman-vérité* is. Recalling Jane Jacobs on maps ("we are all accustomed to believe that maps and reality are necessarily related, or that if they are not, we can make them so by altering reality"), I am reminded of "trap streets" — deliberate errors placed in maps by cartographers to dissuade plagiarism — and of the fake Paris that was built during the First World War to confuse German bombers, complete with a sham Champs-Elysées, Gard du Nord, wooden replica factory buildings, illuminated by Fernand Jacopozzi (the man who went on to light the Eiffel Tower with the Citroën logo).

While I have my phone out, I message Dublin-based Croatian photographer Dragana Jurišić who I know is on a residency in the city. "I'm in Paris for a few days, there's birthday drinks for J. on Friday, Hotel Edgar, Montparnasse at six, you should come along if you are free."

"It's my birthday dinner too. In La Petit Célestine on Seine [sic] on the fourth! How many of you? Do you want to join us — there's about fifteen of my crew."

"I'm not sure how many of us, possibly six. Will let you know."

"Super. This is a good fun place. It's €35 for three courses and it's a late-night place, my Columbian friend's chef friend." She added, "I would love to join forces, could be more fun". She asked if I was in Montparnasse right now, and if I fancied a drink. I told her what I was doing with *Nadja*. "We are at a cemetery," she added.

Jurišić has been assembling a novelist project, *My Own Unknown*, using, as a starting point, a found photograph of her aunt who left Croatia and fled to Paris in the Eighties, where, rumour has it, she worked as a prostitute and spy. One chapter, "L'Inconnue de la Seine", features an unknown young woman whose body was taken from the Seine, and whose death mask became an object of fascination for both the public, and for writers and artists like Man Ray, Nin and Camus. Both female protagonists in Jurišić's work are not entirely real, and she is here to continue work on their, and by extension her own, fictionalised biographies.

I return to the text and plot where, and what, I need to do next. I walk down Boulevard Malesherbes, past La Madeleine, and into Rue Saint-Honoré, looking for a somewhere I've forgotten. I have to go back to the book. "Suddenly, while I am paying no attention whatever to the people on the street, some sudden vividness on the left-hand sidewalk, at the corner of Saint-Georges, makes me almost mechanically knock on the window. It is as if Nadja had just passed by." On to Rue Royale, Rue Saint-Florentin to Place de la Concorde, and I duck inside the Jeu de Paume to take in an exhibition by "realist Surrealist" photographer Eli Lotar, whose work appeared in Bataille's *Documents*.

Toward midnight we reach the Tuileries, where she wants to sit down for a moment. We are in front of a fountain, whose jet she seems to be watching. "Those are your thoughts and mine. Look where they all start from, how high they reach, and then how it's still prettier when they fall back. And then they dissolve immediately, driven back up with the same strength, then there's that broken spurt again, that fall and so on indefinitely."

This fountain is off today. I was sure they passed the Louvre, but I can't find it in my notes. I take a picture anyway, with the corner of the book present, just in case. Across Pont Neuf (which I can find in the book) to Île de la Cité:

The Place Dauphine is certainly one of the most profoundly secluded places I know of, one of the worst wastelands in Paris. Whenever I happen to be there, I feel the desire to go somewhere else gradually ebbing out of me, I have to struggle against myself to get free from a gentle, over-insistent, and finally, crushing embrace.

It is a punishing twenty-eight degrees, the scribbles on the back of my hand are dissolving, the Post-it notes that mark the book are as brittle as dead butterfly wings: "She enjoyed imagining herself as a butterfly whose body consisted of a Mazda (Nadja) bulb toward which rose a charmed snake". I withdraw, decide to call it a day and abandon my wander (and my plans to meet Dragana), the futility of chasing a dead love revealed.

An Exhausting Attempt at Finding a Place in Paris

Steve Finbow

Against the imaginary advice of Charles Baudelaire, my choice of footwear when *flâneuring* is flip-flops. I've *flâneured* in London, New York and Tokyo wearing my trusty Havaianas. At the beginning of summer, the blisters beneath the straps rise and burst, the scabs fall off and two hard ridges of skin form above my medial cuneiforms.

I had three days in Paris to revisit places and to discover new sites. One of these was the Musée Maillol, which had an exhibition of the works of Foujita, a Japanese artist who lived in Paris in the 1920s. The walk from Arcueil would take over an hour. I planned to have a break in Montparnasse cemetery to photograph writers' graves. I had done this eight years ago, but most of the photos had been lost.

The first time I visited Paris was Christmas 1981: Vietnamese food, amphetamine suppositories, cans of 33 Export for breakfast, naked women, a policeman pulling a gun on us, a bruised penis, Man Ray's *Cadeau*, a man on the Métro with a cyst in binary orbit with his head. But, as Barthes wrote, "What right does my present have to speak of my past? Has my present some advantage over my past?" For reasons I won't go into, I didn't visit Paris again until 2008. It was Paris's fault: I blamed it for destroying my life — a life which, in hindsight, I had already been slowly eradicating.

On that occasion, I slowly warmed to the city. We stayed at a hotel near the Square Michel Foucault. We had a passable time and had drinks in the Café de Flore, Les Deux Magots and Brasserie Lipp. I bought Edmund White's *Genet: A Biography* from Shakespeare and Company. I didn't read a page and no longer know its whereabouts. On that visit, according to a notebook, "Paris begins in fits and starts, shorts out, static, flickers, shrugs and begins again. Fractal. Mist lifting off water. Graffiti. The statue of Michel de Montaigne, seated, wearing what look like ballet shoes". Over the past seven years, I have been to Paris on three occasions, once staying in the refurbished Beat Hotel.

It was July 11; the weather was overcast with patches of sun, a breeze made it perfect walking weather. There's not much to write about the journey: noisy traffic, ugly buildings, Bartholdi's Lion of Belfort. I reached the triangle formed by La Rotonde, La Coupole and Le Sélect and walked to the cemetery. Graffitied on a column: SDF75, my initials and the year I first read Arthur Rimbaud.

This was the Paris I remembered. It had history, presence. The Paris I had just walked through was merely present. This is not true of New York and Tokyo; cities that perpetually rebuild themselves. Nodality. In my old notebook, I found, "Why do I chase ghosts? As if I could smell Jean-Paul Sartre's foul breath on the waiter's apron or William Burroughs' farts on the Rue Gît-le-Cœur". Yet, I had asked to be photographed next to a sign at the Hotel des Grands Hommes where André Breton and Philippe Soupault had written *Les Champs magnétiques*.

Before I'd left the hotel, I'd looked at Facebook, the current and precarious depository of our memories, to check which photos of graves I had: Baudelaire, Samuel Beckett, Marguerite Duras, Joris-Karl Huysmans, Tristan Tzara. I didn't have those of Jean Baudrillard, Sartre and Simone de Beauvoir. Checking the map by the gatekeeper's office, I saw that Emil Cioran was also buried here. This was important as I was writing a book in which he was key to the main argument.

The Baudelaire cenotaph was easy to find: it looms up over the tombs like a ship's figurehead. I also planned to visit the Hôtel de Lauzun, where Baudelaire and Théophile Gautier had formed the Club des Hashischins. Why am I so obsessed with photographing writers' graves and the places they had once lived? D.H. Lawrence in Ravello, Georg Wilhelm Friedrich Hegel in Berlin, John Keats in Rome? What am I experiencing when staring at a tombstone, a blue plaque or a notebook under a duty vitrine? Nothing, really. If anything, they are things to see because I don't want to see other things. While living in Sapporo, my favourite place to visit was the Hokkaidō Museum of Literature. I didn't read Japanese, so understood little about the exhibits.

I found Sartre and de Beauvoir's grave. It was littered with train tickets. I'm not sure why. I crossed the cemetery and rediscovered Beckett's grave. According to the map, Cioran's was close — one plot over. I looked at every grave. I clambered over some to check names. It wouldn't be found. I downloaded the map. Division thirteen. I checked the sign. North of the Sainte-Beuve memorial. Nowhere. Cioran: "It is not easy to be nowhere, when no external condition obliges you to do so". But he was nowhere. He wasn't somewhere.

I went to Le Falstaff: Beckett used to drink there. I walked to the museum. The galleries were busy, Foujita's work barely visible among the crowds. People didn't look at the artworks — they stood in front and photographed them. I didn't stay as long as I had planned to. I walked perfunctorily along the Boulevard Saint-Germain, past the famous cafés, down Rue Danton to the Seine, along to Shakespeare and Company to buy a copy of Tao Lin's *Trip*. After twenty minutes, the staff couldn't find a copy. I left. I walked past the sign for Square Michel Foucault, through the Jardin du Luxembourg and back to the cemetery. I retraced my steps. Cioran: "There is no such thing as time, there is only that fear which develops and disguises itself as moments..., which is here, inside us and outside us, omnipresent and invisible" and because I couldn't find the grave. It had become omnipresent and yet remained invisible. After half an hour, I gave up and walked to a bar in Arcueil where I realised I didn't have a book to read while I waited for my never-on-time girlfriend. I took out my phone, googled "Cioran's grave" and found it: "Emil Cioran Rasinari 1911 – Paris 1995". And beneath that "Simone Boué 1919 – 1997".

The next day was hot. I caught a train to Saint-Michel–Notre-Dame and walked to Shakespeare and Company. They hadn't found the book. I purchased a copy of Perec's *An Attempt at Exhausting a Place in Paris* and crossed the bridge to the Île Saint-Louis and stared at the Hôtel de Lauzun. Cioran — "Anxiety is consciousness of fear, a fear to the second degree, a fear reflecting upon itself" and "Inspiration in reverse, anxiety calls us to heel at the slightest impulse, the slightest divagation". I was anxious because I hadn't found his grave, I felt that — although he was important to my work — if I couldn't find his grave, his writing would be reverse inspiration, the work would never be finished.

I walked along the Seine, cut through the streets to Saint-Sulplice, where I planned to have a drink in the Café de la Mairie, the place where Perec may have written the book I'd just purchased. By the time I arrived, I was sweating, my feet black with dirt. There were no chairs available outside, so I headed to the Jardin du Luxembourg, to Boulevard Montparnasse and to the cemetery where I spent forty-five minutes looking for Cioran's grave.

The next day was hotter. I caught the train and went to the Pompidou Centre. Bored after three hours, I walked along the Seine to Galignani, where I looked for the Tao Lin book, but couldn't find it. I crossed the Pont Royal and walked along the Boulevard Raspail down to the cemetery, where I spent thirty minutes looking for Cioran's grave. I even asked someone, but they pointed in the direction where I'd already spent hours searching.

The final day was hotter. I was meeting someone for a drink. I caught the train. I was early and didn't feel like visiting another gallery or bookshop, so I headed through the Latin Quarter and stopped in the Taverne de Cluny for a pre-beer beer. I looked at my notes from eight years ago: "Père Lachaise — we saw the graves of Marcel Proust, Gertrude Stein, Paul Éluard, Guillaume Apollinaire, Raymond Roussel and others I have already forgotten. Later, we sat outside the Taverne de Cluny reading our books, drinking beer. The sacred is enacted in bars, in pubs, in the compulsive community of friends and strangers". Imbrication. Cioran: "The only moments I think of with relief are those when I sought to be nothing for anyone, when I blushed at the notion of leaving the slightest trace in the memory of a single human being".

At a Remove

Cody Delistraty

Few nations are obsessed with the past quite like France. I think back frequently, for instance, to 2002, when one of the far-right National Front's favored rally cries was, "Martel 732, Le Pen 2002!" which attempted to link Jean-Marie Le Pen's anti-Muslim immigration policies to Charles Martel, the Duke and Prince of the Franks in the mid-eighth century, who was known for halting an Islamic advance into Western Europe. The facts aren't exactly correct — these lepénistes were probably referring to the Umayyad invasion of Gaul, which was likely not exactly in 732 CE but rather sometime between 719–759 — but the fact that even in racism, the French insist on a knowledgeable weaponization of the past helps attest to the truism that there is no single French memory; there are only politicized interpretations, myths constructed ex-post for use as present and future justifications.

Today, French intellectuals continue to argue about the lives and proper symbolism of figures going as far back as Joan of Arc. The first Revolution likewise continues to be a central historical moment leveraged by both the left and the right. Every French political party, wrote the historian Robert Gildea in *The Past in French History*, has tried "to develop an interpretation of the Revolution that sustained its goals, and to universalize that interpretation while attacking the legitimacy of rival interpretations". More generally, said the historian Robert Darnton, "History has always been a battleground in France".

The French attention to the past goes beyond even the cerebral and intellectual as it is a country that is, for one, markedly behind the rest of the Western world in its lack of technology; its elites tend toward Catholicism; its art world pushes against the contemporary, tending toward the traditional, sometimes the ancient. A sense of grandeur, regionalism, a fetishization of the farmer, of *la France profonde*, of hyper-designed gardens and urban spaces — in all of this, France seems not so much stuck in its past, as, in fact, preferring to live in it.

This life in the past — this removal from so much of the rest of the world — is, to someone living there, at once freeing and stultifying. I have lived in Paris, off and on, since I was eighteen. I was there first to study at a satellite campus of my American university in a small schoolhouse tucked behind huge blue doors in the sixteenth arrondissement, which has since, regrettably, been converted into a chichi private British high school. I returned to Paris most summers, then did my graduate dissertation research there, before — having worked for a year in New York — returning to Paris for a few more years.

I often wonder why I come and go so frequently, as I still do, but I think it largely comes from this feeling of living at a remove. Paris has always been a place, for me at least, to recharge and to reflect, but rarely has it been a place for me to move forward, in jobs, in relationships, in what is so often called "life". Perhaps that will change. A part of me hopes it doesn't. There is something increasingly rare, increasingly sacred about a place that does not move in lockstep with all of the others. French society might, in many ways, be imprisoned by its allegiance to ideas of resistance, of a paradoxical kind of revolution that has workers taking to the streets to maintain the status quo; but this apparent imprisonment is also a kind of self-exile onto an ideological island. And the allure of that island is a certain freedom. Freedom from the rush toward power and wealth, from the day-to-day, minute-to-minute ethos that says productivity is the only legitimate measurement of oneself, as it so often is in New York and London. Freedom from the obligations of checking the marks of what tends toward that definition of "a normal life": an office job, a significant other, a movement toward marriage, toward retirement, toward property ownership and its ilk. There are romantic Parisian images of taking a coffee at the sidewalk café, but such an image serves best to highlight the most brutal of fallacies of life elsewhere — that is, if a "life" is defined only by a progression toward marriage and up a career ladder, one might as well quit living. What a bore! What a lark!

But working toward freedom takes its toll. Trying to be free is tiring business, and whenever I finally do leave Paris after staying there for a few days, a few months, a few years, when I look out my airplane window, the capital moving fast away from me, I have the distinct feeling of finally being free from trying to be free.

With President Emmanuel Macron, some changes have already arrived — from funded technology incubators in Paris to corporate tax cuts — but as the rest of the world dips into a nationalist, isolationist politics, France also persists in its commitment to liberal democracy[1]. Even in its modernity, France is still running behind. Indeed, often that is for the best.

It's difficult to say if Paris, if France, will continue to be a holdout from so much of the rest of the West. Much has been written on national histories and constructed stories, so while it would be foolish to ask whether France will continue to romanticize its revolts against its monarchs just as we Americans romanticize our own revolt from the Brits (the answer: yes, of course), one wonders whether France *should* throw itself into the future, into the technologies and politics and a more clear-eyed self-historicizing. But I worry. The world needs its places that remain at a remove, that live especially in their constructed pasts even as they manipulate them for present purposes. Without a place like Paris, we're all too often blindly moving forward, able to look up, down, and ahead but rarely inward, where, after all, change must originate. To offer itself up as an ideological island, as a place of existential remove to which to escape is one of Paris' greatest gifts, whether or not it knows that's what it has long provided.

---

1   This piece was written shortly before the rise of the *gilets jaunes* movement (ed.).

The Private Life of Quasimodo

H.P. Tinker

Quasimodo is sitting in the window of an Art Deco café decorated in the style of an American diner. Leaning on an Arne Jacobsen chair in a silver polo neck. Sipping from a bowl of beetroot soup. Quixotic eyes. Prominent cheekbones. Unusually retroussé nose.

Where is Esmeralda? he wonders, glancing around.

Suddenly Dahlia appears like a turn-of-the-century tarot card reader — black silk scarf, long gold necklace, red lipstick, thick black mascara…

"I'm looking for a handsome older gentleman," she says, extending a bunch of ethically-farmed tulips.

(Warm applause undulates around the otherwise empty room.)

"I'm not old," complains Quasimodo.

(Silence.)

"What are you going to call the baby?" he asks, strolling through a bustling, malodorous quarter of the city populated by horse-driven carriages and middle-aged academics dressed in medieval attire.

"Sometimes I want to call the baby Amantine Lucile Aurore," Dahlia says. "Other days I prefer Dido Belle. Mostly though I'd like to call the baby Baroness Elsa von Freytag-Loringhoven…"

"Not all babies are the same," Quasimodo warns her.

"They can change things, cause great disruption. Some have personalities of their own."

"Not mine," says Dahlia.

Dahlia is twenty-nine and speaks of her friends and her friends' babies for some minutes. At the Père Lachaise cemetery she regales him with unlikely facts gleaned from watching late-night documentaries late at night.

"You have a lovely chest," Quasimodo says.

"So do you," says Dahlia.

Quasimodo's new apartment on Rue Notre-Dame-des-Champs smells of newspaper ink, fresh car exhaust, experimental cinema. Tall men in uniforms build beds and wardrobes as he unpacks a pile of brown Gothic paperbacks: Voltaire's *Candide*, Antoine de Saint-Exupery's *The Little Prince*, Raymond Queneau's *Cent Mille Milliards de Poèmes*, Georges Perec's *A Void*, Michel Houellebecq's *Atomised*...

Next morning a neighbour arrives on the doorstep in a cavalier hat.

"I'm d'Artagnan," he says, thrusting a hand into the space between them.

His trademark goatee wispier than in days of yore, d'Artagnan reminisces about the Ancien Régime while Quasimodo makes herbal tea in the kitchen. "We thought we knew it all," he says. "Dining on pâtés, mousses, truffles. Fighting wars, shooting heroin, sleeping with countesses. We thought we could change the world with a lick of eyeliner and a dash of rouge. How wrong we were. Those muskets were useless too. They could blow up in your face and you had to clean them between shots. The accuracy wasn't great either."

D'Artagnan strokes his chin, rubs his face, makes deep,

soulful riffs on the importance of personal hygiene late into the afternoon...

Tuesday. Quasimodo doesn't call his brother again. He opens a bottle of Château Latour even though it's only 3:30pm, a time of day generally considered too early for the traditional opening of a bottle of Château Latour. After several glasses he's convinced his mother and father will come back to life, visit the apartment, dispense kind words and wisdom, straighten him out a little.

Instead, yellowy leaves throw themselves down from the trees outside.

Pretty soon the trees outside are practically naked.

"I think the baby's on the way," Dahlia informs him grimly.

Sitting in the Café de Flore, Quasimodo worries about Dahlia and the baby. A team of student documentary makers are here filming a lengthy close-up of his coffee cup. "Art has become too serious," Quasimodo declares. "Nobody whistles any more. But the time for action has passed. We've all grown older. The time for reflection is upon us..."

Quickly, a colloquial crowd gathers around him. Poets. Models. Dope peddlers. Pimps. Literary agents. The air turning blue with the kind of language many contemporary readers find offensive; the atmosphere bristling with displaced sexuality.

Not mine though, Quasimodo thinks. Everybody else's.

Quasimodo already has a baby of his own, nearly fully grown and causing all sorts of trouble. He recalls standing in the suburb of Saint-Germain-en-Laye years before, watching Esmeralda unleash her almighty fury upon him and anyone else who happened to be in the vicinity. One afternoon, declaring herself Emperor of France, she grabbed a knife, cut off her hair, and left for a Hungarian pianist. That was on Rue Bonaparte where they made the first baby. There was another baby too, Quasimodo remembers, one never quite born.

December. "Hope you're having a good day!" Dahlia says. "I've had the baby now though it was somewhat traumatic getting him here..."

Walking along Boulevard Saint-Michel there's a new smell in town, hot and metallic. Throughout the Latin Quarter, a pandemonium of shouts. Discordant cries. Situationists dancing the Madison. Immigrants being bitch-slapped and punched.

"What is this?" Quasimodo asks a beatnik in black.

"Some lame political shit," the beatnik explains.

Streets swept by machine-gun fire, Quasimodo ducks into La Rotonde. Inside, everything very red: red walls, red drapes, red roses, red wine, red faces.

"I'm worried about Marguerite," says Esmeralda.

"What are you worried about?" asks Quasimodo.

"I'm worried she's going to end up like you."

"Would that really be so bad?"

"Oh, yes. Can you have a word?"

Green crêpes hurtle expeditiously towards them.

"Why do you have such appalling taste in men?" Quasimodo asks.

"How does that explain you?" Esmeralda replies.

"Anybody can get lucky once."

"Well, I fell for your public image. You were never what anyone would call a good-looking man..."

In the courtyard behind his apartment the trees seem to have grown inexplicably overnight. Quasimodo closes his eyes, tries to picture the future, but can't quite see himself in it. Marguerite is on the sofa sickening with something, having watched *The Man in the High Castle* on Netflix. Quasimodo is sickening too, genuine beads of sweat sliding down his forehead.

Marguerite is sixteen and disdainful of almost everything he says and does.

"Thursdays are my worst days of the week," says Marguerite.

"Why's that?" asks Quasimodo.

"Because I come here," she says, glaring at his gold-embroidered breeches.

"Well, your mother wanted me to have a chat..."

"She talks crap, dad," says Marguerite.

"I know," says Quasimodo. "God knows I know."

Quasimodo retreats into the kitchen, contemplates a drink. Am I just a common or garden alcoholic? he wonders, nearly out loud.

Saturday night on the Rue de la Gaîté. Leaning against a zinc bar in a voluminous necktie and velvet three-piece suit. An unshaven philosopher ordering two large cognacs, both for himself. "Monsieur Quasimodo," he says in a mid-Atlantic accent, rather like Cary Grant. "The days come along one after the other. Then a year is gone. Then ten years are gone. Then everything is gone. Then you're gone. It's a cliché, but you think it's going to be all right — and, of course, it never is...'

"In terms of wrestling with your own psyche, I've been there," says Quasimodo. "After guesting in Bardot's New

Year special, I quit bellringing and moved to Hollywood. I met Linda Ronstadt, Henry Winkler, Carole King, Ringo Starr. Hung out with Emilio Estevez and Judd Nelson. Played Charlie Laughton in a biopic. But my career never took off. There was no place for a charismatic hunchback. I lacked the requisite chutzpah. People like Burt Reynolds and Terry Stamp had the charm and the chat, but I saw things in myself I didn't like. I was living a louche life, having a great time. But I was fifteen pounds heavier and looked like Henry James. Anyway, after two decades in exile, countless lovers, a short prison sentence, several religions and a divorce, finally I came home..."

Quasimodo scrunches his face, thinking, thinking, thinking.

"I must have been quite an ass to leave Paris," he says, ruefully downing a Hemingway mojito, a Faulkner mint julep, a Kerouac margarita, a Fitzgerald gin rickey...

Stepping into the night, the more sequestered streets uncannily resemble a dystopian tourist attraction. Flying cars, elevated walkways, gargantuan palaces of steel and glass. Quasimodo suddenly feeling inspired to cook some of his favourite meals again. Maybe his pumpkin polenta. His tofu tagine. Perhaps his crispy kale.

January will be different, Quasimodo thinks.

Soon it is March.

Quasimodo sitting at his antique writing desk, not writing. By now the book industry is undergoing another crisis of identity and popular music is steeped in all kinds of queer introspection. Unexpectedly an old friend invites him over, greeting him barefoot at the door wearing a long white hooded garment similar to the monk's cowl worn by Honoré de Balzac. Petite with cropped hair and feline features, Aphrodite is a visual artist known for running around the Canal Saint-Martin cigar in hand. Her apartment a maze of books, birdcages, half-finished canvases of herself, walls adorned with pages torn from the erotica collection of the Bibliothèque Nationale.

"Let's not talk gender theory or Hélène Cixous," says Aphrodite.

"Okay," says Quasimodo.

"Would you like to put your penis inside me instead?" says Aphrodite.

"Okay," says Quasimodo.

Back at his apartment, Quasimodo sips Château Latour in a bright red Eames chair while Jacques Dutronc sings "I Guess I'll Have to Change My Plans", "September of My Years", "Once Upon a Time", "It Gets Lonely Early", "There's a Flaw in My Flue", "Somewhere Along the Way," "When the World Was Young", "These Foolish Things"…

Christ, thinks Quasimodo, slicing an onion. Soon I'll be five hundred and fifty-seven.

Stabbed in the heart by a thousand tiny memories he crumples to the floor, wine-dark blood cells spilling from his dangling thumb, flowing through the apartment, dampening his once singular resolve.

"What do you think is causing these wounds?" asks Doctor Polanski.

"Isolation," Quasimodo says. "Disappointment. Regret. Disaffection. Rancour. Despair. Humiliation. Regret. Mostly regret…"

"Regret-based melancholy is the worst of all," sighs Doctor Polanski. "It's bottomless, fathomless, all-pervading, and can manifest itself in front of near-total strangers."

He leans forward, adopts a mock-conspiratorial tone.

"Have you seen much of Esmeralda since the divorce?"

"Only in my nightmares," says Quasimodo.

Afterwards there's a downpour of aporia...

Social media shitstorms, life-hacks, suicide bombs...

Lingering beneath the shadow of Notre-Dame, the way a pervert might. Elaborate flames raging in various overly-poetic configurations. His melancholy growing ever more noticeably pronounced...

Weeks later Quasimodo buys a table for the living room and spends several days lacquering it in silent tribute to his father, a man who never lacquered a table in his life. Listening to Django Reinhardt on Spotify, Quasimodo keeps one ear cocked like a dog in front of a fire. Additional time passing him here in the form of minutes, hours, possibly months...

"I've just heard Otis Redding sing 'My Girl'," Dahlia says. "And the weather conditions at the beginning of the song strike me as contradictory. *Can you make sense of them?*"

"I can," says Quasimodo. "They make perfect sense."

"Oh yes!" says Dahlia. "So they do!"

Dahlia is straddling him on a leopard-skin rug, fur tassels spinning on her breasts, a vivid jungle scene tattooed across her back.

"I have straddled other men," Dahlia says.

"That's not surprising," Quasimodo says.

"Women too," Dahlia says.

"That's not surprising either," Quasimodo says.

It's mid-May now and Quasimodo is dressed head-to-toe in grey: grey Nike trainers, grey Levi's, grey cashmere jumper; his iron-coloured pompadour listing to one side. After lunching at Les Assassins and seeing the latest Jean-Luc Godard film, he returns to his new apartment. My new apartment is no longer new, he realises, inspecting the blood spatter speckling the wallpaper and carpet. Suddenly his phone chimes the opening bars of "La Bamba". On the line: Dahlia, slightly exasperated, speaking from a multidisciplinary entropy installation at the Musée d'Art Moderne.

"This may sound twatty," she says, "but you need to view the world the way an artist might. You're making your real world as narrow as you make your imaginative world wide. That statement is actual bullshit, but it amuses me to say it. Anyway, I'll leave you to your internet dating and casual sexual encounters. Have a good evening!"

"I won't," says Quasimodo.

Around 8:35pm Quasimodo doesn't call his brother again. He reads *The Lullaby of a Lover* by George Gascoigne, finishes a bottle of Château Latour, then embarks upon the arduous, surprisingly bittersweet journey, part-memoir, part-metafiction, part-literary criticism, part-architectural monograph, part-psychological ghost story, back across to the other side of the room.

Three Pear-Shaped Pieces

Russell Persson

First

I've named all my name dropping for the night and by Christ it's time for me to walk although another treat of cognac might help us all along.

There is no good sir. No welcome to the evening of the evening. But there my patrons the gentlemen the ladies they go and file out themselves back to their own good homes. A brief gentle walk home. But us here I say there is still no good sir. Just lamps out and the rest going out. Tamped.

Headed home I go and stumble south. The wooden handle of my hammer where it meets the metal head is worn smooth from where I hold it there inside my coat inside my pocket and believe I'm at the ready do believe me. Fucking scoundrels in the shrubs or hiding in the corners. Would as much to be the tack hammer your noggin wants. Headed south and from the Auberge it's mostly downhill until we get us to the Seine. Cocked on evening whisky then it comes to me I've lived a certain life. Wouldn't want this recall to run amiss and so let's take it down. So take this message.

I regulate my life.

This is what I do and when: I rise in early morning. Three hours and five minutes after I become inspired and this goes on for one hour and twenty four minutes. And then I take a lunch. An excellent lunch who takes up no longer than four minutes of my day. For quite soon after I become on horseback to survey the grounds I've come to collect by now. I sweep an arm if you can notice me from where you are. Then this horse I'm off and back to being burdened by the muse who doesn't let me ride. I come indoors to become profound inspired.

In the evening at 7:16 I sit to dinner served. Four minutes after is when I'm done with dinner and then I spend over one full hour on God knows what until we begin the night of symphonic readings out loud. Make of this what you will as of what you've made til now. For then I'm off to bed at the strike of 10:37 night. I sleep soundly unless the day is Tuesday which is when I awake with a start at 3:14 morning and again of this you can what of it would you will.

My food is white as in the whites of eggs and the inside of bread, coconuts, rice, the fat of dead animals, sugar, cotton salad, salt, turnips, shredded bones and certain fish who've been skinned.

When I breathe I breathe distinctly out with pleasure and when I walk I walk with my hands upon my ribs and I see well behind me and crane accordingly to the aft. I wouldn't tell you how I sleep for it would be a true confound. But do let it be known my one eye remains open while the other rests, and so on. And my bed — I'll save you all the time and not go further into what describes such an odd contraption no one would believe in either way but suffice it to say if it'll do to tell let's say a cavity has been cut who saves a room for my dear noggin thank you and good night.

Continue us to walk continue me to walk in due south absolutely.

The Pont Neuf an option this evening.

Though Jesus Christ what with all my cognac I might just with Saint Denis lug my head the half way home tonight to choose where I might rest this awful melon.

With my hands upon my ribs I walk and here and there reach into where in my pocket our night hammer sits. I worry some the handle where it meets the metal head where I lay upon the patina one more thin coat of hand oil or soot from where I've been it is the dust we pick up in the day when we're looking elsewhere.

My stumble my amount I walk me home. The different routes and then the same ones and ones who wouldn't tell the way I wend.

The farther from Montmarte I get. The farther from the Seine and from the Pont Neuf and again we come us up from that black river to the south and what comes with that. In night in time the smell of boiling cows and hides who must in their aroma set out to tell us this is no way to skin a cat. But home it is and I welcome me back to the slum I've kept and kept well hidden from them all.

Second

Well it was like he never thought it through, said the man who moves pianos to his wife. I've not seen a thing like it. Not in all the days I've been.

Soup? said the wife to the man who moves pianos.

The second christing floor, up two flights. We had her legs off this grand of course. No other way to get it up. And him all suited to the nines and dapper bringing up the legs like a boy carrying cord wood I swear, said the man who moves pianos to his wife.

The nut with the pince-nez? I thought he already had a grand up there, said the wife to the man who moves pianos.

Well I tell you he does. The first one we moved up there. It must have been years ago when we lugged that first one up. And then I thought well he must have gotten rid of the first one, but wouldn't I know of a goddamn piano moved in Arcueil? Did he pull it apart and heave it out the window into the street I'm asking? The absolute shit of it all is that his first piano, the one I moved it must have been years ago, is still in his second floor room, right where we left it the first time. Nearly shat my britches. Right where we left it. So Alex, he'd gone ahead to scout the room and comes back down and says there's already a grand in his one room and there's no place else for another. So I go up to his room and he's there and would you believe me if I told you on top of his head was a piece of fabric, a napkin, black, draped over his head like some kind of veil and he's still as a board and he must have heard me stood there and he says, Good sir, I wear this for your protection, so I won't know you've been in my house, and for mine, for I don't prefer the sun. Now Alex, he never said a thing about a black napkin but you think he might have mentioned that little nugget so I stand there and I ask him where we're supposed to put this loving piano we've got now half up his steps and he, get this, he lifts up just a corner of his napkin to see for himself and he points to where his piano is already and says, There. He says, There, just put it on top of this one – I've already cleaned it off for you and so there you go – just put it there.

You see, dear. Not only is he a piece of work, said the wife to the man who moves pianos, but so might you be a piece of work as well.

Third

1. *A Way of Beginning*
What I would like to do this evening is arrange my white collars in their good order of stiffness, from stiff to not, along the outside edge of my top cabinet – and curl this arrangement around if I must.

2. *More of the Same*
I don't hear a soul in the hall so I can now go out to the Parc d'Ecole d'Arcueil. We will need some water for this evening and it is there we'll find an excellent draught. We'll bring two bottles and a bag.

3. *Piece I*
When I'm arranged or near arranged what calls me away is one lone mosquito, possibly desperate but more likely languid and hopeful, sent here I am sure of it by Freemasons who have no objectives of their own but to flounder the plans of others. I'll find you dear buzzing bug. You can not be just a sound forever.

4. *Piece II*
He wants in, sometimes, that Claude. As if he's uncommon. Though in what way is he not? Do we not all answer to

the same muse? Whose his is mine, mine is his. Ungovernable and hidden only by what portion of the moon we choose to see.

5. *Piece III*

A banana becomes white when the pants are off. Almost I could say this goes for some other hobbies. Habits. I wrest the time to become in brief inspired. Oh, the notes come and some go and they come in dull flourish and they come full whittled to the bare unadorned without-pants amount of message I've been on the lookout on.

6. *What's More*

I could have ended even earlier but I say the resolution hangs in air like the best gnat or noseeum. We go about this calmly.

7. *Rehash*

My slow waltz with you my dear my dear self. Me, the sea-bird's nephew. The one who walks slowly with an air of attention, amusement and curiosity and at times inside it's anything other. What stars might gather in their nosey gaze upon my walk I walk me home.

Mirabeau Passing

David Hayden

What is recalled flows over me under the bridge. The sun reaches through the water to my body, its softening tissue weighted below by dense knots of words that descend in a tangle from my mouth into my stomach and intestines. There are three heavy rings on each finger. My boots have long since slipped into the silt. If I turn to left and to right, I can see the faces of the Seine, their silent remembering, their smiles and other contortions.

Time returns as weight and motion: riverine and turbid, holding, shifting particles and pieces of the life above, their shit and coffee cups, all abundance. Navigation is not possible in time, no commerce is possible with its passage, clinging cannot save us, he said. Verbs dissolve in the river, giving its water a flavour we, its inhabitants, cannot identify.

In the day, passing drivers might not be able to bear looking at the river with its massive freight of feeling, stories and silences. We beneath are fluvial and constant, and know the permanence of the intolerable. The days, the journeys, the weeks, the journeys, the years, the journeys, the loves, the journeys, end here. We had children, or not, and we left the children, or the no-children, behind, in our real, in our possible, pasts. We reached out in love and were loved and unloved, and loved and unloved in turn. All that lasted did not last.

I stand on the bridge with you in another time and, later, without you. Down below was my future self. I call out to my past self, and to you where you stood looking down at the river, as it was, unable to see its life in other times.

When night arrives, the bells of some forgotten church bid us rise to the surface where we gaze through smoke into the stars, at their long, continuous arrival, embracing with relief the unmeaning. If we could be seen from the banks we might appear as outsized rotten blooms shivering in a silver garden.

We look up as two cops appear over the green lip of the bridge. One looks back briefly, his arm darts and arcs as he throws a cloth-wrapped something over our heads, that lands with a gulp, beyond sight and touch. Evidence reaches deeper, past knowing and naming, leaving us with the partialities from which we select to make our truths. Hope does violence to hope.

Walkers pass alone together, alone alone, together together, before passing altogether. The hour sounds. We gave each one a number, and the days, the months, the ages, names. The city was Paris. The city is Paris.

The faces of the Seine, the faces of the lost, we turn to each other, arms aloft and aloft, and we reach and link, and bridge from one bank to another, from one time to another, from one love to another: love that had passed away, and desire, the least of love. There is no return, no refrain, only passing, in the river beneath the bridge at Mirabeau.

Flowing, Slow, Violent — A Fantasy

Daniela Cascella

...courante, lente, violente. Courante, lente, violente. Courante, lente, violente. CouranteLenteViolente. In transparencies, limits of the limitless, madness of a sounding memory which busies itself among forbidden thoughts. Courante, lente, violente. Courante, lente, violente. Cour... Coeur... Coeur, my heart, I was sick. Sick to death with the long agony, sick of the stitches in my mouth, sick of waiting for words. I wanted to sing this like a catastrophe, or a kick in the eye. But words failed, senses were leaving me, facts of life of body of mind in transparencies, soon to vanish. First the dark. Then a long stretch of silence. Then the inhale, the deceiving pause in which all seems still. Then no voice. Then the reawakening. Then the words without reason, garbled signal. Then reason found in rhyme. Then the need to lose once again reason. Then the fall, blood, eyes still shut.   Muted recollection of the previous night's conversation after rehearsal —*So what are you going to do? —In truth, I never cared much about Paris-as-literary-milieu, so what? —Ever dream of going back there? — Drea...?* This is when I fell on the ground, from dread. I was so tired and bored with thinking of Paris, of singing of Paris, that I chose a more troublesome encounter. I had to put a rhyme into this. Inappropriate, I know, but no matter.

I'd be cautious with it, so the rhyme would slowly take over then burst, the rhyme and its violent echo, *courante, lente, violente,* the rhyme would burst the stitches, flowing, slow, violent, sighing one unto the other, *courante, lente, violente* sighing, and flowing, slow, violent was that summer evening of the fall, when my mouth started bleeding and it was blood from soul, and from *seul,* only blood of inkept sealed ensouled desire; blood, and aether. Dumbed, the torture began with words imagined from nerves and their outlines, their sounds. Having realized that writing the word "Paris" did not hold Paris, and "sing" certainly did not allow me to sing. It only kept singing in my ears, the word, unsure of the refrain, unsure which song it belonged to, other than the unspoken sealed ensouled inkept song of my stitched-up mouth and bleeding mind, soul, *seul,* alone.   O the incantatory solitude!

So as I said, I was bored, had no words, no voice, had fallen on the carpet. What next? Bitter words, and that rhyme. *Courante, lente, violente.* Couldn't scream, couldn't sing all the clichéd love songs in Paris that I never quite heard but pretended to remember; the images of love songs I never had, the remnants of love songs that never existed, of love that intermittently exists, exhaled they all hammered in my head, in the head of me, hammered, "love", *s'en va,* goes by. And I sought a refrain, a formula which... SHALL WE GO? ...how torturous the wait for the inner rhyme, torturous the voiceless gaps, between the very *courante,* the very *lente,* the very *violente.* Shall we go? Shall we go to the Palais-Royal, a-a-a-a-al. Go, I mean, in my mind, as in this room still I stay, *je demeure,* fallen, on the carpet. The Palais-Royal, only a pretext to think again of the book with the ruin in its title, that paragraph announcing the voices from the Palais-Royal in which it is written that the dead are books. But what is the point of all this if nobody hears, if I'm a ruin? If only I could take some deep resonance from these speechless lungs, blood-filled lungs, if only the sound could be deafening and dispel, dispel the idea of Paris, the idea of Paris like the idea of North, the recluse pianist's broadcast from isolation, when he says that *I've remained, of necessity, an outsider. And the North has remained for me, a convenient place to dream about, spin tall tales about, and, in the end, avoid… Something really does happen to most people who go into the North … they become, in effect, philosophers.* What happens then to people who go to Paris — do they become writers? As if. Oh no. Sometimes they disappear.

This agony, *lente,* this wound that cuts through my neck to the ear, *violente,* all possible beginnings for a song, such as, [*inaudible*], or it could be, [*inaudible*], or it could echo, [*inaudible*], but my mouth is stitched. Teeth, teeth, teeth! Inevitable inaudible counter-bones to breaths of refraction. That evening when a bird came out of my bleeding mouth and took away my voice, I did my best to keep the plumage. On the carpet still I stay, *je demeure, courante, lente, violente,* that evening the mouth started bleeding and it was blood from the mind, then from the cut on the throat, blood of inkept desire, flooding, flowing, *courante.* It kept singing in my ears, I thought I had nothing to sing about Paris but the haunting of a recalled rhyme reveals what I had to say, otherwise what is held after hearing? This is when the inner singing begins. This is how, when I have no voice, the song begins. An uneasy rhyme, and wouldn't it be easier if I was given a catchier one? The mind bends in the constraint of this sound, Paris, Paris, Parisis, De Villeparisis, Madame, *that* book had to make its appearance here somehow, if only as a fleeting hint, but those are the best ones, those hints that generate unexpected significant echoes, hear, Paris, Parisis, Isis, or, as someone better attuned to the city than me once wrote, *remember we are dealing with the goddess Isis. Her forbidding veil is off and not for a long time replaced. She moves now in transparencies. ...do not ask what she is smiling about. ... If you do you must be prepared for other things to happen.* How about the other voices? Oh those are smart. Very smart. They have seen a lot. Seduced, sung. But do not assume that because this voice is silenced or out of tune, it ceases to exist, to desire. So it rains, so it sings. Remember, it sings, not I. Remember the day I understood that the verb "to sing" does not sing, "to write" does not write, and "to bleed" does not bleed. And learned to trust words for what they are, how they sing. *Courante, lente, violente,* their shapes, if only I could sing their rhythm, river-rhythm, flow of words, flowing, slow, violent, and still I stay, *je demeure*, could the song become percussion, buzz then chant-like. It's not the city that escapes me, I do, and the night is mighty chilly, I try to sing a little ditty, but all that comes out is a sigh. Or, a murmur. Perhaps the song should begin in the Musée Gustave Moreau, that dizzying accumulation of pictures, that painterly phantasmagoria where I once thought I heard the murmur of lost desire, perhaps the song should be a dizzying ditty and partially secret like those figures hidden under thick layers of paint, like myself in the city and the murmurs I heard that day, hidden layers of lost desire, as if trapped in a canvas. The song should be sung in the pitch of voice of someone stitched inside a dream of that top room with only slits on the wall, paintings hanging all around, and no doors. If from my lips some chords on Paris, if from my stitched lips some words on Paris. Once I pronounced them, and if I pronounced them I want to hear them over and over, while in my head I hear a sigh of lost desire. Lock all the fine rounded words in the room upstairs. Sing clipped beginnings of song with stitched lips. Despite the stitched lips, the rhyme, *courante, lente, violente*. And this is when I empty my mind from Paris, city of folly, empty for me. To empty my mind from constraints of Paris, from clichés of constraint such as to exhaust a place in Paris, oh no, not the Oulipoists, to exhume a place in Paris, to exhume a plaice in Paris, plaice, fish, soluble fish, oh no, not the Surrealists, plaice, palaice, palais, I need to go to the Palais Royal, in the book with the ruin it its title the palace is a conglomerate of frayed layers of history, will anyone exhume me from beneath these layers of history, no, not exhume, it's exhaust. Exhale? I only I hear my constrained breath against teeth, teeth, teeth.

Courante, lente, violente, the rhyme ended up here as a transparent layer for an insight. A veil. Behind, the image of you escapes me, but always comes back. I will leave the coincidence as it is. To be willing to unravel it, would lead to disappointment. Now I want you in this sealed room of paintings in which we are imprisoned. But you say, no, you are tired, you quieten. And I fall, and in my fall I hear, my lack of words taking you away.

Do you know the things Swedenborg did not tell — even less than the things Huysmans wrote? *Do you know the Song of Paris, how every century she had taken civilisation and made it dance to her tune? Built it and sung it and dressed it, prepared it for the table, for the night assembly, for the bed? For prayer, for wit, for treachery, for rhetoric, for devotion, for the song's life and death?* I need a map, one I cannot look at because it doesn't exist other than in words, as a title and as a story called *Mappa Mundi*, the tale of a character, or a person, who disappears abducted by a shadow in Paris. *This* is how I like to read about the city. *It is of no use, or not much use, to know it only as a spree, or as an aesthetic jolt, returning very sophisticated about it. ... After the spree a veil is drawn, a sober, noli me tangere veil. Isis, whose face on a first swift initiation you think you have seen, even to the colour of her eyes, Isis you believe you have kissed, withdraws... and for lover and mistress you are left with an image, remote as Sainte Geneviève where she stands looking upstream, an inviolable city behind her.* Upstream, flowing, *courante, lente, violente*, garbled signal, garbled signal. I want to lift this veil and wake up in the Musée de Cluny, in front of the Lady and the Unicorn tapestries, to encounter the enigma of the inscription À MON SEUL DÉSIR for my only desire. But from this fall I won't wake up, still I stay, they will find me on the carpet, ruined on the floor. So it ends and begins anew, with no song, with a rhyme, with no reason, *courante, lente, violente*, shall we go?, the ruin, the rhyme, the ruin, curtain, curtain, *courante*...

L'amour s'en va comme cette eau courante
L'amour s'en va
Comme la vie est lente
Et comme l'Espérance est violente.

Vienne la nuit sonne l'heure
Les jours s'en vont je demeure

All love goes by as water to the sea
All love goes by
How slow life seems to me
How violent the hope of love can be

Let night come on bells end the day
The days go by me still I stay

From Guillaume Apollinaire, *Le Pont Mirabeau* (tr. Richard Wilbur)

Moods and Materials

A dream, 13/14 June 2018
André Breton, *Soluble Fish*
Edgar Allan Poe, *The Pit and the Pendulum*
Georges Perec, *An Attempt at Exhausting a Place in Paris* (tr. Marc Lowenthal)
Giorgio Manganelli, *Discorso dell'ombra e dello stemma*
Glenn Gould, *The Idea of North*
Henri Michaux, "My Properties" and "The Night Moves" in *Darkness Falls* (tr. David Ball)
Marcel Proust, *À la recherche du temps perdu*
Mary Butts, "Mappa Mundi" in *The Complete Stories*
Robert Aldrich, *Kiss Me Deadly*
Roberto Calasso, *The Ruin of Kasch* (tr. Richard Dixon)
Various broken and patched up recollections, summer 2018

Peacock Pie in Paris

Adrian Grafe

Hélène Berr (1921–1944)
The following lines are freely indebted to some passages from:
Hélène Berr, Journal 1942–1944, *preface by Patrick Modiano,*
Tallandier: Paris, 2008

I first saw her at the Institut *library,*
On Rue de l'Ecole-de-Médecine.
"Do you have Peacock Pie?"
They didn't. "I have it and will gladly lend it to you."
We met at the Keats lecture the next day.
"Keep the book as long as you like."
"I'll return it to you at the end of the year."
She told me her name was Hélène.
She told me many things over the months that followed.

I took the 92 bus from Montparnasse to the Etoile,
And walked along Avenue Victor Hugo.
By the time I reached 40, Rue de Villejust,
The famous poet's address, I was holding my breath.
The concierge handed me a book
Along with a card addressed to me. It read:
"You wake to the softest light, the deepest blue".
I breathed anew.

This afternoon I chatted in the Sorbonne courtyard with
Jane Austen — I mean the girl doing her thesis on
Jane Austen.
These students all have the gift
Of making you feel they like you.
Today's Keats lecture I found baffling.
But I had no doubt it was full of fire and poetry.

Boulevard Saint-Michel was bathed in sunlight,
Crowded and lively. I felt the familiar joy
As I approached Rue Soufflot.
From there down to Boulevard Saint-Germain
I always feel I'm in wonderland.

Sitting by the duck-pond in the Luxembourg,
I watched the children's sailboats
On their curving voyages across the water.
Someone said: "The Germans are going to win the war".
I protested as best I could: "Beauty is not beauty
If some people are free to enjoy it and others are not".

In the Latin Quarter I met a friend.
I was wearing my jacket
With the yellow star sewn into the lapel.
I was scared it would break up our friendship.
But such a thing did not cross his mind.
We walked together to the Champ-de-Mars.
Never did a park seem more aptly named:
There were Kraut soldiers goose-stepping up and down
With their necks thrown back. I couldn't help laughing.

This morning I talked with Jane Austen
At her place on Rue Claude Bernard.
Her father had died in a concentration camp.
"They will pay for this," I told her.
She replied, "They will, but that won't bring the dead back
to life".
Her street is so hospitable.
A few days before, just down the road,
A woman had given birth on the pavement.

When I left Jane, there was a sudden downpour:
The streets were empty, and I had Paris all to myself.
I walked across Place du Carrousel.
The Louvre stood stark against the sky,
Like a whale or what used to be the map of Europe.

From the *Institut* I walked to Saint-Séverin,
Then crossed Notre-Dame Bridge
And sat down in the gardens behind the cathedral.
A storm broke out. Hailstones pelted my skin.
I could have stayed there forever.
But the keeper threw me out on seeing my yellow star.

At the last Keats lecture of the year
Hélène, true to her word, gave me my book back.
Though I kept an eye out for her at the Institut
I never saw her again after that.
She had wrapped it in tissue paper and tied it with a ribbon.
On a blank card, above her signature she had written:
"A joy forever! Perhaps this is the only copy of Peacock Pie *in*
Paris".

Dreams of the Dead - IX

Alex Pheby

Samuel Beckett dreamt this dream in/of Paris in/of the rooms above Shakespeare and Company.

On the table there are two photographs: one is *of* a tiger, the other is *on* a Vichy regime ID card. The tiger growls as it approaches — it must have been photographed with a very long lens, since these animals are aggressive; no one armed only with a camera would be a match for it.

On the ID card is an old man with glasses and an eye patch, thin and neurotic, but with an intensity of stare that is intimidating. There are other things on the table, certainly — a saucer from which the cup is missing and into which tea has been poured to cool, the guide sheet from a pad of letter paper, three or four cough lozenges rewrapped in crinkled cellophane, that kind of thing — but these two photographs stand out since you are a human being and notice danger and faces. So should you make a pattern of these two things? Draw a conclusion from them? Despite the frailty of the man, he has the spirit of a tiger and should not be taken for granted? That would be too neat.

Beside the table, one either side, are *deux nègres* singing from prayer books, their insultingly thick lips mouthing the words to different songs on the same subject, but frozen in place in a world where their music soothes only their owner, and any rebellious inclinations they might have in the quiets of their minds are subservient to the dinner music they produce: their song is an *apéritif* for the dreamer of this dream.

You have a ham sandwich in your lap on wax paper. It is too perfect for you to eat. White bread, with the crusts cut off, wafers of pig (which are *haram*) unsalted butter and no mustard. What conclusions can you draw about a person who wishes, but fails, to eat food like this, whilst being sung to by slaves?

Draw no conclusions — they are not warranted.

Outside the room in which you sit a girl is making noise, and you ignore her. You ignore that you are ignoring her, and turn your attention to the back of the room where the man identified by the ID card is sitting in an armchair with an open book on his lap. Beside him is a cat with a kink in its tail. There is no wax paper, but he has a fountain pen, the tip of which is pressed to the page of the book in front of him, unmoving. Surely this is something from which conclusions may be drawn, even if minstrels (genderless) and forbidden sandwiches (neither *kosher* nor *halal*) are not worthy of them?

Resist the temptation, since this is a dream, which is a slippery species of thing, and it can be strangled easily if you can only get a grip on it before it squirms away.

She's at it again, calling from the hallway. Doesn't she understand that she is indoors? She should use her indoor voice! She is not a goatherd on the side of an alp, calling the flock in. It is exasperating to have the attention nagged at constantly, especially in a dream where intrusions from the other world can bring everything to an end in an instant.

If there is a bird outside the window; or the tolling of Emmanuel, Marie, Gabriel, Anne Geneviève, Denis, Marcel, Étienne, Benoît-Joseph, Maurice, and Jean-Marie; or flagstones being lifted (to reveal *la plage*) and hurled, they will encroach on the carefully constructed fantasy. It is as fragile as a bubble and can be burst by simply turning your mind to it.

What is so important anyway? Don't pay her any mind, it's not worth the biscuit.

The figure in the chair is not round-headed, but he has spent a great deal of time in Italy speculating on ideas with more and less success. His work is contradictory, marrying the ineffable with the very much effable, poetry with the everyday, fact and myth, but today he is absolutely motionless. He is like a corpse, or like a puppet, or like a puppet constructed from a corpse, and the positioning of his chair against the undrawn curtains is suspicious. Is there someone behind there, hidden, waiting to perpetrate a fraud on the dreamer? You scan the hem of the curtain, which is faded and threadbare red velvet (if it makes any difference), and indeed, there are a pair of feet, the toes arched so they bring to mind the talons of an eagle, perched on a branch. They march in place, anxiously or excitedly; it is impossible to tell which.

They are a girl's feet. Are they her feet? You cannot hear her now in the hallway, so it is not impossible that she has left the shop, gone into the courtyard, climbed up the drainpipe, made it to the window ledge, slipped the latch with a metal ruler or T-square, opened the window, climbed in through the open window, and now stands behind the curtain.

Puppets can be moved by rods as well as strings, and ventriloquists hollow out a block of wood and place a mechanism inside that allows them to move the mouth, and they slip their arm into the corpse's sleeve to give the impression that the puppet has one hand that is still alive. Is this what she has done, so that now she shuffles impatiently, waiting for the performance to begin?

No, there she is again in the hallway, calling for you.

But a fake medium can arrange things in a room so that the voices of the dead come from offstage, using a gramophone or pipework such as used on a ship to talk from one deck to another. There are many forms of amplification that one can rig up very easily that could make it seem as if she was in one place when in fact she is in another.

You return your attention to the writer, to his corpse, to his puppet, but if you are hoping to be distracted from her by something your master will say or do you are unlucky, since the body remains utterly still and there is about his face the quality of a funerary mask such as that of gold made for the mummy of Tutankhamun, or Agamemnon's that found its way to the tribe of the Mycenae, though neither of those wore glasses and an eyepatch.

It is surprisingly difficult to ignore something when you are aware of the effort, which is why it is always important to keep yourself occupied. Writing books is a good way of distracting yourself from almost anything — it is such an involved process that it is hard to think of anything else, even when it is in your interests to do so — but if you do not have the talent to write books of your own, or you are always in the presence of people who are very much better at it than you are, you can distract yourself by paying very close attention to the writings of these people as an apprentice carpenter pays attention to his master. The novice can watch carefully all the things the old hand does and, in the privacy afforded you once your master has laid down their tools for the night and has gone to be fêted in *Chez Francis* and *Le Fouquet's* and *Les Deux Magots*, attempt a panel of your own devising, a *bas relief* in wood to a similar but not identical scheme as that worked on by your master, and attempt to make the same scene using the same techniques and hope one day either for your skill to grow greater than your master's or for your master's skill to diminish, or for your master to die.

During this uncomfortable period of pupillage, which feels a little like a prolonged arse-fucking, you can alleviate your resentment by making subtle and snide allusions to the faults of your master, who is only a human being, after all, and you can represent him, or his family, in a less than flattering light, but in ways that are entirely deniable, and thereby have the best of both worlds, in that your master will know what you have done but will be unable to chide you for it since that looks an awful lot like paranoia, and to admit you represented something so close to reality that it was recognisable even when disguised is to admit that the apprentice possesses a degree of skill his master has yet to admit exists...

You are interrupted when the corpse moves.

If the puppeteer is trying for verisimilitude, she is not successful: the effect is unnerving and uncanny, jerky like a seafront fortune-telling-booth swami, gears with thick teeth grinding and belts slipping. The voice she gives him is nothing like his own, except for the Irish accent, though her slight Triestine twang ruins this, too.

—Thunder! Lightning! Fire!

She moves her free hand in a circle, tracing the progress of all things in a great meaningless loop and she raises the arm of the corpse, the fingers of which have been set to form the Egyptian hieroglyph for "hand".

In the hallway there is a great pounding and shaking on the wooden floorboards, as if a gymnast is taking the run up to the horse in preparation for a vault. It is so loud that you turn, and through the crack in the door you can see her dancing: a lithe and lugubrious fish from the waist up, a stamping and angry tribesman from the waist down. She bangs her feet as hard as she can, rattling the ornaments precariously balanced on the picture rail, and makes sinuous and alluring convulsions of the chest and neck. In this distraction you fail to notice the approach of the corpse, the breath of which you suddenly feel on your cheek, fanned by her wings into his dead and golden phallus.

This is all so much nonsense.

If you wished to resolve the meaning of this dreamscape you could certainly make an attempt — the etymology of words is so wide-ranging that, with a dictionary, a thesaurus, and enough time, an explanation can be made of any string of random images, once they are transcribed. The same goes for the contexts of things, which can be piled up then sifted through as an archaeologist sifts through the dirt at an excavation site. Which is not to say that things have no meaning, since you know what these things mean by feel. The dream provokes in you guilt and anxiety, and you know that she is the source of it.

If anyone examines dreams they only do so because they know there is a requirement to do so, and they know this because they understand the relevance of the dreams already. The examination is an excuse, confirmation of ideas you do not have the courage to avow for yourself, so you look to the ineffable world to provide a backbone that you do not yourself possess. You will turn to a painting to tell you what you know of the world, to music, to a book, and in there you will pick and choose those things you recognise, and from them build a shield against your own prejudices and certainties, create armour for your intuitions, as if they are too weak to live on their own; like a crab that has shed its carapace, you will seek out a discarded shell and live in that.

The corpse is on your lap now, or you are on its, and one of you is ventriloquizing the other, though neither of you knows quite who is doing what. She is back behind the curtain, and even in the dream you know that you are satirising yourself — symbolism of this kind is so obvious, so transparent to you, that it can only be a product of those dreams you have as you approach the morning, dreams that are losing their form, losing their dreaminess, and into which your conscious mind is beginning to encroach, blinking and curious, to find where it is the night-time self lives, and it is bringing with it all the self-consciousness that typifies waking life, all the taboos, all the defences. It is taking the piss out of you, as you sleep, and you wake at that realisation to find that you left the radio on the night before, that it is past eight, that others in the house are up, and that it is raining hard outside, enough to empty the streets of the breakfasting tourists.

Your mouth is stale and your teeth want licking, but you are dry with the dehydration a person feels when they have drunk up all that was in the house. Your bladder is holding it all, tight against the waistband of his pyjamas. The young Parisian bucks would find an erection down there, their engorgement shutting off the valve preventatively, but you will have to make the crooked-backed, cold-footed journey to the end of the corridor soon, regardless of how your head is, or whether, if you laid back down and turned on your other side, you could return to that room and see behind the curtain whether it was she who was manipulating the old man's corpse.

Where is she now? You should know, but it's easy to let things slide when you are as busy as you are.

First things first. You slip the dressing gown from the hanger where it hangs wedged in the door of the wardrobe, and slip it over your shoulders, slip your feet into your slippers and mince across the room. We are all old now, and there is no sympathy for anyone, but when you return you will go to the dressing table and take out paper and a pen and write to her, at least.

Or you will not.

You haven't written for years, haven't thought about her ten minutes past waking. On the way to take a piss you will be called to from downstairs — perhaps news you have been waiting for, perhaps a personable good morning from someone who deserves a personable reply, perhaps an irritable "what time do you call this?" — whatever it is it will overwrite the obligations of the dream world, replace them with things that are more certain, less internal, things that are practical, and you are awake now, and shouldn't you attend to these things first? You forget that which does not press hard enough on your attention. The bladder will not allow itself to be forgotten, the stomach, the bowel; all of these things know how to blackmail you into doing what they wish. Other people too, a business partner, the rain, the wind, Paris, all of these things are here, in front of you, unavoidable. It is no surprise to anyone that your purview is not infinite — you cannot contain everything in your consciousness at all times. You can scarcely remember your telephone number, or the way to the bank, or whether or not you have watered the flowers, and there are some things that can only be properly addressed once all the pressing things of the world have been silenced behind closed eyes, and in the respectful hush that falls on a person in their own house after their bedtime.

Defunge

Richard Marshall

Beckett's grave was the last place I visited when last in
Paris. I took the air there willingly, more so than elsewhere,
according to the doomed verbs and mists and disjecta,
nothing much to write home about but nevertheless in the
lowest deep a lower deep, like an undertaker's, or lapida-
tionist's. It must have been January or late December, both
with their crass tenacity of life and its diligent pains written
out in the moment, a little Paris snow to last a little more
as a finish, a last time living for the theme I'd given the
place, an original French to cleave constituents apart, which
were, truth be told, melancholic mixed with overzealous.
All alone and without commiseration, it was a vivid
nothing between the lunulae, a moment grave-swaddled
and parenthetic, to be honest. What was I wanting? Well,
I was playing fast and balls with desires and lacks. So the
moment at the grave went off half-cocked. I wished to
see Paris gone, from the old stand where it loomed in a
proportion of vast invention, as he'd say how it is, a Paris
erect and rigid in the deepening gloom completely cut
adrift from any reality other than that which it manifests
by its mere presence in language, rightly or very wrongly
as you might suppose. Fuckit, the whisky bears a grudge
against the decanter. In the darkening late afternoon as
if all colours ebbed and ashen I didn't feel like rejoicing,

to my knowledge, nor speaking up, not being deaf, and never gave way to reverie or meditation. I had crammed up with things, all 735,840,000 heart thumps when first time round, a youthful twenty, years before, with the intention of meeting him, an abortion in the end at the dimmening window of Les Éditions de Minuit office 7, Rue Bernard-Palissy and no elegance of diction would relieve me now, him gone and my own winding sheet writhing somewhere in its cupboard, every day less moribund. Before the graveyard deadlight I'd taken a day traipsing to the convulsive spaces, spits, glasses, matches, sands, beers, floors, doors where Bataille, Beckett, Giacometti once came and goed, hung about in the grey ripe cold outside the Bibliothèque Nationale, froze before the École des Chartes before striding like I might attain a life goal by a kind of short-circuit to 3 Rue de Lille and then to 259 Rue Saint-Honoré, where Bataille and Beckett as pure figments of sun corpseless heads shadowed net curtains of black crêpe drying on black trees. Ghosts. I drank a bit in profound apathy of death thinking of the Chinese jar and the perpetual movement in its stillness, half thinking of getting out to 59 Rue Saint-Étienne in the village of Vézelay where Bataille dead to the world kept house unknown, but opted not to leave Paris, I being perhaps a little unconscious by then. I toured round looking for addresses for each of the trio, each address a pause which gives you pause, Balthus's studio at 3 Cour de Rohan where Bataille holed up, then Beckett's early inexistent centre of a formless place, minimally less on the way to inexistence as he put it, 16 Rue de Condé for starters. I barely thought I might go out to Ussy to the east and never did. Instead, after more beer to hasten my misadvantages, I shilly-shallied at the École Normale Supérieure on Rue d'Ulm, but was barred from getting in to Beckett's room on the first floor overlooking the road by an official who gave me hardly a glance before shooing me off. I got the view from it anyway by reading; "the bare tree, dripping; then, behind, smoke from the janitor's chimney-pot, rising stiff like a pine of ashes; then, beyond, beyond the world, pouring a little light up the gully of the street that westers to the Luxembourg...". And felt the satisfaction of cheating the authorities with this. There were other blanks I registered: the café Cochon de Lait in Rue de Corneille was no longer there, nor so the Hôtel Corneille on the very same road. I flew around through the cold to Joyce's flat at Square Robiac, to the top of the Hotel Trianon at 1 bis Rue de Vaugirard just around the corner from the Rue de Corneille. As fast as can reasonably be expected, and saying no more than needs be, I went to Beckett's first address in the city — 12 Rue de la Grande Chaumière — and then to the Hôtel Libéria at No. 9 from where Beckett first ventured out to speak with Giacometti. Such was this long circuit, like love requited as Neary has it, it included the place where Beckett was stabbed by a pimp along the Avenue d'Orléans (now Avenue du Général Leclerc) then off to Broussais hospital where he recovered. What next in the corpse light? To a studio at the top of No. 6 Rue des Favorites before vagitating to the outside vantage of his seventh-floor flat in an apartment block at 38 Boulevard Saint-Jacques with the prison in its brevity across the way. Mid-afternoon I endured more oblivion outside the Salle Wagram or "Multicolor", Avenue de Wagram, where he'd gamble, and then later outside where Beckett would play his billiards at Les Trois Mosquetaires on Avenue du Maine. Perhaps a little later I found the Falstaff on the Rue de Montparnasse, the Rosebud just around the corner on Rue Delambre and the Closerie des Lilas on Boulevard de Montparnasse, before setting down again for more drinks out of the cold in the yellow dimness of some antepenultimate café. But I forget the order and the details are shaky. And so then the final leg: first plunging inside the Petit Café PLM in the Hôtel Saint-Jacques on the boulevard of that same saint, a curiously bleached and impersonal place in which he oversaw his last hurrahs and murmurings. But not quite the very last. Life has to begin as well as end, was all Hazlitt could say to cure our fear of dying. I was more or less drunk by the time I reached the Tiers Temps nursing home at 26 Rue Rémy-Dumoncel, on the way passing the Giacometti studio at 46 Rue Hippolyte-Maindron in Montparnasse, where Beckett and Giacometti tried out a tree for Godot. After lurking about in the abyssal cold outside the place where Beckett in spite of all turned blessed as the dead that die, that the rain rains on, that the sun shines on, etc., I started out to the cemetery for a final glimpse of Paris. The sun extinguished and dropped and a last thought in the freezing gloam was his: "...to be buried in lava and not turn a hair, it is then that a man shows what stuff he is made of. To know you can do better next time, unrecognisably better, and that there is no next time, and that it is a blessing there is not, there is a thought to be going on with". I went on with it.

Not-Beckett

Toby Litt

In a high hall, Oxford, the American biographer (*great* biographer) Hugh Kenner (is that worth saying?) was speaking — of Oscar Wilde, I think. I don't remember what else he said during his lecture; I was thirty rows back, among the other undergraduates, perhaps the back row. And I was doubtful, wishing for Derrida or dead-Barthes or other "theory", not biographical fallacy. But at one still vivid point, in a raised voice, with reverence — this was 1987, or 1988 — Kenner said, up toward the ceiling, "There is one great Modernist, alive," pause, "in *Paris*." Or perhaps the forgotten lecture was on Ezra Pound, about whom I was especially doubtful (apart from his dead-on editing job on *The Waste Land*) (by deceased Modernist T.S. Eliot, but written by him in a living-dead state). There was another pause, after "Paris" ceased echoing, a pause for everyone so close to the parquet floor — who already knew he meant Beckett — to form each their own image of what living Sam was up to, that Parisian moment. Afternoon. Writing or not-writing — most likely not-writing. And if not-writing, which for Beckett was more active an activity than writing is for most writers — if not-writing, then in a café, with a coffee, photogenic, as in John Minihan's great photograph of him. Kenner insisted, during that silence, which (for me, at least) lasted for the next five years: we were in Oxford,

446

not Paris; we were not Modernists, we were post-Modernists; and above all, we were certainly not, and were never going to be, Samuel Beckett.

Above is what I wrote, before Googling. Where I found I was not wholly wrong. Hugh Kenner gave the F.W. Bateson Memorial lecture, in Oxford, on 18 February 1987. But this is what his first words were: "To commence with good news: the Last Modernist is well in Paris where he lives under the name of Beckett." Last, not Great; Last to mean great. I misremembered the rhythm. And he spoke the vivid name, rather than letting an educated room infer it. But clearly, thirty years later, I haven't forgotten the angle of the wound. We were — I was not-Paris, not-not-writing, not-Beckett.

Paris, Isidore Isou, and Me

Andrew Hussey

I met Isidore Isou only once.

This was in April 1999 when I was working on a biography of the Situationist writer Guy Debord. I needed to speak to Isou because in the 1940s Debord and Isou had been close friends, with the former in the role of disciple to the latter. For a short while Debord had been a member of the avant-garde movement founded by Isou called *lettrisme* (or "Lettrism" in English). They had quickly fallen out, however, and despised each other since. "Debord was like a Nazi," Isou told me, "Worse than a Nazi."

Debord shot himself through the heart in November 1994. But this suicide only made things worse for Isou. Debord became posthumously famous for his book *The Society of the Spectacle,* written in 1967 but now considered a text that prophesied the contemporary world of iPhones and social networks — the new "civilisation of the image" as he put it. Isou was jealous that Debord was now also being written about outside France, mainly in Britain and America. His work appeared on university syllabuses and his ideas were claimed as a major influence on all forms of countercultures, from the near-revolution of May '68 to punk rock and rave culture. For Isou, however, Debord was no great thinker; he was no more than a drunk, a plagiarist and a betrayer. Given the level of hate that had simmered away between them for nearly fifty years, I was amazed that Isou had agreed to speak to me at all.

Isou was then seventy-four years old. He had been in bad health for some time and had been unable to walk for several months. He lived in Paris in two small rooms at the top of a building at 42 Rue Saint-André-des-Arts. He had been here since 1965, never leaving the Left Bank except for a few trips to Israel. Legend has it that he had paid off the mortgage by selling a sculpture given to him by Alberto Giacometti.

The apartment was simple and austere: a table, a chair, a bed, no paintings or other images on the walls. The bathroom was used to store paintings; the bath itself contained several medium-sized works. Isou preferred to use a public bathhouse. The three rooms of the apartment were laid out like a long corridor, with windows overlooking a courtyard. This was the common pattern of cheap Left Bank hotels, which was what the apartment had once been. Rather than a place to live, this was a place to consume ideas and books which passed through the apartment as fast as Isou could devour them.

The apartment was also dense with books and newspapers and I noted straight away that Isou was reading simultaneously two huge volumes — the first on Kurt Swchwitters; the second a compendium of Dadaist texts. Isou had not left his apartment for two years and received no visitors apart from a nurse and his friend Roland Sabatier, a filmmaker and artist, who had tight control over the still active group of *lettristes* in Paris.

The room was baking hot, becoming unbearable as the afternoon lengthened. Isou was taking medication for a degenerative condition that led him to drool and slobber on occasion, making him hard to understand at times. The black propaganda from Debord and his supporters was that Isou was totally mad, but it soon became clear — as Isou kept making sense and even cracked jokes — that this was not the case. Happily, we soon left Guy Debord and the tedious intricacies of avant-garde rivalry behind. Instead Isou began to tell me another, altogether more compelling story. It was the story of his life, which he had never talked about before, and certainly not to anyone outside the charmed circle of *lettriste* devotees.

All of that was nearly twenty years ago and it has taken me that long to get round to writing Isou's story, which is the book I am working on now. I left Paris after 1999, published my book on Debord and then some others. Although based in the UK as an academic, I also spent a good part of the intervening years travelling, writing and teaching in North Africa, mainly in Tangier. In 2003 I came back to Paris on a sabbatical, and in 2006 settled here for good. It was not long after this that I started to pick up the threads of Isou's tale, listened to the tapes I had made of our meeting, and started to realise that here was a story that was both old and contemporary — as old and contemporary as Paris itself.

It goes like this. Isidore Isou has largely been forgotten or ignored by cultural historians. This is partly because he believed something which was absurd and impossible. He was a fanatic who held the fantastical belief that he was the Jewish Messiah sent to lead all Humanity to redemption. His most tragic belief was that through the philosophy and practice of *lettrisme* he could find the secret of immortality.

When, as he grew older, his body began to break down, the realisation that he would die like other humans destroyed his mental stability. Ignored by critics and diagnosed by psychiatrists, Isou saw himself as trapped in Kafka's Castle. He could see no way out and his pain intensified.

Amongst the many challenges of writing about Isou is the fact that he does not often stand still or always make sense: he is grandiose, exasperating, self-regarding, brilliant, piercing and poetic; often all in the space of the same page. So it was that when I started writing this book two years ago, I had no idea where it might take me.

I started to learn Romanian, mainly to decipher Isou's earliest diaries. He was a teenager during the war, like Anne Frank, and his account of life as a Jew under the German Occupation is adolescent, funny and frightening. As I read other accounts of the Romanian Holocaust, many still unpublished, I found myself lost in the murky shadows of wartime Romania and what it was like to be a Jew there. I thought I would be more sure-footed when I came to look at Isou in the context of post-war France, but his ideas and creativity often accelerate at such a pace that it could make you dizzy (his associates and disciples all report the same experience). His mental breakdown is still pretty much uncharted territory, with only occasional flashes of illumination from his wartime traumas to light the way.

As I have been writing this book I have been reminded of *Journey to the End of the Night*, the great novel by Louis-Ferdinand Céline which takes us through the madness of the mid-twentieth century through the eyes of its Chaplinesque anti-hero called Bardamu. Isou was an admirer of Céline, even though Céline was a pro-Hitler anti-Semite, who sometimes shocked the German authorities in Occupied Paris with his venom. Isou and Céline share, however, a visionary method. What brings them together as writers is the fact that — to quote André Gide (on Céline) —— they "do not describe reality but the hallucination which reality provokes". It is perhaps worth mentioning here that I fell in love with Céline at the age of sixteen (reading Ralph Manheim's translation), and his books were why I came to Paris in the first place, and started to properly learn French.

For me the importance of Isou is that, like Céline, he gives us a ground-level account of history in real time. Following Isou's own journey has taken me to Romania, Israel, Italy, Switzerland and Germany; to abandoned death camps and a run-down apartment in the *banlieues* of Paris — where the walls are hung with invaluable paintings that Isou gave to a former *lettriste* camp follower.

Isou's daughter, Catherine Goldstein, is also part of the story. As a schoolgirl she hated the Sunday afternoons she was forced to spend with him (he was long since divorced from her mother Jacqueline), when he would drill her in mathematics and as an apprentice genius. She is now a distinguished Professor of Mathematics at the University of Paris, and acknowledges that for all his eccentricity, Isou knew something that was true.

In our conversations, Catherine and I have returned again and again to the Hasidic tradition of Jewish mysticism in which Isou had been raised, which he lived and breathed as a child. There is one singular belief in this tradition which Isou never lost sight of. This is a belief that is at the core of being an *Ostjude*, a Jew from the East, and it is contained in the formula that "man is the language of God". You can find this belief at work in the paintings of Marc Chagall or the writings of Elie Wiesel, as well as countless rabbis and mystics from the Jewish Orient. From this point of view, for all its convoluted abstractions, Isou's *lettrisme* does not necessarily make immediate sense, but it does suddenly come into focus.

As I began to write this book, many of Isou's closest *lettriste* associates cautioned me against it. They had various reasons: they did not want me to shatter their faith in their idol, they were worried that I would make them look foolish, I did not understand the hermetic art of *lettrisme* which they owned and, worst of all, it would be "an Anglo-Saxon work of biography" — the kind of book I had already written about French literary figures, most notably the Situationist Guy Debord, and so it would be vulgar, simple-minded and sensationalist. When I told Roland Sabatier, who has been a faithful *lettriste* since 1963, that I was going to travel back to Romania to retrace Isou's steps, he told me that it would be a pointless "journey for no reason" as Isou never talked about the past.

Sabatier is wrong. Isou's life was an extraordinary voyage through the mid-twentieth century. Retracing his steps — recreating his story as a journey — is the only way to get near to seeing the world as he saw it, and then to understanding it as he understood it. Isou, like all Eastern Jews of his generation, feared most of all being consumed by and then lost to the murderous historical forces at work in his era. "Whatever I write," he said in his autobiography, "I write it because I am a Jew, and I am afraid."

Isou wrote this seventy years ago, when he first arrived in Paris in August 1945. Much has changed in the city since then, but there is much here too that he would find familiar and unchanged, including Jew-hatred. That is not the only reason why I want to write about Isou — I am also captivated by his mad, capricious, overweening and sometimes (but not often) heroic self — but it is the reason why I feel the *need* to write this book right now.

Le Palace

Nicholas Rombes

To understand what it's like at Le Palace, in May 1978, you have to understand what it's like in the red van, and to understand what it's like in the van you have to understand Natalie. But no one understands Natalie. Natalie and her green hair. Her bruise-colored tattoos. How can you understand someone if she doesn't understand herself? That was Roland's theory at least. But I never saw it that way. Maybe that's why Nat and I hit it off so well. That and the fact that she and I were both from Ohio and that she missed it as much if not more than I did. The street names in Ohio: Dutch Road. Mechanic Street. Cherry Lane. Finzel Road. But in Paris? Surrounding Le Palace? Montmartre, d'Uzès, Feydeau. They broke my mouth.

Everything that happened back then happened, first, in Toledo, Ohio. There was no other world than Toledo, in 1978. It was the real world. The world of the present. And everything that happened made it possible, at last, for us to arrive in Paris.

Which in turn replaced Toledo as the real world.

*

We were due at Le Palace, that glittery dump, at 7:00 and it was already 7:30. The van had broken down again on a

455

terrible, guttered stretch of Rue Chauchat. By broken down I mean tire blown and ran out of gas, and by ran out I mean Roland wasn't paying attention to the gas gauge. For all his talk of signs and mythologies he was a simple man. A simple man in belted khakis and worn penny loafers. And also: soft, deceptive eyes. And also: nobody who knew him called him Roland back then. To us, he was RB. How you read the gas gauge didn't matter anyway because it had been stuck on one-quarter of a tank for months now. RB was the drummer and the driver of the van. Our sixty-three-year-old drummer. At that time, he was still at the Collège de France. He was also Nat's occasional lover although Nat would not describe it that way and neither would RB. He who hated binaries ended up loving someone who was the opposite. For there was something between Nat and RB that I would call love even if they couldn't see it for themselves. We'd all had the sentimentality pounded out of us by a remorseless shellacking of ego-blows, shattered hopes, and epic disappointments, both in our personal lives and in what Nat continued to refer to as the *culture industry* long after that phrase fell out of fashion. And so the word love never touched our lips.

Even while standing at the side of the road at twilight with the wet taxis we could feel the end. RB had used bolts from his drum kit as makeshift lug nuts and as much as he'd wanted them to hold they hadn't of course, having come loose, probably, miles back and flying off into the black dirt of some farmer's field. And so there was Roland with his old, arthritic hands hunched in the dark beside the red van, his long unwashed hair some sort of temporary disguise that was threatening to become permanent. It was said that RB had ghostwritten tracts for a notorious Satanist (is there any other kind?) in the 1960s while vacationing in Biarritz during the Satanic-ritual-abuse hysteria which, he said, had only served to shield the real Satanists, who preferred adults to children. He'd read a repressed early draft of *Le Roi en jaune*, one that included a level of explicit, blood-on-the-crosses sensation that wrecked the mythology of it all.

But this was 1978, not 1895, and Le Palace was to be our final show.

"We're fucked," RB had said, in that soft, nasal way of his, the draft of a passing taxi carrying his words away. In French of course. It was one of his favorite phrases and so it didn't mean much. Crouched down by the blown tire I could see his body breathing and felt a sudden and deep sympathy for him. His old man shoulders. His pink silk neck scarf loose and dirty. His time in the desert unlearning theory had unleashed something in him that he was finding hard to put away. Like many men of his generation he was acutely aware that he was no longer needed, that he was obsolete, that the forces of deconstruction that he himself had loosed had now, paradoxically, made him irrelevant. Plus the Satanists were back in fashion again as the Seventies petered out, and darker than ever. I walked over and put my hand on RB's shoulder and offered to help.

He stood up slowly and looked at me with his wet eyes that said what his mouth had said moments ago, and I realized that his *we're fucked* was meant in a more universal sense, as in *we're fucked in this universe*. The thing about Roland is that there was never anything cynical or nihilistic about what he said. The *fuckedness* he was talking about was something that bound us all together, made us a team, gave us a reason.

"Let's go then," he said, climbing back into the driver's seat. It turns out we made it to Le Palace by 8:00 and we weren't even due to take the upper stage until 9:00. It was a warm night, ten years after May '68. Like I said. And here we were, booked at Le Palace, RB's hands and shirt stained in black oil and exhaust dust, and Natalie — I've left Natalie with her pale grass-green hair out of this for good reason — on the verge of some sort of epochal breakdown, and me in my American denim wondering how we were going to make a complete set out of just three songs, the only songs we knew.

But as we took the stage all fear drained away. Roland at his drums. Nat at her keyboard. Me at the mic. The famous and the not-famous mixing in the crowd, the black Paris night leaking in, the swell of a century pushing at the walls. *Each of us has his own rhythm of suffering* RB liked to say, and yet the rhythm that night was not of suffering but of joy, the terrible joy of RB's last days, and of Nat and her green hair beckoning us deeper into some morally fucked jungle, the red van outside like a fading portal to Hell; Le Palace itself suddenly free from the dead weight of its own legend, our music like the wail of an alien drone.

A palace of noise, with many rooms. It was Natalie who took us deeper into the blackness, deeper than we had ever gone before, and with us the audience. Curtains of sound and gradually her Minimoog became a sonic weapon slaughtering the sorts of thoughts that held so many of us hostage to the worst parts of ourselves. Gradually the chants of *mort, mort, mort* were countered by *vie, vie, vie* and we all paused. RB flung his drumsticks into the audience. Natalie's Minimoog gradually ascended and levitated twenty feet above the stage and floated out above the audience. And though my mouth was closed you could hear my song, our song, the last song we would play together.

Two years later RB would be dead, run down by a laundry truck of all things. And Nat would become a teacher and then disappear into the jungles of Peru. Paris would once again become a closed city, *saboteurs* controlling the streets at night. As for me, I adopted Roland's daughter, the daughter no one knew about, and raised her and took care of her, as I promised Roland I would. I see her now, from my small balcony, walking down Rue Biot, on her way to visit. She will pause and wave. *Papa!* The sun will catch her watch and I will unlatch the door in anticipation of her arrival.

Petite vilaine

Susana Medina

Living from hand to mouth
was a prerequisite to Rue Marguerite Duras.
She might transmigrate to the Louvre
as Brexit is no game,
though, argh, the Far Right
has also been on the rise in France.
Duras said:
"Sometimes I think Le Pen should be killed.
Not me. But if there was someone brave enough to do it."
Did Beckett meet her?
Did Córtazar meet her?
A punk tried to plunge
into Córtazar's grave.
He was restrained.

There might have been chance encounters.
In any case, many of her special friends
are now all gathered in the same point in space,
which she once circled on the map of Paris.
It was the time of interrailing
and urchin shenanigans,
café au lait at Gare du Nord, every year,
and she learnt to dematerialize croissants

from nearby tables,
and on one occasion,
after two *cafés au lait*,
on checking into the toilet,
a glimpse of the brasserie's innards and an exit sign
which led to
an irresistible industrial spiral staircase
which flew into the streets.
An intrepid traveller,
down she went, fast, fast,
green velvet ivy cap hat,
skin and gaze so young,
bill unpaid.

The main square
suddenly materialized an out-of-breath overweight waiter
who'd been chasing her.
And catching her eyes, he yelled:
Petite vilaine!
And the words
sounded so beautiful and archaic,
she beamed a smile.
And out-of-breath, he grinned back.
And what a tough job!
And the debt was settled,
and the moment glowed
and survived
recorded in the Annals of the Absurd.

And off she glided
to the angels of Montparnasse Cemetery,

a rendezvous with her beloved word magicians,
exquisite corpses feted with plants, metaphysical pebbles
and tube tickets.

Existentialism is Gay

Isabel Waidner

In the summer of 2004 I took a short adult learning course called "Existentialism", or "Existentialist Philosophy" — I can't remember for sure and neither can I find any trace of it online. The course was run by Birkbeck but held at the London School of Economics on the Strand. I lived in Camden at the time. I'd been reading European philosophy since my late teens (Camden public libraries held and may still hold significant Euro philosophy collections, including works in German original). I'd been attending open lectures at Goldsmiths for years ("feminism" stood for "queer" at Goldsmiths, we all flocked there). But this was my first foray into a university setting as an officially enrolled student — I was thirty, although I looked younger. There were no formal entry requirements to the course, and, crucially, I was entitled to a substantial discount (75% off, or maybe it was even free) as a housing benefit claimant. I worked full-time in retail, but needed my Central London rent topped up.

Tuesday evenings at the LSE, keen adult learners, tables arranged in a U probably. I have no recollection of the lecturer (a sobering realization — I'm a university lecturer now). What I remember is Frank. I hadn't seen Frank for a couple of years, but like me, they were here to swat up on existentialism.

Frank and I used to work together in a café on D'Arblay Street, Soho. Kitchen staff, cooking potato mash by the bucketload, "lifting" Somerfield's readymade pasta sauce with curly parsley and a splash of tamari. Microwaves pinging. Mountains of washing up. Frank disengaged from the more physical tasks — mopping the floor, cleaning the toilets, taking the bins out, taking the biscuit — for existential reasons. Frank didn't go there, they counted themselves out. Instead, they stood by the counter, poised, performing their own brand of mild-mannered gender and sexuality, not lifting a finger. Fair enough, we all thought, including the manager. I picked up the slack and still I thought "fair enough". I still do. We'd created a working environment which supported idiosyncrasy and subcultural flair in that café.

Frank! Fancy meeting you here — What you up to? (This, during small group work in "Existentialism, Week 1".) Shooting a film. Want to be in it? Sure — And you, what you up to? Oh, nothing, I said. Writing a novel. Editing a journal — the ICA bookshop is stocking it. Want to contribute to the next issue? At the time, I didn't ask Frank why they'd signed up for a course on, of all things, existentialism. What was in it for a British Malaysian Fine Art graduate in their mid-twenties? And what, for that matter, was in it for me (an EU working-class self-identified writer)? I haven't asked myself that until now — what was the investment?

When I came to the UK in 1996 for the sole purpose of coming out, I brought one book — the recently published red-and-black Rowohlt paperback edition of Sartre's *Tagebücher: Les carnets de la drôle de guerre (September 1939 -*

März 1940), in German. I still have it, this is its blurb (Google translate, my edit):

> The reservist Jean-Paul Sartre, weather observer of an artillery unit, pursues his favourite occupation. He writes. For up to thirteen hours a day. The ~~stupid~~ stupefying military environment in which the thirty-four-year-old — already a star ~~in~~ on the ~~fictional heaven~~ literary firmament at the time — inspires him: in his diary, the only one he ever kept, he notes observations, literary stories, philosophical reflections. We find ~~bacteria~~ germs of later works, such as entire sections from *Being and Nothingness* or his autobiographical novel, *The Words*. The diaries are the fascinating document of the young genius. The paperback edition contains — for the first time in German translation — the lost but recently rediscovered first book of the diaries.

Simply put, Sartre's *Carnets de la drôle de guerre* made me want to become a writer. ("He writes.") ("For up to thirteen hours a day"—) ("His favourite occupation.") As I saw it, writing gave purpose|control|power to Sartre's existence, temporarily suspended by the Second World War. For me, life was whatever might be the opposite of "suspended" (to do list: find a job, find a room, get to know at least a single soul in the UK), but life could do with some purpose injected into it. Something a bit aspirational ("young genius"), something beyond sheer survival ("germs of later works").

Unlike Sartre, who found himself stationed at Marmoutier or Morsbronn with soldiers called Pieter or

Paul, I found myself working in kitchens, lately with Frank. Like Sartre ("up to thirteen hours a day"), I wrote a lot. Unlike Sartre, I wasn't already a star in "fictional heaven". Unlike Sartre, I wasn't publishing with Gallimard, nor did I expect to be (no sense of entitlement). So why I thought Sartre's philosophy — existentialism — should make for a fitting analytics through which to think my own writing and experience is beyond me.

"Young genius", the blurb says. "Young genius" — *not* educated at Cours Hattmer (an elite private school in Paris) and the École Normale Supérieure. "Young genius", it says, and "x-beliebiger Soldat" (any old soldier). It does *not* say, "Jean-Paul's *maman* was the first cousin of Nobel Prize laureate Albert Schweitzer". "X-BELIEBIGER SOLDAT" IT SAYS — I just checked!

Euro philosophy has taught me many things, but the way it buries its situatedness, obscures the conditions of its possibility, is problematic. The word "genius" does burying work — in blurbs, and elsewhere. Replace "genius" with "privilege", I say. Here is the blurb in plain English (German; even French): "The *Carnets de la drôle de guerre* are the work of a highly educated white man from an extremely privileged background with some talent and a childhood characterized by paternal loss and bullying that gets channelled into literary ambition." Something along those lines.

White middle-class writing is so normalized, its specificity disappears. Now in my forties, I don't need an announcement or contextualizing statement. I read two sentences of something, anything, and I see it; it's all there. But I didn't see it at twenty, nor at thirty; not really. It's like having friends in yr mid-twenties who are cash-poor like you. Like you, they are artists or writers, they wear clothes from Oxfam or ASOS. You work in similarly crappy jobs, you share a flat in Whitechapel or Bethnal Green. Occasionally, yr friends' parents visit the flat. Yr parents never visit. Over time it transpires, yr friends' parents pay their share of the rent, plus bills. It also transpires that many of yr friends have degrees from Oxbridge. You don't know exactly what that means, an Oxbridge degree, not in your twenties you don't. Class plays out differently in yr country of origin (yr deadcountry), so it takes you a minute (years) to learn to interpret British class signifiers correctly, to learn how class works in Britain. When you reach yr thirties, yr friends find themselves in jobs you'd never have access to — you didn't even know they'd applied! (Did they ever apply?) Their careers take off, and you're still working in catering, love, in yr mid-thirties. Eventually, you *do* learn how class works in Britain — from your working-class peers, reading cultural theory, critical race theory, queer theory. You stop Euro philosophising. Yr ontological takes make way for urgent critiques of power in yr writing. You're getting a handle on it, now that you're forty.

I wonder what might have been possible had some brilliant uni professor or hourly-paid lecturer introduced me to theoretical approaches that might have helped me to actually make sense of my experiences, as well as those of my working-class peers? At the very least, it might have made me a better writer, sooner.

The question remains: why did I care about the weatherman in the first place? Why bring the *Carnets de la drôle de guerre* to London in '96? Sartre's play *Huis Clos* (*No Exit*) was on the curriculum at the German secondary school I attended (a good state school with a mixed working- and middle-class demographic). *Huis Clos* had a lesbian in it, that's why. We didn't have the internet in the early Nineties — I, closeted, was sold on *Huis Clos*. Its lesbian, Inès, was one of the first I ever encountered.

Existentialism has fag appeal. Must message Frank —

Going through my drawer just now — what th fk, I kept the "Existentialism" course booklet. I don't have a sentimental attachment to things; I tend not to keep things (a defence mechanism I developed having lost everything once). (Should unlearn.) So what th fk made me hold on to a badly photocopied, stapled together booklet containing set readings, over the course of five London moves (Camden, Highgate, King's Cross, Camden, Brixton, Crystal Palace)? I studied, that's what. I was a student. I, student. Once, when I was studying (on a six-week adult learning class at Birkbeck —). For a minute, I was a student, and not just self-educating all of the time. I was an actual student, as good as a star in fictional heaven.

Week 1: Introduction. Week 2: Being and Nothingness (An Essay on Phenomenological Ontology). Week 3: She Came To Stay (Novel). Week 4: The Second Sex. Week 5: Photo of young white French philosophers being social, smoking. Week 5: No Exit! Week 6: missing. According to the booklet, the course was called "Sartre and de Beauvoir", not "Existen-tialism". It gives me the name of the lecturer, I go on their Wiki page: They published several monographs on European Philosophy and worked at the Adult Education Department at Birkbeck starting in 1995. "When the courses at Birkbeck were cut as a cost-saving measure in 2010—"

ADULT LEARNING COURSES AT BIRKBECK WERE CUT AS A COST-SAVING MEASURE IN 2010. 2010 is the year the Tories got into government. The year the ConDem coalition government started dismantling welfare. The year the ConDem coalition government capped housing benefit with immediate effect, which meant that the amount paid no longer reflected the rents in Central London, effectively cleansing the capital of the working class. The year the ConDem coalition government trebled tuition fees at university.

What Sartre did share with me — and possibly anyone, say Stuart Hall, who ever migrated from any country to England — was a preoccupation with the weather, and that's it. It's obvious that my writing should not be like Sartre's — nor like the writing of most of my literary contemporaries. My writing should be like Frank's perfect refusal, like criticality and transparency, like urgency, like asking for it, like getting some, like giving something back. It's taken me years to figure it out. I blame existentialism.

The Identity of Indiscernibles

Nicholas Blincoe

Martin's father worked at Fothergills for forty years, and six months after he retired he could barely remember a day of it. Can you explain that, he had asked? Martin had no answer. When his father left the mill, Martin was a Cambridge professor, the author of five books, and two dozen other papers. He had spent more than half his life obsessed with philosophy. Why would that end? How could he turn it off?

Easily, it turned out. He had taken leave when his wife was ill. When she died, there was nothing left in the tank. Martin retired formally, and never thought about the problems that had consumed his career. If he came across old notes in the back of a book, he struggled to remember what the words meant: "rigid designators", "the indiscernibility of identicals". He knew, but barely... barely... barely at all.

He was only thinking about philosophy that day because he was meeting Norris. Norris Hammond was the Challis Professor at the University of Sydney, so some philosophy must be fresh in his mind. He was already at the table in La Coupole when Martin arrived; the same man, full of hail-fellow bluster, even fatter than he was eight years ago. They had become friends at Harvard in the Fifties, and remained drinking buddies at conferences. Hooking up for a weekend in Paris was a new experience. The two men hugged: Norris was a hugger. Immediately, he began complaining that it took a series of letters to organise their holiday.

"A fucking letter, Marty! Who needs that? It's the fucking Nineties, embrace it."

"What can I do? I got out before the advent of electronic mail. What am I missing?"

"Aw, you haven't got a fucking clue, mate. It's not just for the departmental goss: it's the whole of life. Get on to AOL and get an account, so your pals can get in touch without taking three fucking months. I'm serious, mate." Norris waved at a waiter, simultaneously pointing at his highball glass. The drink was soda pink and filled with bubbles, probably Dubonnet. It looked like Martin was drinking the same thing. When in Paris, do like the fat Australian, etc.

"Listen, mate, I hate to put business before pleasure, but Ruth is desperate to get hold of you. She knows I'm seeing you, and she's giving me earache. Or locked caps ache, I guess. Email after email after email."

"Ruth who?"

"Barking Ruth."

"Ruth Barcan?"

Norris rolled his eyes upwards. "Holy Mother. She is fearsome, mate. She's got this petition, and everyone has to sign. You know she's on the board of the American Phil Soc, as well as the Symbolic Logic Soc, and now she's the President of the International Institute. Trust an ex-fucking-communist organiser to be methodical, right? Everyone has to toe her line. You know her dad was a trade-union leader, right? The United Textile Workers of fucking Brooklyn, I bet."

"My dad was in textiles," Martin said. "I think Ruth's father was a printer."

"See. You know her. You know what a ball-ache she is."

"What's the petition?"

"She wants to stop Cambridge giving an award to that charlatan Jacques La Kak."

"Lacan? The psychotherapist?"

"No. The other one. The deconstruction clown."

"Jacques Derrida?"

"That's the chap. Have you read him?"

"No."

"Yeah? But absolute fucking codswallop, right, mate?"

"I suppose so. What's Ruth got against him?"

"She's saying, if Cambridge hands out this award, it brings the entire profession into disrepute. She's still angry about the argument Derrida had with John Searle. The pair were supposed to have a face-off but Derrida avoided the debate by making *ad hominem* attacks and inventing quotes."

Martin remembered the affair. It was ten years ago, so why rehash it? Martin and Searle had their own history of disagreements. A philosophical argument need not lead to personal ill-will, but Martin was not going to run to Searle's defence, given a choice.

"What's Ruth's problem? Searle is tough enough. If he feels aggrieved, he can take care of himself."

"Ruth was at Yale when this Derrida joker was a visiting Professor in the English department," Norris said. "She's had direct experience of him. He was always sneering, looking down his long French nose at her, and not beyond that genteel European anti-Semitic shit, either."

Martin thought he understood, now. "So the petition is about racism?"

"No, mate. It's about bringing philosophical argument into disrepute." Norris was finishing his second highball. "Listen. This lunch is on me, and we're having the full spectrum *fruits de mer*, okay? The set of all possible sets."

Martin looked across to a nearby table where a three-tier cake stand dripped with lobsters and shellfish. "Fine. But, listen. I've never read Derrida. I don't teach any more. Can you just tell Ruth I've gone gaga in retirement."

Norris laughed. "No way, mate. She wants you. There's no way out of it." Norris opened his wallet and took out a long strip of paper like a ticker tape. It held an enormously long telephone number. "Call her. And don't make a twat of yourself and forget the time difference with New York."

They drank three bottles of champagne with the seafood feast, on top of the earlier aperitifs, and the later digestifs. As they staggered to the pavement, Martin asked who else had signed Ruth's petition. Norris reeled off a list of names. The biggest came last.

"She's even got Van to sign."

"She's cornered Van! So why the bloody hell is she worrying about me?"

"Because you're the Cambridge Professor Emeritus, mate. It's the politics. Ruth needs a Cambridge man to make the petition stick. She isn't going to let you get out of this. Remember: her Barcan's bad, but her biting's worse."

Martin woke glumly after a late-afternoon nap. He was hungover, and he felt trampled. He walked down the narrow creaking stairs to book a transatlantic call at the hotel desk.

"I've been told to speak to an angry American logician."

He held out the paper with Ruth's number to the young woman.

"Very good, sir. You can dial direct from your room. You must simply place a zero before the long number to reach the line external." She picked up the pen on its chain and wrote a "0" at the front of the number. "Like that."

This felt like an impossible barrier. He knew he was being ridiculous.

"She's started a petition against a famous French philosopher. Perhaps you've heard of him? Jacques Derrida?"

"No, sir."

"Then I don't expect you know John Searle. Anyway, whatever the effective cause, at bottom it's the same old conflict between the English-speaking world and the Continent. I don't know how it looks from your end, but in my circles it's always portrayed as a fight for stubborn Anglo-American common sense, against a very French tolerance for tyranny and grandiosity."

The desk clerk pushed the paper back across the counter to Martin. "The first zero gets an outside line, sir."

"I'm sorry. I'm using you as a sounding board. I can't say I understand it myself. Our great transatlantic divide. We talk about it as a cosmic ideological battle, but we ignore just how recent the Anglo-American tradition is. It barely goes back three generations, and we all know each other. I met Ruth at Harvard, when I followed my supervisor John Austin over in 1955. Then, when the poor man died of cancer at just forty-eight, my notes became the basis of his posthumous book, *How to Do Things with Words.*"

Which then became the basis of all John Searle's work, though Martin thought it bore little relation to anything that Austin had said.

"Sir. Do you need my help?"

"My point is, the whole lineage is so short. At Harvard, I was part of the circle around Willard Van Orman Quine, and of course Van had studied with Alfred North Whitehead, which explains the Anglo-American thing, because Whitehead had worked with Russell at Cambridge. I eventually became the Bertrand Russell Professor of Logic, of course, so that seals the circle. You could say Austin was my philosophical father, and Van was a kind of stepfather. He is brilliant but really quite a self-enclosed man. I'd say, our relationship was based on a deep cordiality, not the genuine warmth I had with Austin."

"Sir. Perhaps I could direct you to a telephone in our business centre?"

"Would you? That's very kind of you."

He followed her down a passageway beside the stairs. He had chosen a small hotel on the Left Bank, while Norris had opted for a huge five star in Montparnasse. Martin touched one of the heavy sixteenth-century beams set into the plaster wall.

"It's incredible so much of medieval Paris has survived revolution and war and the grand plans of Haussmann. There's really nothing comparable left in London. But of course, there was no Paris Blitz; France fell so quickly in 1940."

This seemed more pointed than he intended.

"I was only twelve years old in 1940, which is really

what marks the generations. Van and Austin were both in military intelligence. The work they had begun with Whitehead became the basis of the new field of cryptography, with these astonishing semi-clockwork computers capable of encoding and transmitting messages way beyond anything human. Which led to machine languages, and ultimately to electronic mail. Van is an astonishing figure, really. You know, he basically invented binary languages, so we have him to blame."

Martin pointed at the Minitel console on the little desk, and laughed. The business centre turned out to be an alcove beneath a black timber lintel. The woman spread out Ruth's telephone number between two long fingers, and began dialling.

"Van had a horror of illogicality," Martin said. "He would grow distraught if he got caught in a rambling conversation, though he always thought he successfully hid his anxiety. His sanity literally depended upon logic, yet he knew he was imposing an artificial order on the world. Formal symbolic languages are not a part of the world: they are lesser than the world. In the same way that the code is different from the natural language. Otherwise, it wouldn't *be* a code. The difference sustains the symbolic language, but isn't expressible in the language. It's an extra something. A spark of life."

"The line is ringing, sir."

She wasn't at all slow about hurrying off and leaving him.

Martin tried to compose his thoughts, as he sat in what was essentially a cubbyhole. His generation had ignored the difference between the code and the language. Ruth Barcan, Norris Hampton, as well as Saul Kripke, Noam

Chomsky and all the others, they broke with Van. Yes, okay, there was a difference between the symbolic language and the target language, but no, this difference was not a difference in kind because the rules passed from one to the other, without obstruction, one level always collapsing and merging into the other.

Ruth answered the phone.

"Ruth? It's Martin. You were trying to get in touch with me?"

"Martin. At last! It's Martin Miller." She shouted this off-phone, perhaps to a roommate, or perhaps to her house plants. "Where have you been hiding this past month? I couldn't get hold of you, Martin! I didn't know what had happened. If you had found a rock to crawl under."

"It wasn't a rock, Ruth. Just early retirement. Listen, Norris filled me in on this petition…"

"It's not a petition, it's a letter. To the *Times* of London. Let me read the text …"

"Ruth. One second. I'm calling long-distance from Paris, and it's a hotel phone." Mentioning this felt like penny-pinching. "Ruth, I wanted to tell you personally, out of respect for our long friendship, but I can't help. I've never read Derrida. Frankly, these days I wouldn't know where to begin reading him."

"Of course you haven't read him! No one reads Monsieur Derrida outside of Cultural Studies departments." Her voice was louder and slower as she pronounced the words Cultural Studies.

"I also wanted to call to express my horror if it's true you suffered anti-Semitic abuse from Derrida."

"Who told you that? Norris? Can't that man ever get

his facts straight? Monsieur Derrida is Jewish, Martin. Of course, he's never had the least problem cosying up to the most odious anti-Semitic snobs at Yale. But that's a different matter."

Ruth spoke to Martin as though he was an idiot, which he was, he supposed.

"I'm sorry, Ruth. Norris only told me half a story. So what is this about? Not the affair with John Searle?"

"Well, of course it is about John Searle. In the broadest sense, it's all about John Searle. Monsieur Derrida took refuge in the most bizarre straw-men arguments rather than deal with Searle directly, as though debating an American philosopher was beneath him. And that is the point, because it is his preferred *modus operandi*, avoiding rigour and clarity and instead going for showy put-downs and *ad hominem* attacks."

How often had Ruth Barcan suffered condescension and ridicule in her career? It had always been a struggle for her. Her greatest achievement was a proof of the necessity of identity, but no one paid it the least attention until Saul Kripke offered what amounted to the exact same proof. You could not even argue that Kripke had plagiarised Ruth. No one had even noticed Ruth's work, but everyone was bowled over by Kripke's. God knows why she had never got so angry when Kripke was lauded as a genius.

Martin was woken by a boot kicking at his door. He had fallen asleep across his bed, wearing his underwear and a sweater. There were books scattered across the bedspread and others spines akimbo on the floor.

Norris was yelling from the corridor. "Marty! Marty! Are

you alive or dead?"

Martin opened the door. "I was asleep. What time is it?"

"It's past three." Norris looked past him to the room. "You didn't hear the phone? Oh, mate. You only unplugged the bloody phone."

Martin opened and closed both his eyes and his mouth. His mouth felt furry, his eyes felt as though they had been salt-cured, they were so dry and sore. Norris pushed past him and plugged the phone back in to the wall. It immediately started ringing. Norris answered it.

"He's fine. He was fast asleep like Goldilocks, while I'm stood like a fool outside the Louvre waiting for him."

He replaced the phone.

"Jesus, Marty! Did you pull an all-nighter." Norris at last saw the names on the book covers. "Oh, fuck, mate. You've not been reading Derrida?"

"I don't think I had a choice."

"Christ! Marty, mate! No wonder you look like shit. How many books are there? You must have emptied the shelves at Shakespeare and Company. Did you spend the whole night reading?"

"Pretty much."

"So what did you learn?"

"Van shouldn't have a problem with Derrida. They have the same criticism of symbolic logic."

"Oh, mate, no! One sleepless night and you're seduced? Jacques bats his eyes and now you want to bridge the Anglo-American European divide?"

"Derrida isn't called Jacques, and he's not European, either. He's Jackie from Algeria, and the reason he's using Van's argument is because he was sat in Van's class with us."

This pulled Norris up. "He's Jackie! Jacques Derrida is Algerian Jackie?"

Norris knew who Martin was talking about. They were the three Stooges at Harvard. Fat Norris. Thin Martin. Little Jackie.

"You've got to be mistaken, Marty. It's a different bloke. Jackie was a mathematician. And he was at Harvard to avoid the Algerian war."

"He had got into an elite French university on a maths scholarship. And he had come to Harvard to avoid the French draft. You remember: he was a North African, Arab-speaking Jew. He would have been on the losing side however the war turned out." Martin looked for a book with a photograph on the flyleaf. He handed it to Norris.

Norris stared at the picture. "How am I supposed to tell? The guy's got all this bouffy white hair."

"Jackie was twenty-eight when we were at Harvard. That book is his memoirs. There's not much in it, but he does talk about growing up in Algeria under the Vichy-backed government. He missed two years of education because they kicked the Jews out of state schools. It was a miracle that he got the maths scholarship."

The book was called *Circumfession*. A pun on Jackie's bris. You could complain about the dick joke, but then Kripke's circle were always smirking over their dick jokes: their rigid and flaccid designators. Dick jokes bridged the Anglo-American Continental divide.

Norris said, "Where's his criticism of formal logic?"

The collection containing the essay was on the bed. Martin thumbed through to the opening page.

Norris peered at the title. "Is that how they spell

480

'difference' in French?"

"No. He changed the spelling by switching one of the 'e's' for an 'a'. *'Différance'*. But it doesn't alter the pronunciation. Either way, 'a' or 'e', the words are indiscernible. It's an essay on logic and indiscernibility, and it uses Van's objection to Ruth and Kripke."

"Oh, fuck's sake, mate. The two words are spelled different: they aren't indiscernible at all." Norris read out the first line of Jackie's essay. *"'I will speak therefore of a letter. Of the first letter."* He groaned and snapped the book shut. "You've lost it, Marty. That's nothing to do with the Willard Van Quine I know."

"Van argues that any notion of identity depends upon an unspoken appeal to immediacy: to the space and time in which two similar objects will be revealed as one and the same. That's what Jackie's calling *'différance'*, it's his word for a difference that defers identity."

Norris cast the book on the bed. "You're saying that the Jackie we used to know is living in Paris, inhabiting Jacques Derrida's body? And when we catch them together, they become one and the same?"

"Or they never do. Because our Jackie was a twenty-eight-year-old North African kid with neat black hair."

Norris clicked his fingers. "The fucker was with us when Ruth gave one of her papers. The three of us. If Derrida understands all of her shit, why doesn't he just say so and put her petition to rest."

"Is that what we should tell him to do? Play up and play the game? Play by our rules? If they hate him, I can't see a rational argument is going to help change anyone's mind."

"We're philosophers, we have to believe it could. What

the fuck else except rational argument could change someone's mind?" Norris picked up the memoirs again and took another look at the picture. "This is Jackie. Seriously? Thirty-five years later, and he's still Van's good son?"

The Parting Sea

Evan Lavender-Smith

I walked across the park along the stone path, through the flock of pigeons. I approached the bench and sat down next to her. She looked angry. Had I done something wrong?

"Have I done something wrong?" I asked her.

"Why did you kick that pigeon?" she replied.

Kick a pigeon? What's she talking about? I didn't kick a pigeon. I'm not a child.

"I didn't kick a pigeon."

"I saw you do it. I saw it with my own eyes."

"I walked through the flock and they all moved out of the way. It must have been the angle you were watching me from."

"Don't lie," she said. "Just admit it. And then we can move on."

Move on from what? I'm not a child, obviously, nor am I the type of adult to kick a pigeon — especially here, where kicking pigeons is the type of behavior I've been trying so hard to avoid. American behavior. Although I can barely speak any French, I've been using as little English as possible, gesturing with my hands, with my head, with my face. My sneakers haven't seen the light of day since we arrived. I'm not even wearing my baseball cap.

No, of course I didn't kick a pigeon. Who does she think I am?

"But I can't admit to something I didn't do," I said.

"You're lying," she said. "I can tell. I can always tell."

"Obviously you can't. Because I'm telling the truth."

She scoffed, turned away.

Had my foot touched a pigeon, without my realizing it? But I distinctly remember walking through the flock and making a mental note of what happened: *the parting sea of pigeons*. I remember wishing I had some birdseed on my person. Why would I have wished for a pigeon's sustenance, on the one hand, and its harm, on the other? Why would I have made a mental note in opposition to that which I perceived?

"Look," I said, pointing in the direction of the tower, "I walked from over there, straight toward you. Even if I had kicked a pigeon, you wouldn't have been able to tell, because from your perspective, you wouldn't have been able to see the gap between my foot and the pigeon. Couldn't it be the case that the angle you watched me from simply made it appear as if I'd kicked a pigeon, when in reality I hadn't? Can't you admit that you might be wrong?"

"I saw you swing your leg back," she said. "I saw the pigeon fly through the air. Not because it was flying, but because it had been kicked. First you were walking at a normal pace. And then you trained your sights on a pigeon, sped up, and kicked it. Like a soccer ball."

Impossible. I hate soccer — and with a special passion lately. France playing in the World Cup is the reason we've run into all these cordoned off streets and squares. So many rowdy spectators everywhere, peering up at impromptu jumbotrons. We haven't been able to get to where we need to go. When it comes to sports, I thought it was Americans who were supposed to be the crazy ones, but we're way more civilized about them than the French are. Our cities never come to a screeching halt like this. We don't gather in huge crowds to watch a bunch of guys in short shorts stand around doing nothing for hours on end. *Boot*, French for goal, is one of the few words I've learned while here, despite my having heard the word shouted only two, maybe three times. I know I would never pretend that a pigeon — or anything else, for that matter — is a soccer ball. It would never occur to me.

She continued, "Or a football."

But I do like football. The American kind. Every year from September to February I try to keep my Sundays free. I was even on a football team in middle school. I guess I could see myself pretending something other than a football is a football. In fact, I know I've done that very thing many times in my life. Running up to something other than a football, pretending it's a football on a kickoff tee, kicking it as hard as I can. But just because I've done that in the past doesn't mean I did it just now, with a pigeon. Besides, I made the mental note. I wished for birdseed.

"You're so embarrassing to me," she said. "I'm sick of it. You need to admit to the childish things you do if you're ever going to become a real adult. People in Paris don't kick pigeons."

But I'm a person in Paris. And she's claiming I kicked a pigeon. She's not being logical.

"You mean people native to Paris," I said. "Otherwise, it would follow that I didn't kick one."

She turned away.

I closed my eyes, trying to visualize having walked

485

toward her along the stone path. My walk across the park had happened only moments before, and yet the memory of it now felt very distant. As distant as breakfast. No, even more distant than that. Years distant, perhaps. As distant as middle school. But I can still remember things from way back then, can't I? Yes, of course I can. So why wouldn't I be able to remember having kicked a pigeon just now, if I had?

We had croissants for breakfast. She had one, I had two. One of my croissants was a regular croissant, the other, like hers, a chocolate croissant. A pain au chocolat. And coffee. I smoked a cigarette afterward. When I was finished with it, I suggested that she dump the water from the stylish white ashtray and place the ashtray in her purse. We were the only ones seated at the café's little patio; the waiter hadn't been by in ages. "Don't forget we're leaving tomorrow," I whispered to her. "Who knows whether we'll get another chance like this?" She zipped up her purse, flamboyantly, without the ashtray inside.

And what about middle school? In seventh grade, I remember, we were forced to memorize the capitals of all the European nations. Paris was always difficult because somehow I'd gotten it in my head that France was a city rather than a country. And I knew that a city couldn't be the capital of another city. What was the name of the imaginary country I imagined Paris to be the capital of, I wonder?

I turned to her. She was still looking away.

I bet it was Texas. I also remember Mr Payton giving me a C in geography.

"Listen," she said, turning back to me. "I know you think

that you're right and I'm wrong, or that we've reached some sort of impasse due to the subjective nature of human perception, but the fact of the matter is this. You kicked that pigeon and you just don't want to admit it. Or — and I'd like to believe this isn't the case, because to my mind it would be worse than if you're lying — you're the type of person who kicks a pigeon and it counts as such a trivial, unremarkable event, like turning a doorknob or tying your shoes, that it doesn't even get recorded in your memory banks." She paused, took a breath, continued. "What I need you to do is choose one of the following two options. Either you're A, a liar, or B, a sociopath. If you don't choose right now, then I'm afraid this relationship isn't going to last much longer. I'm sick of your shenanigans, of all your nonsense. I'm at the end of my rope here."

Shenanigans? Nonsense? Liar or sociopath — that's nonsensical. Aren't I being the logical one here? What am I missing?

I was coming from that little bodega or whatever. I bought a pack of cigarettes. I remember the cashier placing the pack on the counter. He spoke a number I didn't understand. I fished through my wallet for an amount of euros I imagined to be enough to cover the cost. I placed the bills on the counter. He looked down at them, then he looked up at me, and then he said something I didn't understand. Except for the word *américain*. He slid two of the bills back across the counter in my direction.

How is that memory any more or less trivial than a memory of turning a doorknob or tying my shoes?

I thought of my shoes, these very uncomfortable boots I've been wearing for two weeks straight. My feet hurt so bad; I should be wearing my Nikes. Can I remember lacing up my boots this morning?

I strained my memory to picture us back in the hotel room. I was so glad to be putting on a fresh pair of underwear, having finally done laundry the night before. I put on my shirt — but then I had to take it off again because I'd forgotten to put on deodorant. I didn't want to accidentally touch the white chalky deodorant stick to my shirt, because this is a black shirt, and I worried that were I to do the thing where I reach up through the bottom of the shirt with the stick of deodorant in my hand, the white of it might touch the black of my shirt and leave a mark. My uncomfortable skinny jeans were crumpled on the floor; I struggled to shimmy them on. I put on a fresh pair of socks. I put on my boots. But, it's true, I don't remember tying them. And I certainly don't remember turning the doorknob to the hotel room as we headed out to breakfast.

So maybe she's right, after all. Maybe I am a sociopath.

I looked down at my boots. Wait a minute, I thought to myself, these are Chelsea boots. They don't even have laces. That's why I don't remember tying them!

"But look," I said, motioning to my feet. "The only reason I don't remember tying my shoes is because these boots don't have any laces!"

"Liar," she said, "or sociopath."

I could see the stone path in the distance. Closing my eyes again, I tried to picture myself walking along it. I watched my laceless boots carry me forward, through the parting sea of pigeons. But is that a real memory? Or am I imagining a series of events that didn't actually occur? Is what I'm seeing in my head right now a series of events that bears only some vague structural resemblance to the events as they actually occurred? Am I merely borrowing selective details from the real events, like the texture of the stone path as I remember it, the height of the green grass, the pebbled leather of my uncomfortable Chelsea boots? But I had wished for birdseed — that's a real memory, I'm sure of it. And I'd made the mental note. I hadn't noted, *the parting sea of pigeons, save one, the pigeon I kicked out of the way, with this extremely uncomfortable boot, like a teed-up football.*

So, assuming I did kick a pigeon, which I know I didn't, I guess I'd have to go with sociopath, even though I'm pretty sure I'm not a sociopath. But, still, B would be the better choice, because I'm more certain that I'm not lying about kicking a pigeon than I am about not remembering having kicked a pigeon. Unless she's willing to concede that she might be in the wrong, which, clearly, she's not willing to do. Or unless she's up for giving me a third option. C, intermittent amnesiac. Or, better, C, benevolent mnemonic revisionist. But I know that if I ask for a third option she's likely to stand up from the bench and walk away. Probably for good.

I turned to her and asked, "Do you think I could have a third option?"

She stood up from the bench, grabbed her purse, and walked away in the direction opposite the park.

I sat still for a long moment. I tried to feel regret about having asked for a third option, but I couldn't, because I felt so victimized by having been given only two.

I removed a cigarette from my pack and lit it. My thoughts returned to middle school. Coach had positioned me at placekicker, I remember, not because I was any good at kicking a football, but because it was the position reserved for the scrawniest kid on the team. Placekickers aren't often tackled, nor are they often required to tackle somebody else. The problem I'd had was that my kickoffs and field goal attempts suffered from a pronounced, seemingly incurable slice. As a right-footed kicker, whenever I kicked the ball it spun and curved wildly to the right. This was because my legs weren't strong. They still aren't. My legs don't look so skinny just because of these ridiculous skinny jeans she's forcing me to wear, but because they're actually very skinny. A strong-legged right-footed kicker would be able to pull his kickoffs and field goals, I imagine—that is, have the football spin and curve to the left — something I've never been able to do.

I dropped my cigarette butt and, with the toe of my right boot, snuffed it out on the ground. I stood from the bench and began walking toward the park. There wasn't a single pigeon in sight.

But, as I approached the stone path, an object lying on the grass began to resolve in my vision. From my perspective, walking toward the tower and the bodega or whatever, the object lay on the stone path's right side. When I reached it, I saw that it was a dead pigeon. I looked down at it for a moment — what a shame, what a poor little pigeon — and then I looked back toward the bench. I turned and again walked in the direction of the tower, about thirty yards on, the farthest I was ever able to kick a football. Again I turned around and faced the bench.

As I looked on with the same perspective I'd had when originally walking through the park, I noted that the dead pigeon lay on the left side of the stone path. I was absolutely certain that I hadn't deviated from the path when I'd walked toward her. Therefore, even if I had kicked the pigeon, it would not have landed on the left side of the path, as the dead pigeon in the distance was now lying, on account of my incurable slice as a placekicker.

All remaining doubt flew from me. She was wrong. The choices she should have offered were these: either A, someone else kicked that pigeon to death; or B, the pigeon died of natural causes.

At the airport the next morning, I tried to explain to her about my kickoff slice, and about how the dead pigeon I'd found after she left lay on the left side of the stone path. But, still, she broke up with me on the flight home, before we'd even made it halfway to America.

Celesteville's Burning: A Work in Regress[1]

Andrew Gallix

Zut, zut, zut, zut.
— Marcel Proust, *À la recherche du temps perdu*

Sostène Zanzibar was not feeling himself that day; someone else was. A journalist from an English paper. Name of Lauren. Lauren Ipsum. Something along those lines. The interview had gone remarkably well. Such probing questions. Very stimulating, very in-depth. There was no denying that Ms Ipsum was thoroughly a young woman. Hang on, cross that out. Was a thorough young woman. Very thorough indeed.

In a bid to impress her host, she had taken up gesticulation with all the fervour of a new convert. It was a joy to behold. Her impeccably-manicured hands would suddenly flutter away from the warmth of her lap, describing graceful ellipses as if trying to conjure up words that could not possibly exist. Ever. In any language. *Even French.*

Yet Lauren had struggled to comprehend the answers to some (if not most) of her questions. The fact that the

---

1   This is an abridged version of a story published on *The White Review*'s website in September 2011.

former bore little (if any) relation to the latter did not help. Neither did Zanzibar's scattergun delivery, nor his baffling habit of peppering his sentences with arcane references to Heidegger and Blanchot. Whenever he switched to pidgin English, he would sound like Jacques Derrida dubbed by Inspector Clouseau, which proved an even greater source of confusion, frankly.

At one point, the ink ran out of her biro, whereupon Zanzibar produced a pencil from his inside pocket with a little flourish. "Men," he said, "alwez ave two pencculs." He almost winked, but thought better of it.

*

Published in late 1986, *Je suis la Femme Bigorneau* was a *succès de scandale* which took the literary establishment by storm; a *cause célèbre* that turned Zanzibar overnight into the *enfant terrible* of French letters. Like Leos Carax's film *Mauvais sang*, also released at the end of that year, it seemed to capture the zeitgeist, polarising opinion along a generational fault line. Louis Pauwels, editor of *Le Figaro Magazine*, claimed the novella was a perfect illustration of the "mental AIDS" afflicting the nation's youth. "Makes Schopenhauer sound positively chipper," wrote Josyanne Savigneau in her full-page rave review for *Le Monde*. "The kind of book that exists on the slippery cusp between pure genius and utter gibberish," wrote a critic at *Le Matin de Paris*. "Bof!" Philippe Sollers is reported to have said, when sounded on the subject, mid-*pied de porc farci grillé*, at Brasserie Lipp. Zanzibar was all over the gossip columns too. He dated Béatrice Dalle (who had recently starred in

Betty Blue), wrote a song for Étienne Daho, appeared in a video with Les Rita Mitsouko (playing the glockenspiel), spent his nights at the ultra-hip Bains Douches nightclub and was headbutted by Jean d'Ormesson during *Apostrophes*, the highly influential TV show. His parents — René and Monique — told *Actuel* that they had always known, deep down, that Sostène was special. "*On sentait bien qu'il allait devenir artiste ou écrivain,*" said his mum. "*C'était vraiment un chieur,*" his father concurred. They confided that they had done their level best to make him as miserable as possible throughout his childhood, so as to provide him with a lifetime of neuroses that would feed his future creative endeavours. "*N'empêche qu'on a drôlement bien réussi notre coup,*" said René, beaming with paternal pride: it was the gift that keeps giving. Zanzibar, however, was overwhelmed by his new-found notoriety. Béatrice Dalle soon left him and he started dabbling in too many drugs. Rumour has it that he could drink the likes of Antoine Blondin, Serge Gainsbourg or Alain Pacadis under the table. His next three books were minor bestsellers, and one of them was even turned into a film with Juliette Binoche (*La Bonniche*, 1991), but Zanzibar was never able to replicate the impact of *Bigorneau*, which he always likened to his seminal first orgasm (1979). Each new novel resembled an increasingly faded photocopy of the original blueprint, giving rise to what Sam Jordison recently described in *The Guardian* as "a sense of perpetual déjà vu on a dimmer switch". *Bref*, his work seemed condemned to a gradual, but irreversible, running down; a depletion of vital energy that implied a dismal future of erectile dysfunction, hair loss and growing inertia.

*

The journalist's black Moleskin notebook lay open, face down, on the coffee table. After an hour or so, weighty topics had been dropped in favour of increasingly flirtatious small talk. Zanzibar got up to refill her glass and, instinctively, she got up too and now they were kissing, deep and slow, their tongues going round and round and round like the ground bass number in the background, and he gently lifted up her summer frock as the melody soared over the looping bassline, and their bodies were grinding, their tongues intertwining, her head spinning and she found herself reclining in a Le Corbusier-style chaise longue. "*J'aime quand ça s'incarne,*" she whispered, drawing him hither with her long legs that he now sported nonchalantly over his shoulders. Leaning on her forearms, she tilted her head back, closed her eyes and bit her lower lip. A slow intake of breath — like a deep drag on a Gitane — subsided into a faint, low-pitched moan, not dissimilar to the sound a puppy makes when kicked.

"Thanks," she said, upon leaving. Zanzibar stared at the outstretched hand last seen clasping his erect penis. "For having me?" she added by way of explanation, but the high-rising terminal transformed her statement into a question. A final probing question that she left dangling like one of Fat Pat's earrings as she departed with a toss of hair and rustle of chiffon. She was marching past Erwin the cat who, curled up on a beanbag, did not even bother to look up. She was making her way down the transparent spiral staircase that seemed — like her — to be wound around nothing. Zanzibar just stood there, in the doorway, buffeted by the fragrant breeze she had generated. With closed eyes, he breathed in a lungful of her absence and just stood there. He just stood there, caught in her slipstream. Winded, he just stood there. He just stood there. "*Putain*!" he muttered, finally closing the door.

*

The presidential candidate emerged from the sea to spontaneous cries of "*Vive la République!*". She was naked save for a tricolor sash — "*Un rien m'habille*" — that bisected the perkiest pair of Delacrucian tits to have ever stalked Le Touquet Plage. "*Tu vois, là,*" said a young father to his son, "*ce sont les deux mammelles de la France.*" As he pointed, tears welled up in his grateful eyes. Everything would be all right now. *Everything.* The crowd parted and Mme Royal glided by. Majestically. Regally. Eponymously... Photographers had a field day, fireworks were let off, babies were brandished, a brass band struck up the national anthem and, just when he was about to get an eyeful, Zanzibar found himself back home in his bathroom. He was standing in front of the mirror, trying to remove his contact lenses, which (as he would discover after plucking out an eyeball) he had forgotten to put in. The eye he was now staring at, and that stared back at him intermittently as he rolled it around in the palm of his hand, resembled a large white egg with a black dot inside — or rather the drawing of a white egg. The black dot alone contained more atoms than all the *penceuls* in the world.

*

Zanzibar was seated at one of the little round tables dotting the semicircle of cobbled stones outside the Théâtre de l'Europe. He had opted for the last row, furthest away from the road, with the steps leading up to the theatre right behind him. He was the only one there now, a couple of German tourists having just departed. The sun was shining; birds were chirping in the nearby Luxembourg Gardens: summer was in the air. A waiter — as stylish as he was young — brought over an espresso and a glass of water, which he placed gingerly beside Zanzibar's copy of *Le Monde*. They had devoted a whole page to *l'affaire Zanzibar*. It was all over the papers, blogs, social networks, podcasts, and news bulletins — both radio and television, local and national. There was no escaping it, and that was precisely why he was seated at one of the little round tables dotting the semicircle of cobbled stones outside the Théâtre de l'Europe.

A 58 bus turned into Rue de l'Odéon. Zanzibar followed its slow progress past the clothes shop where the original Shakespeare and Company once stood. It stopped outside the pharmacy at the other end, on the other side, where an attractive woman he vaguely recognised — but could not quite place — alighted before walking back in his general direction. As she crossed the road, he identified the one-night-stand graphologist who, a few months back, had publicly pooh-poohed his cunnilingus technique, describing the result as a series of "indecipherable chicken-scratch squiggles". Name of Amélie. Or possibly Emilie. Something along those lines. It was she too, he now realised, who had played the part of the presidential candidate in that strange dream that was still haunting him. Thankfully, she had not noticed Zanzibar and picked a table in the second row, next to an olive tree in a square metal pot. With an uncanny sense of apropos, she ordered a kir royal. No sooner had the waiter scuttled away than she proceeded to hitch up her maxi dress until vast swathes of tanned, toned thigh were exposed to the warm rays. She completed this pre-prandial routine by crossing her legs and lowering, visor-style, the designer sunglasses that had been perched on her head, like a tiara. Zanzibar's beady eyes darted from the rear view of the graphologist to the restaurant facing him on the left, back to the graphologist's signature legs, and on to the Flammarion building facing him on the right. He repeated this circuit many times with meticulous, almost obsessive, care until the person he was waiting for finally emerged from the building.

Théodule Meuniaire was a thirty-something publishing whizz-kid with rock star good looks, who — it was an open secret — was largely responsible for reviving Zanzibar's flagging career. He lingered for a few minutes outside Flammarion, talking to someone on his mobile, apparently in a foreign language (probably *franglais*), then walked over to his car (a grey Porsche) that was parked only a few metres away. He opened the door, removed his jacket and hung it on a hook inside. Before closing the door, he hooted twice in brief succession while looking over at the pavement café. He waved. Zanzibar quickly unfolded his paper and hid behind it. Peering over his crumpled copy of *Le Monde*, he saw the graphologist lift up her sunglasses with one hand and wave back with the other. A broad smile had now lit up her face. She sprinkled a few coins on the table and skipped across the road to join her date.

ANDREW GALLIX

They kissed like models in a Doisneau picture and walked, hand in hand, to La Méditerranée, the plush restaurant with its blue exterior and Cocteau decorations. Once they had disappeared from view, Zanzibar called the waiter and whispered something in his ear. *"Bien entendu, Monsieur, au-cun souci,"* he said. Zanzibar got up and ran over to examine the grey Porsche. Lauren Ipsum's horn-rimmed glasses (which, as he recalled, she had removed just before shaking her long hair loose) taunted him from the leather dashboard where they had been conspicuously displayed. With closed eyes, he breathed in a lungful of absence and just stood there. He just stood there, in front of the grey Porsche with the horn-rimmed glasses on the leather dashboard. For a minute or so, he just stood there. He just stood there. *"Putain!"* he muttered, before making his way back.

The waiter smiled at him and Zanzibar felt obliged to order another espresso. He checked his emails on his iPhone, then glanced at the latest tweets, most of which revolved around *"l'Affaire"*. After a brief recap, the article in *Le Monde* focused on the prime-time television show, to be broadcast live that very evening, during which a confrontation between Meuniaire and himself was to take place. Whether it would or not was a moot point, not least because the programme consisted of a series of announcements for nominally forthcoming — but, in reality, constantly deferred — features, followed by lengthy commercial breaks, themselves followed by further announcements, and so on until the closing credits. Although quite taken with the concept of a show that was forever in the process of becoming, Zanzibar had no intention whatsoever of being party to this masquerade. He was equally determined to ensure his rival did not make it to the studio either, and that was — more precisely — why he was seated at one of the little round tables dotting the semicircle of cobbled stones outside the Théâtre de l'Europe.

He looked up, squinting into the sun, just in time to see Meuniaire and the graphologist glide past in the grey Porsche with the horn-rimmed glasses on the leather dashboard.

Putain!

*

In 1992, having finally acknowledged that there was little lead in his *penceul* left, Sostène Zanzibar embarked on an ill-fated prequel to Genesis. Although this grandiose project would occupy him for the best part of two decades, we have precious little to show for it. A few meagre excerpts appeared at irregular intervals in obscure Japanese style magazines whose prohibitive cover prices were inversely proportional to their confidential circulations. The rest of this "work in regress," as he liked to describe it, was destroyed. One night, in November 2009, the author deleted the computer files containing the typescript and burned all the print-outs — ream upon ream — he had archived over the years. According to legend, he then took a taxi to Denfert-Rochereau, uncovered a manhole and disappeared down the Catacombs where he spent the following fortnight listening to the same album over and over again on a battered old ghetto blaster believed to have once belonged to Don Letts.

Franco-Swiss all-girl band Les Péronelles (think

Shangri-Las meet The Slits) always maintained that they had rounded off their first (and last) album (*Trois fois rien*, 1983) with a hidden track. "L'Arlésienne" was so well hidden, however, that no one had ever found it. With time, it became the Holy Grail of Franco-Swiss rock criticism. An early issue of *Les Inrockuptibles* contained a six-page feature ("A l'écoute de l'inouï") devoted to this unheard melody. It included interviews with the producer and sound engineer as well as cultural luminaries such as Patrick Eudeline, Gérard Genette, Jean Baudrillard, John Cage, and assorted roadies.

Listening to this ten-minute stretch of silence over and over again was a Zen-like experience at first. Soon, though, Zanzibar was able to recognise, and even anticipate, every hum, hiss and crackle on the track: its teeny tiny tinny tinnitus quality. The song had to be concealed *behind*, or perhaps even *within*, this silence that was not quite silence. It had to. He even thought he could sense its presence in the same, almost physical, way one is always aware of being observed. It was just out of earshot; a mere whisper away.

By the middle of the second week, a melody had emerged from the static and wormed itself into his eardrums. It was the sound of music leaking from a commuter's headphones on public transport. It was the sound of a distant party carried on the wind of time, ebbing and flowing. It was the sound of mythical monsters plumbing the murky depths of ancient oceans. It was the sound of half a dozen rashers sizzling away like nobody's business in Lauren Ipsum's big fuck-off frying pan. Above all, it was the sound of a wannabe troglodyte slowly going out of his mind.

By the end of the second week, the melody had disappeared. It had never been there in the first place; not really. Zanzibar, now at his wit's end, had a rare eureka moment. The ghost track was not concealed *behind*, or even *within*, the silence — it was that silence itself. He had been listening to it all along, or rather he had not: all along, he had been listening into it for something else. There was, however, nothing else: no *behind* or *within*; no depth or beyond. Zanzibar had finally acceded to a heightened sense of hearing. He was now firmly convinced that this recording of real silence — silence that was not quite silence — constituted, *en soi*, some kind of irreducible message. Communication stripped back to its bare essentials; atomised — *degré zéro*.

The author's discovery could not but chime with his long-standing interest in the many-worlds interpretation of quantum mechanics. Whenever he wrestled with the blank page and the blank page won, Zanzibar would shrug it off as being of little import since it meant, ipso facto, that another version of himself was scribbling away in some parallel universe. Although this explanation was offered in jest, the author started thinking of his alter ego — hard at work on the Great Novel *he* was not working on — with increasing regularity. Some would say that these thoughts even blossomed into a beautiful, full-blown obsession.

In the early days, Zanzibar had tried his hand at *creatio ex nihilo*. Did not work. He then had a go at recreating the world within a whopping great *Gesammtkuntswerk*. This proved equally unfruitful. The words he used to conjure things up simply recorded their absence, instead of preserving them for all eternity: *Evanescence, ou la naissance d'Eva* (1992) expressed nothing but itself — if that. Writing *something*, as opposed to writing *about* something, seemed to be the way forward — or rather backward, as it implied rediscovering some prelapsarian language that merged with the reality of things. *Chemin faisant*, as he strived to bridge the gap between signifier and signified, Zanzibar also hoped to recapture some of that old magic which had inspired *Bigorneau* back in the day: a *soupçon* of oomph; *un peu de* welly. In the event, he did neither. Every single volume he ever published had thus been an approximate translation — and ultimately a failed instantiation — of the ideal book in his head. Were his novels, then, simply intimations or imitations of his other self's works: dim echoes, pale copies? Were they inferior versions of the masterpieces his doppel-gänger could come up with given half the chance? Zanzibar thought long and hard about all this, finally electing to stop writing in order to let his more talented likeness — whom he pictured as slightly better-endowed and -looking than himself — get on with it.

Flammarion ruthlessly exploited Zanzibar's disappearance by encouraging the hypothesis of a suicide. Meuniaire claimed on television that this, *après tout*, would only be in keeping with his "fundamentally nihilistic outlook". Arthur Cravan and Jacques Rigaut were frequently invoked by literary journalists in support of this argument. As a result, Zanzibar's back catalogue flew off the shelves, with *Bigorneau* topping the bestseller lists once again. Of course, the second stage of this cunning marketing strategy — i.e. cashing in on Zanzibar's miraculous reappearance by bringing out a new book asap — was jeopardised by the author's decision to down *penceuls*. Meuniaire was promptly dispatched to resolve this delicate problem. As expected, Zanzibar adopted a hardline position (*"C'est une question de principe, un-point-c'est-tout!"*) but proved far more amenable as soon as Flammarion threatened to sue. A compromise was finally thrashed out between the two parties, down at Les Deux Magots, where many a bottle of Perrier-Jouët was downed, almost *cul sec*.

Zanzibar, who had always tried and failed to convey the inadequacy of words with words, came up with the concept of a novel printed in disappearing ink. Once read, each word would vanish forever, the full text living on in people's minds — retold, reinterpreted, reinvented... "There's no such thing as original fiction," he said, a little worse for wear, "Novels can't be set in stone." He climbed on the table and, punching the air, began chanting, *"Li-bé-rez le texte! Li-bé-rez le texte!"* After a few phone calls, Meuniaire put a damper on proceedings: the project was too complex to pull off from a technical point of view, and would be far too expensive anyway. So it was back to the drawing board: *"Une autre bouteille, s'il vous plaît!"* They finally decided that Zanzibar would write an entire novel in longhand, using disappearing ink, and that Flammarion would publish a facsimile of the manuscript — blank page after blank page: *"Garçon, une autre bouteille!"* What better way to say something without saying it? *"Allez hop, on fête ça, une autre bouteille!"* What better way to express the idea that the writer has *nothing* to express? *"Vous nous remettrez la même chose."* In between hiccups, Zanzibar explained that his blank book would somehow retain traces of the novel that had once graced them. He then spoke confusedly of palimpsests and the tradition of erasure in contemporary poetry;

the word *biffure* was used thrice. When he started claiming that the absent text would be a kind of manifestation, *en creux*, of the Great Novel his other self was composing in a parallel universe, Meuniaire decided to call it a day.

It was probably that night, as he was walking home to clear his head, that he resolved to publish *Le Roman invisible* under his own name. Two grown men — intellectuals! French ones at that! — claiming rights to a blank book was bound to make the front pages. It also made Meuniaire shitloads of money as *Le Roman invisible* became the must-have accessory of that *rentrée littéraire*. Suddenly, it was not only *subversif* and *jubilatoire* (two adjectives which, by law, must feature in all French book reviews) but also *incontournable* and, paradoxically, everywhere to be seen. The fact that it doubled up as a handy memo pad turned it into a top seller in the run-up to Christmas too. With the royalties, Meuniaire treated himself to a luxury yacht worthy of a Russian oligarch. He called it *Authorship* (*en anglais dans le texte*).

*

A laundry van stopped outside the Michelet Odéon hotel. The words *Maison Binger* were painted on the side in quaint curlicue letters. A young man in a crisp beige uniform jumped out, leaving the door wide open. Zanzibar made a wild dash for it. The keys were in the ignition; the driver was talking to a pretty receptionist: the race was on.

The van picked up speed, crushing the asphalt beneath its burning wheels, like a shirt-collar under a Morphy Richards. Meuniaire's grey Porsche was still only a dot in the distance, but it was growing bigger by the second. It contained more atoms than all the *penceuls* in the world. Soon, those atoms would be spilled all over the leather dashboard and horn-rimmed glasses like chicken-scratch squiggles. Zanzibar was already living in the future. He could see it all, now, with blinding clarity. The shattered glass. The chromium twisted into the shape of Byzantine rings. The gory action painting on the tarmac. The charred corpses in their chariot of fire. He was hunched over the steering wheel, headbutting the windshield, laughing manically, whooping and hollering, with the wind in his combover and imaginary music blaring away in his ears. Four cars now separated him from his prey. He was closing in.

Just as he was about to go for the kill, the grey Porsche lurched into the outside lane. A sudden but steady — and, indeed, uninterrupted — flow of traffic prevented Zanzibar from giving chase. This being Paris, no one saw fit to let him go: steaming ahead was a woman's prerogative and a man's virility test. To make matters worse, the cars in his lane had now ground to a halt in what seemed like the mother of all tailbacks. Those on the left-hand side, however, continued to race past as if taking part in a dry run for Le Mans. Watching them whizz by made him a little drowsy after a while. Feeling his eyes glaze over, he stretched, and noticed two large white eggs with black dots inside. The eyes belonged to the Michelin Man who was towering above him benignly from a billboard.

Zanzibar fell asleep and was transported back to the tiny village in Burgundy where he spent his summer holidays as a child. His grandparents' house with the dark-green shutters and, across the road, the plot of land where his grandfather grew tomatoes and carrots and beans. Halfway up the hill, there was a water pump that looked like an obscene squat robot with a chunky, phallic-looking spout. It said POMPES LEMAIRE and TOURNEZ LENTEMENT (although there was no water in it) and it was green, but a lighter shade than the shutters. On the same side, further up, when you had almost reached the top, there was a little convenience store — the only one for miles. People used to go there to give and receive telephone calls. At the other end of the village there was a big barn, and on the door of this barn there was an advertisement with the Michelin Man. It was already old and faded by the early Seventies. Going back there, he thought, now waking up and rubbing his eyes, would be a little like visiting the setting of his past following the detonation of a neutron bomb. Zanzibar looked up at the billboard again, and it was at this juncture that he realised that there was no driver in the car in front. And none in the one in front of that. And so on.

Putain!

Night was beginning to fall. He wondered how long it would take to drive back to the past, and if the Michelin Man would still be waiting for him there.

The Map Rather Than the Territory

Jeffrey Zuckerman

I had the directions figured out: land at Orly, take the light rail to the RER, then the RER to Saint-Michel, then Line 4 and after a few stops I would get out and lug my suitcase to the Airbnb.

Since I didn't have a European SIM card yet, I would have to go off a Google Map of Paris downloaded to my phone. With no data and only sporadic access to Wi-Fi to geolocate myself, I navigated the city by the gleaming five-point stars Google let me pin on the map. One star for my apartment in Oberkampf; one for the apartment of the author I'd meet a few hours after that. One star for the restaurant where I ate lunch with a different author the next day. Another for the bookstore that this author had told me to visit.

I never did bother with getting a SIM card on that trip. Or the one after. I kept the phone's data turned off, kept the Wi-Fi on, and kept checking where I was every so often. I starred practically all the McDonald's locations because they had free Wi-Fi. Some of the Métro stations did, too. Every museum was good for that. One time, utterly lost, I stepped into a café and asked the server if the place had

508

Wi-Fi. He grinned and took my phone and logged me in. (I was so grateful I ordered four pastries, all of them to go.)

Now, sitting in front of my laptop in New York City, with a new book to translate into English, I pull out my phone, open the map of Paris, and constellations fill the screen. The city's a bit ovoid, lying on its side, and I can't see the city for the stars.

I put my two fingers on the screen, spread them apart, and the city zooms into focus. From the southernmost star of Marie Darrieussecq's apartment to the northernmost one by the Parc de la Villette, where the first novel I translated (a murder mystery) was set, this pixel city is more familiar to me than the real-life one. And why not? What I hold in my hands is my own condensation, my own interpretation of the reality I have seen again and again.

The Paris I walk through is complicated, dense, constantly swerving between filmic cliché and unending surprise. The names — the Opéra Bastille, Rue du Cherche-Midi, Montmartre — are so laden with meaning that they, and the history they encapsulate, threaten to turn the city into an unending mille-feuille of signifiers surrounding a nearly-forgotten signified. The streets blur together, one Haussmannian façade after another. I only ever feel properly oriented when I'm standing in an inner courtyard, or with a friend inside a restaurant I recognize, or in one of the many apartments I rent and return to again and again. In places that are contained, places that I have thoroughly mapped in my mind.

And as I think on the city in its full grandeur, I find myself falling in love with the map rather than the territory.

The stars I plant on the screen are memories, specific memories, ones that I replay again and again in my head long after returning to the United States.

The star I worked hardest to find is the one for Thomas Clerc's apartment. He spends four hundred pages describing everything inside it, and all he mentions of its outside is that it's on the Rue du Faubourg-Saint-Martin. I had to watch a documentary about the apartment and catch an accidental glimpse of a storefront through a window to get something I could look for in Google's Street View. And now the star is nothing but a memorial: the author has moved his life and his possessions to the eighteenth arrondissement. If I walk past the doorway to the courtyard to Thomas Clerc's apartment, I won't be able to go in — so I have to keep on walking toward the hulking arch of the Porte Saint-Martin. The only memento I have is the star on my map.

I look up from my phone with its map and focus my eyes on my laptop in New York City. I stare at the last paragraph I translated. Reread the English, reread the original French. The French is a welter of meanings, and every time I try to preserve the language's ambiguity I find my translations pinning down specific interpretations, specific perspectives. Any other translator would have done this paragraph differently.

And rightly so: translating my way through this book is every bit like tracing my own particular itinerary through the convoluted streets and hidden corners of this city. Any other translator would inevitably walk through Paris under a constellation of wholly idiosyncratic stars.

Still Paris

Sam Jordison

The Paris I love is probably an unreal city. But then, this is the twenty-first century. Nothing else is genuine either. And at least the Paris I love is fun. If it's a dream, at least it's a good one.

I'll try to share it with you. But before I do, a bit of throat-clearing self-justification. I know that what follows is fantasy. I also know (if you'll allow an apparent paradox) that it's largely a cliché. You'll have seen a very similar version of Paris in guidebooks, late-period Woody Allen films and soppy love songs. You might even have seen some of my favourite visions flickering around the edges of the real Paris. Or set down on other pages in this very book. I don't try to claim originality. But that shouldn't be an issue. One of the best things about this reverie is the fact that we can all share it. Anyway. Here are some of the stand-out details:

Serge Gainsbourg. Naturally.

Notre-Dame and hearing a stupid voice in my head shouting "The bells!"

Bridges. The river surging below, lovers kissing, all that stuff. (In my dream I also have very powerful bolt cutters to remove all the locks. When I snap them, it feels like I'm breaking bits of stupid. This is important.)

Buildings. So many of them so extraordinary that they

blur and blend into one lovely, golden stone vision. And sure, plenty of them are as overdone as wedding cakes, but they're still beautiful. After all, if you can't have crenellations, flying buttresses, or gargoyles in Paris, where can you have them?

The sewery smells you get on a street café on summer mornings when they've just sprayed the pavements. I enjoy these with coffee and a brief cheering interaction with a waiter in my appalling French.

1968 and sticking it to The Man. The revolution, the barricades, the Commune. Or at least, the idea that some people had that things could be better.

Coleman Hawkins and Miles Davis and Thelonious Monk and all the other jazz musicians finding refuge and respect away from home.

The Lost Generation, Ford Madox Ford, *The Transatlantic Review* and Hemingway starting out, and people doing real work.

Proust. Zola. All of them. All the things that have happened here. And all the other books. The books. The writers. The dreams about books. The idea that books might make things better. The bad books. The good books. The words in the books. The potential.

I'm a journalist and publisher myself, so of course the printed page dominates my dreams of Paris. I'm also anglophone. And as I say, my French is pretty bad. So, as you might expect, these dreams centre around the English bookshop Shakespeare and Company. Around Allen Ginsberg, more than half a century ago, stripped naked, reading *Howl*, destroyed by madness. Don DeLillo talking more cogently to a rapt audience just a few years back. And all the hundreds of writers in between. The ones we've forgotten. The ones who will become immortal. The ones who never published anything but dreamed that they might. The ones who did finish a book, and couldn't believe that it was on those shelves, in that city. And all the readers. The casual browsers. The intent listeners. The Tumbleweeds. Those are my favourite. The people who come in and give up some of their time in exchange for a place to sleep in the shop and the promise that they will write something about who they are and what they have experienced before they leave...

I've been lucky enough to sneak a peak at a few of these testimonies. They are gathered in a flat above the shop in green binders, a neat orderly row of them. These look like perfectly ordinary office ledgers, if maybe a little old-fashioned. In another place, they might contain accounts, or order books, or maybe lists of phone numbers. Here, they contain magic.

They contain brief snatches of hundreds of lives. And lives caught at their brightest moments. The writing is generally accompanied by ever so slightly blurred passport photos, attached to the page with rusting staples. Most of them coming from the age before digital selfie technology, taken by machines whose shutter-falls were unpredictable and which gave no second chances. By modern standards, they look off guard, and all the more revealing. The writing is similar: snatched, grabbed, youthful and unpolished and fantastic.

Some of the accounts are brief and only sketch the bare facts. Most are long and adjectival, the prose in thrall to

Jack Kerouac, full of bounce and excitement and — oh boy! — sudden exclamations. Because: why not? Most of these people are on the road. They are excited, exhilarated, joyful. They speak of escape and adventure.

Most of the pages I've read were written by people in their early twenties, in between university and the rest of life. Briefly jumping off the track that was taking them to mortgage and marriage and Midwestern comfort. Or to law school. Or to more uncertainty. Some were escaping Vietnam. Some were fleeing brown and beige lives in 1970s Britain. Some just wanted a cheap place to stay. One I saw came all the way from Pakistan. They nearly all share dreams about art, immortality and the things that count. They've helped create a legend. They've helped serve literature up fresh. They've worked towards something that might just last.

The flip side of that is that many of the accounts are freighted with sadness. The writers know they're enjoying a fleeting experience. Time is about to start grinding into them — and they'll maybe never have as much fun again. Soon they will have to turn and face the not-so-strange. The everyday world is waiting. They will fade out of that world faster than those beautiful, youthful pictures preserved upstairs at Shakespeare and Company.

But I at least hope those Tumbleweeds carried some of their youthful dreams with them. Dreams built on the dream of George Whitman who founded the shop as a socialist utopia, and recreation of Sylvia Beach's original shop and original dream...

I hope for those dreams especially because it feels now more than ever that personal legends matter. They change things. Lawrence Durrell, one of the earliest regulars at Whitman's shop, once said: "Every man carries a little myth-making machine inside him which operates often without him knowing it. Thus you might say that we live by a very exacting kind of poetic logic — since we get exactly what we ask for, no more and no less".

Lovely. Except, of course, it depends what people ask for. And at the moment, those in power seem to be asking to live in an Ayn Rand novel. The people who run the UK and the USA treat her ideas about "enlightened self interest" and destroying the state as serious propositions instead of weak excuses for being abysmally selfish. Boris Johnson, Donald Trump, Rand Paul (obviously), Daniel Hannan, Douglas Carswell, Paul Ryan, Alan Greenspan: name a wanker and they'll name Ayn Rand as a major influence. Sajid Javid, the UK Home Secretary at the time of writing (but probably not for much longer, the way things are going) once said that he read scenes from *The Fountainhead* aloud to his wife while wooing her. Yes, he did.

Which is part of the reason the world's such a mess. I also attribute our collective failure of imagination to Milton Friedman. Friedman, friend of Reagan and Thatcher and the most influential economist of the 1980s and 1990s. Blame him for the financial weirdness that has done so much to undermine our reality. Blame him for every politician you've heard shitting on about "the discipline of the markets" or injecting "consumer choice" into places it really oughtn't to go. You've also come under his spell if you've suffered Britain's appalling privatised train service, or if you've worked for a state institution that's been destroyed because an overpaid CEO from the "business community" has come in and made everything run on "market principles". Also, if you've been pushed from a plane or murdered in the streets in Pinochet's Chile. But that's another story. Closer to home, Friedman is one of the major proponents of the ideas that privatisation is a panacea, that the state can't run anything, that end users of services are actually consumers and that things work best if they are given the illusion of choice about how they use those services...

I go on. But Friedman matters. Partly because you should know who has screwed you. But also because he was so instrumental in helping reality slip from its moorings. We're living in his dream. He ushered us into a world "governed" by markets — which turned out to be a world that wasn't properly governed at all. His ideas gave us the baffling paradoxical recession of 2007 and 2008, when everything simultaneously went to shit and remained just the same. There were no shortages of resources or food or innovation. Everything you could touch was still basically working. But somewhere in our collective consciousness, it all stopped functioning. A series of fantastical deals on unrealisable mortgages wrapped us all up into an economic death spiral that we couldn't understand, because it had no relation to anything that was happening on the ground, but which still made us all materially poorer...

...it's been strange. And that just about brings us to Donald Trump, who has taken advantage of the anger and uncertainty generated by the Great Recession. And he's also amped up the evil dreams. One of the many weird things about Trump is that he believes (as much as he believes in anything) in the Power of Positive Thinking. He was a close associate[1] of Norman Vincent Peale who told his followers to "prayerise, visualise, actualise". Imagine the world different, in other words. Attitudes matter more than "facts", said Peale. And so it came to pass that if Trump said it didn't rain at his inauguration, that was the new reality. Even though there were water drops bouncing off his nose. If Trump said he was going to "Make America Great Again", he was. Even though he wasn't.

Meanwhile, in Britain, we have Boris Johnson's self-described "Brexit dream". Nostalgic visions of a stronger, happier, whiter Britain that never existed. "Experts" derided in favour of "faith" and the Dunkirk Spirit. "We need to take one decision now before all others — and that is to believe in this country and what it can do," said Boris when he resigned as Foreign Secretary, as if Britain were a tooth fairy and Brexit would leave 20p under all our pillows, if only we wished hard enough. It was utter bollocks. But also just the kind of nonsense that has so successfully consumed the world, and helped destroy the better dreams. Martin Luther King, the post-war rebuilding of a peaceful Europe, Gandhi and give peace a chance. They all seem old-fashioned now, don't they? So what do we have? Well, not much. But maybe Paris?

Okay. I know Paris isn't immune. The nightmares of the twenty-first century have attacked even my unreal

---

1   I was going to write "friend" but he doesn't have friends, does he? Anyway, Peale officiated at Trump's first wedding. Later on, the prayers at Trump's inauguration were led by a preacher who believed in "prosperity gospel", a direct descendant of Peale's visualisation nonsense.

version of the city. The flowers outside the Bataclan testify to the penetrating power of bad dreams. Yet still, for me, it provides a kind of refuge. When I leave *Daily Mail* island on the Eurostar and walk down to Shakespeare and Company I can feel for a short time that I'm stepping into a better dream. A better collection of dreams. Maybe, in the power of words and collective creative endeavour a way to start to fight back. And certainly, a better, kinder version of reality. A bulwark against all the other madness.

At least allow me that.

The House of George[1]

Paul Ewen

Paris remains on high terrorist alert, and there's a notable presence of heavily armed police. Hemingway didn't write about counter-terrorism during his time in Paris, nor does it come up in the numerous campus novels that mention the city, such as *The Marriage Plot*, *The Rules of Attraction*, *Old School* or Paul Auster's *Innocent*. Paris is supposed to be a city of love and romance, not ultra-violence. Of course, Victor Hugo, France's most famous writing son, didn't skimp on the bloodshed. Even *The Hunchback of Notre-Dame* has its share of wanton death and demise. Today, however, I find it easier and more comforting to equate the heightened security and sub-machine guns with my own visit, as an international author of repute.

Shakespeare and Company is directly across the Seine from Notre-Dame cathedral, where Hugo crushed many people with falling beams, or had them perish from melting metal. The bookshop, made from rickety old wood, is not on fire. Portable shelves are arranged outside, and the public idly browse these, without fear of death. I rub my hands with excitement, and also for warmth. Although a cloudless day, it is most bitterly cold. Inside is cluttered, rustic and warm. Books are piled, almost to ceiling height,

---

1   This is an extract from *Francis Plug: Writer in Residence* (Galley Beggar Press, 2018)

on wonky weathered boards. My own novel is displayed just inside the door, and I murmur my approval, catching the eyes of customers, nodding a good deal and pointing. The cashier's desk is like something you might have purchased castor sugar from in yester times. Awkwardly, I ask the young, English-speaking grocer for Adam, who is chairing my evening talk. In this role, Adam has interviewed John Berger, Naomi Klein and Ethan Hawke, and in two days' time will be taking Don DeLillo's measure. But when he arrives, he doesn't strike me as some foreboding David Frost figure. Instead, he is a young, quietly spoken Englishman, tall and bespectacled, without pretensions or uplifted fighting fists. He escorts me out of the shop, back in through a secret adjacent door, and up a spiralling, concrete-strewn staircase.

Adam: Sorry about the mess. We're getting a lift put in.

A third-floor door is marked with a hand-written sign announcing: THE HOUSE OF GEORGE. This, Adam explains, is where George Whitman, the original proprietor, lived until his death, aged ninety-eight. Now, for my three nights in Paris, it will house me. I feel like I'm stepping into some massive shoes, possibly suede, hand-sewn overnight by little French elves. At the back of an entranceway piled haphazardly with books, is a round wooden table offering magnificent window-side views of Notre-Dame. Wow. It's literally right there. An old typewriter sits silently on a side desk, and a passageway leads past a small kitchen to the rear. Adam directs me through to George's former bedroom, with its oak beam ceiling, writing desk, and more books shelved from floor to ceiling. There are towels, toothpaste, and even an in-house cat. Agatha, a stray, was discovered down in the shop's Crime section, before being named after its most famous practitioner.

Adam: Are you okay with cats?

Francis Plug: For dogs we kings should have lions, and for cats, tigers.

Adam: Sorry?

FP: Just messing. I'm not Louis XI. A little cat is fine.

My inaugural French event takes place in less than two hours. Adam leaves me to settle in and get my head together. In English, this translates as downing some fast ones. Sitting at the round table, I watch the lowering sun turn Notre-Dame the same colour as my whisky. The old cathedral was bombed and bullet-holed during the Second World War, and until the 1990s, was apparently black, covered in old soot. But tonight it gleams wonderfully golden. Agatha's purr sounds like the rotating blades of a hovering helicopter. She is sprawled across my midriff, literally hosing my black jumper with tortoiseshell fur. What will my fashionable Parisian audience have to say about this?

FP: Bad cat!

Prior to show time, Adam, and Octavia, a fellow worker in Shakespeare and Company, join me at the table for red wine and a chat. Their demeanours are relaxed and friendly, but I suspect, like the BBC team, they're ascertaining my suitability for public display; in this case, within their famous shop. When Adam mentions that the audio of my event will be piped around every floor, later appearing as a podcast on their website and related social media, I begin a quiet chant.

FP: Non timebo millia populi circumdantis me: exsurge, Domine; salvum me fac, Deus!

Adam: Sorry, what's that you're saying?

FP: It's from *The Hunchback of Notre-Dame*. It means, "I will not fear the thousands of the people gathered together about me: arise, O Lord; save me O my God!" Something along those lines.

We descend the pocked and dust-strewn staircase, stopping at a side door.

Adam: You go first because you're sitting on the far side.

On the other side of the door, unbelievably, is a stage. A small modest stage, granted, but a stage nonetheless. In front of it is a packed house of people, seated, standing and staring. It's like we've just emerged through some kind of portal. It's also like that dream where you're standing before your entire school in the nuddy.

FP: Shit a brick!

When Charles Bukowski visited Paris, he drank openly from wine bottles on live French TV. This was beamed out to sixty million viewers. He didn't talk at Shakespeare and Company, but his European escapades were collected in a book entitled *Shakespeare Never Did This*. I didn't bring my whisky bottle downstairs because I'm not Charles Bukowski, although, like him, I do enjoy frequenting pubs. In truth, I forgot it because I'd been offered the red wine, which I finished. Now, instead of whisky, there are many French faces, staring, staring. Cat hairs! In *The Hunchback of Notre-Dame*, Quasimodo is honoured in the annual Festival of Fools. Tonight, I too have been given a platform and a stage. Just as a hunchback, hidden away in his bell tower, can produce the most exquisite sounds, so too may a writer, from their solitary room, produce a work that stirs the soul. Yet when the hunchback, or the writer, appears before the public, they are nothing short of grotesque.

Adam gets the interview underway by introducing me and suggesting I stand before a plastic lectern to read from my book. With my jumper temporarily obscured, I take the opportunity to give it a vigorous rub-down. The light and cheerful section I've chosen to read is therefore delivered in a manner befitting my physical exertions, which could be misconstrued as abject fury, or an uncontrollable form of mental illness. Bloody cat! Returning to my seat, I continue to pick at the hairs, pretending they are logs, and my thumb and forefinger are steel claws, connected to a shore-based crane. It gives my fingers something to do, in lieu of a drink.

Adam: Thanks, Francis. In your book you allude to writers being woefully unprepared for their new public realities. You were determined not to be one of these writers yourself. How successful have you been in this regard, do you think?

FP: Not terribly. I wasn't prepared for that door over there, straight onto the stage. And I forgot to bring a drink with me, which doesn't show much foresight either. Actually, I probably should have read my book again, to get up to speed. It's supposed to be very good. A chirpy siren belonging to a French emergency vehicle can be heard passing outside. This causes me to sit forward on my seat, in case I need to make a run for it.

Adam: It's not just stage pressure, is it? There's also the pressure of maintaining a social media presence.

FP: No, I stay well clear of that carry-on. Otherwise, you know, I'll just end up writing stuff like, "Mick down the pub is a flaming dickhead". Or: "Graham down the pub is",

I don't know, "a big-eared knob". Or: "Bill down the pub is a stupid arse..."

Adam: Right.

I feel like James in his giant peach, except my peach is much, much smaller, and the pecking seagulls are really, really hungry. Another siren can be heard, and this time I get up and move towards the stage door.

Adam: Oh... Francis?

FP: It's all right, Adam. I'm just going to get a drink.

Adam: I'm sure we can ask someone...

FP: No, no, no.

As well as my whisky, I return with a glass, so I'm not openly drinking from the bottle.

FP: There. Next question?

At some point, the questions and answers begin blurring into each other and I find myself asking questions, having run out of answers. Or, I simply make statements, hoping these may suffice as answers to other people's questions. God knows what I'm spurting out, on stage, in the world's most famous bookshop. God knows, and also the billions of people around the world who'll have access to the podcast.

Afterwards, I sign a few books, although the state of my signature probably won't be of use to those wishing to engage in identity fraud, for instance. Adam and friends whisk me off to a nearby bistro where I use hand gestures, unsuccessfully, to depict the very large drink I desire. We progress to some outer Paris pubs, and after more drinks, I tell Adam I'm ready to be interviewed on live French television. Nothing has been pre-arranged in this regard, and even with Adam's phone calls, and my background interjections, citing the BBC and David Attenborough, there are no available slots. More drinks are consumed, and I find myself outside, in a large square. Here victims of terrorism are remembered with candles, peace banners, and graffiti. The cold no longer affects me, but seeing this is all rather sobering.

The Hunchback of Notre-Dame opens with Parisians being awakened by the noisy peal of bells. Although bedding down directly opposite those peals, I sleep like a log. A real log, not an imaginary cat hair log, at the dockyards. Quasimodo was deaf too. When I finally awake, Agatha is sound asleep on my legs. If there have been any murders in the night, she has no interest in solving them. The windows must be triple-glazed. Despite the busy traffic out on Quai de Montebello, very little filters in. French sirens, I've noticed, are chirpier than English ones. They're more up for a laugh. The bells are more cheerful too. Compared to Big Ben, the toll of Notre-Dame is proper fun times. Big Ben's peal, when you actually listen to it, closely, is basically saying, "Kill yourself."

Insects have bored holes in the ceiling beams. Unlike George Orwell's Parisian room, however, no ants are visible, marching in formation. As rooms go, in this most famous of cities, George Whitman's must rate as the very finest. This isn't an exclusive, opulent, exorbitant hotel. The richest billionaire in the world can't stay here. This room, with its much-loved predecessor, its unique, personalised book collection, and its very special fur-hosing cat, is by invitation only, for bookish types. For once, the struggling, lowly writer wins. Any greedy, billionaire shits staying over in Paris, you totally lose.

There's a knock at the door. A woman, in her mid-fifties

perhaps, stands in the stairwell outside. She looks like she's just stolen 101 Dalmatians. Still unbathed, I am showered with words of the French language.

FP: Lordy! Brakes on, madame!

Woman: Sylvia?

FP: Non, non! Back, back! Moi? Lion tamer! Siegfried and Roy? Oui? Oui, moi!

Woman: [In perfect English.] Ah, yes, I see. You are Roy. Yes, definitely Roy.

FP: Whoah, madame. Roy? Non, non…

Woman: You think I'm a beast you can tame, Roy?

FP: Non, non. I cannot even tame your little French cats, with all the hairs.

Woman: Pardon?

FP: Look, I have to shower. I have the sweaty pong, oui?

Woman: Cheap whisky, that is what I smell. Listen Roy, you must pass this message to Sylvia… [A veritable stream of unintelligible French.]

FP: Ha, ha! You bet!

It's nearly lunchtime when I'm finally in a state to face France. The stairwell is crowded with strong French workmen excavating the lift shaft. I nod politely, keen to hide my ignorance of their language and construction matters. In spite of this, the void between us is all too apparent. While they are covered in plaster and general building debris, I remain blanketed in friendly cat fur. For eight hundred years, until the Eiffel Tower's construction, Notre-Dame was the tallest building in France. By the early nineteenth century, it was in total disrepair. Hugo's novel is widely credited with attracting positive attention for the cathedral, which ultimately helped save it. My novel, I fear, may send the Old Naval College the other way. It's possible to ascend the massive towers, although if you're terribly hungover, I wouldn't recommend it. You have to queue outside, for one thing, and if you stand in the freezing cold for well over an hour, you end up resembling the gargoyles protruding from the exterior walls and edifices. Still, if you're lucky, you may see French policemen race past, on rollerblades!

FP: [Singing.] Hands up! Baby, hands up!

The cathedral steps very nearly did me in, for real. I actually thought I might die. There are 387 steps in all, and after the first twenty, it felt like I was shouldering a massive barrel-shaped hunch, containing sherry.

FP: Mercy! Domine; salvum me fac, Deus!

Tourist: Is he all right?

Hugo lets us imagine a view from the cathedral's lofty heights in 1482. The spectator, on arriving, out of breath, upon this summit, was first of all struck by a dazzling confusion of roofs, chimneys, streets, bridges, squares, spires, steeples. All burst upon the eye at once. Little has changed in that sense. Especially the "out of breath' part. As well as seeing gargoyles up close, and the Eiffel Tower in the distance, Notre-Dame offers a bird's-eye view of Shakespeare and Company. It's possible to see the third floor window to the House of George, where Agatha, from this height, would best resemble a fur ball. While it's wonderful to take in the broad expanse of Paris, without threat of the cathedral being stormed by an angry mob, that warm bookshop room does beckon.

The kitchen and table area in the House of George is also used, I discover, by employees of the shop. Collectively known as "Tumbleweeds", they tend to be visitors to Paris from all parts of the world, who receive free board in exchange for two hours' work a day. Before and after their shifts, they congregate in here, at the window-side table, to eat and to chat. Although exhausted from my epic cathedral climb, an Austrian woman, who attended my talk, is keen to pick my brain.

Austrian Woman: It was interesting, your interview, but sometimes a bit confusing.

FP: What do you mean?

Austrian Woman: Well, Adam would ask you a question, and then you would talk about something else, not relevant to the question.

FP: Hmm. I think I was expanding on his questions. Taking them to the next level.

Austrian Woman: No. I don't think so. Like he asked about your attendance at the Booker Prize ceremony, and you started talking about the foot-flushing system of French toilets.

FP: I was really, really tired. Have you ever travelled all the way from London to Paris? Oh my word. It's such a demanding journey. Exhausting.

Austrian Woman: You were shouting, "VROOM-VROOM!"

FP: I suppose they'll be wanting you downstairs now, won't they? At the coalface...?

Sylvia drops by with her young son Gabriel. Given the worldwide fame of her bookshop, with its illustrious past, Sylvia is arguably more of a celebrity than many of the authors she stocks. So it's like having a celebrity turn up at your house, out of the blue, to say hi. Except, of course, this house is hers. Gabriel is two, and he's a bit tired and grizzly. To keep him entertained, I do a repetitive dance, in a German techno style, with piston-like hands. It doesn't seem to cheer him up at all, so I do it faster.

Sylvia: Anyway, I better get this one home.

FP: Oh, before I forget… a woman dropped by, at the door there. She had a message for you. Something about killing all the Dalmatians? I think a ransom was required…

As they leave, I pretend to shoot Agatha dead, blam, blam, blam, and Gabriel is briefly appeased.

On Rue Descartes, not far from the Pantheon, I pass La Maison de Verlaine, a restaurant dedicated to Paul Verlaine. It was in this building that Verlaine died of alcoholism and misery. A plaque on the same building denotes that Ernest Hemingway was also resident between 1921 and 1925. A bar nearby serves drinks, and all that talk of death and alcoholism and misery has made me thirsty. The bartender resembles the young woman who stares out from the bar in Manet's *The Bar at the Folies-Bergère*, except there's fewer mirrors and bottles, and she's actually looking down, at her phone. When I awake, it's the middle of the night. I'm slumped against a wall, on the side of a cobblestone street. After much squinting and refocusing, the street reveals itself as Rue Mouffetard, which kind of rings a bell. A pigeon lies splattered on the road. Like me, it was given wings for flight, but has ended up sprawled on the ground, wedged in the cobbled ruts. Just around the corner is George Orwell's street, Rue du Pot-de-Fer. It's a very sing-songy name, something you appreciate more when you sing it aloud, to the tune of "Chanson D'Amour". As I walk slowly back towards the Seine, I sing that street, passing through other

Parisian streets, which may be songs also.

FP: RUE. DU POT. DE FERRR. LAT DE DAT DE DAT!

When I awake, it's an overcast morning. When I awake again, as in now, it's a bright and sunny afternoon. The cold, however, prevails. Most of those braving the outdoors stand stiffly, arms pulled down, as if preparing to jump into a swimming pool fully clothed. In desperate need of sustenance, I surrender to a café near my bookshop home, requesting an English breakfast. When served, it is completely foreign to me. The waitress, who isn't English, or French, speaks English.

Waitress: Everything okay?

FP: Wonderful. I must say, I'm very impressed with all the driver-less cars zipping around out there. Compared to England, France is so advanced, such a high-tech country.

Waitress: Driver-less cars? Really? I have not noticed any.

FP: You must have. Every single car, virtually. Only front passengers.

Waitress: Ah. You see, here in France, the steering wheels are on the left side.

FP: [Pause.] I work at a university.

Don DeLillo's symposium is being held, in part, at the Sorbonne, a famous university just down the road. One of the Sorbonne's most infamous alumni is the Japanese student Issei Sagawa, who, in the early 1980s, killed a fellow student and ate various parts of her body. Japan still hunts and kills whales, and you have to wonder if this is actually just Issei Sagawa, serving his own voracious appetite. Although not registered for the symposium, I'm hoping I can blag my way in by capitalising on my language difficulties. Besides, as a scholar presently reading *White*

Noise, perhaps I can actually bring something to the party. If nothing else, it's a good chance to find out what happens at these conference things. If David Lodge's *Small World* is anything to go by, academics deliver papers on the subject in question, and then they drink loads and everyone makes out. But are the drinks free? I'm going to find out. No I'm not. At the Sorbonne's main entrance, on Rue Saint-Jacques, uniformed guards are demanding ID, and even patting down selected entrants. On the pavement opposite, two police officers wield huge sub-machine guns. Walking around the block, to the reception entrance on Rue de la Sorbonne, I encounter further security types in blue uniforms and peaked hats. Back on Rue Saint-Jacques, I try to reason with the guards.

FP: Eh… I am… how you say… "Writer" [scribbling on air] in "Residence" [hands pressed in air like roof gable] at the University of Greenwich [undulating hand, like ship on waves], England, Angleterre [Benny Hill peace sign, cross eyes, tongue out].

Guard: [Shrugging shoulders.]

FP: Eh… I… don't eat… people. I… eat… English breakfasts. Or…I would, if… you… knew how… to make them.

The guard, out of patience, steers me on my way.

FP: Eh… my university has two domes, two [two fingers]. Yours, only one [one finger].

Don DeLillo is not staying in the House of George, although I bet he wishes it were so. The organisers of his symposium, at which he is scheduled to talk, as a "living writer", have probably lumbered him with some swanky hotel, in a room previously occupied by a retired couple dipping into an immense pension accrued from a shameful company for which they performed boring, soul-destroying work. Tonight however, Don DeLillo is meeting interviewer Adam around the third floor table. Agatha is probably welcome, but I've been asked to stay scarce. It's my final night in Paris, and I'm going to see Don DeLillo in the world's most famous bookshop. As a visiting author myself, I've even been reserved a special seat. Turns out I'll need it. A queue starts forming outside at least two hours beforehand, and once the sun departs, it's blinking cold. Leaving the event attendees to form into ice sculptures, I go off in search of a hot-stuff pub.

Dear Anna,
Bonjour from gay Paree!
    The other night, I performed live on stage here in France, to a crowd of people. A bit like Jay-Z. There was even a special artists' entrance door, and when I came through it, there they were, my waiting crowd. Yay, it's Francis! They weren't screaming with excitement, although at one point I did have a sort of encore, in the sense that I went off the stage and then came back on again.
    Paris is the city of lovers, and also a place to die of alcoholism and misery, or to be shot dead for trying to be funny, or where a "friend" might eat you. Did you know that French drivers drive on the right? Of course you did. Everyone knows that!
Love, Uncle Francis.

Shakespeare and Company has wonderfully rickety features, but it's somewhat lacking in space. Books are the priority, creating walls of their own, while the airy bits for people compete with wooden beams, jutting shelves, and tourist bags. When needed as a venue, it must squeeze the punters around the nooks, seating the chosen, accommodating the lucky. Returning from the pub, I am ushered past the shivering folk still queuing outside, and in through the ram-packed crowd. As opposed to my minor interest talk upstairs, Don DeLillo is appearing on the ground floor, in the very heart of the shop. Unlike George Orwell's grim experiences in Paris, I am being personally escorted like a star, to my own reserved seat. Yet again I'm counting my blessings. It's best, in such situations, to act cool, and maintain a sense of humility. But arriving directly from the pub, I can't help smiling broadly at my good fortune, giving thumbs up to strangers, and also laughing lightly. My reserved bench seat is against a right wall, in the thick of it. Others are stuck behind supporting posts, or in back rooms, or even, I suspect, listening in from upstairs. Two modest chairs await, like theatre props, on a stage that's the height of a hand. The stage backdrop, being bookshelves, is a mass of colourful covers and spines. The same plastic lectern I used is going to serve for Don DeLillo. But I can't say I spoke at the same lectern as him, because when I did he hadn't. Although technically Don DeLillo could claim to have talked at the same plinth as me. I really hope he does. I'm yet to break America. Let's hope he's not allergic to cats.

Kristin Scott Thomas, the actress, has just sat down, right next to me. With her, to her right, is Bella Freud, the fashion designer. They were both personally escorted to their seats by Sylvia, who's also famous. Check me out! Kristin Scott Thomas has recently finished a run at the

Old Vic, but tonight an author's on stage, and she's in the audience, watching the show.

FP: Hi, Francis Plug.

Kristin Scott Thomas: Hello.

FP: I didn't see either of you at my event a couple of nights back.

Kristin Scott Thomas: No.

FP: Were you stuck in the queue, outside?

Kristin Scott Thomas: No, we weren't.

An announcement on the tannoy asks us to avoid any photography and filming, and to switch off our phones.

FP: It's like being at the cinema, isn't it? At one of your films.

Kristin Scott Thomas shudders, even though she's in here, where it's warm. Don DeLillo, seventy-nine, is about the same height and build as me, so premium-sized, as opposed to bulk-buy/economy pack. He explores death a great deal in his work, and tonight, both he and Adam are wearing grey, like the skin of dead people. Adam says he is honoured to welcome Don DeLillo, one of the most important and influential writers of recent decades. Don DeLillo stands to read an extract from his novel *Falling Man*, which is printed on A4 pages. The passage concerns events immediately following the attack on the World Trade Center towers. Don DeLillo's turtleneck jumper is grey. Adam wears an open grey cardigan with a lighter grey shirt beneath. "Everything is grey," Don DeLillo reads.

FP: Oh my word!

Nudging Kristin Scott Thomas, I point at the grey clothing, mouthing the words, "Everything is grey." When she displays both perplexity and annoyance, I don't think it's an act. The shop is incredibly quiet during the reading, given the mass of people and the proximity to the roary road by the splashy Seine. The odd scrape of a stool, one cough. An old boy to my left is wearing a black leather jacket, and this rubs and squeaks purely on account of his breathing.

FP: [Whispering.] You sir, need an oiling.

Old Boy: [Whispering.] Pardon me?

FP: [Whispering.] You need an oiling.

Before sitting down, Don DeLillo passes his reading glasses to a woman in the front row, who is of a similar age. Perhaps it's his wife. Or maybe that was the author equivalent of throwing your underwear into the crowd. Adam asks about the 9/11-related reading. Don DeLillo mentions that his book *Underworld* had the twin towers on the cover, four years before they went down. He also covered the subject of terrorism in his novel *Mao II* back in 1991. A character in this book remarks: "Years ago I used to think it was possible for a novelist to alter the inner life of a culture. Now bomb-makers and gunmen have that territory".

Don DeLillo: Terrorism has become a major element in our lives. It sometimes seems as though terror and war are covering much of the planet. And in fact, it is that way, isn't it?

It's reassuring to hear that when he first began, he didn't have loads of author mates either.

Don DeLillo: When I started I didn't know any writers. I knew no one in the publishing industry and I didn't have any writer friends.

We're in the same boat there. If Don DeLillo comes to the Greenwich Book Festival, he'll be my friend for life. He also found enormous beauty and power in James Joyce's *Ulysses*. He points out that both Joyce and Hemingway had close associations with Shakespeare and Company. James Joyce used the original shop as an office, and owner Sylvia Beach first published *Ulysses* in its entirety in 1922.

After the event's conclusion, Don DeLillo is set up at a book-signing table out back, near the children's section. As we wait in the queue, one of the "tumbleweeds" comes around with free glasses of red wine. They know, I assume, that meeting one of the most important and influential writers of recent decades demands courage.

FP: Two, please.

Don DeLillo gets me to confirm the spelling of Plug, in relation to the number of "u"s.

FP: Just the one. Although when my work is translated into Hungarian, who knows?

Don DeLillo: Are you a writer?

FP: Yes, I am. In fact, I did an event here myself, just two nights back. Although it was less an "author" event and more a toxic airborne event.

Don DeLillo: I see.

FP: I tried to visit your symposium, at the university, but they stopped me, with sub-machine guns.

Don DeLillo: Is that a fact?

FP: Yes. I thought about bursting through the guards, sprinting, darting, weaving, to the symposium. But then I thought, what if this symposium thing's actually just really boring? So I thought, stuff it, and went and found a pub/bistro place.

Don DeLillo: I think you made a wise decision.

FP: Of course, when you arrive at the University of

Greenwich, for your Book Festival engagement, there won't be any sub-machine guns at all. No way. Just a proper English cooked breakfast. I suppose you'll be wanting crispy bacon. Hash browns?

Don DeLillo: Sorry, what was this? A book festival in Greenwich?

FP: Yes, not your New York Greenwich, obviously. With all that neon lighting and mirrored sunglasses and graffiti. No, this is the royal one, in London. With the nuclear power station. And Henry Prick...

The two chairs remain on the little stage. Don DeLillo's, seat, alas, is no longer warm. After grabbing a copy of my book from the shelf near the door, I begin reading from the same plastic lectern as Don DeLillo, to empty stools.

Anchovies

Brian Dillon

On a sunny morning in June 1990, my father fell down dead in the street as he walked home from mass. I had just turned twenty-one. My mother had died five years before, and now my two brothers and I lived on as best we could in our slightly decaying semi in the Dublin suburbs. I stayed out of it as much as possible for the rest of the summer, stacking shelves by day in my university's library, and meeting up with friends in town at night, eking out a coffee or a pint till it was time to head home — if that was the word. In the autumn I went back to college, and it must have been a month or so later that my friend Austin and I decided we would spend a few days in Paris at the end of the year. He had been working as a bus conductor all summer, and I was living off my slim inheritance, so there was money. Still, it seemed amazing to me that you could sit on a freezing pavement outside the Stag's Head pub and suck on your cigarette and say yes, why not: *we'll go to Paris for New Year*. Aside from a school trip to Stratford-upon-Avon, I had never been out of Ireland. I owned nothing that resembled luggage.

Where did we think we were going? Paris, imaginary city. Of course I had grown up with the usual clichés, but the city was made in my mind at that time out of randomly assembled and absurdly skewed images, figments of a restricted, overreaching adolescence. There were the backdrops to films by Jean-Luc Godard and Éric Rohmer, photographs by Eugène Atget (I'd read about him in Walter Benjamin) from eighty years earlier, my very small knowledge of Surrealism and Existentialism. Almost nothing contemporary. At school I had been a middling student of French, then at college given it up after one month and an embarrassing grammar test. I studied literature and philosophy instead, and cursed for the next three years (actually, I'm still cursing) my idiotic decision to quit the native language of half the writers I gave a damn about. A few months into the last year of my degree, I was thrilled at the idea of Paris largely because of all the French critics and theorists I had been reading in translation. Out of scattershot encounters with Derrida, Foucault, Cixous and Kristeva, I fantasized a city that bristled with profound, radical, stylish thought. I simply wanted to be near it all — why?

Our innocence was appalling. We smoked our heads off on the plane, got totally lost at Charles de Gaulle and arrived on the Left Bank quite giddy from the Métro: the crowds, the stares, the guy who apologized for pissing on our shoes as we crested the escalator. Somebody had told Austin that it was possible to stay at the Irish College, a couple of streets south of the Panthéon. (This institution, founded by an Irish priest in the sixteenth century, is now the Centre Culturel Irlandais.) But we had not thought to phone ahead and find out if there was accommodation available, or how much it cost. The nun who opened the door on Rue des Irlandais eyed us like we were idiots, but took pity and found us a couple of rooms. I recall a bare refectory the next morning, and trying to extract ourselves from conversation with a seminarian, or a young priest, whom we callowly despised. And on my way back to my room, spotting the writer Anthony Cronin — biographer of Samuel Beckett and Flann O'Brien — scurrying to his own small room at the end of the passage. Cronin was at the time cultural advisor to the lavishly corrupt Taoiseach, Charles Haughey.

The days went by in a frenzy of seeing, almost all of it from the street. Our funds, it turned out, did not stretch to museum tickets, and so instead we trudged around gawping, only half intent, and stumbled on places of interest as much as sought them out. Awful to relate: we got the Métro to Père Lachaise to see the grave of Jim Morrison. But at least we also took in Jacob Epstein's tomb for Oscar Wilde. We trekked up to Montmartre, and the Sacré-Coeur, and happened *en route* upon the house on Avenue Junot that Adolf Loos built in 1926 for Tristan Tzara. (At the time, I had no idea who Loos was, but I'd discovered a volume of Tzara's Dadaist manifestos in the local library in my mid-teens, and been thrilled by his collage methods of making Dada poems, and by his winning facetiousness: "Work yourself up and sharpen your wings. [...] Punch yourself in the face and drop dead".) Austin had borrowed a camera from a friend's father, and we took black-and-white photographs of each other smoking in front of Rodin's statue of Balzac at the junction of the Boulevard du Montparnasse and Boulevard Raspail.

What else? We found a flea market where Austin bought a 12" copy of "Lemon Incest" by Serge Gains-bourg, and I bought some sort of mouldy leather satchel that lacked a shoulder strap and was anyway too small for practical use. Outside a bookshop I spotted a selection of issues of *L'Arc*, the literary and philosophical journal edited by Stéphane Cordier between 1958 and his death in 1986 — I bought the issues devoted to Freud and Surrealism, and a 1977 number on "La crise dans la tête". Back at the College, we arranged these items, and a carton of Gauloises, on the small desk in Austin's room, and photographed them. Who knows what we were trying to prove. In the evenings, we went looking for the cheapest restaurants, and at least once emerged giggling with amazement at our own ignorance: we had thought anchovies were vegetables, and been surprised to find our pizzas so fishy. And each night on our way back to Rue des Irlandais we stopped at the Mayflower, a touristy bar on Rue Descartes, to drink Belgian beer and talk about what to do with our lives. Austin had given up his art-school ambitions for a more practical degree in healthcare, but I — I wanted to be a writer.

I wanted to be a writer because I had been reading Roland Barthes, and not I think because of anybody else. In the library where I'd found *Seven Dada Manifestos and Lampisteries*, there was a copy of *Image-Music-Text* that I had borrowed when I was fifteen, made neither head nor tail of, but persisted and took out again a year later, after my mother died. This time I was seduced: by Barthes's style as much as thought. He was the reason I went to university, the reason I would soon, in my third year, start actually to do some work, begin dreaming of a life in which academia was the route to becoming the writer I hoped to be. (It wasn't, of course.) Barthes had only been dead for a decade. On Monday 25 February, he attended a lunch with François Mitterrand, who was not yet president and liked to surround himself regularly with advanced writers, artists, thinkers. After lunch, where he had expected to be bored, Barthes set off to walk home alone to his apartment on Rue Servandoni. Around a quarter to four, he went to cross the street in front of the Collège de France, and was knocked down by a laundry van. He lingered for a month after the accident, and died of "pulmonary complications" on 25 March. He was sixty-four.

Where had I read about Barthes's death? Fleetingly I suppose in newspaper or magazine articles, because biography was not at that time a part of the secondary academic literature on Barthes. I had not yet read his autobiography-of-sorts, *Roland Barthes*, nor the diaristic pieces in *Incidents*, which was not translated until 1992. There was Italo Calvino's 1980 essay "In Memory of Roland Barthes", with its recollection of meeting Barthes on the street with a cigarette dangling from his mouth, "in the manner of those who were young before the war". But that sort of detail was scarce; Barthes's life and his demise remained aspects of dim legend, worlds away. So that when I told Austin about him one night at the Mayflower, it seemed apt and amusing, in this city that was not yet real for us, to race drunkenly round to Rue des Écoles, and on the steps in front of the statue of physiologist Claude Bernard, start shouting at passersby: "Où est le sang de Roland Barthes?" During the day, sober, I had made Austin hang around Rue Descartes, home of the Collège International de Philosophie, in the absurd hope we might spot Derrida, then its director, going about his business.

Paris then was for this very timid, awkwardly ambitious boy not yet the Paris of adult dreams or delusions, let alone a real place. In the past three decades I have been back perhaps a dozen times as a tourist. And many others for work. I have even made friends. I've given talks at the Pompidou, read my books at Shakespeare and Company, pored over the mineral collection of the Surrealist writer Roger Caillois in the stores of the Muséum national d'histoire naturelle. I've sat in Sophie Calle's kitchen with the artist and her taxidermy collection, and on the photographer William Klein's couch while he pointed at me and said: "Well, Delphine [Seyrig] was sitting right there when she told Alain [Resnais] she'd be in his film..." The anxious orphan of 1990 would not believe it, even if he had heard of half those people. I think about him and his friend every time I pass through the city, and especially the ways innocence, timidity and a limiting pretension — our total failure to get up to very much in Paris, or get beyond our rituals and reference points — set us up for more daring flights and actual adventures.

Belfast to Paris

Robert McLiam Wilson

Irish writers in exile? Seriously, who do Irish writers think they are? Nobody was kicking me out of Ireland (nobody was begging me to stay either). No Irish writer is exiled anymore. We're just low-skilled immigrants with pretensions. And cardigans.

Anyway, I'm from Belfast. It can be hard to say what country that's actually in. Northern Ireland is a comedy routine, a two-minute sketch. My homeland is the laughable landmass, a nub of an island. Me, I was born in a cartographical cartoon.

But despite all that, I feel rather proud of coming from Belfast. Not so long ago, European Union research found that the Northern Irish were *measurably* the ugliest people in the EU and, in addition, the most inveterate and committed masturbators. I am *not* making this up. You can check. There is something about that which makes me weep with patriotic pride.

What a strange place it is. It is the politically-obsessed country with no politics. The land of warm, friendly natives with a millennium of violence behind them. The enchanted, literary isle where no one has heard of Pushkin. Ireland is a country of paradox that cannot endure contradiction. What's not to love about that?

Well, quite a lot, actually.

It is *surpassing* hard for an Irishman to write about Ireland without lapsing into very vulgar language indeed. So may I put it like this? We, the Irish, the faithfully infidel Irish, we're really annoying. Aren't we though? Can we admit this stuff now? We're *dicks*.

As an Irishman, there is something that strikes you the moment you set foot on the Continent. Ok, maybe not that very moment, but certainly when you wake up the next morning. Jesus, you think to yourself, I can just *walk* to Vladivostok. The sudden realization that you are part of a continent brings your central nervous system to a halt.

You Brits are island-folk. It's written in your DNA. You *smell* of it. And it changes everything about you. But you are some considerable way less insular, less *islandish* than we are. Compared with us, you are very Big-Time-Charlies indeed.

Belfast to Paris. You'd think that settling down on a big old land-mass might have expanded my horizons a little. Not so much, it seems. The typical expat experience is like a certain kind of guy changing girlfriends. The new one can do no wrong. The old one is the repository of all the world's faults. While everyone around him struggles to see any true difference.

Those who leave their country are generally in a state of dudgeon, high or otherwise. Dudgeon. How I love that word! Dudgeon is the expat manifesto, the exilic philosophy. The difference between a writer and the whiny, bibulous expat propping up the local ouzo or grappa bar is that the writer expects that people will rather admire his dudgeon. That stuff might have worked for Byron or Voltaire but it cuts no ice in the Internet Age. Deep in the *émigré* soul is this giant, childish sulk. It makes us pretty stupid. And it is, predictably, a hostage to fortune. For what happens when the new country makes that same journey into weary familiarity?

More dudgeon, that's what.

The brand new exile marvels tediously about how much better the new place is than the old one. Oh, the light, the food, the glory and grace of the people and their ever elegant subjunctive. I did plenty of that when I first came here. And Paris has much that Belfast never had. The air is often warm. There is sometimes perfume in the breeze. You can watch teenagers reading Plato or Spinoza on the Métro. Delightfully, almost everyone smokes.

The city is, undeniably, pretty special. If you want to know what an eighty-year-old lady in four-inch heels looks like, come to Paris. We have thousands.

It's a big city with a constant migrainous buzz, a teeth-grinding tinnitus of traffic and tumult. But on a good day, the roar and chatter can disappear suddenly, leaving your ears to ring in the silence while you overhear whispered intimacies at café tables and the faltering steps of a man walking past, miraculously balancing a huge rolled-up carpet on his head. Or those two perfect children playing with a spinning-top in a sudden splash of sun on the pavement. Your heart lifts at the loveliness and then the city buzz starts up again and the migraine returns.

Meanwhile, you are also having an adventure with a foreign language. Which seems to do something unsettling to the laws of time. For it takes ten or twelve years to sound like a five-year-old. The upside being that everyone finds you adorable.

For a while.

But forget the croissants and the *passé simple*, it's really all about geophysics. Like you, I come from a country with no sky. I'd never seen the moon go through all its phases. Not in one single month. In clear-skied night-time Paris, it was almost the first thing I saw. I watched it change from a hint to a slice, a fingernail to a lemon-rind. Then this miraculous big ball that shone brighter than I knew was possible. That kind of thing changes the way you think, it changes the colour of your eyes. What else had I missed, crouching under my damp roof of Irish cloud!

People have such ludicrous notions of some fairytale Paris. All baguettes, moustaches and *cinq-à-sept*. And Parisians, a little like the Irish, while they despise the myth, are really quite content that it should be believed.

That first flush of expat love never entirely fades but soon enough, you start noticing stuff, inconvenient stuff.

I'm sorry but I have to stop here. I need to break the fourth wall for a moment. I hope you will understand why. I wrote all of that more than a month ago. And now I need to speak to you from the heart. Without artifice, without comedy or charm. I need to speak to you not as a writer but as a man. As I'm sure you know, something dreadful happened here recently. And I wrote all that *before*.

And a month ago, I continued in the same vein, querulous and mocking. I gave Paris and Parisians some good old grief. I talked of their bizarre hatred of pigeons, their unforgivable music and their prissy language that no one speaks. Lots of funny, cheeky stuff. How even Parisians don't like Parisians. You'd have liked it. I'm pretty good at funny and cheeky. But I can't do that now. Quite clearly, I *cannot* do that now. Not yet, at any rate.

But that was not all. When I tell you that this was originally called "An Irishman in Pre-War Paris", perhaps you'll understand. It was unbroadcastably, unforgivably prescient. I wrote that Paris absolutely throbs with tension and threat. That I had not known what menace truly was until I came to Paris. I wrote that the city was a circled wagon-train in an old cowboy film. That the poor and multiple minorities lived in the suburbs and that those suburbs were a thick ring of rage around this theme park of a city. I wrote that I had already been attacked more in Paris than I ever was in Belfast. I wondered if it had something to do with my face. I wrote about sincere, committed murderers and about lighting fuses and standing well back. I wrote about a secret civil war. *I used those words.*

Then I wrote this. Which I quote in full:

There is such enmity here, such readiness. It can feel like war. Anyone who says I'm exaggerating simply doesn't know the city. You can't spend all your time objecting to racism or hatred in Paris. You wouldn't have time to feed the cat or brush your teeth. Whisper it, tell no one... but France is a country that is increasingly and silently at war with itself. On the secret battlefield of its dark mutterings and suppressed hatreds, Paris can feel like the front line.

That was then and this is now. I'm taking a risk in quoting it. Because I wrote all that when I had no real reason to write it. Certainly no justification. After the horror at

Charlie Hebdo, I read the thing again, and I felt sick. Because this is about as serious as it gets.

I know what writers are. Writers are creatures of matchless stupidity and lunatic vanity. When something like this happens, they welter in their own irrelevance and impotence. Then they claim that every word they ever wrote predicted whatever horror or trauma has happened. I hope I am not doing this. I'm speaking to you as a man not as a writer. And as a human being, sometimes, just sometimes, you don't want to be right! Sometimes, that's the *last* thing you want to be. There are times when you want to be astoundingly, embarrassingly wrong. I hope no one can doubt that.

There are two things to be said from this. First — if someone as idiotic and shallow as I am can spot this stuff and point it out, it's kinda bad news for those who couldn't. If it seemed so uneasily apparent to this Mick dimwit, why weren't the smart people talking about it? Were they on holiday?

And secondly, when I had finished this a month ago, I was, for the first time in my so-called career, worried. I was anxious about how it might make me *seem*. I'd never worried about that before. I'd never worried about anything before. But there I was, lying awake at night, biting my nails. Worrying. Would I appear exaggerated, alarmist... even a little bit... you know what I mean... *dodgy*?

Actually, I think, the central question is why couldn't I sleep? It's about truth. I couldn't sleep because I couldn't help feeling that this was a truth I really shouldn't tell. An uncomfortable truth. A deeply inconvenient one.

Which is odd. Because everyone pretty much knows

the depth and width of their own good faith. I know I do. And all serious people ask themselves questions about it every single day. If you fail to tell a truth you see or hear because you are worried how you might *seem* then you are the exact opposite of *Charlie Hebdo*. Free speech is absolutely binary. It's either total or it does not exist. And the opposite of truth is not lies. The opposite of truth is euphemism.

It's now more than a week later and my rage and despair has become a hangover, it's a bad taste in my mouth. What do I feel now? What do you care? And frankly, you don't wanna know. But I'm gonna tell you anyway.

I feel experienced. That's the gift of my Belfast birth. I feel experienced. Parisians are being searched when entering shops? I was doing that stuff when I was eight. There are cops and soldiers everywhere? When I first left Northern Ireland, I found it grotesque that there were not. I hate my experience. It disgusts me.

I also feel tenderness. For them, my sweet French friends. I watch them march and stand, light candles and look bewildered. I hear them call me up and ask me if what they're feeling is normal. And I *can't* answer them. Because I can't remember that far back. I can't remember a time that felt anything like the first time.

But they should have their badges, their marches and vigils. It's a consolation and a distraction. I understand that they feel that they have to do something. If marching makes them feel better then march, by all means, march. And I really don't want to say what I am going to say.

It will make no difference at all.

It will not be they who decide when this will stop.

I was a child when the first such campaign happened in

Belfast. I still remember the giant posters. SEVEN YEARS ARE ENOUGH! Even as a child, I laughed.

Yes, I feel overwhelmed with tenderness for the French (and hey, that's not always how people feel about them, believe me). I hope they never have my experience. I hope they never hear a bomb explode a mile away and turn to someone and say "sounded like Montparnasse...?" and then immediately go back to what they were doing. I hope they never learn the trick of switching on the news when the sport comes on just to avoid the body count in their city that day. I hope, I truly hope that they never end up sounding like me.

So, let me go back to being a writer. Let me say at the top of my voice. Paris is still *Paris*. Triumphantly so. A city that has endured worse and better. I didn't know what stubborn meant until I came here. Read some Balzac, it hasn't changed that much. It's still the place that invented sex and the afternoon. The city where a choccy bun can be so disgracefully sublime that it can make you dance in the street. The city of the most beautiful children I have ever seen. The city where this Irishman learned to drink. Where you can have communist councillors and binmen with PhDs. The city where knowledge is your friend and pleasure is your pal. Paris is still and will always be the city where the streets flow like rivers and the sky is still sometimes full of stars.

Missing Paris

Rob Doyle

Recently I flew back to Dublin for a few days from Berlin, where I am living now. When I moved here at the start of the summer, I sublet my room in the Dublin suburb of Kimmage to the boyfriend of one of my housemates. I stored my belongings — mostly books — in plastic crates in the attic. I intended to return at the end of the summer: my rent was quite low and, that being rare in Dublin, I didn't want to give up the room. As the summer ended, however, I decided I was better off in Berlin, and contacted the subletting tenant to tell him he could take over the rental.

After I landed in Dublin, I drove to Kimmage with my father, and he helped me transport the crates back to our small family home in Crumlin. (Crumlin and Kimmage, incidentally, are the two cheapest tiles on the Dublin edition of the *Monopoly* board — the ones marked with brown strips.) In Berlin I rent a room in Friedrichshain, with a balcony on which my flatmate, an artist in her fifties, cultivates an explosion of plants that I water whenever she's away. At the weekends, I can hear the boom of the Funktion One soundsystem at the nearby Berghain nightclub (which is also a day club; my preferred time for going there is after breakfast on Sundays, when the queue is short and the garden area opens).

Unloading the crates in my childhood bedroom (repurposed by my retired father as a room for listening to Bob Dylan while reading about Bob Dylan) made me acutely aware that I'm thirty-five years old and don't really have a home of my own — a place to *put my stuff* — and that maybe I should think about settling down.

One of the books I unpacked was *Paris*, a collection of some five-hundred photographs by Eugène Atget published by Taschen. I bought *Paris* after I left Paris, where I lived, on and off, between the spring of 2015 and the winter of 2017. I bought the book after I started missing Paris, so that I could miss it more. Atget's photographs would be an aid to missing. From the 1890s until his death at the age of seventy in 1927, Atget obsessively photographed a Paris that was vanishing before his eyes, overlaid by modernity. His main motive was to sell his photographs to the painters he observed at work in Montparnasse, for use as memory aids. When the Surrealist photographer Man Ray became enthused after Atget showed him his work, the latter insisted that his photographs were "just documents" (the sign he hung on the door of a studio in the fifth arrondissement around 1890 said as much: "Documents pour Artistes"). When four of his photographs were published in *La Révolution surréaliste* magazine in 1926, Atget stuck to his self-effacing guns and insisted that he not be credited for his contribution.

As Paris was transformed by "Haussmannization" at the end of the nineteenth century — grand boulevards and gridded streets replacing disorderly neighbourhoods — Atget began to consciously regard himself as an artisan documentarian of *le vieux Paris*. In his most evocative photographs of the old Paris he was already missing, there is something else missing too: people. Streets are deserted; quays and canal banks are desolate; the interiors of homes and small businesses are empty, as if the city has been evacuated. Walter Benjamin noted that Atget photographed Paris as if it were the scene of a crime: the witnesses have fled, though here and there a prostitute stands her ground in a doorway, peering brazenly into Atget's lens. For Benjamin, the nature of the crime for which Atget gathered evidence was historical, but perhaps it was also metaphysical (the killing of time?). Whatever dark deed went down, some of the photographs appear to be haunted by its victims. For instance, a ghostly little girl crossing the Boulevard Sérurier in the nineteenth arrondissement: she is transparent, flickering between our shadowy world and some other dimension. Two more children peer furtively from behind a gate, likewise neither here nor there. Near them, an old woman in a dark shawl sits on a bench with her face turned towards the camera. Unlike the children, she is wholly substantial, as if age has solidified her. I have no great understanding of the techniques photographers apply to their craft,[1] so I can't

---

1   I take photos on my phone with sporadic enthusiasm and no sense of what I am doing beyond pointing and clicking. Recently, on my girlfriend's request, I photographed my erect penis, then sent her the image via WhatsApp. It was my first dick-pic. Surprisingly, whenever I see the photo as I scroll though my collection, I find myself aroused by the cock's firmness, its heft, its strutting obscenity. I wonder what that most confusing of Parisian authors, Jacques Lacan, would have made of the *jouissance* of a heterosexual man who, holding a sleek mobile device in his palm, is excited by the image of his own erect cock filling its bright

say what kind of overlay effect has been used here, but it's easy to believe that Atget wanted to depict the city as a (missing) place that haunted him as it haunted itself.

Many of the human figures who *have* stuck around Atget's crime-scene city, like the hookers, stand in clusters and gawp at Atget's lens as if he were an extraterrestrial *flâneur*. Although photography was no longer a new technology in Atget's time and more compact cameras were available, he took his pictures on a cumbersome, twenty-kilo, tripod-supported contraption that he lugged all over the city. It probably did look a bit like an alien spacecraft, or like the metallic capsule from which Arnie emerges in *The Terminator*, having hurtled back from the future — back from our future, perhaps, where unseen cameras document not a crime that has already happened, but one we are all presumed guilty of longing to commit.

These gawking figures on Atget's streets likewise seem to have been transported from elsewhere: namely, from India, where it is a common experience for foreign travellers to arrive in some village or town and find that men on the street stop and stare at them, without the slightest self-consciousness. One of Atget's photographs shows a blind man sitting by the side of a street at Bastille. Staring at him, we wonder if he knows he is being photographed, and if he doesn't, whether this constitutes a more serious violation than the unnerving stare of a stranger in the street, which at least alerts us to the fact that we are being scrutinized. We

---

screen. I wonder too if in some future age, more intrepid dick-pic snappers than I will be praised for generating unintended art, as Atget was for his "documents" of the old Paris.

feel we are appraising the blind man for his vulnerability to robbery or assault — or perhaps the crime we are contemplating is more subtle. As the twentieth century passed in a time-lapse blur and everything on Earth got snapped in the camera's insatiable gaze, postmodern theorists warned of a threat to reality itself, which, crushed beneath mass media, seemed to be disappearing into its representations. No longer was the camera a witness to metaphysical crime; it now *perpetrated* the crime. Jean Baudrillard suggested that the unnatural smiles of people who pose for photographs are like the behaviour of an animal who plays dead to avoid detection by a predator. Relentless and ubiquitous, the camera had become not only predator but Terminator, carrying out the total extermination of the real — *The Perfect Crime*, in Baudrillard's reckoning.

When I bought Atget's *Paris*, the sections I perused most keenly were those devoted to the arrondissements where I lived and spent my time: the nineteenth, tenth, twentieth, eleventh, fifth. Disappointingly, Atget did not take many photos of the nineteenth, where I lived when I first moved to Paris. I had hoped especially to find photographs of the Parc des Buttes Chaumont, where I used to jog in the mornings and, in the evenings, watch the sun set on the Paris skyline from its steep grassy vantage. While I was living next to the Buttes Chaumont (having moved there following a break-up), the French-Argentine director Gaspar Noé's film *Love* was released in cinemas. On its opening night I arrived early at a quayside cinema by the Bassin de la Villette, expecting a long queue of French cinema lovers as keen as I was to see the latest work by this maverick filmmaker. There was no queue at all: I was handed a pair of 3D glasses by the usherette, then I sat in a near-empty theatre, the lone loner amidst two or three couples viewing this film that was inelegantly marketed as a "3D porno". I may as well have been Bruno, the hapless sex-addict in Michel Houellebecq's novel *The Elementary Particles*, who ashamedly jerks off in the porn cinemas that once operated around the Latin Quarter. Despite its lacklustre reception among Parisians, I found *Love* magnificent — especially the scene in which the young American protagonist flashes back to the moment he met his lover, on the viewing point at the top of the Parc des Buttes Chaumont. In a trance of infatuation, the pair walk down the pathway that winds from the summit to the gates of the park, as Paris lights up the swirling dusk behind them — I could see my house from here! *Love* may be a 3D porno, but that scene is exquisitely wistful.

The next time I lived in Paris (in the tenth arrondissement), like the protagonist in Noé's film, I was very much in love — with a woman who flew over to stay a few times in my studio loft opposite the Gare de l'Est train station. One of the things I loved about her was her wistful attraction to the quality of wistfulness — in art, people, places. To her, wistfulness was almost a moral category. "She's not *wistful*," she would declare by way of dismissing somebody. Geoff Dyer's 1998 novel *Paris Trance*, which I had read several times before I ever lived in Paris, must be the most wistful novel ever written about the city, and perhaps about any other city too. It really couldn't be any more wistful. Reading it imparts an exquisite ache that lingers like the memory of someone you missed even while they were there. One way to define wistfulness: the sadness of finding a beautiful experience tainted by the awareness of its passing, even while knowing that beauty is predicated on evanescence. Much of *Paris Trance*, a love story, is set in the eleventh arrondissement — in bars and clubs on Oberkampf and Parmentier — but its final pages unfold on the French coast, where four friends are entranced by a happiness that we know is destined to be shattered. As an evocation of transience, the novel's closing image

> A military jet pulled through the sky, very high. Beyond that was the uncertain region where sky turned into space, where everything began to peter out, where distance ceased to be measured as space, only as light. The plane itself was no more than a dot, would probably have been invisible but for the vapour trail easing out behind it.

resonates across the millennia with the final stanza of a classic text of Mahayana Buddhism, the *Diamond Sutra*:

> *As stars, a fault of vision, as a lamp*
> *A mock show, as dew drops, or a bubble,*
> *A dream, a lightning flash, or cloud,*
> *So one should view what is conditioned.*

Despite all talk of crime scenes, Eugène Atget's Paris, like Geoff Dyer's, is inevitably a zone of intense wistfulness, a remembrance of things in their passing. An archivist of nostalgia, Atget photographed chunks of the present that were crumbling into the past, his mission impelled by the erasures of a looming future. Some of his most suggestive work depicts the poorer arrondissements away from the splendour and opulence of the centre, pushed up against the Périphérique that encloses Paris from the now-notorious *banlieues* beyond. In shots of the city's down-at-heel southeast that have the cosy-seedy atmosphere of Georges Simenon's crime novels, narrow canals run through vacant laneways, past sullen houses. Out past Bercy, a towpath on the Seine leads away from the city to the drab eastern outskirts. It is a bleak, wet day. Once again the view is deserted — or seems to be, until I spot two huddled figures in the middle-distance. It is my friend Liam and I, heads downturned against the rain. We took walks out there on winter Sundays, keen to look beyond the enclave of Paris proper, which we suspected of being a dream, an ether of lost past sustained by a film of nostalgia. On Sunday mornings, we would separately take public transport and meet where we had left off last time, and there resume our march into the *banlieues*. Along the way we would stop to drink in garishly fluorescent working-class bars whose total lack of charm generated its own kind of self-assurance. We eventually made it out to the eccentric postmodern high-rise blocks at Noisy-le-Grand, whose looming geometries of cube and cylinder saw them used as locations for dystopian sci-fi films. I took a few photos on those walks, most of them destined to be archived on the cloud and never seen by anyone else, like old photograph albums buried in a closet.

As I scan through the cloud at these and other photos I took in Paris, some of the memories they evoke are unexpectedly painful, or prompt me to consider elements of my time there in a new and starker light. In this sense, photographs can be evidence not of a crime but of an unhappiness one would rather forget, preferring to cover it up with nostalgic, wistful images like those of Eugène Atget as we can only see them now. Nevertheless, I still miss Paris, the way I remember missing it even while I wandered its photogenic streets. That is why I keep moving, I think: to find new places to miss. In the shimmer of nostalgia cast by the refraction of memory, perception and desire, I make a kind of home.

Contributors

Jeremy Allen is a music, film and culture journalist who has written for the BBC, *Guardian*, *Independent*, *Quietus*, *Stool Pigeon*, *NME*, *Record Collector*, *Prog*, *Huck* and more. His flawed heroes include Rainer Werner Fassbinder, Nina Simone and Serge Gainsbourg, the latter of whom he has written sleeve notes for (posthumously, of course). Allen lived and worked in Paris until recently and now resides in an obscure Surrey village with his partner Claire and son Jean Genie. @jeres

Anna Aslanyan is a freelance journalist and translator. She writes, mainly about books and the arts, for the *London Review of Books*, *Times Literary Supplement* and other publications. Her first book, a popular history of translation, will be published by Profile Books. @anna_aslanyan

Will Ashon is the author of a series of occasionally-read books including *Strange Labyrinth* (2017) and *Chamber Music* (2018), both from Granta. @willashon

Nicholas Blincoe is the author of six novels, including the CWA award-winning *Manchester Slingback* (Picador, 1998), and two histories: *Bethlehem* (Nation Books, 2017) and *More Noble Than War* (Nation Books, 2019) a history of football in Palestine and Israel. He also writes for theatre and film, and his scripts have won the Beckett Award (*Cue Deadly*, 2003) and iFeatures Award (*Eight Minutes Idle*, 2012). His PhD is on Jacques Derrida's use of economics. @NicholasBlincoe

Owen Booth is the author of *What We're Teaching Our Sons* (4th Estate, 2018). His short stories have been published in *The White Review, Gorse, The Moth, Hotel, 3:AM Magazine* and *Best British Short Stories*, among others. He won the 2015 *White Review* Short Story Prize. https://owen-booth.com/ @owenbooth

Gavin James Bower was born in Burnley, Lancashire and graduated from the University of Sheffield. The author of two novels — *Dazed & Aroused* (Quartet Books, 2009), *Made in Britain* (Quartet Books, 2011) — and one non-fiction work — *Claude Cahun: The Soldier With No Name* (Zero Books, 2013). As a journalist, he has contributed to the *Guardian, Independent, Independent on Sunday* and *Sunday Telegraph*. He joined the writing team for *EastEnders* in 2014. @gavin-jamesbower

Tom Bradley has published twenty-seven volumes of poetry, fiction, essays and screenplays with houses in the USA, England, Canada and Japan. His latest blank verse epics are *Energeticum/Phantasticum: a Profane Epyllion* and *Useful Despair as Taught to the Hemorrhaging Slave of an Obese Eunuch*, both published by MadHat Press in 2017 and 2018, respectively. http://tombradley.org/

Donari Braxton is a Brooklyn-based writer, filmmaker and photographer. He has received support and awards from Sundance, TriBeCa, NPR, IFP, Film Independent and Berlinale Talents, amongst other institutions. *Out of My Hand*, the narrative feature that he wrote and produced, premiered at the 2015 Berlin International Film Festival. He was later nominated for the John Cassavetes Independent Spirit Award for his work on the project. Most recently, he was awarded the San Francisco Film Society's KRF Grant & Fellowship for his new feature in development, *Above*. Outside of his feature endeavours, his images, editorials and shorts have frequently been featured in such publications as *GQ*, *Details* and *Playboy* magazines. http://donaribraxton.com/

Daniela Cascella (Italy/UK) writes through sound, literature and art. She has published three books that articulate various tensions and points of contact between creative and critical writing across disciplines: *Singed: Muted Voice-Transmissions, After the Fire* (Equus Press, 2017), *F.M.R.L. Footnotes, Mirages, Refrains and Leftovers of Writing Sound* (Zero Books, 2015) and *En Abîme: Listening, Reading, Writing. An Archival Fiction* (Zero Books, 2012). http://www.danielacascella.com/

David Collard writes regularly for the *Times Literary Supplement, Literary Review* and other journals. He is the author of *About a Girl* (CB editions, 2016). He lives and works in London, where he divides his time. @David-Collard1

Emily S. Cooper is a poet and essayist from the north-west of Ireland. Her work has been published in *The Stinging Fly, Irish Times* and banshee.

Toby Litt was born in Ampthill, Bedfordshire. He has

worked as a teacher, bookseller and subtitler. A graduate of Malcolm Bradbury's Creative Writing MA at the University of East Anglia, Toby is best known for writing his books — from Adventures in Capitalism (1996) to Patience (Galley Beggar Press, 2019) — in alphabetical order. He is a Granta Best of Young British Novelist and a regular on Radio 3's The Verb. His story "John and John" won the Manchester Fiction Prize, and his most recent short story collection, Life-like, was shortlisted for the Edgehill Prize and longlisted for the Frank O'Connor International Short Story Prize. Toby teaches creative writing at Birkbeck College.

Susanna Crossman is an Anglo-French writer. Co-author of the French novel, *L'Hôpital, le dessous des cartes* (LEH, 2015), her work has appeared in *Versopolis*, *ZenoPress*, *The Creative Review*, *3:AM Magazine*, *Litro* and elsewhere. Nominated for Best of The Net (2018) for her non-fiction, her fiction has been shortlisted for the Bristol Prize and Glimmertrain. She regularly collaborates on international hybrid projects with academics, artists, filmmakers and musicians. https://susanna-crossman.squarespace.com/ @crossmansusanna

Elsa Court is a French-born journalist and academic. She is an expat culture columnist for the *Financial Times* and a literary criticism editor at *Review 31*. She is the author of *Émigré Representations of the American Roadside 1955-85: Explorations in Literature, Film, and Photography* (Palgrave MacMillan, 2019). Her essays and book reviews have appeared in the *Times Literary Supplement*, *Los Angeles Review of Books*, *London Review of Books* blog, and elsewhere. She lives in London, and teaches French cinema and culture at Oxford University. @ElsaCourt

Thom Cuell is the Editorial Director of independent publishing company Dodo Ink, and Senior Editor of the journal *Minor Literature[s]*. His writing has appeared in *3:AM Magazine* and *Review 31*. He edited Dostoyevsky Wannabe's Cities series on *Manchester* (2018). @TheWorkshyFop

Cody Delistraty is a writer based in New York and Paris. He writes essays for the *New York Times*, *Paris Review* and *Frieze*, among others. He is at work on his first novel. https://delistraty.com/ @Delistraty

Brian Dillon's books include *Essayism* (Fitzcarraldo Editions, 2017), *The Great Explosion* (Penguin, 2015), *Objects in This Mirror: Essays* (Sternberg Press, 2014) and *I Am Sitting in a Room* (Cabinet Books, 2012). He is an editor of *Cabinet* magazine, and teaches writing at the Royal College of Art, London. @briangdillon

Rob Doyle's first novel, *Here Are the Young Men*, was published in 2014 by Bloomsbury and the Lilliput Press. It was one of *Hot Press* magazine's "20 Greatest Irish Novels 1916-2016", and is currently being adapted for film. His second book, *This Is the Ritual* (Bloomsbury/Lilliput, 2016) was a book of the year in the *Irish Times*, *Sunday Times* and *New Statesman*. Rob is the editor of *The Other Irish Tradition* (Dalkey Archive Press, 2018) and *In This Skull Hotel Where I Never Sleep* (Broken Dimanche Press, 2018). His writing has also appeared in the *Guardian*, *Irish Times*, *Dublin Review*, *Vice*, and elsewhere. His third book will be published by

Bloomsbury in early 2020. https://robdoyle.net/

Nathan Dragon has been published in *NOON Annual*, *New York Tyrant*, *Egress* and *3:AM. Magazine*. Dragon lives in Salem, MA and is currently finishing a book of short fiction. https://nathandragon.wordpress.com/

Lauren Elkin is an award-winning writer and translator, most recently the author of *Flâneuse: Women Walk the City* (Chatto & Windus, 2016). Her next book, *Art Monsters* (Chatto & Windus), looks at an aesthetics of monstrosity in the last century of women's writing, art, music, and fashion. She lives in Paris. @LaurenElkin

Wendy Erskine lives in Belfast. She is the author of *Sweet Home* (The Stinging Fly Press, 2018), a collection of short stories. Her writing has also appeared in several issues of *The Stinging Fly*, as well as in *Being Various: New Irish Short Stories* (Faber & Faber, 2019), *Stinging Fly Stories* (2018), *Winter Papers* (2018), *Female Lines: New Writing by Women from Northern Ireland* (New Island Books, 2017) and on BBC Radio 4. @WednesdayErskine

Gerard Evans wrote for years under the nom de plume George Berger. After working for *Sounds*, he wrote *Dance Before The Storm: The Official Story Of The Levellers* (Virgin, 1998) and *The Story Of Crass* (Omnibus, 2006) among other things. He is also vocalist for punk band Flowers in the Dustbin and teaches mindfulness in Brighton, UK. Together with writer Jon Wilde, he recently released *The Turning Point* (Zen 23, 2018), a book about mindfulness. https://zen23.co.uk/

Paul Ewen is a New Zealand writer based in south London. His first book, *London Pub Reviews* (Shoes with Rockets, 2008), was called "a cross between *Blade Runner* and *Coronation Street*" (Waterstones). His first novel, *Francis Plug: How To Be A Public Author* (Galley Beggar Press, 2014), appeared on numerous Books of the Year lists, won a Society of Authors McKitterick Prize, and was described by the *Sunday Times* as "a brilliant, deranged new comic creation". His new Francis Plug novel, *Writer in Residence* (Galley Beggar Press, 2018), has been called "Glorious... another outstandingly funny book" (*Guardian*), and seen him heralded "the saviour of comic fiction" (*Spectator*). @GalleyBeggars

Utahna Faith is a writer, farmer, mama, who lives in New Orleans. Her stories have appeared in *Flash Fiction Forward* and *Exquisite Corpse: A Journal of Letters and Life*. She is working on a novel entitled *Daylights Out of Me*. @utahna

Gerry Feehily is the author of *Gunk* (Galley Beggar / 3:AM Press, 2014) and *Fever* (Parthian, 2008). He lives in Paris.

Natalie Ferris is a Leverhulme Trust Early Career Fellow in the School of Literatures, Languages & Cultures at the University of Edinburgh. She has contributed art and literary criticism to publications such as *Frieze*, *The Guardian*, *The White Review*, *Tate Etc.* and is currently finalising her monograph *Abstraction in Post-War British Literature 1945-1980* for publication. https://edinburgh.academia.edu/NatalieFerris @ResidntPheasant

Steve Finbow's fiction includes *Balzac of the*

Badlands (Future Fiction London, 2009), *Tougher Than Anything in the Animal Kingdom* (Grievous Jones Press, 2011), *Nothing Matters* (Snubnose Press, 2012) and *Down Among the Dead* (Number Thirteen Press, 2014). His biography of Allen Ginsberg in Reaktion's Critical Lives series was published in 2011. His other works include *Grave Desire: A Cultural History of Necrophilia* (Zero Books, 2014), *Notes From the Sick Room* (Repeater Books, 2017) and *Death-Mort-Tod: A European Book of the Dead* (Infinity Land Press, 2018). He is currently working on a book called *Being & Happiness*. He lives in France. http://indifferentmultiplicities.blogspot.com/ @stevefinbow

Tristan Foster is a writer from Sydney, Australia. His short story collection *Letter to the Author of the Letter to the Father* (2018) is published by Transmission Press. He is co-editor-in-chief of *3:AM Magazine*. https://tristanfoster.wordpress.com/ @tristan_foster

Steven J. Fowler is a writer and artist who works in poetry, fiction, theatre, video, photography, visual art, sound art and performance. He has published seven collections of poetry, three of artworks, four of collaborative poetry, plus volumes of selected essays and selected collaborations. He has been commissioned by Tate Modern, BBC Radio 3, Tate Britain, the London Sinfonietta, Wellcome Collection and Liverpool Biennial. http://www.stevenj-fowler.com/ @stevenjfowler

Andrew Gallix is an Anglo-French writer and freelance journalist who teaches at Sorbonne Université (Paris IV)

and edits *3:AM Magazine*. His work has appeared in the *Guardian, Irish Times, Times Literary Supplement, Financial Times, Independent, Literary Review, New Statesman*, BBC Radio 3 and elsewhere. He co-edited *Punk is Dead: Modernity Killed Every Night* (Zero Books, 2017). Andrew divides his time between Scylla and Charybdis. https://andrewgallix.com/ @andrewgallix

Greg Gerke's work has appeared in the *Paris Review Daily, Kenyon Review Online, Denver Quarterly, Quarterly West, Mississippi Review, LIT, Film Quarterly*, and elsewhere. He is the author of *He Lives in Brooklyn* (Queen's Ferry Press, 2015). http://www.greggerke.com/ @Greg_Gerke

Jonathan Gibbs is a writer and critic based in London. He has published two novels: *Randall, or The Painted Grape* (Galley Beggar Press, 2016) and *The Large Door* (Boiler House, 2019). He lectures in Creative and Professional Writing at St Mary's University, Twickenham, and curates the "Personal Anthology" short fiction project: https://apersonalanthology.com/ @tiny_camels

Niven Govinden is the author of five novels, *We Are the New Romantics* (Bloomsbury, 2004), *Graffiti My Soul* (Canongate, 2007), *Black Bread White Beer* (The Friday Project, 2012), *All the Days and Nights* (The Friday Project, 2014) and *This Brutal House* (Dialogue Books, 2019). *Black Bread White Beer* won the 2013 Fiction Uncovered Prize and was longlisted for the DSC Prize. *All the Days And Nights* was longlisted for the Foli Prize and shortlisted for the Green Carnation Prize. @niven_govinden

Adrian Grafe grew up in Oxfordshire, and lives in Paris. An English professor at Université d'Artois, he has published many articles and book reviews on poetry, and several books, including *Edward Thomas: Roads from Arras*, a multi-author essay collection co-edited with Andrew McKeown (Cambridge Scholars, 2018).

Julian Hanna is Assistant Professor at Madeira Interactive Technologies Institute in Portugal. His creative work has featured in *The Atlantic*, *3:AM Magazine*, *Berfrois*, *Minor Literature[s]* and elsewhere. He writes a blog called *Crap Futures* with the Paris-based designer James Auger, which provides a nice excuse to visit the city. He is the author of *The Manifesto Handbook* (Zero Books, 2019) and *Manifestos from the Machine Age to the Digital Age* (Palgrave Macmillan). http://crapfutures.tumblr.com @julianisland & @crapfutures

Owen Hatherley writes regularly on aesthetics and politics for, among others, *Architectural Review*, *Dezeen*, *The Guardian* and *Prospect*. He is the author of several books, most recently *Landscapes of Communism* (Penguin, 2015), *The Ministry of Nostalgia* (Verso, 2016), *The Chaplin Machine* (Pluto, 2016, based on a PhD thesis accepted by Birkbeck College in 2011), *Trans-Europe Express* (Penguin, 2018) and *The Adventures of Owen Hatherley in the Post-Soviet Space* (Repeater, 2018). He is the culture editor of *Tribune*.

David Hayden's work has appeared in *The Stinging Fly*, *Granta* and *Zoetrope All-Story*. His collection of stories, *Darker With the Lights On* (Little Island Press), came out in 2017. He is currently working on a novel. @seventydys

Tomoé Hill is a contributing editor at *Minor Literature[s]*. Her reviews and essays have appeared in *Numéro Cinq, 3:AM Magazine, Berfrois, Lapsus Lima* and elsewhere. She was co-author of the XX and XY series reviewing classic erotic literature for *The Amorist*, and is currently working on *Normal/Hunger*, a memoir about sex and identity. She lives in London. @CuriosoTheGreat

Andrew Robert Hodgson is author of the novel *Reperfusion* (WPS&B, 2012), the novelesque *Mnemic Symbols* (Dostoyevsky Wannabe, 2019) and monograph *The Post-War Experimental Novel* (Bloomsbury, 2019). He is translator from the French of Roland Topor's *Head-to-toe Portrait of Suzanne* (Atlas Press, 2018) and from the Danish, Carl Julius Salomonsen's *Modern Forms of Art and Contagious Mental Illness* (New Documents, 2019). @andhodgson

Jennifer Hodgson is a writer and critic from Hull. She edited *The Unmapped Country* (& Other Stories, 2018), a collection of stories by the writer Ann Quin. Her next book will be about Quin's life and work. https://jenniferhodgson.co.uk/ @jenniferhodgson

John Holten's first novel *The Readymades* was published in 2011 by Broken Dimanche Press, the "fictional" art press he co-founded in Berlin in 2009. It was followed up by the novel *Oslo, Norway* in 2015. Holten has collaborated with many visual artists on texts and publications in recent years. He has been awarded Literature Bursaries from the Arts Council of Ireland, most recently in 2017. *The Readymades* is republished in Ireland by gorse editions. http://www.

johnholten.com/ @brokendimanche

Stewart Home is an award-winning visual artist and the author of fifteen novels, seven works of cultural commentary, one collection of stories and one collection of poetry. His most recent book is *Re-Enter The Dragon: Genre Theory, Brucesploitation & the Sleazy Joys of Lowbrow Cinema* (The LedaTape Organisation, 2018). Home was born and lives in London. When he isn't shredding copies of his own books as live art, he likes to entertain audiences by standing on his head spewing obscenities. https://www. stewarthomesociety.org/ @stewarthome1

Andrew Hussey is Professor of Cultural History at the School of Advanced Study, University of London and a Paris resident. He has written several books including *The Game of War: The Life and Death of Guy Debord* (Cape, 2001), *Paris: The Secret History* (Penguin, 2006) and *The French Intifada: The Long War Between France and its Arabs* (Granta, 2015). He is a regular contributor to the *Guardian* and *New Statesman* and is the writer/presenter of several BBC documentaries. He was awarded an OBE in 2011 for services to Anglo–French cultural relations.

Heidi James is the author of three novels: *Carbon* (Blatt Books, 2009), *Wounding* (Bluemoose Books, 2014) and *So the Doves* (Bluemoose Books, 2017), which was a *Sunday Times* Crime Novel of the Month. Her novella *The Mesmerist's Daughter* (Neon Press, 2015) won the Saboteur Award. Her essays, poetry and short stories have appeared in numerous publications and anthologies. She has an MA in Creative

Writing and a PhD in English Literature and is the 2015 recipient of the Dr. Rajini Pani Outstanding Faculty Award. https://heidijames.me/ @heidipearljames

Rosalind Jana is an author, journalist and poet. She has written for many publications including *British Vogue, Buzzfeed, Dazed & Confused, AnOther*, BBC Radio 4, *Refinery29, Broadly* and *Suitcase*. Her debut non-fiction book *Notes on Being Teenage* came out with Hachette (Wayland) in 2016. She has performed her poetry widely, with her first collection *Branch and Vein* available through the New River Press. http://www.rosalindjana.com/ @rosalindjana

Sam Jordison is an author, journalist and publisher. He is the co-director of the award-winning independent publisher Galley Beggar Press. He also writes about books for *The Guardian* and has published several works of non-fiction including *Enemies Of The People* (about Brexit and Trump and the people behind them both), *Crap Towns* (about the worst places to live in the UK) and, most recently, *The 10 Worst Of Everything* (pretty self-explanatory). He lives in Norwich. http://galleybeggar.co.uk, https://www.theguardian.com/profile/samjordison @samjordison

Richard Kovitch is a London-based writer, director and producer, whose work has won awards in Europe and the US. He works regularly for the BBC and Channel 4. His writing on film and music has been published by *3:AM Magazine* and *Gorse*. His debut feature documentary *Penny Slinger — Out Of The Shadows* was released to worldwide

acclaim in 2017. https://www.richardkovitch.com/ @
RKovitch_

Evan Lavender-Smith's writing has been published by
*Arts & Letters, BOMB, Colorado Review, Denver Quarterly, Egress,
Harvard Review, Hobart, New England Review, The Southern
Review, The White Review* and many other magazines and
websites. He is the author of *Avatar* (Six Gallery Press, 2011)
and *From Old Notebooks* (Dzanc Books, 2013), the founding
editor of Noemi Press, and an assistant professor in the MFA
program at Virginia Tech. http://el-s.net/ @elavendersmith

Sophie Mackintosh won the 2016 *White Review* short-
story prize and the 2016 Virago/*Stylist* short-story compe-
tition, and has been published in *Granta* and *The Stinging
Fly*. Her debut novel, *The Water Cure* (Hamish Hamilton) was
longlisted for the 2018 Man Booker Prize. http://sophie-
mackintosh.co.uk/ @fairfairisles

Richard Marshall has been a contributing editor at *3:AM
Magazine* since 2000. He is the author of *Philosophy at 3:AM*
(OUP, 2014) and *Ethics at 3:AM* (OUP, 2017) which collects
some of the interviews with leading philosophers he has
undertaken at *3:AM Magazine* in the ongoing "End Times"
series. He likes to bide his time.

Susana Medina is the author of *Philosophical Toys* (Dalkey
Archive Press, 2015), offspring of which are the short films
Buñuel's Philosophical Toys and *Leather-Bound Stories* (co-di-
rected with Derek Ogbourne); *Red Tales* (bilingual ed.
co-translated with Rosie Marteau, Araña editorial, 2012);

Poem 66 (bilingual ed. trans. R. Marteau, Good Morning Menagerie, 2018/the runner-up in their Translation Contest), and *Souvenirs del Accidente* (Germanía, 2004). She has been awarded the Max Aub Short Story International Prize and an ACE Writing Grant for *Spinning Days of Night*. http://www.susanamedina.net/SUSANA_MEDINA.html @ SusanaMedina_

Tom McCarthy is a novelist whose work has been translated into more than twenty languages. His first novel, *Remainder* (2005) won the 2008 Believer Book Award and was recently adapted for the cinema. His third, *C* (Jonathan Cape), was a 2010 Booker Prize finalist, as was his fourth, *Satin Island* (Jonathan Cape), in 2015. McCarthy is also the author of the study *Tintin and the Secret of Literature* (Granta, 2006), and of the essay collection *Typewriters, Bombs, Jellyfish* (New York Review Books, 2017). He contributes regularly to publications such as the *New York Times*, *London Review of Books*, *Harper's* and *Artforum*. In 2013 he was awarded the inaugural Windham Campbell Prize for Fiction by Yale University. He lives in Berlin.

Robert McLiam Wilson is the author of three novels: *Ripley Bogle* (Andre Deutsch, 1989), *Manfred's Pain* (Picador, 1992) and *Eureka Street* (Harvill Secker, 1996). *Ripley Bogle* won the Rooney Prize and the Hughes Prize in 1989, as well as a Betty Trask Award and the Irish Book Awards in 1990. In 2003 McLiam Wilson featured among *Granta*'s 20 "Best of Young British Novelists". Originally from Belfast, he now lives in Paris, where he writes for *Charlie Hebdo*. @Parisbob2001

Jo Mortimer lived in Paris for a few years, working and studying an MA in Paris Studies: History and Culture. During this time she was lucky enough to meet and walk with Will Self. She is now tucked away in the foothills of the South Downs, UK, working as a proofreader and room guide in Virginia Woolf's home. Step by step, the novel is coming together and a few short stories can be found online and in print. www.joproofreader.com @JoMortimer2903

Yelena Moskovich is a Soviet-born, American and French artist and writer, author of *Virtuoso* (Serpent's Tail, 2019) and *The Natashas* (Serpent's Tail, 2016). She studied theatre at Emerson College, Boston, and in France at the Lecoq School of Physical Theatre and Université Paris VIII. Her plays and performances have been produced in the US, Canada, France and Sweden. She has also written for the *New Statesman*, *Paris Review*, *The Happy Reader* and *3:AM Magazine*, and in French for *Mixt(e) Magazine*. Yelena won the 2017 Galley Beggar Press Short Story Prize. In 2018, she was a curator and exhibiting artist for the Los Angeles Queer Biennial. https://www.yelenamoskovich.com/ @yelenamoskovich

Russell Persson lives in Reno, Nevada. His work has appeared in The Quarterly, Unsaid, 3:AM Magazine, New York Tyrant, Fantastic Floridas, Hotel, and Territory. His novel The Way of Florida was published in 2017 by Little Island Press.

Alex Pheby teaches at the University of Greenwich. He is the author of *Grace* (Two Ravens Press, 2009), *Playthings*

(Galley Beggar Press, 2015) — shortlisted for the 2016 Wellcome Book Prize — and *Lucia* (Galley Beggar Press, 2018). @alexpheby

Ashton Politanoff lives in Redondo Beach, California. His writing has appeared in *NOON, Conjunctions, Egress, New York Tyrant,* and elsewhere. https://ashtonpolitanoff.com/ @APolitanoff

Max Porter is the author of *Lanny* (Faber & Faber, 2019) and *Grief Is the Thing with Feathers* (Faber & Faber, 2015), which won the *Sunday Times*/Peter, Fraser & Dunlop Young Writer of the Year, the International Dylan Thomas Prize, the Europese Literatuurprijs and the BAMB Readers' Award and was shortlisted for the *Guardian* First Book Award as well as the Goldsmiths Prize. It has been translated into twenty-seven languages. He lives in Bath with his family. https://www.maxporter.co.uk/ @maxjohnporter

Chris Power's short story collection *Mothers* (Faber & Faber) was published in 2018. His column, "A Brief Survey of the Short Story" has appeared in *The Guardian* since 2007. He has written for the BBC, *New York Times, Wall Street Journal* and *New Statesman*. His fiction has been published in *Granta, The Stinging Fly, Dublin Review,* and *White Review,* and broadcast on BBC Radio 4. He lives with his family in London. https://www.theguardian.com/books/series/abriefsurveyoftheshortstory @chris_power

Cal Revely-Calder is a writer and editor based in London.

Adam Roberts was born in England and has lived in Paris for over 20 years. He is the editor of the *Invisible Paris* online resource and author of the *Paris Cityscopes* guide (Reaktion Books, 2017). He was the Paris contributor to the *World Atlas of Street Food* (Thames & Hudson, 2017), and has collaborated with numerous media sources including the *Guardian*, *Irish Times*, and CNN. http://parisisinvisible.blogspot.com/

Nicholas Rombes, a professor of English at the University of Detroit Mercy, is author of the novel *The Absolution of Roberto Acestes Laing* (Two Dollar Radio, 2014) and director of the film *The Removals* (2016). A revised, second edition of his book *Cinema in the Digital Age* was published in 2017. In 2018 he was a keynote speaker at the International Cinema in the Digital Age Conference in Tehran, Iran. https://thehappinessengine.net/ @Requiem102

C.D. Rose is the editor of *The Biographical Dictionary of Literary Failure* (Melville House, 2014) and author of *Who's Who When Everyone's Someone Else* (Melville House, 2018). His short fiction has appeared in *Gorse, The Lonely Crowd,* and *Lighthouse* magazines, as well as *Best British Short Stories 2018* (Salt). Originally from Manchester, he is now at home anywhere there are dark bars, dusty libraries and good second-hand bookshops. @cdrose_writer

Lee Rourke is the author of three novels, *The Canal* (Melville House Press, 2010), *Vulgar Things* (Fourth Estate, 2014) and *Glitch* (Dead Ink, 2019), as well as two poetry collections, *Varroa Destructor* (3:AM Press, 2013) and

Vantablack (Dostoyevsky Wannabe, 2019). @LeeRourke

Nicholas Royle is the author of three short story collections — *Mortality* (Serpent's Tail, 2006), *Ornithology* (Confingo Publishing, 2017) and *The Dummy & Other Uncanny Stories* (The Swan River Press, 2018) — and seven novels, most recently *First Novel* (Jonathan Cape, 2013). Reader in Creative Writing at Manchester Metropolitan University, he also runs Nightjar Press and is head judge of the Manchester Fiction Prize. http://www.nicholasroyle.com/# @nicholasroyle

Kathryn Scanlan is the author of *Aug 9—Fog* (Farrar, Straus & Giroux and Little Island Press, 2019) and *The Dominant Animal* (Little Island Press, 2019, and Farrar, Straus & Giroux, 2020). Her stories have appeared in *NOON, Fence, Granta,* and *Egress*. She lives in Los Angeles. @K_Scanlan_

Adam Scovell is a writer and filmmaker from Merseyside now based in London. His writing has featured in *Sight & Sound, Little White Lies* and *The Quietus*. He runs the website, *Celluloid Wicker Man,* and completed his PhD at Goldsmiths University in 2018. In 2015, he worked with Robert Macfarlane on a short adaptation of his *Sunday Times* bestseller, *Holloway*. His books include *Folk Horror: Hours Dreadful and Things Strange* (Auteur, 2017), *Mothlight* (Influx Press, 2019) and *How Pale the Winter Has Made Us* (Influx Press, 2020). https://celluloidwickerman.com/ @adamscovell

Fernando Sdrigotti was born in Rosario, Argentina. His writing in English and Spanish has been widely published in print and online. His books include *Dysfunctional Males* (LCG Editores, 2017), *Shitstorm* (Open Pen, 2018), *Departure Lounge Music* (LCG Editores 2018) and *Grey Tropic* (Dostoyevsky Wannabe, 2019; co-authored with Martin Dean). He lives in London. https://www.fernando-sdrigotti.com/ @f_sd

Will Self is an English novelist, journalist, political commentator and broadcasting personality. He is the author of eleven novels, five collections of short stories, three novellas, and five collections of non-fiction. His work has been translated into 22 languages. *Umbrella* (2012) was shortlisted for the Man Booker Prize. https://will-self.com/ @wself

Richard Skinner is a writer working across fiction, life-writing, essays, non-fiction and poetry. He has published three novels with Faber & Faber, three books of non-fiction and three books of poetry. His work has been nominated for several prizes and is published in eight languages. Richard is Director of the Fiction Programme at Faber Academy. https://richardskinner.weebly.com/ @RichardNSkinner

Christiana Spens is the author of several books, including *Death of a Ladies' Man* (3:AM Press, 2012), *Shooting Hipsters: Rethinking Dissent in the Age of PR* (Repeater Books, 2016) and *The Portrayal and Punishment of Terrorists in Western Media* (Palgrave Macmillan, 2019). She read Philosophy at Cambridge and earned her PhD in International Relations at St. Andrews. She currently writes on art and politics for *Art Quarterly, Studio International, Prospect* and other publications. https://www.christiana-spens.com/ @ChristianaSpens

H.P. Tinker is a Manchester-based short story writer and author of *The Swank Bisexual Wine Bar of Modernity* (Social Disease, 2007) and *The Girl Who Ate New York* (East London Press, 2015). His fiction has appeared in *Ambit, 3:AM Magazine, Best British Short Stories, The Mammoth Book of Best British Crime,* and several other places. He is slightly older than he used to be.

Susan Tomaselli is founder and editor of Gorse journal, and editor at Gorse Editions. Her essays have been published in The Guardian, The Stinging Fly, The Irish Times, The Elysian: Creative Responses (New Binary Press, 2017), and elsewhere. She is currently working on a novel-in-essays on memory, trauma, technology, and failure, called Traces.

Dylan Trigg is an FWF Lise Meitner Senior Fellow at the University of Vienna, Department of Philosophy. He has previously held research and teaching positions at the University of Memphis, University College Dublin, and Husserl Archives, École Normale Supérieure. Trigg is the author of several books, including: *Topophobia: A Phenomenology of Anxiety* (Bloomsbury, 2016); *The Thing: A Phenomenology of Horror* (Zero Books, 2014); and *The Memory of Place: A Phenomenology of the Uncanny* (Ohio University Press, 2012). With Dorothée Legrand, he is co-editor of *Unconsciousness Between Phenomenology and Psychoanalysis*

(Springer, 2017). Trigg's works have been translated into French, German, and Russian. http://www.dylantrigg.com/

Laura Waddell is a publisher and writer based in Glasgow, Scotland. Her writing has featured in publications including the *Guardian*, *Times Literary Supplement*, *McSweeney's*, *3:AM Magazine*, and the books *Nasty Women*, *Know Your Place: Essays on the Working Class by the Working Class*, and *The Digital Critic: Literary Culture Online*. She sits on the board of Scottish PEN and *Gutter Magazine*. https://lauraewaddell. com/ @lauraewaddell

Isabel Waidner is a writer and critical theorist. Their books include *Gaudy Bauble* (Dostoyevsky Wannabe, 2017) which was shortlisted for the Republic of Consciousness Prize for Small Presses, and *Liberating the Canon: An Anthology of Innovative Literature* (ed., Dostoyevsky Wannabe, 2018). Waidner's articles, essays and short fiction have appeared in journals including *3:AM Magazine*, *Cambridge Literary Review*, *Configurations*, *Gorse*, *The Happy Hypocrite*, *Minor Literature[s]* and *The Quietus*. They are the curator of the reading series *Queers Read This* at the Institute for Contemporary Art, and a lecturer at Roehampton University, London. @isabelwaidner

Joanna Walsh is the author of seven books. The latest, *Break.up* (2018), is published by Semiotext(e). https:// badaude.wixsite.com/joannawalsh @badaude

Stuart Walton is a cultural historian, novelist and book critic. His publications include *In the Realm of the Senses: A Materialist Theory of Seeing and Feeling* (Zero Books, 2016);

Introducing Theodor Adorno (Zero Books, 2017); *A Natural History of Human Emotions* (Dean Street Press, 2016); *Intoxicology: A Cultural History of Drink and Drugs* (second edition, Dean Street Press, 2016); a monograph on the chilli pepper, *The Devil's Dinner* (St Martin's Press, 2018); and a novel, *The First Day in Paradise* (Roundfire, 2016). He has written widely on food and drink, and is a past chairman of the Circle of Wine Writers. @StuartWalton1

Will Wiles is a writer on architecture. He is the author of three novels: *Care of Wooden Floors* (4th Estate, 2012) which won a Betty Trask Award, *The Way Inn* (4th Estate, 2014), shortlisted for the Encore Award, and *Plume* (4th Estate, 2019), a hallucinatory vision of contemporary London, the city where he lives. @WillWiles

Eley Williams' collection of prose, *Attrib. and Other Stories* (Influx Press, 2017), was awarded both the Republic of Consciousness Prize and the James Tait Black Memorial Prize 2018. With stories anthologised in *The Penguin Book of the Contemporary British Short Story* (Penguin Classics, 2018), *Liberating the Canon* (Dostoyevsky Wannabe, 2018) and *Not Here: A Queer Anthology of Loneliness* (Pilot Press, 2017), she is a recent Fellow of the MacDowell Colony and was granted Fellowship of the Royal Society of Literature. She teaches at Royal Holloway, University of London and is co-editor for fiction at *3:AM Magazine*. http://www.eleywilliams.com/ @GiantRatSumatra

Jeffrey Zuckerman is a New York-based translator of French novels, from Ananda Devi's *Eve Out of Her Ruins*

(Les Fugitives, 2016) to Jean-Jacques Schuhl's *Dusty Pink* (Semiotext(e), 2018). He has contributed to the *New Republic*, *Paris Review Daily*, *White Review* and *VICE*. His titles have been shortlisted for the TA First Translation Prize, the Best Translated Book Award, and the Albertine Prize, and he has been awarded the CLMP Firecracker Award and a French Voices grant for his translations. He is a recipient of a PEN/Heim Translation Fund grant for his ongoing work on the short stories of Hervé Guibert. @J_Zuckerman

Repeater Books

is dedicated to the creation of a new reality. The landscape of twenty-first-century arts and letters is faded and inert, riven by fashionable cynicism, egotistical self-reference and a nostalgia for the recent past. Repeater intends to add its voice to those movements that wish to enter history and assert control over its currents, gathering together scattered and isolated voices with those who have already called for an escape from Capitalist Realism. Our desire is to publish in every sphere and genre, combining vigorous dissent and a pragmatic willingness to succeed where messianic abstraction and quiescent co-option have stalled: abstention is not an option: we are alive and we don't agree.